Beyond Liberal Democracy

Beyond Liberal Democracy

Political Thinking
for an East Asian Context

Daniel A. Bell

PRINCETON UNIVERSITY PRESS

PRINCETON AND OXFORD

Published by Princeton University Press, 41 William Street, Princeton, New Jersey 08540
In the United Kingdom: Princeton University Press, 3 Market Place, Woodstock,
Oxfordshire OX20 1SY

Library of Congress Cataloging-in-Publication Data

Bell, Daniel (Daniel A.)
    Beyond liberal democracy : political thinking for an East Asian context /
Daniel A. Bell.
        p.   cm.
    ISBN-13: 978-0-691-12307-3 (alk. paper)
    ISBN-10: 0-691-12307-1 (alk. paper)
    ISBN-13: 978-0-691-12308-0 (pbk. : alk. paper)
    ISBN-10: 0-691-12308-X (pbk. : alk. paper)
        1. Democracy—East Asia.   2. Human rights—East Asia.   3. Capitalism—
East Asia.   4. East Asia—Politics and government.   I. Title.
    JQ1499.A91B45 2006
    321.8095—dc22   2006002730

British Library Cataloging-in-Publication Data is available

This book has been composed in Sabon

Printed on acid-free paper. ∞

pup.princeton.edu

Printed in the United States of America

In memory of Don Bell

Father and writer

CONTENTS

ACKNOWLEDGMENTS

THIS BOOK was written over a stretch of two years. The first year was my sabbatical year at Stanford's Center for Advanced Study in the Behavioral Sciences (CASBS). *Pace* the occasional mountain lion attack, it was an ideal setting for thinking and writing. I am grateful for the administrative support and funding provided by CASBS and, above all, for the many friendships that developed over the course of the year. I would also like to thank the City University of Hong Kong, which cofunded my sabbatical. I owe special thanks to then head of department Ian Holliday and then Dean Matthew Chen for facilitating this arrangement.

The second year was spent at Tsinghua University (Beijing). I am particularly grateful to Professor Wan Junren for his strong support and warm welcome. I would also like to thank my colleagues in the department of philosophy for conversations and friendship that have made my stay in Beijing both enjoyable and stimulating.

I have received numerous comments on earlier drafts of the book. I am most grateful to the two readers for Princeton University Press—Joseph Chan and one anonymous referee—for reports that have helped me sharpen the argument. I would also like the following individuals for valuable comments on individual chapters: Sia Ackermark, Peter Baehr, Bai Tongdong, Charles Blattberg, Leah Briones, Joe Carens, Ci Jiwei, Jean-Marc Coicaud, John Delury, Avner de-Shalit, Paul Dumouchel, Chris Eisgruber, Fan Ruiping, Steve Geisz, Jonas Grimheden, Hahm Chaibong, Hahm Chaihark, He Baogang, Ian Holliday, Philip Ivanhoe, Leigh Kathryn Jenko, Will Kymlicka, Theresa Lee, Linda Li, Li Qiang, Liang Zhiping, Huichieh Loy, Roy Mill, Kathleen Much, Paik Wooyeal, Randy Peerenboom, Franklin Perkins, Elaine Scarry, Song Bing, Tan Sorhoon, Michael Walzer, Ben Wong, and Chan-Liang Wu. I would also like to thank I-Chung Chen, Tom Chu, Mike Dowdle, Fan Ruiping, Russell Arben Fox, Krzysztof Gawlikowski, Tom Gold, He Baogang, Huang Ko-wu, Kanishka Jayasuriya, Will Kymlicka, Ethan Leib, Linda Li, Liu Wenjia, Jeff McMahan, Christopher McNally, Andrew Murphy, Antony Ou, Randy Peerenboom, Thomas Pogge, Edmund Ryden, Sing Ming, Frank Upham, T. Y. Wang, and Xiao Qiang for sending material that has been useful for my book.

Let me also thank my research assistants at Stanford, Rakhi Patel and Zhang Chenchen; and in Beijing, Chang Huili, Li Wanquan, Tu Wenjuan, and Zhang Yanliang. Thanks also to Anita O'Brien for careful copy editing. I have been learning Chinese for several years, and I would like to thank my teachers. I owe special thanks to three graduate students in Beijing who have generously offered their time to help me improve my classical Chinese: Kong Xinfeng, Liu Wenjia, and Wu Yun. The translations are my own, unless indicated otherwise, and I do not want to implicate my teachers if there are any mistakes!

Over half of the book consists of new material. However, I have been thinking and writing about some of these topics for a long time, and the book draws on some previous work that has been substantially revised and updated. I wish to thank several publishers for permission to incorporate previously published material:

Chapter 4 draws on my essay (cowritten with Joseph H. Carens), "The Ethical Dilemmas of International Human Rights and Humanitarian NGOs: Reflections on a Dialogue between Practitioners and Theorists," *Human Rights Quarterly*, May 2004; and on my introduction to *Ethics in Action: The Ethical Challenges of International Human Rights NGOs*, coedited with Jean-Marc Coicaud (New York: Cambridge University Press, 2006).

Chapter 5 draws on my essay (cowritten with Paik Wooyeal), "Citizenship and State-Sponsored Physical Education: Ancient Greece and Ancient China," *Review of Politics*, May 2004.

Chapter 7 draws on my contribution to *Democratization and Identity: Regimes and Ethnicity in Southeast Asia*, ed. Susan J. Henders (Lanham, MD: Lexington Books, 2004).

Chapter 8 draws on my essay, "Teaching in a Multicultural Context: Lessons from Singapore," *Dissent*, Spring 2000.

Chapter 9 draws on my contribution to *Confucianism for the Modern World*, ed. Daniel A. Bell and Hahm Chaibong (New York: Cambridge University Press, 2003).

Chapter 11 draws on my contribution (cowritten with Nicola Piper) to *Multiculturalism in Asia: Theoretical Perspectives*, ed. Will Kymlicka and He Baogang (Oxford: Oxford University Press, 2005).

I am most grateful to my editor, Ian Malcolm, for his support and interest in the project; to Joe Carens, Paik Wooyeal, and Nicola Piper, who cowrote earlier versions of chapters 4, 5, and 11, respectively; to my dear friend Tatiana Sayig, who designed the cover; and to my wife Song Bing, our child Julien Song Bell, my mother, Anthony, Valérie, Oliver, grandmother, as well as family members in China, for emotional support. I dedicate this book to my father, Don Bell, who left this world on March 8, 2003. If I like writing books, it's because of him.

Beyond Liberal Democracy

1

Introduction: One Size Doesn't Fit All

IN MAY 2002 the eminent American legal theorist Ronald Dworkin toured several Chinese universities and delivered lectures on human rights. The Chinese translation of his renowned book *Taking Rights Seriously* had been topping the best-seller lists for several weeks and his public lectures drew literally thousands of people. At the time, Professor Dworkin's tour was compared to the visits to China eight decades ago by John Dewey and Bertrand Russell. China had once again been opening up to the West, and it looked like another opportunity for cross-cultural exchanges and mutual learning by the leading intellectuals of "East" and "West."

Dworkin began his lectures by "conceding" that the human rights discourse is uniquely Western, but he argued that this "fact" does not bear on the question of the normative worth of human rights. If the concept of human rights is morally defensible, then the uniquely Western history of human rights should not be used as an excuse to prevent its application in non-Western contexts, including China. Dworkin proceeded to sketch a view of human rights self-consciously inspired by the liberal thinkers of the Enlightenment. He posited two moral principles (moral equality and self-direction) that support civil and political rights and then showed that these principles can underpin critiques of contemporary Chinese legal and political practices. He then challenged his audience to come up with competing principles based on "Asian values" that would justify violations of civil and political rights. The audience, however, failed to rise to the challenge; perhaps the idea of mounting a compelling oral defense of an alternative Asian philosophy in a brief question-and-answer period, particularly in a context where there may be political constraints, linguistic barriers, and cultural aversions to public intellectual battles, struck members of the audience as, to put it neutrally, inappropriate.

Those expressing "enthusiasm for liberal values," Dworkin noted, did voice their views: "all the scholars and almost all the students who spoke about the issue on various occasions insisted that there was no important difference between Western values or conceptions of human rights and their own." One member of the audience "said of course the fundamental situation of human beings is the same everywhere, that there should be no more talk of distinctive Chinese values, that China must begin what he called a 'renaissance' of liberal individualistic values. When he finished, the large audience clapped loudly." Nevertheless, Dworkin found it peculiar that members of the audience did not seem to share his desire to discuss specific cases of human rights violations, leading him to conclude that Chinese academic discourse remains "eerily abstract in a country whose government treats itself as above the law."[1] What Dworkin seems to have learned from his trip, in short, is that Chinese academics cannot mount a successful defense of an Asian philosophy even when given the opportunity to do so. The only question that remains is how to implement liberal individualism in China, which apparently requires greater moral courage and concrete thinking on the part of Chinese academics.

Not surprisingly, Dworkin's visit generated less-than-friendly responses. Professor Liufang Fang, who teaches law at the Chinese University of Political Science and Law, opens his critique with a sarcastic account of the college students who attended Dworkin's lectures because they "did not want to miss the festival-like event." They could hardly hear anything, but "being squeezed in the crowd itself was a joy to many of the students." Professor Dworkin, meanwhile, "unilaterally believed that his China tour was a valuable opportunity for China to be privy to his ideas of liberty." Ironically, he was taken for a ride by the Chinese government. His visit had been organized to showcase China's new freedoms, and the government knew full well that Chinese academics would not argue publicly about the details of particularly sensitive cases. Dworkin seemed unaware of the risks that China-based academics would incur by publicly endorsing his condemnation of the Chinese government's handling of such cases. As Professor Fang puts it, "the truth is that the degree of freedom of speech is negatively correlated with the risks borne by the speaker." Moreover, Dworkin seemed unaware of the extent to which "general discussions" of legal issues by China-based academics have led to substantial improvements of legal practice. Had Dworkin been better informed, he would not have made facile comments

---

[1] See Ronald Dworkin, "Taking Rights Seriously in Beijing," *The New York Review of Books*, vol. 49, no. 14 (26 September 2002). Ironically, the dean of Beijing University's School of Law (China's leading law school), Professor Zhu Suli, is most famous for his critique of abstract theorizing in law and has also translated many of Richard Posner's works into Chinese. For an excellent account of Zhu Suli's work in English, see Frank Upham, "Who Will Find the Defendant If He Stays with His Sheep? Justice in Rural China?" *The Yale Law Journal*, vol. 114, no. 7 (May 2005), 1675–1718. Zhu's colleague, Professor He Weifang, has openly and courageously campaigned for an improvement of civil and political rights in China, and his efforts have been credited for recent reforms of laws protecting the rights of migrant workers.

regarding the "eerily abstract" Chinese discourse. Professor Fang concludes his essay by suggesting that Chinese professors should spend more time reading, thinking, and writing instead of wasting time on "hot events."[2]

Even scholars otherwise sympathetic to Dworkin's theory reacted with dismay. The philosopher Jiwei Ci expresses broad agreement with the two principles of ethical individualism spelled out in Dworkin's article "Taking Rights Seriously in Beijing," and he praises Dworkin for critically evaluating his own society on the basis of his moral theory in other works. However, Dworkin's theory "went out the window" when he addressed the Chinese audience. Rather than appealing to his radical first principle (which underpins his critique of economic inequality), he stuck to American political common sense that equates human rights with civil and political rights. As a result, Professor Ci notes, "the United States, and the West as a whole, emerge triumphantly above the threshold, well-placed to sit in judgment of the human rights record of the rest of the world. . . . When Dworkin leaves the Euro-American academic context and takes on the role of observer and critic of China's human rights record, he can come pretty close to an uncritical identification with the mainstream values of the West, at times almost sounding like its moral and political spokesman."[3]

How could things have gone so wrong? Yes, Dworkin should have been better acquainted with the contemporary Chinese political context and the situation of Chinese academics in particular.[4] His less-than-modest demeanor and hectoring tone did not help. The deeper problem, however, is that Dworkin made no serious attempt to learn about Chinese philosophy, to identify aspects worth defending and learning from, and to relate his own ideas to those of Chinese political traditions such

[2] Liufang Fang, "Taking Academic Games Seriously," *Perspectives*, vol. 3, no. 7 (www .oycf.org/Perspectives/19_123102/takingAcademic.htm, visited 19 July 2003). Professor Fang's views are criticized by Yanan Peng. In my view, Peng's critique is unfair (e.g., he argues that "Professor Fang chooses to believe the government" in specific legal cases, but Fang's argument is that Dworkin did not have sufficient information to pass judgment, not that he should have sided with the government). Even Peng, however, implicitly criticizes Dworkin by noting that foreigners must "understand their Chinese audience before they give speeches." Yanan Peng, "Taking Dworkin Seriously," *Perspectives*, vol. 4, no. 1.

[3] Jiwei Ci, "Taking the Reasons for Human Rights Seriously (in China)," ms. on file with author. Ci views Dworkin's misuse of human rights in the Chinese context as typical of a wider phenomenon, and he argues that the human rights discourse has been so tainted with such misuses that it should be dropped altogether. A more abstract version of this manuscript, without discussion of China or Dworkin, was published in *Political Theory*, vol. 33, no. 2 (April 2005), 243–65.

[4] Dworkin's article includes such bizarre statements as "It is important to remember that the professoriate and the intellectuals in China are almost all young."

as Confucianism and Legalism. Whereas earlier luminaries such as Dewey and Russell had expressed their admiration of Chinese culture and argued for a synthesis of "East" and "West,"[5] Dworkin merely put forward his own ideas and identified fellow "liberals,"[6] and the "debate" rarely moved beyond this starting point.

The Uniquely Parochial Development of Liberal Democracy

Unfortunately, Dworkin's experience is not atypical. Few, if any, Western liberal democratic theorists in the post–World War II era have sought to learn from the traditions and experiences of East Asian societies. Although derived entirely from the norms and practices of Western societies, their theories are presented as universally valid, and defenders of "Asian values" are viewed as archaic or politically dangerous.

This blind faith in the universal potential of liberal democracy would not be so worrisome if it did not take the form of U.S. government policy to promote human rights and democracy abroad, regardless of local

[5] Part of the explanation for the difference may be the relatively short length of Dworkin's visit (two weeks). In the 1920s it would have been unthinkable to plan such a short trip to China (Dewey came for one year and decided to stay for a second). Given the length and inconvenience of the travel and the fact that travelers would be cut off from their home cultures for prolonged periods, this kind of trip provided an incentive for relatively serious commitment to learning the culture of the far-away destination. In our day of rapid intraplanetary travel (and global e-mail), it is possible to pop in and pop out, and no serious cost is attached to limiting oneself to a superficial understanding of the "distant" culture.

Prior to the twentieth century, several Western political thinkers did make efforts to engage with East Asian thought. However, they were working with unreliable translations and reports, and they tended to oscillate between the extremes of uncritical and idealized endorsement of the "Eastern way" (e.g., Voltaire and Leibniz) to blanket condemnation of East Asian political thought and practice as belonging to "prehistory" and thus inappropriate for modern societies (e.g., Hegel, Marx, and Mill). See J. J. Clarke, *Oriental Enlightenment: The Encounter between Asian and Western Thought* (London and New York: RoutledgeCurzon, 1997).

[6] It is worth asking whether the "liberals" Professor Dworkin allegedly encountered during his visit to China shared much more than a common label. Notwithstanding their own self-identification, did these Chinese "liberals" really identify with Dworkin's priorities and political outlooks? Richard Nisbett's findings offer reason for doubt. In value surveys, Beijing University students reported holding "Western" values such as independence more strongly than Westerners did. However, when the investigators "described scenarios that tacitly pitted values against one another and asked participants how they would behave in those situations, or would prefer others to behave, [they] obtained results that matched the intuitions of Asian and American scholars who study Asia." Nisbett, *The Geography of Thought: How Asians and Westerners Think Differently . . . and Why* (New York: The Free Press, 2003), 221–22.

habits, needs, and traditions.[7] Notwithstanding the rather huge gap between liberal democratic ideals and the reality at home,[8] and the repeated history of misadventures abroad due (at least partly) to ignorance of local conditions (Guatemala, Iran, Vietnam, Iraq),[9] nothing seems to shake the faith in the universal potential of Western-style liberal democracy in official circles.[10]

This is not to deny that academic defenders of liberal democracy have cast doubt on the means employed by U.S. foreign policy makers. Amy Chua has put forward an argument against promoting electoral democracy and free markets in poor societies on the grounds that they empower resentful majority groups who proceed to target relatively well-off minority groups. Thus, the U.S. foreign policy establishment should not recklessly push for immediate adoption of democratic practices that took root slowly even in relatively prosperous and stable Western societies. However, Chua does not seem to doubt that the "West is best" and that liberal democracy should be the long-term goal.[11] Samuel Huntington, for his part, argues against exporting democratic ideals for now and the foreseeable future. Although he upholds these ideals, they are appropriate only in (Western) cultures with particular histories, and they will lead

---

[7] In contemporary U.S. foreign policy, the most enthusiastic defenders of expansionism grounded in the idea that American-style liberal principles should be exported to the rest of the world tend to be labeled as "neoconservatives," but President Woodrow Wilson (a Democrat) is perhaps the main intellectual inspiration for expansionism. See Lloyd A. Ambrosius, *Wilsonianism: Woodrow Wilson and His Legacy in American Foreign Relations* (New York: Palgrave Macmillan, 2002).

[8] I do not mean to deny that there are substantial differences between liberal democracies in different Western countries (consider the differences between Sweden and the United States). In this book, I will be working with a definition of liberal democracy that draws mainly on the theories of Anglo-American liberal political theorists and the values and practices of U.S.-style liberal democracy.

[9] Even apparent success stories could have been more "successful" had the political relevance of local knowledge been taken more seriously. It could be argued that Japan would have surrendered earlier (thus avoiding much bloodshed) if President Truman had followed the advice of Japan experts in the State Department who opposed the demand for unconditional surrender on the grounds that a promise to protect the imperial throne would increase the likelihood of surrender. See Ian Buruma, *Inventing Japan: From Empire to Economic Miracle 1853–1964* (London: Weidenfeld & Nicolson, 2003), 102.

[10] Of course, some forms of missionary zeal are more overt than others. In 1997 a senior Chinese official briefed American visitors from the U.S. Congress on China's domestic and international challenges. In the question period, one member of Congress asked, "I just want to know if you've accepted Jesus Christ as your personal savior." Quoted in Robert M. Hathaway, "The Lingering Legacy of Tiananmen," *Foreign Affairs* (September/October 2003).

[11] Amy Chua, *World on Fire: How Exporting Free Market Democracy Breeds Ethnic Hatred and Global Instability* (New York: Doubleday, 2003), 13, 263–64.

to clashes in non-Western "civilizations" with different histories and cultural outlooks. On the home front, the United States is under threat from multiculturalists who threaten to dilute Western civilization: "The futures of the United States and of the West depend upon Americans reaffirming their commitment to Western civilization."[12] Thus, the U.S. government should stick to buttressing Western values at home and build up walls against foreign influence, at least until conditions change for the better in the non-Western world. In neither case do these critics of expansionist U.S. foreign policy suggest that liberal democracy can be substantially enriched by engaging with the principles and practices of non-Western political traditions.

In short, defenders of liberal democracy, notwithstanding different interpretations of implications for U.S. foreign policy, do not seem to doubt that the "West is best." This helps to explain why Western liberal democrats, *pace* occasional lip service to openness, fail to allow engagement with the non-Western world to challenge the normative underpinnings of their preset views. They serve, de facto, as secular preachers of the democratic faith, blind to the possibility of defensible alternatives that may be worth learning from. Here the asymmetry with East Asia[13] is most striking. Since the late nineteenth century, the dominant trend has been to recognize (and act upon) the importance of learning from Western political theories and practices. It would be almost unthinkable for contemporary East Asian political thinkers and actors to uphold political theories and practices that owe nothing to liberal democracy.[14]

This sad state of affairs, at the level of both Western-style political theory and political practice, is not, fortunately, replicated in other domains. The modern history of Western painting has been immeasurably enriched, consciously so, by its encounter with East Asian art. French Impressionists and post-Impressionists were directly inspired by Japanese prints. Occasionally, this took the form of slavish imitation and incorporation of Japanese themes. At its best, however, familiarity with the Japanese tradition led to subtle incorporation of Japanese techniques

---

[12] Samuel P. Huntington, *The Clash of Civilizations and the Remaking of World Order* (New York: Simon & Schuster, 1996), 307. See also Samuel P. Huntington, *Who Are We?: The Challenges to America's Identity* (New York: Simon & Schuster, 2004).

[13] In this book, the term "East Asia" refers to countries in the East Asian region that have been subject to prolonged Chinese cultural influence and that have demonstrated economic prowess in the post–World War II era: mainland China, Hong Kong, Taiwan, South Korea, and Japan. Singapore is also included because it is predominantly Chinese, though it is located in the Southeast Asian region. I will not say as much about Vietnam because of its relatively undeveloped economic status and unique recent history (i.e., the fact that Vietnamese are still recovering from what they call the American War).

[14] North Korea is an obvious exception. This point refers to East Asian countries that are economically and culturally integrated with the rest of the world.

and styles, to the point that they were both unmistakable yet almost impossible to separate from the whole. Vincent van Gogh, who had spent several years studying Japanese art, told his brother Theo that his landscape drawings from the Arles period did not look Japanese but "really are, more so than others."[15] By the twentieth century East Asian thought and art did not just influence formal and visual techniques, they also provided the philosophical inspiration for some revolutionary developments in Western art. For example, "the parallels between the free existentialist gestures of Pollock, Kline or Soulages and Zen ink painting [the Zen ink flingers of the thirteenth century] seem too close to be mere chance."[16] In some cases, the influence was direct, as in Paul Klee's expressive distortion of form inspired by his immersion in Chinese poetry.[17]

Until recently, Western medicine had developed largely impervious to East Asian influence, but there has been a rapprochement of late. Acupuncture is widely practiced in the United States to treat back and other pains (and it is often covered by medical insurance, which is the ultimate test of social acceptance in the American context). Herbal remedies are increasingly used, and recent emphasis on the links between lifestyle and health parallels the Chinese idea that patients should be treated as wholes, not simply as carriers of this or that defective physical part. "Alternative medicine" has been relabeled "complementary medicine" by the U.S. medical establishment, partly to make it sound more acceptable. Medical professionals in Western countries have not (yet?) reached the point of routinely prescribing mixtures of Western chemical drugs and Chinese herbal medicines, as in Japan and China, but it is not implausible to surmise that we may be heading that way.

In psychology, too, there is growing awareness of critical differences between Westerners and East Asians, along with the concomitant idea that both "sides" can be enriched by mutual learning. The social psychologist Richard Nisbett, following intriguing questions by his then student (now collaborator) Kaiping Peng, has engaged in comparative research that points to profound cognitive differences between Westerners and East Asians. In one famous experiment, Nisbett showed an

---

[15] Michael Sullivan, *The Meeting of Eastern and Western Art* (Berkeley: University of California Press, 1997), 235. Sullivan's book traces the history of mutual learning between Western and East Asian art, focusing largely on influence that has enriched the history of art. If an equivalent book were to be written on political theory, the chapter on "The Western liberal democratic response to East Asian political thought" would be very short indeed.

[16] Ibid., 244.

[17] Klee steeped himself in Chinese poetry from 1917 to 1923, and during this period he wrote to his wife, "J'ai le temps de lire beaucoup, et je deviens de plus en plus chinois" [I have time to do lots of reading, and I'm becoming more and more Chinese]. Quoted in ibid., 251.

animated underwater scene to two groups of students and found striking differences in their responses: American students focused on a big
fish swimming among smaller fish, whereas the Japanese students made
observations about the background environment.[18] Drawing on such
experiments, Nisbett argues that Westerners typically have a strong interest in categorization and analytical separation, and East Asians rely
more on contextual and background knowledge. These contrasting cognitive patterns are explained with reference to different philosophical
backgrounds, language structures, and child-rearing practices. While
they are not impervious to change (Asian Americans scored midway on
most tests), they express pervasive and long-lasting differences that have
implications for reforming such apparently "culturally neutral" practices
as IQ tests. Nisbett also surveys the advantages and disadvantages of
Western and Asian thinking styles, concluding with a normative plea for
mutual enrichment.[19]

Once again, Western liberal democratic theory stands out by its apparent imperviousness to developments in East Asia and elsewhere in
the non-Western world. This insularity would not be so worrisome if
East Asian political traditions and practices had nothing of value and it
really was just a matter of exporting Western political ways or building
barriers until the non-Western world becomes more "civilized" and
hence willing and able to implement Western-style liberal democratic
practices.

My own view, not surprisingly, is different. I will argue that that there
are morally legitimate alternatives to Western-style liberal democracy in
the East Asian region. What is right for East Asians does not simply involve implementing Western-style political practices when the opportunity presents itself; it involves drawing upon East Asian political realities
and cultural traditions that are defensible to contemporary East Asians.
They may also be defensible to contemporary Western-style liberal
democrats, in which case they may be worth learning from.[20] But there
may also be areas of conflict, in which case the Western-style liberal
democrat should tolerate, if not respect, areas of justifiable difference.

---

[18] A Japanese friend of mine joked that the different result can be explained by the fact
that Japanese find fish boring because they eat so much sushi and thus find it more interesting to focus on the relatively novel background.

[19] Nisbett, *The Geography of Thought*. See also David Wong, "Relational and Autonomous Selves," *Journal of Chinese Philosophy*, vol. 31, no. 4 (December 2004), 422.

[20] It may also be possible to learn from East Asian political realities and cultural traditions that are not defensible to contemporary East Asians. For example, certain practices
meant to foster social ties in the workplace that may be widely viewed as overly burden-
some in Japan can help to inspire reform in Western companies that seek to remedy the
problem of worker alienation.

In this book, I will try to show that the main hallmarks of liberal democracy—human rights, democracy, and capitalism—have been substantially modified during the course of transmission to East Asian societies that have not been shaped by liberalism to nearly the same extent. The normative argument points to the dangers of implementing Western-style models and proposes alternative justifications and practices that may be more appropriate for East Asian societies. If human rights, democracy, and capitalism are to take root and produce beneficial outcomes in East Asia, they must be adjusted to contemporary East Asian political and economic realities and to the values of nonliberal East Asian political traditions such as Confucianism and Legalism. Local knowledge is therefore essential for realistic and morally informed contributions to debates on political reform in the region, as well as for mutual learning and enrichment of political theories.

The book is divided into three sections that correspond to the main hallmarks of liberal democracy. Each section opens with a chapter that discusses the historical and philosophical roots of legitimate East Asian alternatives to Western-style human rights, democracy, and capitalism, respectively, followed by chapters that focus more directly on contemporary themes.

Human Rights for an East Asian Context

Western democracies are *constitutional* democracies, meaning that their constitutional systems are meant to protect certain individual rights. These rights are held to be so fundamental that they "trump" the ephemeral decisions of democratically elected politicians in cases of conflict. When this notion is exported abroad, it takes the form of campaigns to promote human rights, and non-Western governments are criticized for failing to live up to these standards. But is it really appropriate to uphold standards of human rights derived from the Western experience in East Asian societies?

Chapter 2 discusses what may be the mother of all human rights debates: what, if anything, justifies warfare and the consequent killing of people for particular ends? Western debates on just and unjust war have largely ignored Chinese contributions, and my essay is an attempt to formulate a Confucian perspective that draws primarily on the philosophy of Mencius. Of course, Mencius did not develop his theories with reference to the language of human rights. In substance, however, there are some parallels between Mencius's ideas on warfare and those of contemporary theorists of just war who deploy the language of human rights.

Mencius upholds an ideal theory of sage-kings who govern the world by means of rites and virtues rather than coercion. This kind of theory cannot provide much, if any, guidance for the real world, particularly when rulers must decide whether or not to go to war. However, Mencius also puts forward principles designed to provide practical, morally informed guidance in the nonideal world of competing states, and he draws implications for the pursuit of warfare. He is severely critical of rulers who launched ruthless wars of conquest simply to increase their territory. But he does not oppose war in principle. States can defend themselves if the ruler is supported by the people. Mencius also argues that wars of conquest can be justified if the aim is to bring peace to foreign lands, so long as particular conditions are in place: the conquerors must try to liberate the people who are being oppressed by tyrants, the people must welcome their conquerors, and the wars of conquest are led by virtuous rulers who can make a plausible claim to have the world's support. The chapter ends with an argument that seemingly historical debates may have important implications for present-day East Asian societies.

The next two chapters turn to more contemporary debates on human rights. The most visible challenge to Western ideas of human rights has come from the "Asian values" school. This debate, however, has generated more heat than light. Chapter 3 aims to get beyond the rhetoric and identify relatively persuasive East Asian criticisms of traditional Western approaches to the human rights. It is made explicit at the outset that the debate turns on the merits of publicly contested rights that fall outside the sphere of customary international law. Drawing on several East–West dialogues on human rights, four separate East Asian challenges are discussed: (1) the argument that situation-specific justifications for the temporary curtailment of particular human rights can only be countered following the acquisition of substantial local knowledge; (2) the argument that East Asian cultural traditions can provide the resources to justify and increase local commitment to practices that in the West are typically realized through a human rights regime (as opposed to the claim that the Western liberal tradition is the only moral foundation for human rights values and practices); (3) the argument that distinctive East Asian conceptions of vital human interests may justify some political practices that differ from human rights regimes typically endorsed in Western liberal countries; and (4) the argument that the current "West-centric" human rights regime needs to be modified to incorporate East Asian viewpoints. The chapter ends with my own doubts regarding the practical use of further cross-cultural dialogues between academics on human rights theory.

Chapter 4 incorporates the views of practitioners, and it turns out that the lack of a truly universal foundation for human rights is not the main obstacle for human rights organizations operating in the East Asian region. Drawing on dialogues between representatives of international human rights nongovernmental organizations (INGOs) and human rights theorists, I discuss the actual challenges encountered by INGOs during the course of their work: the challenge of cultural conflict; the challenge of dealing with global poverty; the challenge of dealing with states that restrict the activities of INGOs; and the challenge of fund raising. Different ways of dealing with these challenges have advantages and disadvantages that vary in importance from context to context, and any satisfactory solution must bear this in mind. Normative views, however, can help to determine outcomes in truly hard cases—when the advantages and disadvantages of different approaches seem comparable—and the chapter ends with reflections on implications for INGOs operating in East Asia.

DEMOCRACY FOR AN EAST ASIAN CONTEXT

The next four chapters assess the possibility and desirability of implementing Western-style democracy in East Asia. One of the bulwarks of liberal democracy is the idea that, at minimum, the political community's most powerful decision-makers should be chosen by the people in free and fair competitive elections. These days, it is also widely argued that democratic values should be promoted in other spheres, such as schools that educate future citizens. Once again, the question is whether it is appropriate to export liberal models derived from the Western experience to East Asian societies. There are reasons to be cautious about implementing liberal notions of democratic rule, and this section examines the possibility of justifiable East Asian variations of these models.

The origin of democratic citizenship can be traced to ancient Athenians. The Athenians recognized that the educational system is crucial for the purpose of cultivating democratic virtues, and they devised elaborate mechanisms for doing so. The main purpose of the Athenian educational system, including intellectual and physical education, was to prepare future citizens for the competitive, rough-and-tumble arena of democratic politics. State-sponsored physical education was an important component of the educational system, and chapter 5 compares the ancient Greek system of physical education with the approach to physical education in ancient China of the Warring States period.

In ancient Greece, the need to train future citizens underpinned state-sponsored physical education in two ways. First, the citizens of diverse

Greek polities fought hard to maintain their political independence, though the sense of cultural commonality allowed for international sporting competitions that provided the forums for the expression of the "political difference within cultural unity" principle. Second, the material surplus of largely commercial societies and freedom from family obligations provided sufficient leisure time for a class of male citizens to perfect their human bodies and train for physical excellence. The tight link between the Greek conception of active citizenship and state-sponsored physical education may not be a legacy worth preserving, however. Greek-style civic republicanism upholds the glorification of warfare and underpins a highly competitive mode of life, including macho pride in athletic rivalry. In ancient China, different social conditions underpinned the Confucian view that physical activity should be tied to the pursuit of nonmilitaristic virtues and that the test of success should be its contribution to moral and intellectual development rather than victory in warfare and international sporting competitions.

The chapter ends with some general reflections on the ideal of active citizenship for the East Asian context. Even if it is possible to detach this ideal from its problematic ancient Greek features, the main problem is that it threatens to overwhelm all our other communal commitments, particularly ties to the family. In East Asian societies with a Confucian heritage, the family has long been regarded as the key to the good life, and the republican tradition is so far removed from people's self-understandings that it is a complete nonstarter. Most people have devoted time and energy to family and other "local" obligations, with political decision making left to an educated, public-spirited elite.

Elite politics does not rule out democratic participation by ordinary citizens, but democracy will take minimal forms, not much more demanding than visiting the voting booth every few years. Chapter 6 points to the Confucian underpinnings of elite politics in East Asia and sketches an ideal that reconciles minimal democracy with elite politics. Confucian political culture places great emphasis on the quality of political rulers. The main task of the educational system is to identify and empower the wise and public-spirited elite, and the common people are not presumed to possess the capabilities necessary for substantial political participation. In imperial China, the meritocratic ideal was institutionalized by means of the civil service examination system. This system was of course imperfect, but neo-Confucian thinkers put forward ideas for reform that may still be relevant for the modern world. Huang Zongxi, for example, argued for a political institution composed of representatives selected on the basis of competitive examinations that test for both memorization and independent thought. Combined with a democratically elected lower house, Huang's proposal could institutionalize dual commitments to "rule by the people" and rule by a talented and public-spirited elite. This chapter ends with suggestions for dealing with conflicts between the two houses and some reflections on the possibility and desirability of strong meritocratic rule.

This ideal, admittedly, has yet to be institutionalized, and the "realist" will favor thinking about political problems in ways that draw on existing practices and institutions. The next two chapters are less speculative: they both focus on the tension between democracy and the interests of minority groups and draw some lessons for East Asian societies. Chapter 7 evaluates the likely effects of democratic elections on minority groups in the East Asian region. It is argued that some less-than-democratic political systems in the region have helped to secure the interests of minority groups and that democratization can be detrimental to those interests. More specifically, democracy can harm minority interests by promoting a form of nation building centered on the culture of the majority group. The experience of several East Asian countries shows that democracy may pose special dangers to vulnerable ethnocultural minority groups because nation-building projects centered on the majority culture can marginalize or eliminate expressions of minority traditions and languages.

This argument should not be too controversial; on reflection, most people will likely accept that democratic rule is generally advantageous for majorities and sometimes for minorities, but that it may also hinder legitimate minority rights, depending on the context. The problem, however, is that leading liberal defenders of minority rights, such as Will Kymlicka, fail to concede the possibility of trade-offs between majority rule and minority rights. More worrisome, this utopian view informs the practices of Western-based prodemocracy forces, perhaps causing real harm to minority groups. Thus, outside prodemocracy forces need to investigate the local reality to determine the likely effects of democratization on minority groups in the region. If democracy is likely to be disadvantageous to minority groups in particular contexts, prodemocracy forces should consider the possibility of focusing their energies elsewhere. The chapter ends with some reflections on the possible dangers of democratization in China for the Taiwanese minority.

The foregoing suggests that even minimal democracy needs to be underpinned by citizens that display political virtues such as tolerance and respect for difference. Chapter 8 puts forward ideas for educating such citizens. One of the teaching methods designed to improve democratic education is public recognition of the intellectual contributions of different groups, including those historically marginalized. In the East Asian context, this means reaching beyond the works of Great White European Males to include works by Asian thinkers that may resonate more with the interests and cultural backgrounds of the students. The aim is not so much to transmit specific moral content from particular traditions as to identify significant contributions by authors of scholarly traditions that students take pride in and that seem to address their concerns, thus increasing the students' desire to learn and participate in classroom discussion, and, one hopes, improving their ability to participate intelligently as adults in the political processes that shape their society.

This argument is supported by my own experience teaching political theory at the National University of Singapore. To give greater recognition to Asian civilizations in the course curriculum, I assigned Han Fei Zi, an ancient Chinese Legalist thinker, as a starting point for the course. Han Fei was an original and politically influential proponent of realpolitik who anticipated many of the arguments in Machiavelli's *The Prince*, and my assumption was that Han Fei and other Chinese thinkers would generate more interest in the predominantly Chinese Singapore context. To my surprise, the decision to discuss the contributions of Chinese thinkers led to hate mail and strong dissatisfaction among minority Malay and Indian students. The following year, the curriculum was expanded to include the contributions of Malay and Indian thinkers and the course was far more successful, judging by the lively discussion in tutorial groups.

The lesson, of course, is that the teacher should make an effort to design a curriculum that draws on the scholarly contributions of all ethnic groups in the class. From the political point of view, a curriculum that ignores the contributions of minority groups can only exacerbate the marginalization and sense of political alienation of those groups in society at large. An inclusive curriculum, on the other hand, provides the foundation for social cohesion and political participation by all groups. The normative vision animating this proposal is not a political community composed of active, public-spirited citizens from all ethnic groups; that, to repeat, would be both unrealistic and undesirable in Western societies, and even more far-fetched in East Asia. But if "minimal democracy"—in the sense of very occasional participation by the people in the public affairs of the day—is to be workable, it is important for all sectors of society to feel a stake in the outcome, to be motivated by slightly more than crude self-interest, and to respect the rights of minority groups. And that is where fully inclusive democratic education can help. The chapter ends with an argument that democratic education should be further tailored to the East Asian context, with open recognition of the value of political elitism and greater emphasis on the virtue of humility.

Capitalism for an East Asian Context

The next three chapters address the question of whether liberal models of capitalism are appropriate for the East Asian context. Liberal democracy is not simply a political system. It is also an economic system that is dominated by owners of capital who hire wage laborers and produce for profit, that is, capitalism. The main virtue of capitalism is that it facilitates economic and technological development more rapidly than other forms of economic organization. The fact that Western liberal democracies first embraced capitalism largely explains their current economic prowess relative to the rest of the world. Several East Asian societies have recently embarked on the "capitalist road" and seem likely to challenge the economic dominance of Western democracies in the future. But capitalism does not take the same forms in all times and places. There are different ways of organizing the market and of dealing with its negative consequences. In East Asia, as we will see, some of these variations may be normatively appealing as well.

East Asian countries such as Japan and Korea have managed to combine rapid economic development with relatively egalitarian distributions of income. Economic development has been less egalitarian in China, but the state's policies in the economic reform era have helped to lift tens of millions out of poverty. Chapter 9 discusses Confucian perspectives on wealth distribution underpinning economic policies in East Asia. The aim here is not to deny the importance of other explanatory factors, but to suggest that Confucianism facilitates and helps to maintain certain characteristic features of East Asian capitalism.

Throughout Chinese history, Confucians opposed heavy-handed Legalist government control and warned of the negative effects of state intervention in the economy. This did not translate, however, into endorsement of an unfettered private property rights regime. Rather, Confucians defended constraints on the free market in the name of more fundamental values. These constraints have influenced the workings of East Asian economies and continue to do so today.

First, the state has an obligation to secure the conditions for people's basic material welfare, an obligation that has priority over competing political goods. The government realizes this aim, according to Mencius, by means of the "well-field system" that allows farmers to make productive use of land while ensuring that enough food is supplied to the non-farming classes. Chinese rulers adapted the principles of this system to their own circumstances, and even Deng Xiaoping's rural land reform program may have been influenced by Mencius's ideas.

Second, Confucians argued that ownership rights should be vested in the family, not the individual, so as to encourage the realization of "family values" such as filial piety, the care of elderly parents. Family joint ownership was institutionalized in traditional legal systems—for example, junior members of families could not be accused of stealing, but only of appropriating (for their own use) family property. While modern East Asian countries have incorporated "individualistic" conceptions of

property rights to a certain extent, they still tend, in both law and morality, to regard property as an asset of the whole family, including elderly
parents. This feature of East Asian–style property rights has the advantage that needy members of the family are less likely to be deprived of
the means of subsistence. However, Confucian familism can be criticized
for its haphazard legal implementation. The chapter ends with some
thoughts on the prospects of exporting Confucian-style constraints on
property rights to countries outside East Asia.

The next two chapters deal more directly with contemporary capitalist
phenomena in East Asia. Chapter 10 tries to steer between the extremes
of universalizing claims made on behalf of the liberal Anglo-American
form of capitalism and glorification of the East Asian approach that preceded the Asian economic crisis of the late 1990s. It attempts to identify
the features of East Asian capitalism that seem, prima facie, to serve desirable social and political purposes while also being compatible with, if
not beneficial for, the requirements of economic productivity in an age of
intense international competition. These features owe something to East
Asia's common cultural background, but not every East Asian country
partakes of all these features.

East Asian capitalism is characterized by several features that serve to
promote economic productivity. These features include a strong, autonomous state that takes an active role in regulating the economy,
heavy reliance on social networks to "grease the wheels" of economic
transactions, a tendency to rely on family members in management and
ownership positions of firms, and group-based business cooperation.
East Asian capitalism is also characterized by several features that serve
to secure the welfare of those vulnerable to the negative effects of capitalist development. These include active state intervention to secure
widespread access to education and curtailment of Western-style property rights as well as an indirect, less interventionist approach that relies
on informal, relational bonds to secure care for the needy. The chapter
ends by drawing implications for public policy. I argue that the East
Asian emphasis on affective ties within the workplace can justify policies
that curb the imperatives of economic productivity, but that the larger
challenge will be to ensure that such policies do not radically undermine
family ties.

Chapter 11 assesses the typical East Asian response to an unfortunate
but characteristic feature of global capitalism—the fact that many people in poor countries lack decent work opportunities and therefore are
drawn to relatively rich countries to do the low-status and difficult work
that locals are unwilling to do. I focus on the case of domestic workers
who migrate to wealthy territories to help with housework and care for
needy family members. They are perhaps the most vulnerable group of

all residents, but they are denied equal rights in East Asian societies, no matter how long they stay.

Liberal political theorists argue that such an arrangement is fundamentally unjust, and that long-term migrant workers should be put on the road to equal citizenship. Their argument mirrors the emerging pattern in most Western liberal democracies. In East Asia, however, migrant domestic workers typically have other concerns and do not regard equal citizenship as an important goal. Were they to do so, they would likely be deported, and the door would be closed to other migrant domestic workers. The East Asian approach to migrant workers seems morally suspect, but it has comparative advantages. The fact that the door is closed to equal rights has the benefit that more doors are open to temporary contract workers. In most Western countries, few foreign domestic workers are officially admitted, though many work illegally without any legal protections whatsoever. The choice, in reality, is between Western-style, formal equal rights for all workers combined with high rates of illegal employment of foreigners and Asian-style reliance on large numbers of contract workers with legal protection but without the hope of equal rights. In the West, the liberal political culture places higher priority on the justice of legal forms, and there may be greater willingness to accept substantial harm in the social world for the sake of preserving laws that conform to liberal democratic principles. In East Asia, by contrast, the authorities prefer to enact nonliberal laws that allow for large numbers of migrant domestic workers to engage temporarily in legally protected work in their territories. And from the perspective of people in poor sending countries and regions, the East Asian approach may be preferable. The cultural particularities in East Asia, such as the idea of extending family-like norms to nonfamily members, may also justify different solutions to the question of how best to secure the interests of migrant domestic workers. The chapter ends with a discussion of migrant domestic workers in mainland Chinese cities: it turns out that similar questions and prescriptions may also arise at the national level.

A Note on the Culturally Sensitive Approach to Political Theorizing

These essays may be provocative. In my view, however, the pervasive and politically influential view that liberal democracy is the final destination of human social evolution is sufficiently wrong-headed that it is better to err on the side of critique. East Asian societies, by and large, have been relatively successful in adapting to the requirements of modernity.

To the extent that East Asian countries need to reform, they should be
very cautious about implementing liberal models that fail to work properly at home, never mind in contexts with radically different cultures and
priorities. Put positively, the traditional values of East Asia provide am-
ple resources for thinking about social and political change.

The role of "traditional values," however, may seem somewhat obscure. If the aim is to explain policy outcomes, the effects of economic
and political factors often seem more immediate and less controversial.
But culture can also play an important role. It provides an intellectual
framework for sociopolitical alternatives and the motivational resources
for policy implementation, and certain paths thus become more likely.
Let me be more precise. Culture can help to explain the *origin* of policies
and institutional arrangements. Traditional Confucian concerns for securing the basic means of subsistence, for example, may have made East
Asian legislators emotionally and intellectually committed to relatively
egalitarian forms of economic development. Culture can also help to explain the *stability* of policies and institutional arrangements. Legislators
in Singapore may have been primarily motivated by the need to minimize state welfare expenditures when they forced adult children to provide material support for their elderly parents, but this policy may prove
to be long-lasting at least partly because it resonates with people's traditional and deeply felt concern for filial piety. Culture can also help to
explain the *failure* of policies. Japanese policymakers, in their haste to
modernize, copied the "shareholder-first" Anglo-Saxon model of corporate governance in the early twentieth century, but this model may have
been short-lived partly because of its incompatibility with deeply held
cultural values that prioritize reciprocal obligations in face-to-face group
contexts (e.g., fellow workers) over obligations to distant outsiders (e.g.,
anonymous shareholders). A similar argument can be made about the
Cultural Revolution's ultimately failed attack on family loyalties. The
culturally sensitive approach, in short, allows for the possibility that
deeply held values provide the motivational resources to influence certain outcomes, both in the minds of legislators and in the minds of people who must follow (or defy) their decisions.

Let me say something about the role of cultural values in thinking
about social and political reform. Short- to medium-term proposals
should not deviate too far from existing social practices (or else they
would not seem realistic). For such proposals, it is more important to
have detailed knowledge of the relevant political and economic context
than knowledge of philosophical traditions. For example, the defense of
differential citizenship rights in Singapore and Hong Kong appeals primarily to economic and political features of those two societies (chapter
11). In the case of medium- to long-term proposals, the constraint of

feasibility is relaxed somewhat and there is more room to seek inspiration from traditional philosophical resources. One example is the proposal for an upper house of government composed of meritocratically selected deputies (chapter 6). Such proposals need to show their potential for addressing the medium- to long-term needs of the particular society. It also helps to speculate about how they might evolve from current practices and institutions, but detailed knowledge of the empirical reality is not essential. Part of the point of putting forward medium- to long-term proposals is the expectation (hope) that they can shape the future, though not necessarily the foreseeable future.

Finally, there is the question of which particular cultural traditions matter for explanatory and normative purposes. Once again, it depends on the context. In East Asia, two main political traditions—Confucianism and Legalism—have shaped and continue to shape understandings informing political practices and ways of dealing with social problems.[21] More precisely, Confucian concerns for the good of the family, material well-being, and the quality of political rulers inform political understandings in the region, as do Legalist calls for strong states and political institutions that reflect the needs of the times. These two traditions have been in constant tension, but both are essential underpinnings of East Asian politics. From a normative standpoint, both traditions have merits and demerits, and which particular aspect to defend depends, once again, on the context and the particular problem at hand.

I have been presenting material from this book at conferences and seminars for several years, and no matter how much I say—to be more precise, because of how much I say—there still seem to be misunderstandings regarding my methodology and my intentions. Hence, the final chapter will attempt to set the record straight—and perhaps the book will end on a lighter note than expected.

[21] John E. Schrecker distinguishes between Confucian-inspired *fengjian* and Legalist-inspired *junxian* and helpfully deploys these ideal types to understand ancient China and the subsequent course of Chinese history. Shrecker, *The Chinese Revolution in Historical Perspective* (New York: Greenwood Press, 1991).

PART ONE

Human Rights for an East Asian Context

2

Just War and Confucianism: Implications for the Contemporary World

Mencius said, "A true king uses virtue and
benevolence, a hegemon uses force under the
pretext of benevolence." Let us first consider
the idea of the hegemon. According to Mencius's
saying, a hegemon uses force to attack others in the
name of benevolent justice. This kind of war is an
unjust war. . . . In ancient times as well as today, most
rulers are very clear regarding political realities, they
won't lightly abandon the cover of virtue to launch
such wars. . . . The best contemporary example is
President Bush's war of invasion against Iraq! He used
the excuses of weapons of mass destruction and
terrorism in order to obtain oil resources and
to consolidate his strategic position in the Middle
East. This is the best example of "using force
under the pretext of benevolence." Bush is
today's hegemonic king.
—Ming Yongquan,
"Are There Just Wars?"[1]

IT MIGHT SEEM odd that the most modern of technologies—the Internet—should be filled with references to ancient Confucian thinkers. Yet that is exactly what happened in response to the Bush administration's wars in/against Afghanistan and Iraq.[2] The theories of Confucians from what subsequently became known as the Warring States era were downloaded from computer to computer in Chinese-speaking households for

[1] Ming Yongquan, "Youmeiyou zhengyi de zhanzheng? Yilun Rujia (wang ba zhi bian)" [Are There Just Wars? A Confucian Debate on True Kings and Hegemons] (http://www.arts.cuhk.hk.hk/~hkshp, visited 11 October 2003).

[2] As were Chinese language newspaper articles—see, e.g., Chen Zhe, "Cong xiangin zhuzi de 'zhanzhengguan' jiedu jinri de Mei A zhi zhan" [Interpreting Today's American-Afghanistan War Using the War Concepts of Various Pre-Qin Thinkers], *Lianhe zaobao*, 11 October 2001.

the purpose of evaluating U.S foreign policy. But what exactly did classical Confucians say regarding just and unjust warfare? And does it make sense to invoke their ideas in today's vastly different political world? Why not simply stick to the language of human rights? These questions will be explored below.

THE IDEAL WORLD VERSUS THE NONIDEAL WORLD

First, however, we need to confront an apparent problem.[3] Whatever the relevance of Confucian political values, they do not seem to bear on the question of war between sovereign states. War involves the use of force to maintain or increase the state's territory. Yet classical Confucianism seems to rule out the possibility that rulers could justifiably use force to exercise authority over a particular territory and establish boundaries between that territory and the rest of the world. Instead, Confucians defended the ideal of *tian xia* (天下, the world under Heaven), a harmonious political order without state boundaries and governed by a sage by means of virtue, without any coercive power at all.[4] Moreover, this harmonious order can and should be attained by means of benevolence and positive example, once again without any coercive power. It is a kind of communism attained by entirely peaceful means, without any revolutionary uprisings.[5] This would seem to rule out the possibility of justifiable use of force. In this view, all wars are bad, and pacifism would seem to be the only justifiable moral stance. But are Confucians really pacifists?[6]

---

[3] This section draws on ideas initially expressed in my essay, "The Making and Unmaking of Boundaries," in *States, Nations, and Borders: The Ethics of Making Boundaries*, ed. Allen Buchanan and Margaret Moore (New York: Cambridge University Press, 2003), 58–62.

[4] See the discussion in chapter 5.

[5] Communism here means a society where the coercive apparatus of the state would have "withered away" and social order is secured by noncoercive means. Beyond that, of course, there are many differences between the ideals of Marx and Confucius. For example, the Confucian ideal is supposed to have existed earlier so it is a matter of recovering the past, whereas communism is meant to lie in the future and can only be implemented once the productive forces provide the material basis for humans to be freed of the need to engage in drudge labor. Another key difference is that Confucian familism would place more informal constraints upon individual action compared to Marx's ideal.

[6] I will argue that Confucians are not pacifists. Edmund Ryden argues that, more generally, "there is no basis in the Chinese tradition for pacifism." Ryden, *Just War and Pacifism: Chinese and Christian Perspectives in Dialogue* (Taipei: Taipei Ricci Institute, 2001), 46.

Confucius himself does point to the possibility of a sage-king who could spread "his peace to all the people" (14.42, Leys; see also 17.6).[7] In this ideal world, the ruler need not resort to coercion or punitive laws:

> Lord Ji Kang asked Confucius about government, saying: "Suppose I were to kill those without the Way to help those with the Way: how about that?" Confucius replied: "You are here to govern; what need is there to kill? If you desire the good, the people will be good. The moral power of the exemplary person is the wind, the virtue of the common person is grass. Under the wind, the grass must bend." (12.19; Leys, modified)

Confucius suggests that the moral power (*de*, 德) of the ideal ruler will eventually attract those living in faraway lands, bringing peace to the whole world and presumably doing away with the need for territorial boundaries between states:

> I have always heard that what worries the head of a state or the chief of a clan is not poverty but the inequitable distribution of wealth, not the lack of population, but the lack of peace. For if wealth is equitably distributed, there will be no poverty, and where there is peace, there is no lack of population. And then, if people who live in far-off lands still resist your attraction, you must draw them to you by the moral power of your civilization; and then, having attracted them, make them enjoy your peace. (16.1; Leys, modified)

Mencius draws on these ideas to elaborate upon the ideal of a sage-king who rules the whole world by noncoercive means. This end can be achieved by gaining the sympathy of the people:

> There is a way to gain the whole world. It is to gain the people, and having gained them one gains the whole world. There is a way to gain the people. Gain their hearts, and then you gain them. (4A.10; Dobson, modified)[8]

---

[7] The translations of *The Analects of Confucius* are based on one of two translations (as indicated in the main text): Simon Leys's translation of *The Analects of Confucius* (New York: Norton, 1997), and Roger T. Ames and Henry Rosemont, Jr.'s translation of *The Analects of Confucius: A Philosophical Translation* (New York: Ballantine Books, 1998). Both these translations have been criticized for excessive extrapolations that seem to make Confucius into a proponent of modern liberalism, and I have occasionally modified the translations (as indicated in the main text with "modified").

[8] The translations of Mencius are based on one of two translations (as indicated in the main text): W.A.C.H. Dobson's translation of *The Works of Mencius* (London: Oxford University Press, 1963), which is helpfully organized by themes; or D. C. Lau's complete translation of *Mencius* (Hong Kong: The Chinese University Press, 1984), vols. 1 and 2, which includes the accompanying Chinese text. I have occasionally modified these translations (as indicated in the main text with "modified").

Mencius argues that the ideal ruler would win people's hearts simply by his[9] benevolence (*ren*, 仁), without relying on the use of force (see 1A.6). Even if people do not seem immediately receptive to Confucian norms, the ruler should not worry. He should cultivate his own personal virtue, people will be inspired by his example, and eventually he will gain the allegiance of the whole world:

> Mencius said, "If others do not respond to your love with love, look into your own benevolence; if others do not respond to your attempts to govern them, look into your own wisdom; if others do not respond to your courtesy, look into your own respect. In other words, look into yourself whenever you fail to achieve your purpose. When you are correct in your person, the whole world will turn to you. (4A.4; Lau, modified)

Mencius even seems to provide a time frame for ultimate success:

> If any lord implements the policies [government] of King Wen [an ideal ruler of the past], he will be ruling over the whole world within seven years. (4A.13; Lau, modified)

From a contemporary perspective,[10] all this might seem like pie-in-the-sky theorizing, of little relevance to the real world. Fortunately, that is not the end of the story. In fact, it would be surprising if Confucius and

---

[9] I use the male personal pronoun because Confucius and Mencius seemed to assume (without argument) that the ideal sage-king would be male. Having said that, Chan Sin Yee argues that Confucius and Mencius did not argue in favor of the biological inferiority of women (in contrast to Aristotle) and that the central values of Confucianism do allow in principle for the equal participation of women in education. See her essays, "Gender and Relationship Roles in the Analects and the Mencius," *Asian Philosophy*, vol. 10, no. 2 (Summer 2000); and "The Confucian Conception of Gender in the Twenty-First Century," *Confucianism for the Modern World*, ed. Daniel A. Bell and Hahm Chaibong (New York: Cambridge University Press, 2003).

[10] This form of idealism also seemed absurdly utopian to Legalist critics of Confucianism in the Warring States era. As Han Fei Zi brilliantly put it, "Now if one says that we must wait for the worthiness of a Yao or a Shun [two sage-kings of the distant past] to bring order to the people of the current age, this is like saying that one should hold out for fine grain and meat in order to save oneself from starvation." Han Fei Zi, in *Readings in Classical Chinese Philosophy*, ed. Philip J. Ivanhoe and Bryan W. Van Norden (New York: Seven Bridges Press, 2001), 135. Sima Qian, China's Han dynasty grand historian, also heaped contempt upon Confucian idealists: "What then shall be said of those scholars of our time, blind to all great issues, and without any appreciation of relative values, who can only bark out their stale formulas about 'virtue' and 'civilization,' condemning the use of military weapons? They will surely bring our country to impotence and dishonor and the loss of her rightful heritage; or, at the very least, they will bring about invasion and rebellion, sacrifice of territory and general enfeeblement." Quoted in Yitzhak Shichor, "Military-Civilian Integration in China: Legacy and Policy," in *Civil-Military Relations, Nation-Building, and National Identity: Comparative Perspectives*, ed. Constantine P. Danopoulos, Dhirendra Vajpeyi, and Amir Bar-or (Westport, CT: Praeger, 2004), 85.

Mencius had not attempted to provide some practical, morally informed guidance in a nonideal political world of sovereign states delimited by territorial boundaries. Consider the fact that *The Analects of Confucius* and *The Works of Mencius* were penned during the Spring and Autumn and Warring States periods (c. 800–221 B.C.E.), a time of ruthless competition for territorial advantage between small walled states. In such a context, it would seem odd, to say the least, for two political thinkers explicitly concerned with practical effect to limit their political advice to quasi-anarchistic principles.[11] This kind of political thinking might have resonated more in the days of imperial China, when rulers saw themselves as governing the largest and most powerful empire in the world surrounded by as-yet-uncivilized barbarians. But China had not yet been unified in the Warring States period.[12] True, Warring States thinkers never quite abandoned the background ideal of universal kinship,[13] but the idea that political thinkers should provide guidance for leaders of a self-conscious, culturally unified, and politically stable community with the potential to spread civilized norms (what later became known as *Zhongguo*, 中國: literally, "Middle Kingdom")[14] would have seem farfetched to thinkers of the time.

Moreover, Mencius suggests that successful sage-kings come in five-hundred-year cycles—or more, since "seven hundred years have now passed since Chou began. As a matter of simple calculation the time is overdue" (2B.13, Dobson; see also 7B.38). Mencius seems to suggest that sage rulers would not last for more than a generation or two,[15] which means that—according to his own theory—the nonideal world of

[11] I say "quasi-anarchistic" because, unlike anarchists, Confucius and Mencius still saw the need for a political ruler to provide for order without coercion. It is worth noting that even Laozi is not, properly speaking, an anarchist because he allowed for the use of military weapons that, if necessary, must be used with "calm restraint" (*Daodejing*, 31 *zhang*).

[12] The first Chinese dynasty was founded in 221 B.C.E. by the ruthless Emperor Qin, who relied on legalist principles that emphasized the use of harsh punishments and quasi-totalitarian control of the whole population. Emperor Qin is notorious for ordering the live burial of Confucian scholars and their books. Imperial China only began to be "Confucianized" during the Han dynasty (206 B.C.E.–220 C.E.).

[13] See Benjamin Schwartz, "The Chinese Perception of Order, Past and Present," in *The Chinese World Order: Traditional China's Foreign Relations*, ed. John K. Fairbank (Cambridge: Harvard University Press, 1968), 279.

[14] The references to *zhongguo* (中國) in Mencius (e.g., 1A.7) refer to the geographical location of the central states in the Warring States era and not to their moral status (i.e., these states were not viewed as the natural heirs of the Zhou dynasty, and there was no particular expectation that they would form the core of a unified empire).

[15] Only one passage in *The Works of Mencius* deals with the question of the succession of sage-kings. Mencius notes that after sage-king Yao's death, his unsagelike son took over. But the people paid homage to Shun, and the sage-Shun assumed the "Mandate of Heaven," ruling for a further twenty-eight years (5A.5).

competing states delimited by territorial boundaries is the reality for
roughly 90 percent of the time. Given the predominance of the nonideal
world, one might have expected Mencius to formulate principles of political guidance for this context as well.

Confucius is even more skeptical concerning the prospects of sage-kings
ever taking power. For one thing, he did not—unlike Mencius[16]—consider
himself to be in the top moral/intellectual category, which is presumably a
requisite for sagehood:

> The Master asked Zigong: "Which is the better, you or Yan Hui?"—"How
> could I compare myself with Yan Hui? From one thing he learns, he deduces
> ten; from one thing I learn, I only deduce two." The Master said: "Indeed,
> you are not his match; and neither am I." (5.9; Leys, modified; see also 7.34)

But even Yan Hui (Confucius's favorite pupil), along with everybody else
Confucius has met, is subject to human weaknesses: "I have yet to meet
the person who is fonder of virtue than of physical beauty" (15.13; Ames
and Rosemont, modified). Nor is Confucius overly confident about the
ability to cultivate one's personal virtue in an honest and non-self-
deceiving way: The Master said: "Alas, I have never seen a man capable
of seeing his own faults and of exposing them in the tribunals of his
heart" (5.27; Leys). Even Yao and Shun, the icons of sagehood, proved
to be deficient:

> Zigong said: "What would you say of a man who showers the people with
> blessings and who could save the multitude? Could he be called benevo-
> lent? The Master said: What has this to do with benevolence? He would be
> a saint! Even Yao and Shun would be deficient in this respect. (6.30; Leys,
> modified; see also 7.26)

In short, both Confucius and Mencius seem to recognize the difficulty,
if not impossibility, of implementing an ideal, nonterritorial political order governed by a wise and virtuous sage-king who inspires the whole
world simply by means of his exemplary moral character. But is there any
evidence that classical Confucians did in fact attempt to provide practical, morally informed guidance for a nonideal world? In my view, many,
if not most, of the passages in *The Analects of Confucius* and *The Works
of Mencius* seem to assume the context of a nonideal political world.[17] It
is difficult to otherwise make sense of, for example, the statement in *The*

---

[16] See 2B.13.

[17] The third "founding father" of Confucianism—Xunzi (c. 310–219 B.C.E.)—more explicitly distinguishes between prescriptions for ideal regimes and those for nonideal ones
(comparable to Aristotle's distinctions in the *Politics*)—see, e.g., Xunzi's distinctions between true kings (*wang*, 王), hegemons (*ba*, 霸), and pure opportunists (11.1a–11.2c), in decreasing order of goodness. Unlike Mencius, Xunzi does recognize that hegemons can be

Analects that "An exemplary person has a moral obligation to serve the state, even if he can foresee that the Way will not prevail" (18.7; Leys, modified). In the same vein, it would seem odd for Mencius—if his only concern was to lecture rulers on the requirements of sagehood—to make the argument that people can transgress traditional norms in hard-luck situations (4A.17), including breaking promises (4B.11) and killing tyrannical rulers (1B.8). More pertinently, the passages on warfare[18] provide direct evidence that Confucius and Mencius allowed for the possibility that the use of force can be justified in nonideal situations.[19] One quote will suffice to make this point:

> Duke Wen of Teng asked, "Teng is a small state, wedged between Qi and Chu. Should I be subservient to Qi or should I be subservient to Chu?"
>
> "This is a question that is beyond me," answered Mencius. "If you insist, there is only one course of action I can suggest. Dig deeper moats and build higher walls and defend them shoulder to shoulder with the people. If they would rather die than desert you, then all is not lost." (1B.13; Lau, modified)

In a nonideal context, the justifiable course of action may be to reinforce, rather than abolish, territorial boundaries between states.[20] If Mencius—

---

partly bad and partly good, and he even suggests that power politics would be the right strategy to adopt by a ruler who is aware of his own incompetence and seeks out capable ministers (11.2c). In this chapter, however, I focus primarily on Mencius and Confucius because Xunzi is a more controversial character who is "blamed" for being a major influence on Legalism. If it turns out that even the relatively "idealistic" Confucian thinkers seek to provide useful guidance for rulers in nonideal contexts, this would make the case for the practical relevance of Confucian theories of just and unjust war even more compelling.

[18] For a more general presentation and analysis of Confucian military thought, see *Zhongguo Ruxue baike quanshu* [Encyclopedia of Confucianism in China] (Beijing: Zhongguo dabaike quanshu chubanshe, 1997), 185–93). It is interesting to note that the otherwise comprehensive English-language *RoutledgeCurzon Encyclopedia of Confucianism*, ed. Xinzhong Yao (London: RoutledgeCurzon, 2003), does not have an entry on Confucianism and War.

[19] Once again, it would be easier to make the case by invoking Xunzi's military thought, with its greater willingness to embrace realpolitik (see, e.g., Book 15, "Debates on the Principles of Warfare"). My strategy, however, is to show that Confucius and Mencius also seem to allow for less-than-ideal solutions to dilemmas in nonideal contexts.

[20] The same sort of reasoning leads contemporary anarchists such as Noam Chomsky to endorse the possibility that walls can have legitimate defensive purposes in the modern world (in the case of Israel, if it decided to build a security wall within its internationally recognized border, although he condemns Israel's current wall as an illegitimate attempt to isolate Palestinians and annex land on the West Bank). Chomsky, "A Wall as a Weapon," *The New York Times*, 23 February 2004, A25.

who is considered to be the most "idealistic" of the Confucians[21]—had only been concerned with the ideal world, he would have urged Duke Wen to rely exclusively on moral power to deal with larger states, in the hope that virtue would attract the good will of people outside and eventually make territorial boundaries obsolete.[22]

My claim, in short, is that several prescriptions in *The Analects of Confucius*[23] and *The Works of Mencius* were meant to apply in a political context of walled states competing for territorial advantage, including the need for morally informed, practical guidance in military affairs.[24]

---

[21] For example, Peter R. Moody, Jr., comments on Mencius's "strong—not to say obsessive—distinction between what is expedient (*li*) and what is right (*i*) [yi], and the conviction that when the right and the expedient conflict, the only valid standard of behavior is the right." Moody, "The Legalism of Han Fei-tzu and Its Affinities with Modern Political Thought," *International Philosophical Quarterly*, vol. 19, no. 3 (September 1979), 321. In the nonideal world, however, Mencius does allow for less-than-ideal prescriptions.

[22] Perhaps because they do not explicitly distinguish between Mencius's prescriptions for the ideal world and those appropriate for the nonideal world, even otherwise sympathetic scholars criticize Mencius for his "unrealistic" theories on warfare. See, e.g., Liang Wei Xian, *Mengzi yanjiu* [Research on Mencius] (Taipei: Wenjin chubanshe 1993), 71–72.

[23] According to E. Bruce Brooks and Taeko A. Brooks, the real Confucius was in fact a warrior who had the misfortune to live at a time when his skills as a charioteer and bowman were becoming obsolete. Brooks and Brooks, *The Original Analects* (New York: Columbia University Press, 1998), 270–71. The myth of Confucius as a learned scholar only emerged after his death. This is a controversial interpretation, but if true it would lend even more support for the thesis that many of the prescriptions in the *Analects* were meant to apply in a nonideal context of competing states.

[24] This Confucian idea that war should be considered nonideal, an unfortunate but occasionally necessary event stemming from difficult circumstances, may seem obvious today (if not always to politicians: Castro said that Khrushchev had "no cojones" [balls] for having averted war during the Cuban missile crisis William Taubman, *Khrushchev: The Man and His Era* [New York: W. W. Norton, 2003], 579); President George W. Bush praised Blair for having had the "cojones" to stand up to antiwar forces in the buildup to the invasion of Iraq; etc.) However, it contrasts with the historical glorification of warfare and the romantic model of the heroic soldier characterized in terms of boldness and masculinity that has been so prominent in Western societies. See, e.g., Kurtis Hagen, "A Chinese Critique on Western Ways of Warfare," *Asian Philosophy*, vol. 6, no. 3 (November 1996) (http://search.epnet.com/direct.asp?an=9702072810&db=aph, visited 12 January 2003), 3–7; see chapter 5 of this book for an account of the ancient Greek view that has contributed much to this view. The mainstream premodern Western view helps to explain why antiwar modernists like Benjamin Constant had to run through the list of prowar arguments in order to show that they had become obsolete. He summarizes his critique of the premodern view with the statement, "La guerre a perdu son charme, comme son utilité" [War has lost its charm as well as its utility]. Constant, *Ecrits Politiques*, ed. Marcel Gauchet (Paris: Gallimard, 1997). 132. There would be no need for a Chinese critic of warfare to argue against the view that war is "charming."

In the next section, I will discuss general Confucian principles that underpin theorizing on just and unjust war. I limit myself to the values espoused by Confucius and Mencius. *The Analects of Confucius* is, of course, the central, founding text in the Confucian tradition, and Mencius, who elaborated and systematized Confucius's ideas, became its most famous exponent.[25] Mencius continues to be the most influential theorist of war and just war in the Confucian tradition, and the third section is devoted to presenting Mencius's views on the topic. The chapter ends by considering the contemporary implications of Confucianism for thinking about just and unjust war.

GENERAL CONFUCIAN PRINCIPLES OF GOOD GOVERNMENT

The topic of just and unjust war must be approached somewhat indirectly. To the extent that Confucius and Mencius evaluated the justice of warfare, it was by means of applying more general ideals regarding good government that have implications for evaluating the justice of warfare. Those ideals are meant to apply in the ideal world, but they are also relevant for the nonideal world. Even in the nonideal world of competing states marked by territorial boundaries, rulers should strive to meet those ideals, to the extent possible.

At a minimum, rulers should strive for peace (*an*, 安, or *ning*, 寧). In an ideal world, Mencius suggests, the whole world (*tian xia*, 天下) would be unified and peaceful (1A.6; 2B12; see also *The Analects*, 14.42). One benevolent ruler would have obtained sovereignty over the whole world without having committed a single unjust deed (2A.2), and no one would be fighting for the sake of gaining territory. At that point, it makes sense to ask, "What need is there for war?" (7B.4, Lau).

In a world of competing states, however, it would be foolish for states to act on the assumption that wars are unnecessary. In the days of early Confucianism, several states were ruled by blood-thirsty tyrants ready and willing to use ruthless means to increase their territory, and this called for different prescriptions. In this nonideal world, Confucians held that smaller countries must prepare to defend themselves. This involves a well-trained army—as Confucius puts it, "To send to war a people that has not been properly taught is wasting them" (13.30, Leys; see also 13.29). Fortified boundaries are also essential—as noted above, Mencius

---

[25] The philosophy of Mencius became the orthodoxy in imperial China from the Song onward, and still today he is "regarded as a fountainhead of inspiration by contemporary Neo-Confucian philosophers." Shu-hsien Liu, *Understanding Confucian Philosophy* (Westport, CT: Greenwood Press, 1988), 55.

urges the governor of a small state to "Dig deeper moats and build higher walls and defend them shoulder to shoulder with the people. If they would rather die than desert you, then all is not lost" (1B.13). Rulers of small states must get the people on their side, train them for self-defense, and fortify territorial boundaries. There is no other way to secure the peace.

Put negatively, boundaries between states would not be justified if they did not serve the value of peace. In his own day, Mencius lamented the fact that boundaries resulted from ruthless wars of conquest:

> Mencius said, "The setting up of border posts in antiquity was to prevent violence. Today they are set up for the purpose of engaging in violence."[26] (7B.8, Dobson; see also 6B.9)

Peace, however, does not simply mean the absence of violence.[27] It also refers to a united world that is governed by benevolence (*ren*, 仁). In an ideal Confucian world, to repeat, one sage-king would rule peacefully over the whole world, without any coercion whatsoever. In a nonideal, multistate world, rulers should still strive to realize the ideal. Even small states can be governed by relatively benign rulers that display benevolence:[28]

> Mencius said, "A hegemon uses force under the pretext of violence. Such a one has no need of the rule of a major state. A True King is one who, practising benevolence, resorts only to virtue. Such a one has no need for a major state. Tang the Successful had a state of only seventy miles square, and King Wen a state of only a hundred miles square. (2A.3; Dobson, modified)

[26] This passage suggests that fixed territorial boundaries existed even in the Golden Days of Antiquity (for the purpose of preventing violence), which suggests once again that Mencius may not have been overly optimistic about the possibility of a borderless world governed by one ruler.

[27] Li Ming Han, "Cong Ruxue de guandian kan heping wenti" [Looking at the Issue of Peace from a Confucian Perspective], in *Dangdai Ruxue fazhan zhi xin qiji* [Opportunities for the Development of Contemporary Confucianism], ed. Liu An Wu (Taipei: Wenjin chubanshe, 1997), 271.

[28] What, one may ask, does *ren* (variously translated as benevolence, humanity, or love) mean? As one may expect, there have been volumes of debate on this question in the Confucian tradition. Confucius himself is (deliberately?) vague, though one passage does provide some insights:

> Zizhang asked Confucius about benevolence. The Master said: "Whoever could spread the five practices everywhere in the world would implement benevolence." "And what are these?" "Courtesy, tolerance, good faith, diligence, generosity. Courtesy wards off insults; tolerance wins over the many; good faith inspires the trust of others; diligence ensures success; generosity confers authority upon others." (17.6; Leys, modified)

But the True King should not be satisfied with a small state. He should try to spread benevolence beyond his borders.[29] The appropriate means, to repeat, is moral power, not force:[30]

> Allegiance which is gained by the use of force is not allegiance of the heart—it is the allegiance which comes from imposing upon weakness. Allegiance which is gained by the exercise of moral power is true allegiance. It is the response of joy felt deeply in the heart. (2A.3, Dobson)

The aim is to attract as many people as possible, including those living in faraway lands:

> It is all a matter of practicing good government [putting benevolence into practice]. But if you were really to do so, then all within the four seas [the whole world] would raise their heads to watch for your coming, desiring you as their ruler. (3B.5, Lau, modified; see also *The Analects*, 13.16)

There are no restrictions—racial, ethnic, or other—to membership in the Confucian state, beyond adherence to benevolence. Everyone can, in principle, be "civilized" (see *The Analects*, 9.14, 15.10).[31]

The key to implementing these ideals of good government is a virtuous and capable ruler.[32] In an ideal world, once again, one virtuous ruler would govern the whole world. The ruler would achieve perfect virtue by observing the correct rites (*li*, 禮), his moral power would have a "civilizing" effect on the people, and there would be no need for coercive laws and regulations. As Confucius put it,

> The practice of benevolence comes down to this: tame the self and restore the rites. Tame the self and restore the rites for but one day, and the whole world will rally to your benevolence. (12.1; Leys, modified; see also Mencius, 2A.3)

---

[29] Mencius, however, suggests that large states based on benevolence will find it easier to "spread the message" abroad: "Today, if a large state were to put into effect government based on benevolence, the rejoicing of the people would be that of a man saved from the gallows" (2A.1; Robson, modified).

[30] If moral power fails, however, then armed force can be justified—see the discussion of punitive expeditions below.

[31] See, e.g., Wu Junsheng, "Tianxia yijia guannian yu shijie heping" [The Concept of One Family under Heaven and World Peace], *Dongfang zazhi*, vol. 10, no. 8 (1977), 9.

[32] In imperial China, of course, Confucian ideals of good government were made to depend on more than the quality of the ruler—such institutions as civil service examinations and censors were designed to help promote those ideals. Still, Confucians typically emphasized the moral quality of the ruler, and this concern continues to influence evaluation of rulers in East Asian societies with a Confucian heritage to a greater extent than would be the case in most Western societies. In Korea, for example, it is quite likely that a publicly exposed liar such as Bill Clinton would have lost the "Mandate of Heaven" (that is, the moral right to rule) and been forced to resign.

In the real world, however, the people will not always be swayed by the personal virtue of the ruler. The ruler should do his best to rely on moral persuasion and exemplary virtue, but some people may not respond to virtue:

> The Master said: "The moral power of the Middle Way is supreme, and yet it is not commonly found in the people anymore." (6.29, Leys; see also 8.9)

Even perfect benevolence will not always be reciprocated: someone might well respond to the benevolence with bad treatment, at which point the exemplary person should conclude that his interlocutor is an "utter reprobate" (4B.28, Dobson). Not surprisingly, Confucius allowed for the use of legal punishments when other mechanisms for promoting moral behavior (and preventing immoral behavior) fail to do their work (12.13, 4.11).[33] Mencius concurred,[34] going so far as to justify the use of the death penalty for those who neglect elderly parents (6B.7; see also 1B.7 and 7A.12).[35]

More worrisome, some rulers in the nonideal, multistate world are positively wicked.[36] In fact, Mencius could not find a single virtuous ruler in his own day, though he seemed to recognize that some were better than others (see, e.g., 6B.7), and some rulers openly claimed to be open to positive influence (see, e.g., 1A.4). This helps to explain why Mencius, like Confucius himself, moved from state to state, hoping to find rulers receptive to his advice. Unfortunately, perhaps, this was not to happen in his lifetime.[37]

Other than manifesting virtue, the ideal ruler should also implement the right *policies*. In practice, this means securing the conditions for people's basic means of subsistence and intellectual/moral development. In the nonideal world, however, there may be conflicting obligations that

[33] See the discussion in Joseph Chan, "A Confucian Perspective on Human Rights for Contemporary China," in *The East Asian Challenge for Human Rights*, ed. Joanne R. Bauer and Daniel A. Bell (New York: Cambridge University Press, 1999), 226–27.

[34] Even in an ideal state, Mencius suggests, the True King will *lighten* (but not eliminate) the penal code (1A.5). In another passage, Mencius says that "when worthy men are in positions of authority . . . its policies and laws will be made clear to all (2A.4; Dobson). The aim seems to be transparency, not the abolition of punitive laws.

[35] Confucius also seemed to endorse the death penalty, though not as a first resort: "To impose the death penalty without first attempting to reform is cruel" (20.2; Lau).

[36] Later Confucian thinkers—most notably, Huang Zongxi—explicitly drew the implication that there is a need for institutional checks on the ruler's power. See Wm. Theodore de Bary, *Asian Values and Human Rights: A Confucian Communitarian Perspective* (Cambridge: Harvard University Press, 1998), chap. 6.

[37] Confucius himself did not find any rulers receptive to his ideas about good government, and while Mencius had slightly more success—he served briefly as minister in the state of Qi—he soon became disenchanted with political life and reluctantly settled for a teaching career.

need to be prioritized. According to the *Analects*, the obligation to secure the basic means of subsistence of the people should have priority:

> Ranyou drove the Master's carriage on a trip to Wei. The Master said: "What
> a huge population!" Ranyou said: "When the people are so numerous, what
> more can be done for them?" The Master said, "Make them prosperous."
> Ranyou asked, "When the people are prosperous, what more can be done for
> them?" The Master replied, "Educate them." (13.9; Ames and Rosemont,
> modified)

In the same vein, Mencius argued that there is no point promoting moral
behavior if people are worried about their next meal: "The people will
not have dependable feelings if they are without dependable means of
support. Lacking dependable means of support, they will go astray and
fall into excesses, stopping at nothing" (1A.7; Lau, modified).[38] Depriving the people of their means of support will lead to internal strife, and it
will be impossible to secure the peace. At a minimum, then, the ruler
striving for peace must ensure that the people are well fed.

MENCIUS ON JUST AND UNJUST WAR

Let us see how Mencius drew upon these ideals of good government to
evaluate the justice of warfare. Mencius, to repeat, argued that rulers
have an obligation to promote the peaceful unification the world. As a
consequence, he was critical of rulers who launched bloody wars of conquest simply to increase their territory and engage in economic
plunder—wars that were, unfortunately, all too common in his own day
(see, e.g., 7B.8). He was also critical of "Machiavellian"[39] advisers who
aimed to help rulers achieve their nefarious purposes:

> Mencius said, "Those who serve rulers today promise to enlarge their land-
> holdings and enrich their treasuries and arsenals. They are called 'good
> ministers' but in antiquity they would have been called 'plunderers of the
> people.' To enrich a ruler who is neither attracted to the Way nor inclined
> towards benevolence is to enrich a Qie [an evil king]. Some promise to ne-
> gotiate advantageous treaties for their ruler so that he will be successful in
> war. These, too, are called 'good ministers' but in antiquity they would
> have been called 'plunderers of the people.' To try to make a ruler strong in

---

[38] Mencius also provided concrete guidance for implementation of the "right to food":
see the discussion in chapter 9.

[39] I employ this term because it has come to refer to realpolitik in the English language,
though it would be more precise to refer to proto-Legalist advisers, who outdid Machiavelli himself in their "Machiavellianism" (see chapter 8).

war who is neither attracted to the Way nor bent upon benevolence is to aid a Qie." (6B.9; Robson, modified)

This kind of advice cannot lead to the desirable consequence of a unified world: "No ruler today, pursuing the path they presently follow, without a change of practice, could rule the world for a single day, even supposing he were offered it" (ibid., modified).[40] Mencius suggests that wars of conquest cannot even lead to short-term victories, and that they are disastrous for all parties concerned, including the conqueror's loved ones:[41]

> Mencius said, "King Hui of Liang is the antithesis of benevolence. The man of benevolence brings upon the things he does not love the things he loves. But the man who is not benevolent brings upon the things he loves, the things he does not love." Gongsun Chou said, "What does that mean?" Mencius said, "King Hui of Liang ravished his own people for the sake of territory and went to war. When defeated, he tried again and fearing that he might not succeed he drove the son he loved to fight and his son was sacrificed. This is what I meant by 'bringing upon the things he loves, the things he does not love.'" (7B.1; Robson, modified; see also 1A.7)

An unjust war, in short, is a war that is launched for purposes other than peace and benevolence. In an ideal world—a unified world without any territorial boundaries ruled by a sage-king by means of moral power—all wars are unjust. In the nonideal world, however, some wars can be just. The first kind of just war approximates the modern idea of self-defense. If a small territory is ruled by a capable and virtuous ruler who seeks to promote peace and benevolence, and if that territory is attacked by an unjust would-be hegemon, then the ruler of that territory can justifiably mobilize the people for military action. As noted earlier, Mencius suggested that the leader of the small Teng state threatened by larger neighbors should "dig deeper moats and build higher walls and defend them shoulder to shoulder with the people. If they would rather die than desert you, then all is not lost" (Lau, 1B.13). This passage suggests that the people's support is crucial for successful warfare (see also

---

[40] This prediction, arguably, was proven wrong when the ruthless Qin emperor unified "China" (what was then considered to be the world) using Legalist methods. Perhaps Mencius's claim that the world could not be held for a single day was not meant to be taken too literally, and the fact that this dynasty proved to be relatively short-lived (at least partly due to excessive brutality and consequent unpopularity, according to the standard account) could then be used to support Mencius's point.

[41] Mencius's supposed ideological opponent, Mo Zi, also argued that wars of aggression are bad not just for the defeated state but also for the aggressor state that experiences enormous human wastage and economic loss (see R. James Ferguson, "Inclusive Strategies for Restraining Aggression—Lessons from Classical Chinese Culture," *Asian Philosophy*, vol. 8, no. 1 (March 1998) (http://search.epnet.com/direct.asp?an=2752805&db=aph), 4.

2B.1).[42] It also suggests the people can only be mobilized to fight if they are willing to fight, with the implication that conscription of a reluctant populace would not be effective. Even the ruler himself does not have an obligation to participate in wars of self-defense. In some situations, rulers, no matter how virtuous, will not be able to defend their state against the superior power of larger states, and Mencius does not counsel in favor of suicidal "last stands." Rather, he suggests that abdication is a perfectly legitimate choice:

> Duke Wen of Teng said to Mencius, "Teng is a small state. Though I make every effort to please the large states, I never manage to rid myself of the demands they make upon me. What should I do?" Mencius replied, "In antiquity, when King Tai lived in Pin, the Ti tribes invaded his territory. He offered them furs and silk but still could not get rid of them. He offered them horses and hounds but still could not get rid of them. He offered them pearls and jade but still could not get rid of them. Whereupon he gathered the elders of his people and told them, 'The Ti tribes want to take our land. I have heard it said, a True King does not allow the people to be harmed by interfering with the things upon which their livelihood depends. It will do you less harm to have no king [than to be deprived of your land]. I am going to leave this place.' He left Pin, crossed the Liang mountain, and built a city at the foot of Mount Qi and settled there. The people of Pin said, 'A man of benevolence indeed! We cannot do without him,' and they followed him, as if to a market." (1B.15; Dobson, modified)

The ruler of a small state can flee to a more hospitable environment and start anew, and if he is benevolent, at least some of the people will follow.[43]

The second kind of just war approximates the modern idea of humanitarian intervention—Mencius labels these wars "punitive expeditions"

---

[42] An essay by two high-ranking members of the People's Liberation Army specifically invokes Mencius as part of the philosophical basis for the Chinese military tradition's emphasis on the human factor (in contrast to the Western emphasis on the "weapon factor"), as in Mao's dictum that "Human beings are the most precious in the world. So as long as we have human resource [*sic*], we can work out whatever miracles in the world." Zhang Junbo and Yao Yunzhu, "Differences between Traditional Chinese and Western Military Thinking and Their Philosophical Roots," *Journal of Contemporary China*, vol. 5, no. 1 (July 1996). ⟨http://search.epnet.com/direct.asp?an=9608225143&db=aph, visited 1 December 2003⟩, 10, 5.

[43] Mencius's example points to the relative ease of migration between states in the pre-imperial era. As Zhao Tingyang notes, the "free immigration policy" may help to explain why the Spring and Autumn and Warring States periods were culturally active and creative times in what came to be known as Chinese history: states had to develop their cultural appeal so as to attract people. Zhao Tingyang, "A Philosophical Analysis of World/Empire in Terms of All-under-Heaven," ms. on file with author, 12.

(*zheng*, 征). States can legitimately invade other states if the aim is to bring about global peace and benevolent government. Certain conditions, however, must be in place.[44] First, the "conquerors" must try to liberate people who are being oppressed by tyrants:

> Now the Prince of Yen cruelly mistreated his own people and Your Majesty set out on a punitive expedition. Yen's people thought you were saving them from "flood and fire" [i.e., from tyranny]. (1B.11; Lau, modified)[45]

In the nonideal world, the tyrants are not likely to go down without a fight, and moral power may not work with truly wicked oppressors. Mencius suggests that the liberation of people may require murdering the tyrant: "He killed the ruler and comforted the people, like the fall of timely rain, and the people greatly rejoiced" (1B.11; Lau, modified).[46] Just as people may justly kill their despotic rulers (1B.8), so leaders of punitive expeditions may justly kill tyrants in foreign lands, if need be.[47]

Second, the people must demonstrate, in concrete ways, the fact that they welcome their conquerors:

> When King Wu attacked Yin, he had over three hundred war chariots and three thousand warriors. He said, "Do not be afraid. I come to bring peace, I am not the enemy of the people." And the sound of the people knocking their heads on the ground was like the toppling of the mountain. (7B.4; Lau, modified; see also 1B.10, 1B.11, 3B.5)

[44] Mencius probably had the Warring States context of his own day in mind, and his aim may not have been to present and defend these conditions as universal principles (in contrast to the moral imperative to pursue peace and benevolence that is clearly meant to be universal; I thank Chan-Liang Wu for alerting me to this distinction). In the final section of this chapter, I will argue that the Warring States era shares important similarities with our own international context, so there may be something to learn from prescriptions meant for that era.

[45] This passage implies that it would have been legitimate to punish a ruler who cruelly mistreats his own people, though in this case the ruler being addressed (criticized) by Mencius went on to mistreat the people being "liberated."

[46] Lau translates the character *zhu* (誅) as "punished," but it can (more controversially, perhaps) refer to justified killing. In any case, the tyrant would not likely be "punished" with velvet gloves, and since Mencius allows for regicide by common people it would be odd for him to rule out the possibility that leaders of justified punitive expeditions could kill tyrants in the lands being liberated, if need be.

[47] As Julia Ching and Philip J. Ivanhoe argue, the imperative to liberate an oppressed people does impose certain constraints on what can be done in the name of liberation: most obviously, the conquering army cannot use weapons of mass destruction that would cause large-scale slaughter in the name of liberating an oppressed people. See Julia Ching, "Confucianism and Weapons of Mass Destruction," and Philip J. Ivanhoe, " 'Heaven's Mandate' and the Concept of War in Early Confucianism," both in *Ethics and Weapons of Mass Destruction: Religious and Secular Perspectives*, ed. Sohail H. Hashmi and Steven P. Lee (New York: Cambridge University Press, 2004). In between justified killing of an evil ruler and unjustified large-scale slaughter, however, there will likely be some contestable practices in any punitive expedition.

However, the welcome must be long-lasting, not just immediate. The real challenge is to maintain support for the invading forces after the initial enthusiasm.[48] Even punitive expeditions that were initially justified can go bad, in which case the conquerors should pack up their bags (or, more precisely, their weapons) and leave:

> The people welcomed your army [which had just carried out a punitive expedition] with baskets of rice and bottles of drink. If you kill the old, bind the young, destroy the ancestral temples, and appropriate the ancestral vessels, how can you expect the people's approval? Even before this, the whole world was afraid of the power of Qi. Now you double your land without practicing benevolent government, this will provoke the whole world's armies. If you quickly release the captives, old and young, and stop taking their valuable vessels, set up a ruler in consultation with the people of Yen, and take your army out, all this talk of relief of Yen will then cease. (Lau; 1B.11, modified)

Third, punitive expeditions must be launched by rulers who are at least *potentially* virtuous. The ruler being addressed in the passage quoted above (1B.11) is obviously hypocritical. He was supposed to have liberated the people of Yen from tyranny, but instead he subjected them to more tyranny. However, one can assume that Mencius bothered to talk to such flawed rulers only because he believed that they contained the seeds of virtue within them, or at least that they had sufficient good sense to respond to practical, morally informed advice. In an earlier passage, the same ruler—King Xuan of Qi—is being scolded over and over again by Mencius, who exposes the gap between what he is doing and what he should be doing. King Xuan patiently listens, at one point saying, "Instruct me clearly. Although I am not clever, please let me try to follow your advice" (1A.7; Lau, modified). Mencius may be encouraged by such comments, and he keeps on plugging away. He might not be expecting radical moral transformation on the scale of, say, Emperor Ashoka of India, who adopted and promulgated a tolerant and nonviolent form of Buddhism after several years of atrocious brutality, but Mencius does seem to hold out the hope of substantial moral progress.[49]

Fourth, the leader of justified punitive expeditions must have some moral claim to have the world's support. In his dialogue with the flawed

---

[48] As Xunzi put it, "To annex lands and population is easily done; it is the consolidation of a firm hold on them that is difficult." *Xunzi: A Translation and Study of the Complete Works*, trans. John Knoblock (Stanford: Stanford University Press, 1990), vol. 2, 15.6b, 234.

[49] Confucius, in contrast, seems less concerned with the potential virtue of the ruler. He reports that Guan Zhong became minister of a "murderer" and then succeeded in imposing "his authority over all the states and set the entire world in order; to this very day, the people still reap the benefits of his initiatives" (14.17; Leys). This passage leaves open the possibility that good ministers are sufficient to produce good results for the people, even if the ruler himself does not morally improve.

King Xuan, Mencius points to the example (model) of a justified punitive expedition led by King Tang:

> The Book of History says, "In his punitive expeditions Tang began with
> Ge." The whole world was in sympathy with his cause. When he marched
> on the east, the western tribes complained. When he marched to the south,
> the northern tribes complained. They said, "Why does he not come to us
> first?" (1B.11; Lau, modified)

The ruler, in other words, must have the trust of the world. Without this
trust, punitive expeditions should not be launched. With this trust, even
rulers with bad track records may be regarded as potentially virtuous
leaders who can bring peace to the world.

Of course, the claim to have the trust of the world should not be taken
literally to mean that every single person supports the punitive expedition. If that were the case, the punitive expedition would be unnecessary,
and the actually or potentially virtuous ruler could rely on moral power
to spread good government. At least one person—the tyrant who needs
to be punished or killed—will resist. In the nonideal world, there will be
an element of uncertainty regarding the question of whether or not the
virtuous ruler enjoys the world's support. It may only become clear in
hindsight, when more facts are available and more balanced judgments
can be made.[50]

For Mencius, in short, a defensive war is justified only if an actually or
potentially virtuous and capable ruler (one who aims to provide peace
and benevolent government), with the support of his people, must resort
to violence to protect his territory against would-be conquering hegemons. An offensive war is justified only if it is led by an actually or potentially virtuous ruler who aims to punish oppressive rulers and bring
about global peace. The "conquering" army must be welcomed by the
"conquered" people, and if the welcome is not long-lasting, the conquering army should appoint a local leader in consultation with the conquered
people and withdraw as soon as possible. The punitive expedition should
only be launched if the conquering ruler can make a plausible claim to
have the world's support.

IMPLICATIONS FOR CONTEMPORARY SOCIETIES

Needless to say, this ancient Confucian world is far removed from our
own, and one has to be careful about drawing implications for contem-

---

[50] See Mary I. Bockover, "The *Ren-Dao* of Confucius: A Spiritual Account of Humanity," paper presented at the 2004 annual conference of the Society for Asian and Comparative Philosophy (Asilomar, California, 20–23 June 2004), 16–17.

porary states. But, as Benjamin Schwartz notes, this conglomeration of separate states and principalities "resembled the emerging multi-state system of fifteenth- and sixteenth-century Europe (more, in fact, than did the *polis* of ancient Greece). We even find the emergence of many of the concomitants of the multi-state system—including a rudimentary science of international politics and efforts to achieve collective security."[51] Arguably, the Warring States period also has more in common with the current global system than with imperial China, then held to be the empire (Middle Kingdom) at the center of the world. Ni Le Xiong argues that Spring and Autumn/Warring States period shares five common characteristics with the contemporary international state system: (1) there is no real social authority higher than the state; (2) the higher social authorities exist in form rather than substance (the Zhou Son of Heaven in the case of the pre-Qin system, the United Nations today); (3) national/ state interest is the highest principle that trumps other considerations in cases of conflict; (4) the dominant principle in international relations is the "law of the jungle"; and (5) universal moral principles are invoked as pretexts for realizing state interests.[52] Thus, it should not be entirely surprising if at least some Confucian prescriptions on just and unjust war are held to be relevant for the contemporary world of sovereign states in an "anarchical" global system.[53]

This is not just a theoretical point. As mentioned, Mencius's views serve as a normative reference point for contemporary Chinese social critics opposed to wars of conquest.[54] They also serve to underpin judgments regarding just wars. For example, Gong Gang appeals to the distinction between wars of conquest and justified punitive expeditions to differentiate between recent wars in the Persian Gulf:

---

[51] Benjamin Schwartz, "The Chinese Perception of World Order, Past and Present," 278–79. See also Victoria Tin-Bor Hui, "The Emergence and Demise of Nascent Constitutional Rights: Comparing Ancient China and Early Modern Europe," *The Journal of Political Philosophy*, vol. 9, no. 4 (2001), 374, 401.

[52] Ni Lexiong, "Zhongguo gudai junshi wenhua guannian dui shijie heping de yiyi" [The Implications of Ancient China's Military Cultural Conceptions for World Peace] *Junshi lishi yanjiu* [Military History Research], vol. 2 (2001) (http://www.meet-greatwall.org/gwjs/wen/jswhgn.htm, visited 10 November 2001).

[53] There is, however, one important disanalogy between the Warring States era and the current international system. As discussed in chapter 5, large states in the Warring States era did adhere to the long-term ideal of a world government. In contrast, the international system of sovereign states is now widely held to be a permanent condition (at least since the collapse of missionary communism).

[54] It does not necessarily follow, however, that moral opposition to the global hegemon necessarily leads to opposition to particular wars of conquest. One well-connected Chinese friend of mine privately welcomed the U.S. invasion of Iraq (before it occurred) because he anticipated that it would stretch U.S. military capacities and would leave the country less able to pursue its hegemonic policies in East Asia (e.g., less willing to defend Taiwan in the event of a conflict with the mainland).

Mencius said, "A hegemon uses force under the pretext of benevolence," "a true king uses virtue and benevolence," "The Spring and Autumn Annals acknowledged no just wars. There are only cases of some wars not being as bad as others. A punitive expedition refers to a higher authority attacking a lower one. Peers should not launch punitive expeditions against one another." It is very obvious. One can say that the First Gulf War is a just war authorized by the United Nations, similar to "a guilty duke corrected [punished] by the Son of Heaven." It is like a conflict with a "higher authority attacking a lower one." In this war [the 2003 invasion of Iraq], the United States says it is using force to exercise benevolence, that it is acting as both a true king and a hegemon. But the Second Gulf War is not the same, because without the authorization of the United Nations, the United States and the United Kingdom are attacking an enemy state with vastly different [inferior] power and resources. In this war, the United States is using force under the pretext of benevolence, and it is also maintaining its geopolitical, national security, and economic interests in the name of promoting democracy in the Middle East; it is obviously acting as a global hegemon.[55]

The key difference between the two Gulf Wars is that the first had the stamp of approval from the "symbolic" global institution, the United Nations. While it was led by a "hegemon," the United Nations lent moral legitimacy to the war, just as Mencius suggests that punitive expeditions can be carried out by a ruler with the potential to be a "true king" who brings about global peace. In the messy and dangerous world of competing states, it may be difficult to determine who constitutes the "true king" until long after the fact (of war), but it may not be so difficult to rule out possibilities. The Bush administration's willful disregard of global legitimacy in the second Gulf War shows that it did not even make an effort to gain the trust of the world.[56] One condition—the need to liberate a country from an oppressive tyrant—may have been met,[57] but that is not sufficient, according to Mencian theory.

Still, one may ask, why not use the traditional Western (Christian or Jewish) theories of just and unjust war to make such judgments? These theories are also meant to be universal in scope and arguably continue to be relatively influential in the Western-dominated international system.

[55] Gong Gang, "Shei shi quanqiu lunli de daidao shiwei" [Who is the armed Guard of Global Ethics?], *Nan feng chuang*, September 2003 (http://www.nfcmag.com/news/newsdisp.php3?NewsId=296&mod=, visited 10 November 2001).

[56] Even the "coalition of the willing" was composed of several countries like Italy and Spain where the large majority of citizens opposed the invasion of Iraq without U.N. support.

[57] As argued below, however, Confucians and Western defenders of human rights may disagree over what constitutes tyranny.

A reply is that Mencius, and the ancient Chinese texts more generally, have been less willing to embrace what moderns would consider to be evil in the name of doing good. As Karen Turner explains,

> [I]n the Chinese texts I have found no parallels with the Old Testament's justification for slaughtering wholesale the people of an enemy in a holy war. Nor are the Chinese texts as brutally pragmatic as Aquinas, who was willing to admit that women, children, and fruit trees should be spared from war, but that for crimes against God, an entire city or nation could be justly punished so as to deter other such crimes. The Chinese texts do not regard war as a remedy for the sins of ordinary people unlucky enough to serve an evil regime, but as a punishment for those particular leaders who lead their subjects astray with improper demands. Thus force should be directed only toward the rulers who made the decisions and not toward their subjects.[58]

In this sense, the Mencian theory of just and unjust war is more normatively appealing than the traditional Western just war theory.[59]

So why not use the modern, international language of human rights to make such judgments? Defenders of human rights, needless to say, would not justify the massacre of civilians, no matter what the potential benefits. Michael Walzer, the most celebrated contemporary theorist of just and unjust war, explicitly argues that human rights are at the foundation of wartime morality: "individual rights to (life and liberty) underlie the most important judgments we make about war."[60] The obvious response is that the "we" does not typically include Chinese intellectuals

---

[58] Karen Turner, "War, Punishment, and the Law of Nature in Early Chinese Concepts of the State," *Harvard Journal of Asiatic Studies*, vol. 53, no. 2 (December 1993), 304–5. See also John K. Fairbank, "Introduction: Varieties of the Chinese Military Experience," in *Chinese Ways in Warfare*, ed. Frank A. Kierman, Jr., and John K. Fairbank (Cambridge: Harvard University Press, 1974), 7.

[59] Of course, Mencius's theory can be misused, like any other theory. It could be argued that the act of focusing on rulers rather than the people when thinking about just war can make people in the aggressor state think of war as some sort of police action against one bad man, not as a real war that hurts many real people. Arguably, that is part of what the Bush administration did in order to convince so many Americans that war in Iraq was justified: the administration talked about bringing Saddam Hussein to justice, but it downplayed the fact that a military campaign would likely kill thousands of Iraqi soldiers and civilians. I thank Steve Geisz for this point.

[60] Michael Walzer, *Just and Unjust Wars: A Moral Argument with Historical Illustrations*, 3rd ed. (New York: Basic Books, 2000), 54. Walzer does not, however, construct a philosophical argument in favor of human rights ("How these rights are themselves founded I cannot try to explain here"), so his only argument in favor of using the language of human rights is practical (and therefore it can be defeated by competing practical considerations, as in the case of what may be relatively effective Mencius-inspired arguments for just and unjust war in the Chinese context).

and policymakers. In the Chinese context, the language of human rights, when it has been deployed to justify military intervention abroad, has been tainted by its misuses in the international arena.[61] Given the history of colonial subjugation by Western powers, as well as the ongoing conflicts over economic resources and geopolitical interests, the language of human rights is often seen as an ideology designed to rationalize policies of exploitation and regime change. Even where military intervention in the name of human rights may have been justified—as, arguably, in the case of NATO's war on behalf of the Kosovo Albanians—it is difficult, if not impossible, to overcome Chinese skepticism regarding the "real" motives underlying intervention.[62]

This provides a practical reason for invoking Mencius's theory of just and unjust war (in the Chinese context and other societies with a Confucian heritage, such as Korea). What ultimately matters is the *practice* rather than the theory of human rights. So long as people are protected from torture, genocide, starvation, and other such obvious harms, there is no need to worry about the particular political and philosophical justifications.[63] That is to say that states and other collective agencies should do their best to respect our basic humanity, but whether such practices are backed by human rights morality is secondary. And if Mencius's theory leads to the same judgments regarding the justice of particular wars as theories of wartime morality founded on human rights, then why not deploy his theory in the Chinese context?

Having said that, Mencius's theory will not always lead to the same judgments as theories founded on human rights—but this may speak in favor of Mencius's theory. One key difference between Walzer's view and Mencius's view regards the value of membership in a particular political community. For Walzer, membership in a particular political community is a fundamental human good and also helps to underpin judgments regarding the justice of warfare. Part of the justification for (moral) self-defense is that a common life exists among members of a political com-

---

[61] As a matter of domestic policy, however, the language of human rights is much better received in China, by critics of the regime as well as official government circles. See my review essay, "Human Rights and Social Criticism in Contemporary Chinese Political Theory," *Political Theory*, vol. 32, no. 3 (June 2004), 396–408.

[62] Of course, the (accidental?) bombing of the Chinese embassy in Belgrade sealed the matter in the eyes of (most?) Chinese. I personally experienced the reaction in Hong Kong. The one time I was truly made to feel like an outsider among otherwise sympathetic mainland Chinese friends and family members was when I argued that the war against Serbia was still justified, even after the bombing. I rapidly learned to keep my views to myself, in the interest of maintaining harmony with loved ones!

[63] For a similar view, see Charles Taylor, "Conditions of an Unforced Consensus on Human Rights," in *The East Asian Challenge for Human Rights*, ed. Joanne R. Bauer and Daniel A. Bell (New York: Cambridge University Press, 1999).

munity, one founded on particular cultural ties (linguistic, religious, etc.). If a state is attacked and its members are challenged in their lives and form of political association, then the state can justifiably resort to force to defend its territory (so long as it does its best to secure rights to life and liberty). Conversely, if there is no common life between members of the state, there is no moral justification for self-defense.[64] Those being attacked would be justified in fleeing abroad, and the state would not be justified in conscripting its citizens.

For Mencius, in contrast, there is no moral force attached to valuing one's particular culture or language or religion or distinctive form of political association,[65] and he would certainly reject the idea that valuing particular ties or exclusive forms of common life can justify the resort to armed force in the international arena. The moral justification for the use of armed force lies solely in its necessity to promote the values of peace and benevolence at home and abroad. These values are meant to have universal validity, and the ruler most likely to promote them has the most moral legitimacy and the right to engage in just warfare, if need be. That is why moral/political advisers should seek out such rulers and why common people will (and should) migrate to territories governed by them.[66]

From a contemporary normative standpoint, it could be argued that Mencius's view is more attractive. So many unjust wars have been

[64] Walzer, *Just and Unjust Wars*, 54.

[65] These possibilities are not explicitly mentioned in early Confucianism, though passages in Confucius and Mencius do seem to allow for some sort of pluralism. Confucius famously said: "The exemplary person seeks harmony rather than conformity, the petty person seeks conformity rather than harmony" (13.23). Regarding attachment to particular tracts of land, Mencius does suggest that land may have value and that people can justifiably fight back attempts to conquer their land (1B.15), but the context of the passage suggests that abdication is a better option. (Mencius discusses the option of abdication first and in more detail, and the fighting for land option is presented as somebody else's view, i.e., "people say that . . . ," suggesting some skepticism.) In any case, the value of land for Mencius lies primarily in its importance for people's livelihoods, not in its sentimental value. (Confucius is more straightforward in condemning sentimental attachment to land: "The master said, "Exemplary persons cherish their virtue; petty persons cherish their land"; 4.11; Ames and Rosemont, modified; see also 14.2.) If land elsewhere can yield better harvests and those harvests are more likely to be distributed fairly (e.g., the well-field system), then it would be better to go there in the event of an attack (assuming this is a realistic option). Fan Ruiping has noted that Confucian Chinese have manifested attachment to their homeland because they prefer to be buried near their ancestral tombs (e-mail communication, 11 March 2004), but one cannot draw the implication (from the works of Mencius or Confucius) that people can fight for their homeland in part because they want to be buried near their ancestors.

[66] If the economic conditions are satisfactory and the benefits fairly distributed (i.e., the well-field system is in place), however, Mencius did seem to justify curbs on the freedom of movement (see 3A.3).

fought in the name of preserving and promoting particular communities of character—ancestral homelands, ethnically pure states, linguistic
communities—that any theory, such as Walzer's, allowing for the possibility of justified violence on behalf of this cause may be weakened beyond repair.[67] Imagine, say, a war of self-defense where a soldier must
face the choice between surrender (with guaranteed migration to a
peaceful and relatively wealthy country, but with the likely dilution of
the family's cultural roots) and ferocious fighting (and the probable
killing of civilians in the aggressor state). A modern-day Mencius would
likely recommend the former, but for Walzer it would be a harder call.[68]

The problem may lie with Walzer's particular theory, rather than with
Anglo-American theories of just war founded on human rights. Walzer
himself recognizes that his defense of cultural membership as part of the
justification of self-defense may be the outlying view: "most moral
philosophers working in the Anglo-American tradition disagree with me
precisely on the value of membership. Mine is the minority position, so
if followers of Mencius also disagree, that doesn't distinguish them from
Western philosophers."[69] Let me then point to one feature of the Mencian view that distinguishes it from most contemporary Western accounts of just warfare. For Mencius, as for Confucius, the government
cannot secure the peace if its people are not well fed. Hence, the first obligation of government is to secure the basic means of subsistence of the
people. By extension, the worst thing a government can do—the most serious violation of "human rights," so to speak—would be to deliberately
deprive the people of the means of subsistence (by killing them, not feeding them, not dealing with a plague, etc.). A ruler who engages in such
acts, for the Confucian, would noncontroversially be viewed as an oppressive tyrant, and punitive expeditions against such rulers would be
justified (assuming that the other conditions for punitive expeditions

[67] My own view is that cultural particularity matters from a moral point of view and
can justify such particularistic policies as welfare benefits for fellow citizens (even if more
"bang for the buck" can be achieved by, say, using those funds to help the needy poor in
distant lands), but I would draw the line at (before) allowing for violence on behalf of cultural particularity. This intuition may stem from my experience as a Canadian communitarian (an Israeli communitarian is more likely to be sympathetic to Walzer's view), and it
would, admittedly, need to be developed.

[68] Walzer has controversially defended Britain's policy of terror bombing of German cities
in the early (but not later) days of World War II on the grounds that "no other decision
seemed possible if there was to be any sort of military offensive against Nazi Germany."
Walzer, *Just and Unjust Wars*, 258. In a later work, Walzer further spells out his doctrine of
"supreme emergency," which tries to provide a justification for overriding the rights of inno-
cent people if such immoral acts are necessary to save the community from communal
death. Walzer, *Arguing about War* (New Haven: Yale University Press, 2004), chap. 3.

[69] E-mail communication from Michael Walzer, 10 March 2004.

have also been met). In contrast, the sorts of violations of civil and political rights that might be viewed as constituting tyranny by contemporary Western defenders of human rights, such as systematic denials of the right to free speech or the heavy-handed treatment of political dissenters in the name of social order, would not be viewed as human rights violations sufficiently serious as to justify humanitarian intervention by foreign powers.

Such differences in emphasis can influence judgments of just and unjust warfare in the contemporary world.[70] For Western defenders of human rights, Saddam Hussein was noncontroversially regarded as an oppressive tyrant because he engaged in the systematic violation of civil and political rights: liberal defenders of humanitarian intervention such as Michael Ignatieff and Thomas Friedman supported the invasion of Iraq largely on these grounds.[71] For Confucians, however, so long as the Iraqi people were not being deliberately deprived of the means of subsistence, the intervention could not be justified. The demand (in some liberal circles) that the United States should also consider "liberating" oppressed people in wealthy Saudi Arabia would be even less justified.

In other cases, however, Confucians may be more likely to support punitive expeditions compared to liberal defenders of humanitarian intervention. In cases of deliberately engineered famines, such as Afghanistan government's total road blockade on Kabul in 1996, the Confucian just war theorist would argue for foreign intervention (assuming, as always, that the other conditions for intervention have been met). In contrast, liberal human rights groups such as Amnesty International denounced the shooting and torture of a few victims as human rights violations and treated the manufactured starvation of thousands as background.[72] Similarly, if it is true that the North Korean government has been deliberately promoting policies that result in the starvation of millions of people, the Confucian would have emphasized the need for foreign intervention in North Korea rather than such countries as Iraq.[73]

---

[70] I do not mean to deny that there are also "easy cases" where Confucians and Western defenders of humanitarian intervention would converge on the same judgment. If the government carries out or facilitates the massacre of large sectors of its own population (e.g., the Nazi Holocaust, the Rwanda genocide), then both would justify intervention by foreign powers.

[71] It is worth noting that Walzer himself opposed the invasion because he argued that the Iraqi threat was not imminent and the U.N. inspectors should have been given more time (see Walzer, *Arguing about War*, 143–51).

[72] In response to such cases of apparently misguided priorities, Amnesty has expanded its mission to include economic and social rights: see chapter 4.

[73] Given the likely civilian casualties, however, Confucian critics would likely emphasize other means of opposition, such as remonstrance or targeted killing of the North Korean leaders responsible for the famine.

It is worth asking how much of this matters in practice. Even if Confucian views inform the judgments of critical intellectuals in China, do these judgments really affect the political practices of the Chinese state? Confucian theorists of just war are likely to prove to be just as ineffective as moralizing theorists of human rights in the American context (perhaps even more so, if the society lacks a free press and other public forums for communicating criticisms). It is obvious, for example, that war against Taiwan if it declares formal independence would not meet the Confucian criteria for justifiable punitive expeditions:[74] so long as the Taiwanese government does not kill or starve its people, only moral power could be justifiably employed to bring Taiwan back into the Chinese orbit. But it seems just as obvious that Confucian objections are not likely to hold back the Chinese government in such an eventuality. So what exactly is the utility of Confucian theorizing on just warfare?

A historical perspective may provide some insight. One feature of imperial China was that it did not expand in ways comparable to Western imperial powers, even when it may have had the technical ability to do so. Instead, it established the tributary system, with the "Middle Kingdom" at the center and "peripheral" states on the outside. In this system, the tributary ruler or his representative had to go to China to pay homage in ritual acknowledgment of his vassal status. In return, China guaranteed security and provided economic benefits,[75] while using moral power to spread Confucian norms and allowing traditional ways of life and practices to flourish.[76] Needless to say, the practice often deviated from the ideal.[77] Still, the Confucian-Mencian discourse did help to stabilize the tributary system and curb the excesses of blood-thirsty warriors and greedy merchants.[78] There may be lessons for the future. As

[74] The Confucian would also condemn Taiwan's ethnically motivated proindependence movement because of the Confucian presumption in favor of unity and the lack of value placed upon cultural particularity. But would Taiwan be justified in defending itself if attacked by the mainland? For the Confucian, the judgment would depend partly on the moral character of the Taiwanese ruler, the degree of popular support in Taiwan for that leader, and the likely consequences of other options such as surrender (not so bad if the Chinese Army withdraws soon after invasion and the Chinese government restores the *status quo ante*).

[75] See John K. Fairbank and Ssu-Yu Teng, "On the Ch'ing Tributary System," in *Ch'ing Administration: Three Studies*, ed. John K. Fairbank and Ssu-Yu Teng (Cambridge: Harvard University Press, 1960), 112–13.

[76] See Immanuel C. Y. Hsu, *China's Entrance into the Family of Nations* (Cambridge: Harvard University Press, 1960), 8–9.

[77] See, e.g., Alasdair Ian Johnston, *Cultural Realism: Strategic Culture and Grand Strategy in Chinese History* (Princeton: Princeton University Press, 1995). Johnston focuses on the Ming dynasty's grand strategy against the Mongols, and he is struck by "the prevalence of assumptions and decision axioms that in fact placed a high degree of value on the use of pure violence to resolve security conflicts" (xi). This example may not be typical, however.

[78] See Cho-yun Hsu, "Applying Confucian Ethics in International Relations," *Ethics and International Affairs*, vol. 5 (1991).

China once again establishes itself as an important global power, with the economic and military means to become a regional (or even global) hegemon, it will need to be constrained by more than realpolitik. More than any other discourse, Confucian theorizing on just and unjust warfare has the potential to play the role of constraining China's imperial ventures abroad, just as it did in the past. Put more positively, China would also have the power and the responsibility to carry out punitive expeditions in neighboring states (e.g., if an East Asian state began to carry out a Rwanda-style massacre of its population, China would face international pressure to intervene). The Confucian discourse could provide moral guidance in such cases.[79]

Deploying the Confucian views on just and unjust war as a critical tool to make judgments in history can also influence political actors. Consider, for example, the Great Leap Forward in the late 1950s, which was carried out under radical rural leadership with Mao's blessing. The ostensible goal was to increase rural productivity by means of organizing all of rural China into people's communes, but the actual "result was famine on a gigantic scale, a famine that claimed 20 million lives or more between 1959 and 1962."[80] The key point is the Mao Zedong can and should be held at least partly responsible for the famine. In July 1959 Army Marshal Peng Dehuai pointed out some of the Great Leap's problems at a conference for China's top leaders. Mao's response was to launch a personal denunciation of Peng, purge him from his post as minister of defense, and reassert disastrous policies that led to millions of deaths.[81] From a Confucian perspective, a punitive expedition would have been justified.[82] Of course, such intervention did not occur, but making these sorts of implications explicit can put tyrants on notice if they engage in policies that lead to famine.[83] It is hoped that rulers of the future will think twice before doing so.

[79] It could also be argued that moral considerations will play a greater role than they did in the past. Given the growth of worldwide trade, it is possible that fewer wars will be fought for economic reasons (if it is easier to buy scarce resources, there may be less of a need to fight for them), and more wars fought for moral reasons. I thank Mao Yushi for this point.

[80] Jonathan D. Spence, *The Search for Modern China* (London: Hutchinson, 1990), 583.

[81] Mao could also have taken note of the criticism by Nikita Khrushchev (then Soviet leader) of the new Chinese communes. Instead, Mao attacked Peng Dehuai as a traitor allied with Khrushchev (Taubman, *Khrushchev*, 392).

[82] Assuming, once again, that the other criteria for punitive expeditions have been met. Given the likely civilian casualties (and opposition to such intervention among ordinary Chinese), such criteria would not likely have been met during the Great Leap Forward. However, less extreme means of punishing rulers, such as "smart sanctions" against state leaders and prohibiting travel, could less controversially have been invoked.

[83] Mao himself was well versed in the Confucian tradition and may have been aware of Mencian views on justified violence against rulers, which may help to explain why he turned against Confucianism and affirmed Legalism during the Cultural Revolution. Some rulers in imperial China obviously felt threatened by Mencian ideas regarding justified violence: for example, the founder of the Ming dynasty, Emperor Hong Wu (1368–98),

Confucian theorizing can also have an impact below the highest levers of the state, particularly once the war is already under way. The torture of prisoners at Abu Ghraib in Iraq is a reminder that evil deeds in warfare are committed "unofficially," by soldiers acting without the explicit authority of the top commanders. Nonetheless, these soldiers took implicit cues from the top, which set the tone for a cavalier approach to the protection of prisoners' well-being. Here the Confucian emphasis on the moral quality of political and military leaders may be particularly relevant. In Imperial China, the idea that those carrying out the war should be benevolent informed the practice of appointing generals who were held to be exemplary persons with both moral character and military expertise.[84] One important reason for emphasizing the moral quality of commanders is that they set the moral example for other ordinary soldiers, and their moral power radiates down to lower levels: "under the wind, the grass must bend." If the aim is to sensitize soldiers to moral considerations, the leaders should not, as in Clausewitz's idea of the general, simply be concerned with the practical skills required for victory.

There are, in short, two main reasons for invoking Mencius's theory of just war. The first reason is psychological. If there is rough agreement on the aims of a theory of just war—that it should prohibit wars of conquest and justify certain kinds of wars of self-defense and humanitarian interventions—then one should invoke the theory that is most psychologically compelling to the people being addressed. In the Chinese context, and perhaps in other societies with a Confucian heritage, the theory of Mencius is most likely to have causal power. The comparison here is not just with theories of human rights, but with other Chinese thinkers such as Mozi and Xunzi who have also put forward theories functionally similar to modern theories of just war. Mencius is unambiguously viewed as a "good guy" by most contemporary Chinese, so there is no need to qualify or apologize for aspects of his theory.

The second reason is philosophical, and it speaks to the normative validity of Mencius's theory. Compared to alternative theories, Mencius's theory has several advantages, such as the focus on material well-being and the lack of emphasis on communal particularity as justifications for going to war. Mencius's theory can and should be taught in military academies, both in China and elsewhere. And critical intellectuals should

---

commissioned a special board of scholars to excise passages from Mencius that implied a lack of devotion to the ruler, with the result that eighty-five passages were deleted (see Ivanhoe, " 'Heaven's Mandate' "). In Tokugawa Japan, Mencian ideas inspired rebels to rebellion or martyrdom against the ruling regime, though they were also used to support the authorities on other occasions. John Tucker, "Two Mencian Political Notions in Tokugawa Japan," *Philosophy East and West*, vol. 47, no. 2 (August 1997).

[84] See Hagen, "A Chinese Critique on Western Ways of Warfare," 2, 12.

draw upon Mencius's views to evaluate the justice of wars in the contemporary world. Of course, there is no reason to take Mencius's theory (or any other theory) of just war as the final word on the subject. One lacuna, for example, is the lack of detailed prescriptions for *jus in bello*. Besides arguing against the large-scale slaughter of civilians (7B.3), Mencius did not explicitly draw the implications of his views on just war for just conduct in war.[85] But it should be possible to do so within the broad confines of his theory.

The next two chapters turn to more contemporary debates on human rights in East Asia. In chapter 3, I draw on dialogues with East Asian intellectuals for the purpose of discussing relatively persuasive "East Asian" critiques of Western-style approaches to human rights. Chapter 4 draws on dialogues between human rights theorists and practitioners, and I draw implications for international human rights organizations operating in the East Asian region.

[85] Perhaps because Mencius felt that war is so distasteful, even when it is necessary, he was unwilling to think through in great detail the implications of going to war. In contrast, the more hardnosed Xunzi did go into detail, and he proposed moral guidelines meant to apply once "the drum is sounded" similar to those of contemporary theorists of just warfare, such as not executing prisoners or engaging in the massacre of defenders of a city (see *Xunzi*, trans. Knoblock, 15.1f, 226–27). The actual practice of dealing with the enemy during the Warring States period occasionally went beyond contemporary notions of justice in warfare, such as supplying meat to invaders and adversaries in hot pursuit. Frank A. Kierman, Jr., "Phases and Modes of Combat in Early China," in *Chinese Ways of Warfare*, ed. Frank A. Kierman, Jr., and John K. Fairbank (Cambridge: Harvard University Press, 1974), 37. Julia Ching notes that such practices also made military sense: "a time honored practice was to extend extreme courtesy and generosity to the enemy—capturing and imprisoning them during the fight, but releasing them soon afterward, showered with gifts and kindnesses. The reason? To decrease their will to fight or their desire for vengeance." Ching, "Confucianism and Weapons of Mass Destruction," in *Ethics and Weapons of Mass Destruction: Religious and Secular Perspectives*, ed. Sohail H. Hashimi and Steven P. Lee (New York: Cambridge University Press, 2004), 11, 28.

3

Human Rights and "Values in Asia":
Reflections on East-West Dialogues

IN THE EARLY 1990s the economic and social achievements of modernizing East Asian states became too conspicuous to ignore. Senior Asian statesmen such as Lee Kuan Yew and Dr. Mahathir trumpeted their high GNPs on the world stage, arguing that the "Asian miracle" rested on distinctive "Asian values." The point was to cast doubt on the normative superiority of Western-style human rights and to question the desirability of exporting that model to East Asian societies. If Asians can do well with their own moral values and conceptions of political organization, then why should defenders of Western-style human rights seek to impose their ideas on the rest of the world?

The Asian values debate, unfortunately, generated more heat than light. In retrospect, the substantive problem seems obvious: the debate was neither about Asia nor about values. Asia is a huge and exceptionally diverse landmass, encompassing much of the world's population. It hosts a number of religions, such as Islam, Hinduism, Buddhism, Confucianism, Taoism, Christianity, and Judaism, as well as a myriad of races, ethnicities, customs, and languages. The assumption that Asia has its own cultural essence fundamentally different from that of the West is, to say the least, dubious. In fact, as Tatsuo Inoue has argued, the Asian values thesis ironically owes its roots to Western intellectual imperialism, that is, "Orientalism," the very force that was being criticized by official Asian critics of human rights.[1]

There are no distinctly Asian values, and anything that goes by the name of "Asian values" tends to refer to values that are either narrower (distinctive only to some societies, or parts of societies, in Asia) or broader (the values characterize societies both in and out of Asia) than the stated terms of reference. More surprisingly, perhaps, most claims made on behalf of Asian values were not even about values! Consider some claims typically put forward by politicians under the rubric of Asian values: political rights conflict with economic development; free speech leads to

---

[1] Tatsuo Inoue, "Liberal Democracy and Asian Orientalism," in *The East Asian Challenge for Human Rights*, ed. Joanne R. Bauer and Daniel A. Bell (New York: Cambridge University Press, 1999).

racial and religious conflict; Confucian values promote economic development. Whatever the merits of these claims, they are ultimately empirical claims that must be answered by social scientists, not by moral philosophers. The only way to evaluate these claims is by means of historical and sociological analysis.

Of course, political actors tend to be motivated by considerations other than clear thinking, and it may not be fair to blame elderly Asian politicians for the obfuscating discourse on Asian values.[2] The interesting part, however, is that the debate attracted so much global attention, suggesting the presence of something besides obfuscation and self-promotion. Several East and Southeast Asian societies did modernize quickly, while seeming to build upon traditional values somewhat at odds with Western liberal approaches to human rights. Fortunately, the less publicized but more nuanced views of critical intellectuals in East Asia help to make sense of the key issues underlying the debate. Over the last decade, I have been fortunate to participate in several East–West dialogues on the subject of human rights, and this chapter constitutes my reflections on these dialogues.[3] My aim is to get beyond the rhetoric that has dogged the human rights debate and identify relatively persuasive East Asian criticisms of traditional Western approaches to human rights.

[2] Lee Kuan Yew, to be fair, has backed away from the term "Asian values," arguing that he was referring only to values shared by East Asian countries with a Confucian heritage.

[3] In the mid-1990s the Carnegie Council on Ethics and International Affairs convened several workshops involving dialogues between East Asian and Western intellectuals on the subject of human rights in East Asian societies. The project was planned and administered by Joanne R. Bauer, director of studies at the Carnegie Council. Workshops were held in Hakone (Japan), Bangkok (Thailand), and Seoul (Korea), with a final wrapup session at the Harvard Law School. My reflections on the Hakone workshop appeared as the article "The East Asian Challenge to Human Rights," *Human Rights Quarterly*, vol. 18, no. 3, (August 1996), and my reflections on the Bangkok workshop appeared as the article "Minority Rights: On the Importance of Local Knowledge," *Dissent* (Summer 1996). I have also coedited (with Joanne R. Bauer) a book that is the product of this multiyear project, *The East Asian Challenge for Human Rights*. Chapter 1 of my book *East Meets West: Human Rights and Democracy in East Asia* (Princeton: Princeton University Press, 2000) also draws on the findings of this project. Over the past several years, I have also participated in a multiyear, cross-cultural dialogue on Confucianism convened by Hahm Chaibong then of Yonsei University and UNESCO that has dealt with the topic of human rights (among other topics). I have coedited two books that resulted from this project, *Confucianism for the Modern World*, co-edited with Hahm Chaibong (New York: Cambridge University Press, 2003), and *The Politics of Affective Relations: East Asia and Beyond*, co-edited with Hahm Chaihark (Lanham, MD: Lexington Books, 2004). This chapter draws on all these sources and some unpublished arguments made by East Asian participants at these workshops. My own qualifications and elaborations of these arguments are largely confined to the footnotes and the concluding section. I have also updated the arguments and examples by drawing on other sources.

One can distinguish between four sorts of arguments put forward by East Asian critics of Western approaches to human rights (I do not mean to imply that these arguments are distinctly or uniquely Asian). First, the argument often asserted by East Asian governments that a right must be temporarily curtailed in order to deal with an unfortunate set of particular social and political circumstances. Once the perceived crisis is over, according to this view, then the rights denial is no longer justified. This viewpoint is not in the first instance a "cultural clash" over human rights, as both the government in question and the human rights activist share a common set of moral and political aspirations as an end goal. However, cultural factors can affect the *prioritizing* of rights, which matters when rights conflict and it must be decided which one to sacrifice.

The other challenges to Western liberal conceptions of human rights are more directly disputes over cultural values. Supporters of universal human rights tried to discredit the Asian values discourse by pointing to the diversity of values within the Asian region, but such arguments also undermined their own position. As Randall Peerenboom argues, "if such diversity precludes the common values within the Asian region, then it also precludes *a fortiori* the possibility of *universal values.*"[4] Hence, I will use the term "values in Asia," which is sensitive to the pluralism of values within Asia yet retains the implication that such values can pose challenges to Western liberal approaches to human rights.

The second challenge is an argument over the *justification* of rights. As against the claim that the Western liberal tradition is the only possible moral foundation for human rights, many East Asian human rights activists argue that their own cultural traditions can provide the resources for local justifications of ideas and practices normally realized through a human rights regime in Western countries. This argument is not merely theoretical, it also has strategic importance for advocates of human rights reforms in East Asia.

The third challenge is an argument for moral pluralism. That is, cultural particularities in East Asia may justify a different moral standpoint vis-à-vis the human rights regime typically endorsed by Western governments, scholars, and human rights activists. To repeat, the East Asian region is a complex mix of societies, cultural traditions, and political viewpoints. It is also true that values change significantly over time in response to various internal and external pressures, and this is evident in the region. However, some values in Asia may be more persistent than others and may diverge from some human rights ideas and practices typically endorsed in Western countries. If these values are widely shared by

---

[4] Randall Peerenboom, "Show Me the Money—the Dominance of Wealth in Determining Rights Performance in Asia," *Duke International Law Journal*, vol. 15, no. 1 (2005), 131.

both defenders and critics of the political status quo, there is a strong presumption in favor of respect for those values.

The fourth challenge is the argument that the current "international" human rights regime needs to be modified to incorporate East Asian viewpoints. East Asian critics have argued that the current rights regime has been forged largely on the basis of Western liberal-democratic norms, and that the people of East Asia can contribute positively to the evolution of a truly international human rights discourse in which they had not heretofore played a substantial part. The point here is not to displace human rights in favor of some other set of principles,[5] but rather to allow for the possibility of learning from values in Asia so that the human rights regime reflects the outcome of an international dialogue between peoples of different cultures. The section ends with my own doubts regarding the feasibility of such a project.

TRADE-OFFS AND PRIORITIES

Rights versus Development: A Zero-Sum Game?

A common East Asian argument is that Western-style civil and political liberties need to be sacrificed in order to meet more basic material needs. Most famously, Lee Kuan Yew argues that political leaders in developing countries should be committed to the eradication of poverty above all else: "As prime minister of Singapore, my first task was to lift my country out of the degradation that poverty, ignorance and disease had wrought. Since it was dire poverty that made for such a low priority given to human life, all other things became secondary."[6] If factional opposition threatens to slow down the government's efforts to promote economic development or to plunge the country into civil strife, then in Lee's view tough measures can and should be taken to ensure political stability. Such is the message Lee delivers to receptive audiences in China, Japan, Vietnam, and the Philippines.[7]

Nobel Prize–winning economist Amartya Sen, however, casts doubt on the validity of this proposition.[8] He argues that there is little empiri-

---

[5] See Anthony J. Langlois, *The Politics of Justice and Human Rights: Southeast Asia and Universalist Theory* (Cambridge: Cambridge University Press, 2001).

[6] Nathan Gardels, "Interview with Lee Kuan Yew," *New Perspectives Quarterly*, vol. 9, no. 1 (Winter 1992).

[7] The idea that the government's first obligation is to secure the means of subsistence has Confucian roots and has been influential throughout East Asian societies with a Confucian heritage: see chapter 9.

[8] Unless otherwise specified, the examples from this section were provided by East Asian participants at the workshop held in Hakone, Japan, in June 1995 (see note 3).

cal evidence that civil and political rights lead to disastrous outcomes. Systematic cross-national statistical studies do not support the claim that there is a correlation or a causal connection between authoritarianism and economic success. Civil and political rights in fact help to safeguard economic security in the sense that such rights draw attention to major social disasters and induce an appropriate political response:

> Whether and how a government responds to needs and sufferings may well depend on how much pressure is put on it, and the exercise of political rights (such as voting, criticizing, protesting, and so on) can make a real difference. For example, one of the remarkable facts about famines in the world is that no substantial famine has ever occurred in any country with a democratic form of government and a relatively free press.[9]

Similar to Lee Kuan Yew, the Burmese military junta argues that rights must be curtailed in order to provide the political stability said to underpin economic progress. At least some freedoms, however, need to be restored to allow for economic growth. In the words of Yozo Yokota, then UN Special Rapporteur on Human Rights in Burma: "If the government allows economists to freely engage in research and to make necessary recommendations to improve the economic situation of the country, and if the people are allowed to do business freely by traveling without government restrictions and collecting information and conducting negotiations as they like, there is a great chance that the country would grow rapidly."[10]

The current status of Burma and North Korea—desperately poor countries governed by the region's most repressive rulers—supports Yokota's doubts.

The Need for Specificity

While the general claim that civil and political rights must be sacrificed in the name of economic development may not stand up to social scientific scrutiny, East Asian governments also present narrower justifications for curbing *particular* rights in *particular* contexts for *particular* economic or political purposes. These actions are said to be taken as a short-term measure to secure a more important right or more of that

[9] Amartya Sen, "Human Rights and Economic Achievements," in *The East Asian Challenge for Human Rights*, ed. Joanne R. Bauer and Daniel A. Bell (New York: Cambridge University Press, 1999), 92. If the problem is severe malnutrition, however, the record is not so clear: since Deng's reforms, autocratic China has a better record in this respect than democratic India.

[10] Yozo Yokota, "Economic Development and Human Rights Practice," paper presented at the Hakone workshop (on file with author), 3.

same right in the long term. Xin Chunying, a lawyer working at the Human Rights Center of the Chinese Academy of the Social Sciences, notes that East Asian governments emphasize "the particularity of human rights protection and the priority determined by the specific conditions of each country."[11] Such claims are put forward by government officials but often attract significant local support.

Consider the following examples of situation-specific justifications for the temporary curtailment of particular rights:[12]

1. Kevin Tan, then professor of constitutional law at the National University of Singapore, noted that Singapore in the 1960s was plagued by "the threat of a communist takeover, and communal and ethnic divisions, which pitted Singapore's majority Chinese population against the minority Malays."[13] Tan noted that Singapore made use of emergency powers (originally established by British colonial rulers) to counter these threats when it was expelled from Malaysia in 1965. The Singapore government argued that without these powers, including the authority to detain without trial persons suspected of being subversives, it may not have been able to prevent the country from plunging into civil strife.[14]

2. The Malaysian government sometimes deprives indigenous populations of access to forests and waters, thus restricting their right to a secure cultural context. The Malaysian government asserts that control of such natural resources is necessary for economic development in that country.

3. When Korean President Park issued a threat to execute blackmailers, a capital outflow that was hemorrhaging the country's economy ceased.

4. Post–World War II land reform in Japan, South Korea, and Taiwan would have been much more difficult to accomplish without a U.S. occupying force. If instead there had been a democratic context in each country, the political process may have been captured by landed interests that would have posed serious obstacles to land reform.

[11] Xin Chunying, "East Asian Views of Human Rights," paper presented at the Hakone workshop (on file with author), 9.

[12] East Asian participants at the Hakone workshop gave these examples but did not necessarily endorse them. They were raised as examples of justifications that cannot be rebutted without the acquisition of local knowledge.

[13] Kevin Tan, "Economic Development, Legal Reform, and Rights in Singapore and Taiwan," in *The East Asian Challenge for Human Rights*, ed. Joanne R. Bauer and Daniel A. Bell (New York: Cambridge University Press, 1999), 266.

[14] Needless to say, it is difficult to prove that such powers were necessary to prevent civil strife because the alternative scenario is counterfactual. Experience from other contexts, however, does suggest that civil liberties can contribute to communal strife if left unchecked: the freedom of the press in Rwanda, for example, allowed Hutu demagogues to whip up hatred against the Tutsi minority and thus provided ideological justification for the 1994 genocide. See Chua, *World on Fire*, 168–70.

5. The constitutional right to own property and to receive fair compensation for state acquisition of such property was deliberately left out of Singapore's postindependence constitution because it conflicted with the imperatives of economic development. According to Kevin Tan, the "overall national interest, which required that vast tracts of land be reclaimed and developed for industrial use, was given priority in the passage of the Land Acquisition Act. Two key objectives were secured through the powers accorded under this act, since it allowed the government to acquire land for both industrial development and public housing."[15]

6. The existence of underpaid labor, denied the right to protest,[16] has attracted much international investment in China's coastal regions, leading to high growth rates and increasing opportunities for enrichment. As international enterprises along the coast become increasingly capital- and technology-intensive, foreign firms requiring cheaper labor move inland. There is an argument that the whole process has a spillover effect that, in the end, may benefit much of the country.

7. Although meaningful political participation for people with hearing disabilities requires state subsidies for the use of sign-language interpreters in public forums when political leaders address citizens in an official capacity, and the use of interpreters for the hearing disabled to make their own views known to political officials, as well as the use of subtitles when political candidates speak on television, poor countries such as China, Vietnam, and the Philippines simply cannot afford to provide such services.[17]

Whatever one thinks about these justifications for rights violations, it is important to note that they are not offered as general arguments for repression and hence cannot be refuted by social scientific evidence based on generalizations. What makes these arguments for human rights violations plausible is that they include a description of a pressing social problem (communal strife, capital outflow, lack of economic

---

[15] Tan, "Economic Development," 268.

[16] While the central government does oppose, at least rhetorically, this kind of maltreatment of labor, Dorothy Solinger points out that its own economic policies (decentralizing profit retention to local governments and allowing tax receipts on local industry to be collected and kept locally) have disposed local leaders to solicit rights abusing investors. As Solinger observes, "the problem is pretty complex—it's not just a question of 'the state' and its approach to rights . . . the various echelons of the state may have separate interests and different reasons for their stances on rights." Letter from Dorothy Solinger to Daniel Bell (23 September 1995) (on file with author).

[17] The example of human rights violations against people with hearing disabilities was provided by Akihiko Yonaiyama in a public forum on "The Growth of East Asia and Its Impact on Human Rights," held at the United Nations University in Tokyo, June 1995, following the Hakone workshop.

resources) and an account of why a rights violation (the right to detain without trial, a threat to execute blackmailers, not providing interpreters for the hearing impaired) is the only effective way of dealing with that particular problem.[18] To counter such arguments with the claim that most countries do not have to face similar problems or that not all rights need to be curtailed for purposes of economic development seems beside the point.

Nor is it appropriate to respond to this "Asian" challenge with the claim that human rights are universal and hence cannot be restricted under any circumstances. The so-called Asian side of the debate often concedes that human rights are universal and that ideally governments ought to try to secure as many rights as possible.[19] The point being made here, however, is that certain rights may conflict, and that consequently governments may have to either sacrifice some rights in order to safeguard more important ones or sacrifice a certain right in the short term in order to secure more of that same right in the long term. Put differently, the real East Asian challenge is often not so much a dispute about the ideal of promoting human rights or different cultural "essences" as a plea for recognition of the (alleged) fact that certain East Asian governments often find themselves in the unenviable position of having to cur-

---

[18] It is worth noting that article 4 of the United Nations International Covenant on Civil and Political Rights (1966) explicitly allows for short-term curbs on rights if these are necessary to deal with particular social crises:

> In time of public emergency which threatens the life of the nation and the existence of which is officially proclaimed, the States Parties to the present Covenant may take measures derogating from their obligations under the present Covenant to the extent strictly required by the exigencies of the situation, provided that such measures are not inconsistent with their other obligations under international law and do not involve discrimination solely on the ground of race, color, sex, language, religion or social origin.

[19] For example, article 8 of the Bangkok Declaration adopted by several Asian states in April 1993 states that "while human rights are universal in nature, they must be considered in the context of a dynamic and evolving process of international norm-setting, [and] bearing in mind the significance of national and regional particularities and various historical, cultural and religious backgrounds." Michael W. Dowdle argues that this formulation is wholly consistent with the conception of rights as principles (rather than hard commands) defended by John Rawls and Ronald Dworkin in the context of Anglo-American jurisprudence. Dowdle, "How a Liberal Jurist Defends the Bangkok Declaration," in *Negotiating Culture and Human Rights*," ed. Lynda S. Bell, Andrew J. Nathan, and Ilan Peleg (New York: Columbia University Press, 2001), 125–52. The challenge to the universalization of human rights is more explicit in the case of Islam, however: the Cairo Islamic conference in August 1993 contrasted Islamic values with the UN Declaration. Jose Rubio-Carracedo, "Globalization and Differentiality in Human Rights," in *Beyond Nationalism: Sovereignty and Citizenship*, ed. Fred Dallmayr and Jose M. Rosales (Lanham, MD: Lexington Books, 2001), 277.

tail certain rights in order to secure other more basic rights.[20] To para-
phrase Isaiah Berlin, not all good rights go together, contrary to the optimistic and well-meaning pronouncements of some Western human rights
activists.

When countering plausible government justifications for rights violations of this sort, one can question either the premise that the East Asian
country under question is facing a particular social crisis (for example, a
high risk of intercommunal warfare) requiring immediate political action or the idea that curbing a particular right is the best means of overcoming that crisis.[21] Whatever the tactic, the social critic must be armed
with detailed and historically informed knowledge of the society that
finds itself in a specific, historically contingent condition.[22]

Even if it turns out that (1) the social crisis is real and (2) curbing
rights is the most effective way of overcoming it, such local justifications
for the denial of rights are, as Jack Donnelly put it, "at best a short-run
excuse."[23] Once the economic or political troubles are more or less successfully overcome, then, according to the government's own logic, the

[20] The U.S. government's reaction to the September 11, 2001, terrorist attacks shows
that such arguments are not distinctly Asian. As Randy Peerenboom puts it, "When stable,
Euro-America can afford to preach to developing countries struggling with terrorists about
the value of civil and political rights and the importance of the rule of law. But when faced
with threats, much cherished rights go out the window. If there is anything universal, it
would seem to be disregard for rights whenever there are real or perceived threats to stability or order" (Peerenboom, "Human Rights and Rule of Law: What's the Relationship?",
Georgetown Journal of International Law, vol. 36, no. 3 (2005), 935. The September 11
terrorist attacks have also led to rethinking in some human rights circles regarding the possibility that social crises may justify the temporary curtailment of rights: see, e.g., William
F. Schulz (executive director of Amnesty International U.S.A.), "Security Is a Human Right,
Too: Have Rights Advocates Failed to Face Up to Terrorism?", *The New York Times Magazine*, 18 April 2004, 20.

[21] Of course, human rights groups and NGOs are likely to look harder for feasible alternatives to rights violations than government officials, but if they look and find nothing, it
may be time to move on to something else.

[22] The social critic, in other words, must first concede the possibility of situational constraints on the part of the power holder and then proceed to show (on the basis of a contextual argument) that those constraints do not apply in that particular situation. Social
critics in East Asia may be better culturally prepared to engage in this sort of contextual
criticism. In experimental settings, according to Richard Nisbett, "Americans in general
failed to recognize the role of situational constraints on a speaker's behavior whereas Koreans were able to." Nisbett, *The Geography of Thought*, 190. For whatever concatenation
of historical reasons, there may be perceptual and cognitive processes that make Americans
typically think in "black and white" terms (perhaps helping to explain the readiness to
condemn "foreign" practices without any understanding of different cultures as well as the
popularity of such U.S. presidents as Ronald Reagan and George W. Bush).

[23] Jack Donnelly, "Human Rights and Asian Values: A Defense of 'Western' Universalism," in *The East Asian Challenge for Human Rights*, ed. Joanne R. Bauer and Daniel A.
Bell (New York: Cambridge University Press, 1999), 72.

denial of rights is no longer justified.[24] This leads us once again to the point that the Asian values debate is something of a misnomer. Some government arguments for curtailing rights turn mainly on the validity of empirical facts, not on culture. These arguments are sometimes used to call for curtailing rights in such a way that the traditional cultural values are actually violated. As Amartya Sen observed, the Chinese government justifies its one-child policy by claiming (erroneously, in Sen's view) that it is necessary to deal with the population crisis. In fact, the resulting policy violates, not honors, a deeply held cultural preference for siring male children.[25]

Nonetheless, the argument is not purely a matter of how best to stamp out undesirable cultural values. Traditional values can be widely adhered to and considered defensible by members of a particular community, and this can affect the *prioritizing* of rights. Different societies may rank rights differently, and if they face a similar set of disagreeable circumstances they may come to a different conclusion about the right that needs to be curtailed. For example, U.S. citizens may be more willing to sacrifice a social or economic right in cases of conflict with a civil and political right: if neither the constitution nor a majority of democratically elected representatives support universal access to health care, then the right to health care regardless of income can be curtailed. In contrast, the Chinese may be more willing to sacrifice a civil or political liberty in cases of conflict with a social or economic right: there may be wide support for restrictions on the right to form free labor associations if they are necessary to provide conditions for economic development.[26] Different priorities assigned to rights can also matter when it comes to deciding how to spend scarce resources. For example, East Asian societies with a Confucian heritage will place great emphasis upon the value of education, which may help to explain the large amount of spending on

[24] Note, however, that the "short term" can last a long time, particularly if the social crisis is replaced by another that similarly justifies the rights curtailment. (For example, in the late 1990s, pressure was building on Singapore and Malaysia to repeal internal security acts that allowed indefinite detention without trial because the initial justification, viz., fear of communist takeover, was no longer plausible, but the September 11 terrorist attacks, along with the concomitant fear of terrorist attacks by Islamic "fundamentalists" in Southeast Asia, put an end to that debate.) Moreover, if the main reason for rights curtailment is insufficient economic resources (e.g., few countries can afford to subsidize sign-language interpreters in all political forums so that people with hearing disabilities are guaranteed equal rights to meaningful political participation), then the "short-term" restriction on rights will not "wither away" in the foreseeable future.

[25] Sen, comment at Hakone workshop.

[26] To repeat, I do not mean to imply that such beliefs justifying constraints on civil and political rights are necessarily distinctive to the East Asian region. What I do mean to argue is that they will seem more plausible to a wider array of constituents compared to people in Western liberal democratic countries.

education compared to other societies with similar levels of economic development.[27] Note, however, that these choices are not meant to be celebrated; they reflect the difficult circumstances that may bind political actors in the short to medium term.

In short, these arguments for curtailing rights do not undermine the quest for a truly universal human rights regime: Cultural arguments for the *systematic* denial of basic civil and political rights, as well as economic, social, and cultural rights, cannot withstand critical scrutiny, even allowing for justifiable moral and political differences and for plausible accounts of situation-specific curtailment of particular rights. At best, different cultural values can justify different priorities given to rights in cases of conflict, but both "sides" can agree that such hard choices are unfortunate and hopefully temporary.

The other challenges to Western ideas of human rights are more directly arguments over cultural values. Several East Asian intellectuals have argued that Western-style human rights discourse and instruments have not yet adequately incorporated "values in Asia." The proposed remedies draw on the positive—potential and realized—contributions of East Asian cultural traditions.

ASIAN JUSTIFICATIONS FOR HUMAN RIGHTS

Human Rights: Is Liberalism the Only Moral Foundation?

According to the prominent human rights theorist Jack Donnelly, "the idea that all human beings, simply because they are human, have certain inalienable political rights" was essentially foreign to traditional Asian political thought as well as to premodern Western political thought.[28] The theory of human rights was first fully developed in John Locke's *Second Treatise on Government*. These ideas spread broadly in response to the dual threats to human dignity posed by modern centralized states and socially disruptive free markets in seventeenth-century Europe.

The claim that the concept of human rights is foreign to East Asian political traditions may be out of date: China, for example, has been the

---

[27] China is an exception within the East Asian region. As the official newspaper *China Daily* notes, "in the 1990s, China spent just 2 percent of its GDP on education, growing to more than 2.4 percent in 2003. In 2003, developed Western nations invested an average 6 to 7 percent of their GDP in education, and even in third world countries the average was 4.1 percent." "Experts Say Education Input Vital," *China Daily*, 7 August 2005 (www.china daily.com.cn/English/doc/2005-07/08/content_458397.htm, visited 7 January 2006). As China continues to recover its Confucian tradition, it is hoped that this percentage can increase. In any case, social critics can appeal to the Confucian tradition to argue for an increase.

[28] Donnelly, "Human Rights and Asian Values," 62.

site of a rich discourse on rights for the last century or so, every since the term "rights" began to be translated into the Chinese term *quanli*.[29] Moreover, several East Asian intellectuals argued that values similar to aspects of Western conceptions of human rights can also be found in some "premodern" non-Western traditions. For example, the distinguished Islamic scholar Nurcholish Madjid notes that "Islam too recognizes the right to found a family, the right to privacy, the right to freedom of movement and residence, the right to use one's own language, the right to practice one's own culture and the right to freedom of religion."[30] The University of Hong Kong political philosopher Joseph Chan argues that values similar to aspects of Western conceptions of human rights can also be found in the Confucian tradition.[31] The notion of *ren* (variously translated as benevolence, humanity, or love), for example, expresses the value of impartial concern to relieve human suffering. In Mencius's famous example of a child on the verge of falling into a well, a person with *ren* would be moved by compassion to save the child, not because he or she had personal acquaintance with the child's parents, nor because he or she wanted to win the praise of fellow villagers or friends, but simply because of his or her concern for the suffering of a human person. Such concern shows that Confucianism allows for duties or rights that belong to human persons *simpliciter*, independent of their roles.[32]

In addition, the functional equivalents of some human rights *practices* can be found in Asian traditions. For example, the idea of curbing the ruler's exercise of arbitrary state power figured prominently in Confu-

[29] See Stephen C. Angle, *Human Rights and Chinese Thought: A Cross-Cultural Inquiry* (New York: Cambridge University Press, 2002), and Marina Svensson, *Debating Human Rights in China: A Conceptual and Political History* (Lanham, MD: Rowman and Littlefield, 2002). Angle and Svensson have coedited and translated *The Chinese Human Rights Reader* (Armonk, NY: M. E. Sharpe, 2002), which includes many of the key Chinese-language documents and essays on human rights.

[30] Nurcholish Madjid, "Islam, Modernization and Human Rights: A Preliminary Examination of the Indonesian Case," paper presented at the Hakone workshop (on file with author) (quoting Chandra Muzaffar), 7. Since the downfall of Suharto, Nurcholish Madjid has played an important role in aiding the transition to democratic rule, and his views have been respected partly, if not mainly, because he appeals to Islamic foundations and is personally respected for his religious piety.

[31] In the same vein, Stephen Angle argues that the Chinese rights discourse owes much to neo-Confucian theories about legitimate desires that date back to the sixteenth century. Angle's main argument is not that there is an exact convergence between Western and Chinese views on human rights, but rather that the Chinese background has shaped a distinctively Chinese discourse about rights. I have critically evaluated this argument in my review of Angle's book, "Human Rights and Social Criticism in Contemporary Chinese Political Theory," *Political Theory*, vol. 32, no. 3 (June 2004), 397–400.

[32] See Chan, "A Confucian Perspective on Human Rights," 218.

cian political regimes.[33] Jongryn Mo argues that the Censorate provided an effective institutional restraint on the ruler's power in Choson dynasty Korea. The Censorate consisted of three organs that were explicitly designed to prevent abuse in the exercise of political and administrative agents. The censors were not only judicial and auditing agents, but also voices of dissent and opposition, playing roles similar to that of opposition parties in modern democracies.[34]

There were also functional equivalents of some social and economic rights. Classical Confucians strongly emphasized that the first obligation of government is to feed the people, and this norm was often put into practice in imperial China. In the Song dynasty (960–1279 C.E.), the central government established a granary in each district for the storing of rice that came from the public land as rent. Each of the four classes of people was given rice and sometimes clothes. In the Qing dynasty (1644–1911), there were strict legal sanctions to punish officials who failed to secure the "right to food": "According to the Law Code of the Tsing [Qing] Dynasty, if the officials do not support the four classes, the very sick person and the infirm and superannuated who need public support, they shall be punished by sixty blows of the long stick."[35]

[33] It is rather surprising that Alasdair MacIntyre, known for his supposed hostility to Western-style rights discourse, has argued that modern states necessarily must draw on that discourse in a way that precludes Confucianism: "my view does involve a denial that any modern state, Asian or Western, could embody the values of a Mencius or a Xunzi. The political dimensions of a Confucianism that took either or both of them as its teachers would be those of the local community, not of the state." MacIntyre, "Questions for Confucians: Reflections on the Essays in Comparative Study of Self, Autonomy, and Community," in *Confucian Ethics: A Comparative Study of Self, Autonomy, and Community*, ed. Kwong-loi Shun and David B. Wong (New York: Cambridge University Press, 2004), 217. But if some aspects of Confucian-inspired practices and institutions can serve as the functional equivalent of Western-style practices and institutions that secure civil and political rights, then why take such a hard line against "political Confucianism"? MacIntyre underestimates the potential of Confucian-inspired political institutions, just as he overestimates the potential of Confucian ethics to structure ethical life at the level of local community. Few contemporary adherents of Confucianism regard Confucianism as a "well-defined concept of the kind of community within which relationships could be defined by the relevant norms, and the four virtues would provide the standards for practice" (ibid., 215); rather, Confucianism is viewed as part of the good life, particularly relevant for structuring relationships with elderly parents, but most Confucians freely draw upon other ethical resources such as Christianity and Buddhism for structuring ethical lives.

[34] Jongryn Mo, "The Challenge of Accountability: Implications of the Censorate," in *Confucianism for the Modern World*, ed. Daniel A. Bell and Hahm Chaibong (New York: Cambridge University Press, 2003).

[35] Chen, Huan-Chang, *The Economic Principles of Confucius and His School, vol. 2* (New York: Columbia University Press, 1911), p. 599. Quoted in Joseph Chan, "Giving Priority to the Worst-Off: A Confucian Perspective on Social Welfare," in *Confucianism for the Modern World*, ed. Daniel A. Bell and Hahm Chaibong (New York: Cambridge University Press, 2003), 241–42.

In short, the Western liberal tradition may not be the only moral foundation for realizing the values and practices associated with human rights regimes. But why does this matter, practically speaking?

Increasing Commitment to Human Rights in East Asia: Strategic Considerations

While it may be possible to defend the argument that human rights ideas and practices resonate to some extent with Asian cultural traditions, are there any particular reasons for proponents of human rights to adopt culturally sensitive strategies for the promotion of rights, either instead of, or as a complement to, other strategies? If the ultimate aim of human rights diplomacy is to persuade others of the value of human rights, it is more likely that the struggle to promote human rights can be won if it is fought in ways that build on, rather than challenge, local cultural traditions.[36] To deny the possibility that human rights norms and practices are compatible with Asian traditions translates into dependence on a foreign standard for promoting human rights. This approach has a number of drawbacks.

First, the argument that Western liberalism is the only moral foundation for human rights unwittingly plays into the hands of nasty forces in East Asia who seek to stigmatize human rights voices as "agents of foreign devils" and defamers of indigenous traditions. Similarly, the argument that the development of human rights is contingent on the development of capitalism strengthens the position of antimodernists who oppose human rights, while the argument that human rights is contingent on anthropocentric arguments strengthens advocates of a theocentric view who oppose human rights.[37] Worse, arguments that present a stark choice between religion and human rights (as opposed to an

---

[36] The conception of tradition refers to an ongoing argument about the good of the community whose identity it seeks to define. The cultural traditions of interest to human rights activists, in other words, should be living in the sense that fundamental values still have the capacity to motivate action in the contemporary era. For similar accounts of tradition, see Robert Bellah et al., *Habits of the Heart* (Berkeley: University of California Press, 1985), 27–28, 335–36; and Alasdair MacIntyre, *Whose Justice? Which Rationality?* (London: Duckworth, 1988).

[37] John L. Esposito points out that "[t]oo often analysis and policymaking have been shaped by a liberal secularism that fails to recognize it too represents a world view, not the paradigm for modern society, and can easily degenerate into a 'secularist fundamentalism' that treats alternative views as irrational, extremist, and deviant." Esposito, "Political Islam: Beyond the Green Menace," *Current History*, vol. 93, no. 579 (January 1994), 24. The problem with "secular fundamentalism" is not just that it fails to respect nonliberal cultural traditions, but that it plays into the hands of "religious fundamentalists" who also seek to reject wholesale values and practices associated with the Western liberal tradition.

approach that promises to reconcile religious insights with human rights
ideas) may lead politically moderate religious persons into developing
feelings hostile to human rights positions.[38]

Second, it is a widespread belief within the United States—currently
the dominant voice/actor on the world diplomatic stage—that exporting
U.S. political practices and institutions is necessary for the promotion of
human rights abroad. As Stephen Young, former assistant dean at the
Harvard Law School, puts it,

> Many Americans seem to believe that the constitutional pattern of gover-
> nance in the United States today—as formalized in the Declaration of Inde-
> pendence, the Constitution, and the Bill of Rights—is a necessary prerequi-
> site for protecting human rights. Thus, they evaluate the performance of
> other countries in the field of human rights by comparing their conduct
> with the standards of American politics.[39]

It may well have been feasible to act on this belief in the post–World War
II era, when the United States was powerful enough to insist upon human rights norms. The U.S. capacity to dictate appropriate forms of government to Japan in the immediate post–World War II period is a classic
example. Today, however, the relative economic and military strength of
East Asia means that the United States must now rely primarily on moral
authority to promote human rights in Asia. However, several factors undermine U.S. moral authority in this respect.

Widely publicized social problems in the United States no longer make
it the attractive political model that it may once have been. For example,
Tokyo University's Onuma Yasuaki is an active proponent of human

---

[38] This is not to deny that aspects of religious traditions are inconsistent with contemporary human rights values and practices, but only to suggest that aspects of religious traditions may be supportive of human rights and to offer the possibility that contemporary
members of religious traditions may be able to formulate persuasive interpretations while
excising "contingent" aspects inimical to human rights concerns. See the discussion of Islamic feminism below.

[39] Stephen B. Young, "Human Rights Questions in Southeast Asian Culture: Problems
for American Response," in *The Politics of Human Rights*, ed. Paula Newberg (New York:
New York University Press, 1980), 187. Young then proceeds to criticize this standpoint:
"Although the Anglo-American political and legal tradition has been a forceful expositor
of human rights causes, it is not the only basis upon which to build a political system that
respects individual dignity." Nonetheless, he falls into his own universalist trap when he
fails to distinguish between democracy and human rights, apparently assuming that
Western-style electoral mechanisms are necessary and sufficient to secure basic human
rights (see ibid., 187–88, 209). It is important to keep in mind that nondemocratic governments sometimes do fairly well at securing human rights (e.g., contemporary Hong Kong
or the Republic of Venice for most of the previous millennium), whereas democratic governments can sometimes have atrocious human rights records at home (e.g., Sri Lanka and
El Salvador under Duarte) and abroad (e.g., the United States in Vietnam and Iraq).

rights in Japan, but he is also a harsh critic of the attempt to export the U.S.-style rights regime, which emphasizes civil and political liberties over social and economic rights.[40] Onuma argues that this regime—with its excessive legalism and individualism—contributes to various social diseases, such as high rates of drug use, collapsing families, rampant crime, growing economic inequality, and alienation from the political process.[41]

It is obvious that recent foreign policy developments, particularly since the Iraq War, have undermined U.S. moral credibility in Asia and elsewhere.[42] The tendency to subordinate human rights concerns when they conflict with security and commercial considerations contributes to cynicism regarding the true motivation of U.S. policymakers, not just among government officials, but also among ordinary citizens.[43] The refusal to make amends for past misdeeds such as the Vietnam War further undermines U.S. moral authority in Asia,[44] just as Japan's refusal to accept full responsibility for its war of aggression weakens its own moral authority in Asia. For the foreseeable future, the attempt to export "American ideals" is likely to fall on deaf ears, if not be counterproductive, in the East Asian region.

Third, appeal to the Universal Declaration of Human Rights (UDHR) as a standard for promoting human rights in East Asia is not without drawbacks. Although the UDHR has served as an effective tool in some human rights struggles in East Asia (for example, by human rights cam-

[40] The U.S.-style priority of civil and political rights refers to the official policies of the U.S. government (its invocations of "human rights and democracy" tend to refer to civil and political rights), the works of leading American political philosophers (e.g., John Rawls's *A Theory of Justice*), and U.S.-based human rights groups (e.g., Human Rights First, formerly known as the Lawyers Committee for Human Rights). It is worth noting, however, that the U.S. branch of Amnesty International is explicitly critical of the official U.S. devaluation of economic rights (see the following chapter).

[41] Onuma Yasuaki, "Toward an Intercivilizational Approach to Human Rights," in *The East Asian Challenge for Human Rights*, ed. Joanne R. Bauer and Daniel A. Bell, eds. (New York: Cambridge University Press, 1999), 107.

[42] The lack of moral authority in the rest of world was explicitly recognized by the U.S. State Department when it postponed the annual release of its (2004) Country Reports on Human Rights Practices following the public release of photos depicting the torture ("abuse," as the U.S. government called it) of Iraqi prisoners at Abu Ghraib prison.

[43] On the case of China, see Randall Peerenboom, "Assessing Human Rights in China: Why the Double Standard?," *Cornell International Law Journal*, vol. 38, no. 1 (February 2004), 73, n. 7.

[44] The Bush administration, needless to say, is not likely to apologize for the Vietnam War. More surprisingly, perhaps, the Clinton administration added insult to injury by pressuring the Vietnamese government to repay $145 million in debts incurred by the U.S.-backed government of the former South Vietnam, effectively putting "Hanoi in the position of retroactively footing part of the bill for a war against itself." Clay Chandler, "Ghosts of War Haunt Rubin's Vietnam Trip," *International Herald Tribune*, 11 April 1997.

paigners in the Philippines during Marcos' rule),[45] in many parts of East Asia the UDHR and other U.N. documents are not nearly as relevant.

Since the UDHR was formulated without significant input from East Asia, it is not always clear to East Asians why the UDHR should constitute "our" human rights norms (the Bangkok Declaration was significant because it was the first organized expression of Asian opposition to the UDHR).[46] Although the UDHR is normatively binding, most East Asian states endorsed it for pragmatic, political reasons and not because of a deeply held commitment to the human rights norms it contains. The UDHR thus does not have the normative force and political relevance of a constitution that emerges from genuine dialogue between interested parties keen on finding a long-term solution to a shared political dilemma.[47] The lack of a proper enforcement mechanism for the International Bill of Human Rights, as the UDHR and subsequent documents are called, further reduces the practical viability of this standard.

Another fundamental weakness of the U.N. documents is that they are pitched at too high a level of abstraction (perhaps necessarily so in view of the need to reach agreement among many states) to be of use for many actual social and political problems.[48] For example, does the "right to life" (article 3 of the UDHR) mean that capital punishment should be abolished? It is much easier to secure agreement at the level of high principle than to secure agreement over the application of those principles to

[45] One can explain this phenomenon in part by the fact that the Marcos regime depended to a great extent on U.S. economic and military support. Because of this, Marcos was extremely conscious of his public image before the world. This, in turn, led him to employ legalistic justifications for his policies. As Maria Serena Diokno puts it, "what better way than to apply international instruments he had publicly proclaimed as the guiding principles of his rule?" Letter from Maria Serena Diokno to Daniel Bell (20 November 1995) (on file with author).

[46] Sumner B. Twiss notes that the Chinese delegate to the drafting process of the UDHR argued for the inclusion of the Confucian idea of *ren* in article 1, which was eventually reflected in the idea that human beings are endowed not just with "reason," but also with "conscience." Twiss, "A Constructive Framework for Discussing Confucianism and Human Rights," in *Confucianism and Human Rights*, ed. Wm. Theodore de Bary and Tu Weiming (New York: Columbia University Press, 1998), 41. If that is the only concrete manifestation of an East Asian contribution to the UDHR, however, it won't quell the critics who view it as a "Westcentric" document.

[47] One might also ask why the government's voice should count as the normatively binding final interpretation of human rights issues in East Asia. Ironically, the same critics who point out that East Asian governments illegitimately present their own interpretations of human rights (often self-interested arguments for the denial of rights) as though it represents a society-wide consensus are saying, in effect, that international human standards upheld in the UDHR should be upheld because their governments endorsed this document.

[48] Similar problems arise with principles laid out in state constitutions: on the (mistaken) tendency to think that constitutionalizing property rights is sufficient to secure those rights, see Greg Alexander, "Property in Global Constitution-Making: Avoiding the Formalist Trap" (ms. on file with the author).

particular cases. Moreover, U.N. documents do not provide much guidance when rights conflict or need to be violated preemptively to prevent further violations of rights.

In short, U.S. and "international" justifications for human rights do not seem particularly promising from a tactical point of view, and to be effective human rights activists may need to pay more attention to local justifications for human rights in Asia. There are also positive reasons in favor of drawing on the resources of indigenous cultural traditions to persuade East Asians of the value of human rights.

First, awareness of "values in Asia" allows the human rights activist to draw on the most compelling *justifications* for human rights practices. Many rights battles will be fought within societies according to local norms and justifications. Consider the example of the Sisters in Islam, an autonomous, nongovernmental organization of Muslim women in Malaysia.[49] This group challenges the way that Islam has been (mis)used by powerful forces to justify patriarchal practices, often contravening Islam's central ideas and animating principles. It tries to advocate women's rights in terms that are locally persuasive, meaning that it draws upon Islamic principles for inspiration.[50] For example, the Sisters in Islam submitted a memorandum to the prime minister of Malaysia urging the Federal Parliament not to endorse the *hudud* law passed by the Kelantan state legislature. The *hudud* punishments included such troubling features as the inadmissibility of women as eyewitnesses. Sisters in Islam argued against the endorsement of these punishments by rejecting the crude equation of *hudud* with *Shari'a* and *Shari'a* with Islam that helped to justify the Kelantan enactments. Apparently this campaign was effective, because the Federal Parliament states that it will not pass the Kelantan *hudud* code. The Sisters in Islam also engage in long-term human rights work, such as distributing pamphlets on Quranic conceptions of rights and duties of men and women in the family that provide the basis for a more egalitarian view of gender relations than the regressive ideas typically (and misleadingly) offered in the name of Islam itself. The assumption is that building human rights on traditional cultural resources—on the customs and values that people use to make sense of their lives—is more likely to lead to long-term commitment to human rights ideas and

[49] See Norani Othman, "Grounding Human Rights Arguments in Non-Western Culture: *Shari'a* and the Citizenship Rights of Women in a Modern Islamic State," in *The East Asian Challenge for Human Rights*, ed. Joanne R. Bauer and Daniel A. Bell (New York: Cambridge University Press, 1999). chap. 7.

[50] Similar arguments have been put forward by Islamic feminists in Morocco: see Wendy Kristianasen, "Debats entre femmes en terres d'islam," *Le Monde Diplomatique*, Avril 2004, 20. In Kenya, the argument that female genital cutting is inconsistent with the teachings of the Quran (Koran) has been relatively effective at changing the minds of (former) practitioners of genital cutting. Mark Lacey, "Genital Cutting Shows Signs of Losing Favor in Africa," *The New York Times*, 8 June 2004, A3.

practices. Conversely, the group seems to recognize that defending rights by appealing to "universal human rights" (not to mention Western feminist ideas) is likely to be ineffective, if not counterproductive.[51]

It can be argued that predominantly Islamic societies present a special case, where people's outlooks and "habits of the heart" are profoundly informed by religious values. In this context, it seems obvious that defenders of human rights are more likely to be effective if they work within the dominant tradition. But cultural traditions may also be relevant for human rights activists and democratic reformers elsewhere. For example, Wang Juntao—a long-time democratic activist who spent nearly five years in jail after the 1989 Beijing massacre—argues that many of the key figures in Chinese democracy movements drew inspiration from Confucian values. From the late nineteenth century to the present, nearly all the important figures in the history of democracy movements in mainland China, Taiwan, and Hong Kong tried to revive Confucianism in order to support democratization. Wang Juntao supports this aspiration, partly on the grounds that democracy may be easier to implement in the Chinese context if it can be shown that it need not conflict with traditional political culture: "If Confucianism is consistent with democracy, the traditional culture may be used as a means of promoting democratization in East Asia. At the very least, the political transition will be smoother and easier, with lower costs, since there will be less cultural resistance."[52] Of course, there is an element of speculation here since the "effectiveness" of Confucian—based arguments for democracy remains to be proven in mainland China, but such arguments, at minimum, can be deployed to counter official attempts to use "Confucianism" to justify constraints on democratic rule.

Second, local traditions may shed light on the *groups* most likely to bring about desirable social and political change. For example, Han

---

[51] Note, however, that the strategy adopted by Sisters of Islam is not without controversy. At the Bangkok workshop, a representative of the group was severely criticized by a devout Muslim from Malaysia, who questioned the Islamic credentials of the group, including the fact that some members could not read the Quran in Arabic. Such criticisms suggest that local justifications are most effective if deployed by "true believers" of the tradition: in the case of Islam, if a nonbeliever draws on Islam to push forward values similar to human rights in an Islamic context, the strategic use of the religion is not likely to be viewed as sincere and may be rejected as another form of cultural imperialism. Needless to say, I do not mean to imply that the members of Sisters of Islam are not true believers: in fact, their successes in the Malaysian political area suggests that they are taken seriously by other Muslims. In this case, it appears to be a dispute between competing interpretations of Islam, not between believers and nonbelievers.

[52] Wang Juntao, "Confucian Democrats in Chinese History," in *Confucianism for the Modern World*, ed. Daniel A. Bell and Hahm Chaibong (New York: Cambridge University Press, 2003), 69.

Sangjin of Seoul National University suggests that students from universities in Korea, centers of "cultural authority," could draw on the Confucian tradition of respect for intellectual elites and hence play a crucial role in establishing a society-wide commitment on the need for improving the human rights situation in Korea.[53] It may be that intellectual elites are granted uncommon (by Western standards) amounts of respect in societies shaped by Confucian traditions, with the implication that human rights activists need to target this group in particular, as opposed to investing their hopes in a mythical liberalizing middle class that often supports human rights reforms only insofar as they maintain a political order conducive to the accumulation of wealth.[54]

Third, regardless of the substance or the moral justification for one's arguments, awareness of local traditions may shed light on the appropriate attitude to be employed by human rights activists. For example, Onuma Yasuaki reminds us that "[i]n Japanese culture, modesty is highly valued. Even if one believes in certain values, proselytizing for them is regarded as arrogant, uncivilized, and counterproductive. Instead, one should find ways to induce others to appreciate these values in a quiet and modest manner."[55] This has implications for cross-cultural critics of human rights violations: instead of the high-decibel "naming and shaming" approach[56] that is often seen in East Asia as high-minded and self-righteous, even by dissident intellectuals, criticism of human rights violations in East Asia is often more effective if it is presented in a more subtle and indirect way.

Fourth, local traditions may also make one more sensitive to the possibility of alternative, nonlegalistic mechanisms for the protection of the vital human interests normally secured by a rights regime in a Western context.[57] As Onuma (himself a professor of international law) notes,

[53] Han Sangjin, "Political Liberalization, Stability, and Human Rights" (paper presented at the Hakone workshop, on file with author), 21.

[54] See David Brown and David Martin Jones, "Democratization and the Myth of the Liberalizing Middle Classes," in Daniel A. Bell et al., *Towards Illiberal Democracy in Pacific Asia* (London and New York: Macmillan/St. Antony's College and St. Martin's Press, 1995), 78–106.

[55] Onuma Yasuaki, "In Quest of Intercivilizational Human Rights: 'Universal vs. Relative' Human Rights Viewed from an Asian Perspective," Centre for Asian Pacific Affairs, The Asia Foundation, Occasional Paper no. 2, 1996, 4.

[56] See the discussion in the following chapter of the "naming and shaming" approach defended by Human Rights Watch.

[57] If human rights practices and institutions refer by definition only to the legal protection of individual rights, then, needless to say, nonlegalistic mechanisms for the protection of those same individual rights cannot be termed "human rights practices." However, if the end result is the same—that is, the protection and promotion of vital human interests, which is presumably the whole point of a human rights regime—it is unclear why one should place too much emphasis on this terminological issue.

"legalistic thinking has been rather foreign to many Japanese . . . to re-sort to juridical measures and to enforce one's rights is not appreciated. Rather, one is expected to reach the same goal by resorting to less force-ful measures such as patient negotiations, mediation, and other concilia-tory measures."[58] In such a context, human rights activists can suggest nonjuridical mechanisms for the protection of vital human interests, em-phasizing that legal means are to be employed only as a last resort.[59]

It would seem, then, that strategic considerations of practical rele-vance speak strongly in favor of local justifications for the values and practices that, in the Western world, are normally realized through a hu-man rights regime. Perhaps, however, the deepest and most controversial question remains to be addressed: Can one identify aspects of East Asian cultural traditions relevant not just in the strategic sense of how best to persuade East Asians of the value of a human rights regime, but also in the sense that they may provide a moral foundation for political prac-tices and institutions different from the human rights regimes typically favored in Western countries? It is to this topic that we now turn.

Values in Asia versus Western Liberalism: Justifiable Moral Differences?

A human rights regime is supposed to protect our basic humanity—the fundamental human goods (or needs or interests) that underpin any "rea-sonable" conception of human flourishing. But which human goods are fundamental? There is little public dispute over rights against murder, torture, slavery, and genocide (though, needless to say, many govern-ments continue to engage in nasty deeds off the record). As Singaporean government official Bilahari Kausikan puts it, "It makes a great deal of difference if the West insists on humane standards of behavior by vigor-ously protesting genocide, murder, torture, or slavery. Here there is a

---

[58] Onuma, "In Quest of Intercivilizational Rights," 4. See also Albert H. Y. Chen, "Me-diation, Litigation, and Justice: Confucian Reflections in a Modern Liberal Society," in *Confucianism for the Modern World*, ed. Daniel A. Bell and Hahm Chaibong (New York: Cambridge University Press, 2003) chap. 11. Several areas of conflict, such as traffic and industrial accidents, that would be dominated by private litigation in the United States are settled by administrative procedures in China. William C. Jones points to the imperial roots of such practices and suggests that administrative agencies can also protect and pro-mote freedom in China's future. William C. Jones, "Chinese Law and Liberty," in *Realms of Freedom in Modern China*, ed. William C. Kirby (Stanford: Stanford University Press, 2004), 55–56.

[59] For the view that legalistic human rights language is generally counterproductive (i.e., not just in the East Asian context) given what it is trying to achieve, see Charles Blattberg, "Two Concepts of Cosmopolitanism" (ms. on file with author).

clear consensus on a core of international law that does not admit of any derogation on any grounds."[60] However, beyond this agreed upon core, it may well be possible to identify "civilizational" faultlines with respect to differing conceptions of vital human interests.

To repeat, both Western and Asian cultural traditions are complex and change a great deal in response to various internal and external pressures. Nonetheless, it is possible that most politically relevant actors, both officials and intellectuals, in East Asian societies typically endorse a somewhat different set of fundamental human goods than their counterparts in Western societies now and for the foreseeable future. Different societies may typically have different ideas regarding which human goods must be protected regardless of competing considerations, and which human goods can be legitimately subject to trade-offs with other goods as part of everyday politics. If there is some truth in these propositions, it is essential for purposes of improving mutual understanding and minimizing cross-cultural conflict to take them into account. It may mean that some Western conceptions of human rights are actually culturally specific conceptions of fundamental human goods, not readily accepted elsewhere, too encompassing in some cases and too narrow in others.

Limiting the Set of Human Rights for an East Asian Context

For example, it is not only defenders of "Asian" autocratic rule who question the "American" idea that individuals have a vital interest in speaking freely, so long as they do not physically harm others, along with the political implication that the government has a "sacred" obligation to respect this interest. Consider the case of Dr. Sulak Sivaraksa, a leading prodemocracy activist in Thailand and a nominee for the Nobel Peace Prize. In 1991 the Thai ruler, General Suchinda, pressed charges against Sulak for *lèse-majesté*—derogatory remarks directed at the royal family—and for defaming the general in a speech given at Thammasat University in Thailand. Fearing for his life, Sulak fled the country, but he returned in 1992 to face charges after the Suchinda government had fallen. In court, Sulak did not deny that he had attacked the "dictator" Suchinda, but he did deny the charge of *lèse-majesté*,

---

[60] Bilahari Kausikan, "Asia's Different Standard," *Foreign Policy*, vol. 92 (1993), 39. The consensus, soon breaks down once it comes to the application of general prohibitions to particular cases, as illustrated by disputes over the whether the abuse of Iraqi prisoners constitutes "torture." There may even be disputes over the application of "torture" in everyday, familial settings: an American student of Indian descent told me that her parents forced her to eat spicy food as a child even after she was crying from the pain, telling her that God would punish her if she didn't eat it (if the point of this child-rearing practice was to promote the love of spicy food, it was effective in this case).

referring to the many services he had performed for the royal family. Sulak explains:

> I did not . . . stake my ground on an absolute right to free speech. My defense against the charge of *lèse-majesté* was my innocence of the charge; my defense was my loyalty to the King and the Royal Family and, even where I discussed the use of the charge of *lèse-majesté* in current Siamese political practice, it was to highlight abuse and to point to the ways in which abuse might undermine the monarchy, rather than to defend any theoretical right to commit this action. I am not affirming, nor would I affirm, a right to commit *lèse-majesté*. This aspect of the case is particularly concerned with my being Siamese and belonging to the Siamese cultural tradition.[61]

In other words, Sulak aimed to persuade fellow citizens that the dominant political system should be replaced with an alternative, relatively democratic political structure, but he made it explicit that this did not mean advocating the removal of the existing constraint on direct criticism of the Thai king. Perhaps Sulak, like many Thais, would feel deeply offended, if not personally harmed, by an attack on the king. In such a case—where a constraint on the freedom of speech seems to be endorsed by both defenders and critics of the prevailing political system—there should be a strong presumption[62] in favor of respecting this deviation from American-style free speech.[63]

Other examples put forward by East Asian intellectuals regarding the possibility of narrowing the definition of vital human interests more than would typically be the case in liberal Western countries—hence narrowing the list of rights that belong to the core of the human rights zone—include the following:

> 1. In Singapore, there is a law that empowers the police and immigration officers to " 'test the urine for drugs of any person who behaves in a suspi-

---

[61] Sulak Sivaraksa, "Buddhism and Human Rights," paper presented at the Bangkok workshop on Cultural Sources of Human Rights in East Asia, March 1996 (on file with author).

[62] I do not mean to deny that this presumption can be overridden. For example, the foreign human rights advocate would not have an obligation to refrain from critique of the Thai king if the king were to call for an unjustified war against a neighboring state, even if all Thais support this call. But such an eventuality is very unlikely (at least under the current king, who is widely admired and recognized to be a benevolent ruler), hence the strong presumption in favor of deferring to the "Thai" constraint on free speech.

[63] At the Bangkok workshop (March 1996), Charles Taylor pointed out that relatively uncontroversial laws against hate speech also exist in Canada. It could be argued, however, that the Thai case is more of a deviation from American-style free speech because the core of this ideal is the right to criticize political leaders, which is precisely the right being called into question here.

cious manner. If the result is positive, rehabilitation treatment is compulsory.'"[64] Joseph Chan comments that "[t]his act would be seen by Western liberals as an unjustifiable invasion of privacy. But for some Asians this restriction may be seen as a legitimate trade-off for the value of public safety and health."[65]

2. In democratic South Korea, each household is required to attend monthly neighborhood meetings to receive government directives and discuss local affairs.[66] What may be viewed as a minor inconvenience in Korea would almost certainly outrage most U.S. citizens, and it is likely that the U.S. Supreme Court would strike down a governmental policy that forced citizens to associate for political purposes of this sort as a violation of the First Amendment. Once again there seems to be more willingness in East Asia among the general population to serve the common good by limiting individual freedom, perhaps as a residue of the Confucian cultural tradition.

3. Islamic legal scholar and human rights activist Abdullahi A. An-Na'im offers the following example from Islamic criminal law. According to Islamic law, which is based on the Quran and which Muslims believe to be the literal and final word of God, and on the Sunna, or traditions of the Prophet Muhammad, theft is punishable by the amputation of the right hand and homicide by exact retribution or payment of monetary compensation. An-Na'im notes that

> Islamic law requires the state to fulfill its obligation to secure social and economic justice and to ensure decent standards of living for all its citizens before it can enforce these punishments. The law also provides for very narrow definitions of these offenses, makes an extensive range of defenses against the charge available to the accused person, and requires strict standards of proof. Moreover, Islamic law demands total fairness and equality in law enforcement. In my view, the prerequisite conditions for the enforcement of these punishments are extremely difficult to satisfy in practice and are certainly unlikely to materialize in any Muslim country in the foreseeable future.[67]

Notwithstanding the practical impediments to the legitimate implementation of corporeal punishment under Islamic law, An-Na'im argues that

[64] Joseph Chan, "The Asian Challenge to Universal Human Rights: A Philosophical Appraisal," in *Human Rights and International Relations in the Asia Pacific*, ed. James T. H. Tang (London: Pinter, 1995), 25, 36 (quoting Won Kan Seng, "The Real World of Human Rights," address at the Second World Conference on Human Rights, Vienna, 1993).

[65] Ibid.

[66] Kim Dae Jung, "Is Culture Destiny?", *Foreign Affairs*, November/December 1994, 190.

[67] Abdullahi A. An-Na'im, "Toward a Cross-Cultural Approach to Defining International Standards of Human Rights: The Meaning of Cruel, Inhuman, or Degrading Treatment or Punishment," in *Human Rights in Cross-Cultural Perspectives: A Quest for Consensus* (Philadelphia: University of Pennsylvania Press, 1992), 34.

Islamic criminal law is endorsed in principle by the vast majority of Muslims today,[68] whereas most Western liberals and human rights activists would almost certainly regard it as a violation of the human right not to be subjected to cruel, inhuman, or degrading treatment or punishment.

Expanding the Set of Human Rights for an East Asian Context

The East Asian challenge, however, is not simply an argument for shortening the set or rights typically endorsed by members of Western liberal societies. In some areas, there may be a case for *widening* the scope of fundamental human goods to be protected by a rights regime. In Japanese society, for example, well-developed empathetic ability is regarded as one of the necessary conditions for the pursuit of the good life. Such ability is normally acquired via warm, intimate human relationships in early stages of life, leading Teruhisa Se and Rie Karatsu to argue that "a new right could be included in the category of human rights: a right to be brought up in an intimate community."[69]

Consider also the value of filial piety, what Confucians consider to be "the essential way of learning to be human."[70] East Asian societies influenced by Confucianism strongly emphasize the idea that adult children have a duty to care for elderly parents,[71] a duty to be forsaken only in the most exceptional circumstances.[72] Thus, whereas it is widely seen

---

[68] Ibid.

[69] Teruhisa Se and Rie Karatsu, "A Conception of Human Rights Based on Japanese Culture: Promoting Cross-cultural Debates," *Journal of Human Rights*, vol. 3, no. 3 (September 2004), 283. He and Rie point to the possibility that such new rights can improve the human rights scheme prevailing in Western cultures (ibid., 284–85), though my view is that well-developed empathetic ability is not nearly so central to the Western liberalism and is not likely to be adopted as the foundation for new rights in the West.

[70] Tu Wei-ming, *Confucianism in an Historical Perspective*, Institute of East Asian Philosophies, Occasional Paper and Monograph Series no. 13, 1989, 15.

[71] Interestingly, this moral outlook still seems to inform the practices of Asian immigrants to other societies. According to the *New York Times* (11 July 2001), fewer than one in five whites in the United States help care for or provide financial support for their parents, in-laws, or other relatives, compared with 28 percent of African Americans, 34 percent of Hispanic Americans, and 42 percent of Asian Americans. Those who provide the most care also feel the most guilt that they are not doing enough. Almost three-quarters of Asian Americans say they should do more for their parents, compared with two-thirds of Hispanics, slightly more than half of African Americans, and fewer than half of whites.

[72] The obligations of filial piety do not end with the death of one's parents: equally, if not more important, are the mourning period and the subsequent rituals designed to show ongoing respect for one's parents. In Korea, for example, the large majority of families endorse the practice of ancestor worship. Geir Helgesen, *Democracy and Authority in Korea: The Cultural Dimension in Korean Politics* (Richmond, England: Curzon, 1988), 128. Arnold Schwarznegger expressed a contrasting approach in the film *Pumping Iron*, where he seemed proud of the fact that he chose to train for a body-building competition rather than return home for his father's funeral.

as morally acceptable in the West to commit elderly parents to nursing homes,[73] from an East Asian perspective this often amounts to condemning one's parents to a lonely and psychologically painful death and thus should be considered as a violation of a fundamental human good. In political practice, the value of filial piety means that it is incumbent on East Asian governments to provide the social and economic conditions that facilitate the realization of the duty to care for elderly parents.[74] This can take the form of laws that make it mandatory for children to provide financial support for elderly parents, as in mainland China,[75] Taiwan,[76] Japan, and Singapore, and/or reliance on more indirect methods such as tax breaks and housing benefits that simply make at-home care for the elderly easier, as in Korea, Hong Kong, and Singapore.[77] In some cases, the right to be cared for by adult children is secured in the constitution itself, along with other "constitutional essentials."[78]

In sum, East Asian conceptions of vital human interests may well justify deviations from the human rights standards typically endorsed by liberal theorists, Western governments, and international human rights documents formulated without substantial input from East Asia. The position that different societies can draw different lines between the core

[73] This is not to deny that Westerners sometimes agonize over the decision to commit a parent to an old-age home. It is only to say that, generally speaking, East Asians are more likely to provide personal care for older parents (see also chapter 10).

[74] In the case of elderly parents without family members, Mencius argues that the obligation falls to the state: see the discussion in Chan, "Giving Priority to the Worst-Off," 238–42.

[75] In China's basic courts, appeals by parents for support from their children constitute 5–10 percent of the cases. Upham comments that "Confucian values notwithstanding, the refusal of young Chinese to obey their legal obligation to support their parents is a significant social problem" (Upham, "Who Will Find the Defendant?") (ms. on file with the author). But the fact that young Chinese have such a legal obligation shows the continuing relevance of the value of filial piety (the point is to punish the minority of young Chinese who do not pay the "costs" of this value).

[76] It is interesting to note that laws meant to secure the traditional value of filial piety are not subject to political debate in Taiwan, one of the few areas of consensus in an otherwise highly polarized society where the government seems intent on casting aside manifestations of traditional "Chinese" values and practices (see chapter 6).

[77] The Singapore state, for example, promotes the ideal of "three generations under one roof" by means of policies that give priorities of allocation for publicly subsidized accommodation or additional housing subsidies for newly married couples who live within a certain distance of their old neighborhood where their parents continue to live. Antonio L. Rappa and Sor-hoon Tan, "Political Implications of Confucian Familism," *Asian Philosophy*, vol. 13, nos. 2/3 (July 2003), 90.

[78] The right to be cared for by adult children may not be expressed in rights language—for example, the 1992 Mongolian Constitution specifies the duty to care for elderly parents. But if adult children can be punished for neglecting their parents, the difference is terminological rather than substantive.

of the human rights regime and less important values is not particularly controversial in East Asia.[79] However, many otherwise progressive liberal voices in the West still seem compelled by a tradition of universalist moral reasoning that proposes one final solution to the question of the ideal polity yet paradoxically draws only on the moral aspirations and political practices found in Western societies.

One obvious implication of these reflections is to allow for the possibility of justifiable deviations from Western-style human rights regimes in East Asia. If otherwise critical East Asian voices endorse their government's "autocratic" measures, Western human rights activists need to think twice before intervention. Let me put it differently. Given the extent of human suffering in today's world, with so many obvious and uncontroversial violations of the minimal conditions of human well-being, it is difficult to understand why Western human rights groups would want to spend (scarce) time and money critiquing human rights "violations" that would not be viewed as such by East Asians with no particular axe to grind.

CROSS-CULTURAL DIALOGUES ON HUMAN RIGHTS: WHAT IS THE POINT?

But it is not just a matter of defending parochial attachments to particular nonliberal moralities. Far from arguing that the universalist discourse on human rights should be entirely displaced with particular, tradition-sensitive political language, some critics of Western-style human rights have criticized liberals for not taking universality seriously enough, for failing to do what must be done to make human rights a truly universal ideal. If the ultimate aim is an international order based on universally accepted human rights, the West needs to recognize that human rights have been in constant evolution and allow for the possibility of positive non-Western contributions to this process. Such critics argue for more cross-cultural dialogues on human rights, with the perspective that Asian proposals for improving the current "Westcentric" human rights regime

---

[79] I leave aside the question of cultural differences that may affect different ways of determining the core of human rights *within* societies. For example, newly arrived Hmong immigrants to the United States believe that ritual killings of animals is necessary to heal sick family members, but once the practice became known to residents of Merced, California, the city passed an ordinance banning the slaughter of livestock and poultry within city limits. See Anne Fadiman, *The Spirit Catches You and You Fall Down: A Hmong Child, Her American Doctors, and the Collision of Two Cultures* (New York: Farrar, Straus, and Giroux, 1997), 107–8. Were the Hmong to frame their grievances in terms of the language of human rights, they would have a good case to argue that their basic rights are being violated.

should be welcomed, not feared.[80] These critics—let us label them "cosmopolitan critics of liberalism"—have suggested various means of improving the philosophical coherence and political appeal of human rights. In this section, I discuss their proposals and raise some doubts regarding their feasibility.

As mentioned, there is little debate over the desirability of a core set of human rights, such as prohibitions against slavery, genocide, murder, torture, prolonged arbitrary detention, and systematic racial discrimination.[81] These rights have become part of international customary law, and they are not contested in the public rhetoric of the international arena. But political thinkers and activists around the world can and do take different sides on many pressing human rights concerns that fall outside what Michael Walzer terms the "minimal and universal code."[82] This gray area of debate includes criminal law, family law, women's rights, social and economic rights, the rights of indigenous peoples, and the attempt to universalize Western-style democratic practices. For cosmopolitans, the question is: how can the current "thin" list of universal human rights be expanded to include some contested rights?

The Perils of Inclusive Dialogues

Onuma Yasuaki proposes an "intercivilizational approach to human rights" that would entail dialogue between members of "civilizations" with the aim of achieving the widest possible consensus on human

---

[80] There is less reason to welcome such proposals if they are likely to be motivated by economic or political self-interest, but it still does not mean that seemingly self-interested proposals should be rejected, a priori. In reaction to a suggestion by then Malaysian Prime Minister Mahathir bin Mohamad that the Universal Declaration of Human Rights might be in need of review to allow for more input from developing nations, then U.S. Secretary of State Madeleine Albright vowed that the United States would be "relentless" in opposing review of the UDHR. Leaving aside the point that the United States does a poor job of living up to the social and economic rights enshrined in the UDHR, the problem with Albright's position is the assumption that the particular rights affirmed in the UDHR should be valid for eternity. As Peter Van Ness puts it, "Mahathir should instead [of being condemned] have been encouraged to make a concrete proposal, because one of the basic requirements of achieving and sustaining consensus is to be prepared to reshape global standards whenever better principles are discovered." Van Ness, ed. *Debating Human Rights* (London: Routledge, 1999), 11.

[81] Terrorist groups that justify the mass killing of civilians are an obvious exception. It is interesting to note, however, that even Osama bin Laden does not straightforwardly proclaim responsibility for the September 11 attacks, presumably on the grounds that this would undermine his base of support.

[82] Michael Walzer, *Interpretation and Social Criticism* (Cambridge: Harvard University Press, 1987), 24. See also Walzer, *Thick and Thin* (Notre Dame: University of Notre Dame Press, 1994).

rights.[83] Such a dialogue would seek to address the concern that most international human rights groups interpret and prioritize rights according to the Western liberal tradition and that international human rights instruments have not yet adequately incorporated non-Western views. Onuma's proposal, however, is not without problems. For example, the boundaries between civilizations, if they exist at all, are never easy to delineate, especially when considering the fact there are disputes over these issues even within particular traditions. More serious, this dialogue would exclude those not belonging to the major religious, philosophical, and cultural traditions: marginalized groups and individuals who may be particularly vulnerable to human rights abuses.[84] For example, members of small indigenous tribes, sex workers, refugees, and people who are mentally ill would not have their interests represented at the intercivilizational dialogue on human rights.

Addressing this problem by increasing participation, however, would raise its own set of problems. Amitai Etzioni, for example, proposes a worldwide moral dialogue that would not be limited to representatives of the major civilizations: "Before we can expect to see global mores that have the compelling power of those of various societies, the citizens of the world will have to engage in worldwide moral dialogues."[85] But does it mean that five billion people must participate in the global dialogue? Leaving aside the issue of cost, the main obstacle such megalogues face is getting participants to agree upon anything more than vague aspirations and empty platitudes. Put simply: the more inclusive the deliberations, the more difficult it will be to arrive at any politically meaningful resolutions.

So participation needs to be limited. One might reasonably argue that a representative sample of leaders and citizens from around the world, if the sample were kept small enough, would be able to reach agreement on the global values that are supposed to guide and constrain policymakers. But this leads to a number of questions: Should the dialogue involve political leaders, diplomats, international lawyers, leaders of religious traditions, academics, representatives of nongovernmental organizations, ordinary citizens, or a combination of these? How many from each group? How many from each country? If the outcomes of these deliberations are meant to command international legitimacy and trump

---

[83] Onuma, "Toward an Intercivilizational Approach to Human Rights."

[84] See Neve Gordon, ed., *From the Margins of Globalization: Critical Perspectives on Human Rights* (Lanham, MD: Lexington Books, 2004).

[85] Amitai Etzioni, *The New Golden Rule* (New York: Basic Books, 1996), 236. I have critically evaluated Etzioni's proposals in my essay, "Toward an International Human Rights (and Responsibilities) Regime: Some Obstacles," in *Autonomy and Order: A Communitarian Anthology*, ed. Edward W. Lehman (Lanham, MD: Rowman & Littlefield, 2000), 211–18.

the decisions of national political leaders, there will be endless disputes over the right way to select "representative" participants.

Can Tolerating Disagreement Lead to Meaningful Resolutions?

Following an extended period of study in Thailand with Buddhist practitioners and thinkers, the Catholic philosopher Charles Taylor has put forward another proposal for establishing an unforced, cross-cultural consensus on human rights. He imagines a cross-cultural dialogue between representatives of different traditions. Rather than argue for the universal validity of their views, however, he suggests that participants should allow for the possibility that their own beliefs may be mistaken. This way, participants can learn from each other's moral universe. There will come a point, however, when differences cannot be reconciled. Taylor explicitly recognizes that different groups, countries, religious communities, and civilizations hold incompatible views on theology, metaphysics, and human nature. In response, Taylor argues that a "genuine, unforced consensus" on human rights norms is possible only if we allow for disagreement on the ultimate justifications of these norms. Instead of defending contested foundational values when we encounter points of resistance (and thus condemning the values we do not like in other societies), we should try to abstract from those beliefs for the purpose of working out an "overlapping consensus" of human rights norms. As Taylor puts it, "we should agree on the norms while disagreeing on why they were the right norms, and we would be content to live in this consensus, undisturbed by the differences of profound underlying belief."[86]

While this proposal moves the debate on universal human rights forward, it still faces certain difficulties. For one thing, it may not be realistic to expect that people will be willing to abstract from the values they care deeply about during the course of a global dialogue on human rights. Even if people agree to abstract from culturally specific ways of justifying and implementing norms, the likely outcome is a withdrawal to a highly general, abstract realm of agreement that fails to resolve actual disputes over contested rights. For example, participants in a cross-cultural dialogue can agree on the right to political participation, while radically disagreeing upon what this means in practice: a Singaporean official may argue that competitive elections are sufficient, whereas a Western liberal will argue that meaningful elections must be accompanied by the freedoms of speech and association.

---

[86] Charles Taylor, "Conditions of an Unforced Consensus on Human Rights," in *The East Asian Challenge for Human Rights*, 124.

The Failures of Cross-Cultural Dialogues

The problems noted above are not simply theoretical possibilities. In the last decade or so, there have been many attempts to put forward truly universal moral values, and the response has ranged from hostility to indifference. None has come even close to supplanting the Universal Declaration of Human Rights as a normative frame of reference, notwithstanding the ongoing controversy regarding the "Westcentric" perspective of this document.

The attempt by a group of former heads of state to formulate "A Universal Declaration of Human Responsibilities"[87] illustrates some of the problems with global dialogues. This declaration was supposed to complement the UDHR, but its main effect would have been to dilute it. Most of the declaration consists of vacuous moralizing. Article 3 is not atypical: "Everyone has the responsibility to promote good and to avoid evil in all things." Such platitudes are not necessarily harmful, but they serve to draw attention from the really important rights that do need to be enforced.

The more serious problem is that some sections of the declaration would be politically dangerous if they were taken seriously. Consider article 14: "The freedom of the media to inform the public and to criticize institutions of society and governmental actions, which is essential for a just society, must be used with responsibility and discretion. Freedom of the media carries a special responsibility for accurate and truthful reporting. Sensational reporting that degrades the human person and dignity must at all times be avoided." It is interesting to note that the group of former heads of state includes the father of the "Asian values" debate, Singapore elder statesman Lee Kuan Yew. In Singapore, Lee has often advanced similar arguments about the need for "responsible" journalism that "at all times" avoids "sensational reporting that degrades the human person and dignity." The result? Singaporean newspapers have been completely defanged, and foreign newspapers like the *Asian Wall Street Journal* and the *International Herald Tribune* have had to pay huge damages for having "defamed" members of the Lee family. Not surprisingly, article 14 met with vigorous opposition from journalists.[88] Such opposition ensured that the Universal Declaration of Human Responsibilities never did get far in the UN General Assembly.[89]

---

[87] See http://www.interactioncouncil.org/udhr/declaration/udhr.pdf (visited 2 March 2005).

[88] http://www.wpfc.org/index.jsp?page=Newsletter%20December%2021%201998 (visited 2 March 2005).

[89] The UNESCO effort to develop "A Common Framework for the Ethics of the 21st Century" similarly ended in failure.

In short, the aspiration to develop values of more universal scope with substantive content may not be realizable.[90] Cross-cultural dialogue will lead to either empty platitudes or politically controversial conclusions likely to be rejected by affected constituents. The good news is that no major damage has been done to the human rights movement (other than, perhaps, wasting funds that could have been more productively spent elsewhere). The truth of the matter is that only philosophers and theologians will be deeply concerned about the need to secure truly universal foundations for human rights. For governments concerned with implementing human rights, national laws usually serve as the normative point of reference. For local human rights groups (or their functional equivalent), it is sufficient to ground their work in the local values and traditions that members of the community use to make sense of their moral lives. For international human rights organizations, much of the work will consist in exposing the gap between public allegiance to uncontested rights (such as the right not to be tortured) and sad reality of ongoing abuse. They will not waste time writing about or deliberating about the desirability of practices that everyone condemns at the level of principle. Such organizations will also provide funds and expertise to local and national human rights organizations, and here too the lack of a truly universal foundation for human rights is not an obstacle: everybody agrees on the shared ends.

This is not to deny, of course, that human rights organizations encounter ethical challenges during the course of their work. But practitioners, not academic theorists, are best placed to identify such challenges. Let us then turn to reflections on dialogues that involve the views of practitioners. The next chapter will discuss those challenges, with particular focus on the East Asian region, followed by some normative reflections that may provide some practical guidance for dealing with the challenges.

[90] Fred Dallmayr expresses a more optimistic view: "The point of comparative political theory, in my view, is precisely to move toward a more genuine universalism, and beyond the spurious 'universality' claimed by the Western canon and by some recent intellectual movements." Dallmayr, "Beyond Monologue: For a Comparative Political Theory," *Perspectives on Politics*, vol. 2, no. 2 (June 2004), 253. I do not mean to imply that cross-cultural dialogue and comparative theorizing should not be done (quite the opposite), but the main aim would be to identify areas of justifiable moral difference, thus teaching us "about the diversity and richness of what human beings may reasonably prize, and about the impossibility of reconciling all they prize in just a single ideal" (David Wong, "Comparative Philosophy: Chinese and Western," *Stanford Encyclopedia of Philosophy*, http://plato.stanford.edu/entries/comparphil-chiwes/, 9, visited 18 February 2005), as well as learning from other cultures with the aim of improving flaws in one's own culture.

4

The Ethical Challenges of International Human Rights NGOs: Reflections on Dialogues between Practitioners and Theorists

IN TRADITIONAL liberal theory, national governments were assumed to have the obligation to secure human rights for citizens.[1] Today, however, it is widely recognized that diverse institutions and groups, both higher (the UN, regional organizations) and lower (civil society, the family) than the state, can and should help with the task of implementing human rights. Perhaps the most visible (and controversial) of such nonstate actors are human rights and humanitarian INGOs,[2] agencies specifically

[1] An earlier version of this chapter was presented as the Max Kampelman Annual Lecture on Human Rights and Democracy, Hebrew University, 2 May 2005. The chapter draws on papers presented at a workshop held at the Carnegie Council on Ethics and International Affairs in New York in February 2002, and at a workshop held at the City University of Hong Kong in October 2003, as well as subsequent exchanges and reflections. The New York workshop consisted of papers by high-level representatives of human rights INGOs that discussed the ethical challenges such organizations typically face during the course of their work, with comments by academic theorists of human rights. The Hong Kong workshop consisted of papers by academics that were meant to provide critical reflections on the first workshop, with comments by human rights practitioners. The overall project was coadministered and funded by the United Nations University (Tokyo, New York) and the City University of Hong Kong, with additional funding from the Open Society. An edited book entitled *Ethics in Action* drawing on this project will be published by Cambridge University Press/United Nations Press, coedited by Jean-Marc Coicaud and myself (several papers mentioned in this chapter will be published in that book). I am particularly grateful to my coeditor Jean-Marc Coicaud as well as to Joanne Bauer, Joseph H. Carens, Geneviève Souillac, and Ramesh Thakur for helping to conceptualize and operationalize this project.
[2] An international NGO (INGO) is defined here as an organization with substantial autonomy to decide upon and carry out human rights projects in different regions around the world. According to this definition, the Danish Institute for Human Rights, for example, is an INGO because it has autonomy to decide upon and carry out projects in Asia, Africa, and elsewhere (though its funds come largely from the Danish Ministry of Foreign Affairs and most of its staff is Danish). This chapter does not discuss the ethical challenges of humanitarian INGOs that provide immediate assistance to the world's worst-off people and deliberately strive to maintain political neutrality as they do good. On the ethical dilemmas of humanitarian INGOs, see Daniel A. Bell and Joseph H. Carens, "The Ethical Dilemmas of International Human Rights and Humanitarian NGOs: Reflections on a Dialogue between Practitioners and Theorists," *Human Rights Quarterly*, vol. 26, no. 2 (May 2004), 317–20.

entrusted with the task of making human rights real. They fund human rights projects, actively participate in human rights and humanitarian work, and criticize human rights violations in foreign lands. They work in cooperative networks with each other, with local NGOs, and international organizations. They consult and lobby governments and international organizations, sometimes participating in high-level negotiations and diplomacy for global policy development. They cooperate and negotiate with the same economic and political organizations in the field for the implementation of their projects, whether this be monitoring or assistance. In short, they are generating a new type of political power, the purpose of which is to secure human rights on an international scale, regardless of state boundaries.

Needless to say, good intentions are not always sufficient to produce desirable results. In an imperfect and unpredictable world, INGOs often face ethical challenges that constrain their efforts to do good in foreign lands. Like other organizations, they are constrained by scarce resources and must choose between competing demands. In such cases, long lists of fairly abstract desiderata such as the Universal Declaration of Human Rights that do not take into account real world constraints do not help much.[3] So how do human rights INGOs set their moral priorities? On what basis do they choose how to do good, and where to do it? How should their decisions be critically evaluated? Can their choices be improved? What role, if any, can theorizing about human rights contribute to these questions?

The purpose of this chapter is to discuss the ethical challenges encountered by human rights INGOs as they attempt to do good (with an emphasis on the East Asian region), and to refine thinking on the relative merits and demerits of ways of dealing with those challenges. These organizations are often viewed as "good" counterweights to authoritarian

---

[3] None of the INGO representatives involved in the dialogues suggested that the UDHR and related human rights treaties could provide useful guidance for dealing with the ethical challenges discussed in this chapter (nor did any INGO representatives refer to the works of human rights theorists in their papers). Mona Younis, program officer for the Joyce Mertz-Gilmore Foundation, notes that "At no point in the deliberations [within her foundation regarding funding of human rights projects] were there references to the actual texts, terms or rights in the Universal Declaration of Human Rights or the human rights treaties it has generated. Instead, not unlike the majority of human rights funders today, JM-GF's Board members were moved by an abstract notion of 'human rights' principles that had very little to do with treaties and states' obligations. Indeed, although the power of human rights lies in the obligation of governments, including the U.S., to respect, protect and fulfill rights enumerated in the treaties, human rights funders generally make little use of these as reference points in their funding." Younis, "An Imperfect Process: Funding the Human Rights Movement—A Case Study," paper presented at the New York workshop, February 2002, on file with author, 5–6.

state power and exploitative multinationals or "bad" agents of liberal capitalism and Western values. A more nuanced evaluation of human rights INGOs needs to delineate the typical constraints and dilemmas they face in their attempts to achieve their aims. The idea is to see what kinds of questions and problems emerge when one thinks of human rights from the perspective of people or organizations who have to make choices about how best to promote rights in concrete contexts, rather than simply from the perspective of abstract theory or even general policy recommendations. Such knowledge is essential for minimizing the harm unintentionally done by lack of knowledge of how the world actually works.

On the other hand, INGO practitioners might also benefit from engagement with the ideas of theorists. The conceptual resources, normative frameworks, and historical knowledge provided by academic theorists might help to guide moral prioritizing of human rights INGOs as they choose between different possible ways of doing good. Moral theorizing that is sensitive to actual constraints of practitioners can perhaps provide a sounder basis for decision making than ad hoc adaptation to less-than-ideal circumstances. In short, both theorists and practitioners of human rights can benefit from engagement with each other.

In view of these considerations, a multiyear dialogue on human rights was organized between high-level representatives of human rights INGOs and prominent academics from different backgrounds and disciplines who work on the subject of human rights.[4] This chapter constitutes my reflections on the findings of these workshops. The first four sections discuss the typical ethical challenges encountered by INGOs during the course of their work as well as some of the advantages and disadvantages associated with different ways of dealing with those challenges.[5] The following challenges will be discussed: the challenge of cultural conflict; the challenge dealing with global poverty; the challenge of dealing with states that restrict the activities of INGOs; and the challenge of fund raising.[6]

---

[4] See note 1.

[5] The discussion draws primarily on examples from the Asian region, but I do not mean to imply that these challenges are distinctly Asian. The practical reason for the Asian focus is that we obtained a generous grant from the Open Society that allowed us to invite INGO representatives and academics based in the Asian region.

[6] The list of ethical challenges covers those that generated the most debate at the aforementioned workshops. Had the discussion been less centered on Asia, other challenges may have been the focus of discussion: for example, INGOs working in Israel are often confronted with the problem of legitimacy, that is, they need to answer the criticism that their views do not represent any particular constituency compared to the government they are criticizing (discussion with Ishai Menuchin, researcher for Oxfam, Jerusalem, 5 May 2005). In China, of course, the (unelected) government is less likely to criticize INGOs on such grounds since its own legitimacy may be called into question.

The chapter ends with reflections on implications for INGOs operating in the East Asian region.

The Challenge of Cultural Conflict

Most human rights and humanitarian INGOs are based in the West. With their executives and offices centralized in key Western cities, program officers and coordinators are then sent to the field. As Alex de Waal notes, "[i]n its basic structure, the ethics business is like many global businesses [with] its headquarters in a handful of Western centers, notably New York, Washington and London."[7] From a practical point of view, this may pose a special challenge in foreign lands where detailed knowledge of different linguistic, social, cultural, and economic circumstances is more likely to ensure success.[8] INGO workers are not always familiar with these or trained beforehand to face unexpected complications[9] or to deal with subtle behavioral nuances of people who have different social and political customs. It is not merely a strategic matter of understanding "the other" for the purpose of promoting one's views,

---

[7] Alex de Waal, "The Moral Solipsism of Global Ethics Inc," *London Review of Books*, 23 August 2001, 15. On "human rights imperialism," see de Waal, "Human Rights Organizations and the Political Imagination in the West and Africa," paper presented at the New York workshop (on file with author), 22–23. See also Ravi Nair, "Exploring New Relationships—the Need for Devolution in the International Rights Movement," paper presented at the New York workshop (on file with author). Rieky Stuart, executive director of Oxfam Canada, however, notes that one should be careful about assuming that most people who work globally are from the Western centers because most large international development NGOs today have people from the country in question as the vast majority of their staff, and/or their work may be primarily funding local NGOs. This is increasingly true for human rights INGOs as well (e-mail correspondence, 23 September 2002).

[8] The history of aid projects in the developing world is littered with blunders that could have been avoided with more detailed local knowledge. See, e.g., Michael Edwards, *Future Positive: International Cooperation in the 21st Century* (London: Earthscan, 1999), and Michael Dowdle, "Preserving Indigenous Paradigms in an Age of Globalization: Pragmatic Strategies for the Development of Clinical Legal Aid in China," *Fordham Journal of International Law*, vol. 24, symposium issue (2000), 56–83. According to Ram Mannikalingam of the Rockefeller Foundation, the greatest challenge in terms of learning local knowledge is not so much acquiring basic familiarity with the language, history, and political context for one's projects as the need to figure out and establish ties with the intricate social networks and local power holders that allow for projects to be successfully implemented (what he calls "Small Politics," as opposed to "Big Politics") (comment at New York workshop).

[9] See, e.g., Basil Fernando, "Ethics in Action: Defending the Rights to Life and Article 2 of the ICCPR," paper presented at the New York workshop (on file with author). Fernando argues that Westerners often fail to understand that promoting the right to life may require different tactics in contexts without developed judicial systems.

however. INGO representatives also experience ethical conflicts when they must decide between promoting their (Westcentric) versions of human rights norms and respecting local cultural norms that may differ from these. There are different ways of dealing with this conflict, and below I list some of the possible responses along with their associated advantages and disadvantages.[10]

Challenging Local Cultural Norms

Habitat for Humanity is an INGO that was founded in the United States in 1976 with the goal of helping people to acquire adequate housing, which the organization sees as a basic human right and a prerequisite for the effective enjoyment of many other human rights.[11] According to Steven Weir, the Asia and Pacific director of Habitat, the organization's best-practice standards require that local boards be diverse and representative of the community at large, including 30 percent representation by women. Moreover, many affiliates require that the women's names be included on the land title as a condition of the loan. But Weir adds that these requirements can be contrary to cultural norms and legal regulations in some countries. Still, he suggests that challenging these norms can be effective:

> In most developing countries, reaching gender equity and full participation is a slow process. A typical local affiliate (governing board) begins with the women serving tea, sitting quietly in the back, and evolves to their participation on the family selection and support subcommittees, finally developing into full participation on all committees, often including chairing the family selection and support committees. Some affiliates in traditionally male-dominated societies even eventually elect women as board presidents.[12]

---

[10] The different strategies are presented in increasing order of "cultural sensitivity," but my immediate aim, to repeat, is not to take sides regarding the desirability of particular strategies. I focus on cases where there are arguments to be made on both sides of the question. Thus, I leave aside the (all-too-common) cases of blatant cultural arrogance, where the Western-based INGO is clearly in the wrong. World Vision used to be accused of making aid conditional on conversions in the Philippines and elsewhere, but it has have since disavowed such practices. One funder noted the increase in recent years in Palestinian grantees spending scarce resources on the auditing services of Western auditors, particularly Arthur Andersen. She noted the irony of grantees turning to Arthur Andersen, rather than reputable locals, to demonstrate their trustworthiness to U.S. funders.

[11] The organization is perhaps best known for the involvement of former U.S. President Jimmy Carter in its work (see *Habitat for Humanity International, Jimmy Carter and Habitat*, available at http://www.habitat.org/how/carter).

[12] Steven Weir, "Transformational Development as the Key to Housing Rights," paper presented at the New York workshop (on file with author), 6.

Weir's account here paints a happy outcome. At the same time, he acknowledges that the organization does make compromises with local communities. It does not simply come into a place and insist that it conform to the organization's norms in every respect, including its practices with regard to gender, not only because such a demand would be impractical, but also because it would conflict with the organization's commitment to local participation and control over the process. Trying to challenge local cultural norms so that they can meet the requirements of the human rights INGO has the advantage of improving the lives of vulnerable and marginalized members of the community. The fact that "success" seems to be eventually endorsed by both the beneficiaries and other members of the community lends legitimacy to this approach. However, there may also be some resistance given the developing world's history of experience with "cultural imperialism." It may also be the case that challenging some undesirable community norms may have the effect of unintentionally undermining other valued community norms.[13]

Tolerating Clashing Beliefs

Danish representatives of the Danish Institute for Human Rights (DIHR) oppose the death penalty on moral grounds. Yet they must occasionally work in countries such as China where there is widespread support for the death penalty. As a result, the DIHR must avoid straightforward campaigning for abolition of the death penalty if it is to gain support from the intended recipients of its human rights aid. The same is true in the emerging democracies of Eastern Europe, where local NGOs are often hesitant to promote the abolition of the death penalty: "In the early 1990s, a DIHR partner, an NGO in Lithuania, would not campaign for the abolition of the death penalty. The justification was that it would be too risky and that it, as a newly established NGO, would lose credibility

---

[13] This kind of trade-off was well depicted in Zhang Yimou's film, *The Story of Qiu Ju* (Columbia/Tristar Studios, 1995). The female protagonist, a rural Chinese farmer played by Gong Li, was shown resolutely seeking justice for her husband, who had been physically harmed by a patriarchal village chief. She ultimately "won" her case, but the film ends with serious doubts about the benefits of recourse to legal remedies as opposed to informal mechanisms of conflict resolution. More generally, Zhang seems to be suggesting that the pursuit of liberal ideas about freedom and equality backed by the rule of law comes at the cost of destroying the existing community bonds and relationships of solidarity in the local community. Zhu Suli drew upon the apparent message of this film to cast doubt on the practicability of legal means to resolve conflicts in rural China, arguing that modern legal institutions should not be introduced until the benefits of a rule-of-law social order can be established (see Albert Chen, "Socio-legal Thought and Legal Modernization in Contemporary China: A Case Study of the Jurisprudence of Zhu Suli," ms. on file with author, 11–12), thus triggering off a heated debate in mainland Chinese academic circles.

because the majority of the people, according to public opinion polls, were for the death penalty."[14] In such cases, the INGO tolerates, without endorsing, the dominant cultural belief so that it can successfully pursue other projects designed to improve human rights. At most, the INGO can support projects that may have the effect of reducing the incidence of implementation of the local belief deemed to be inconsistent with what representatives of the INGO consider to be human rights norms. For example, in the case of China, the DIHR supports academic research designed to show that application of the death penalty in some areas may not be widely endorsed, with the hope that such findings can gradually reduce the incidence of application of the death penalty in China.

In the same vein, Ndubisi Obiorah, senior legal officer of Hurilaws in Lagos, Nigeria, noted that many Nigerian NGOs work with INGOs but pointed out that, in relation to the subject of advocacy activities undertaken by INGOs in Nigeria, it would be very difficult, given local cultural and religious beliefs widely prevalent at the present time, to press vigorously for gay and lesbian rights in Nigeria. In such cases—the same sorts of concerns are likely to be present in predominantly Islamic countries elsewhere, such as Malaysia—representatives of human rights INGOs that would otherwise try to promote gay and lesbian rights need, in the immediate to medium term, to refrain from a high-decibel "naming and shaming" approach in acting upon (or speaking about) this aspect of their mandate.[15] They would need to tolerate, without respecting, the negative views of the majority on gay and lesbian rights. This approach carries the advantage that other aspects of their mandate stand a greater chance of success. The cost, however, is that it sends the message that gay and lesbian rights can be sacrificed on the altar of other values.[16] Strong defenders of these rights may well question why the INGO needs to work in such contexts as opposed to other places where they need not suppress an important part of the ethical mandate.

[14] Birgit Lindsnaes, Hans-Otto Sano, and Hatla Thelle (Danish Institute for Human Rights), "Human Rights in Action: Supporting Human Rights Work in Authoritarian Countries," paper presented at the New York workshop (on file with author), 2.

[15] In the long term, however, Obiorah argues that an educational approach that aims to secure over time a greater degree of acceptance of diverse sexual orientations in Nigeria can and should challenge current views in this respect. He adds that "the few gay and lesbian advocacy groups in Nigeria critically need support from INGOs in their efforts to bring about a change in popular attitudes" (e-mail communication, 26 September 2002).

[16] This leads to the question of which rights can be sacrificed on the altar of other values. As Brian Joseph of the National Endowment for Democracy puts it, "what if an INGO cannot work on women's rights or religious minorities' issues, would we find that acceptable?" (e-mail communication, 26 September 2002).

Revising the Principles and Practices of the Human Rights INGO

Amnesty International has had to question whether its concern for universal solidarity leaves adequate space for legitimate manifestations of the particular and the partial. According to Morton Winston, "perhaps the main feature of Amnesty International's ethical culture is its commitment to international solidarity. AI members learn that they can and should work to advance the human rights of persons in distant lands who are suffering violations or abuses."[17] In practice, this took the form of the [No] "Work on Own Country Rule," which prohibited AI members from taking up efforts on individual prisoner appeal cases in their own country and prohibited AI national sections from undertaking specific kinds of research on their own government's human rights practices. There were various practical justifications for this policy,[18] but the most important moral justification was that "it prevent[ed] AI members from doing nothing but a certain kind of 'identity politics' around human rights concerns in their own countries, and reinforces the core ethic of international solidarity."[19]

This policy, however, created problems. In terms of AI's organizational development, it "led to the centralization of the research function in a single headquarters, the International Secretariat (IS) in London, and the specialization of national sections into primarily campaigning, fundraising and membership development organizations."[20] It also meant that some potential members lost their motivation to join once they found out they could not do research on their own country.[21] Finally, the policy

---

[17] Morton E. Winston, "Assessing the Effectiveness of International Human Rights NGOs: Amnesty International," in *NGOs and Human Rights: Promise and Performance*, ed. Claude E. Welch, Jr. (Philadelphia: University of Pennsylvania Press, 2001), 31.

[18] For example, the likelihood that local sympathies may bias one's judgment and also that the own country rule helps protect AI members and their families and friends from government harassment and retaliation. According to Andre Frankovits, executive director of the Human Rights Council of Australia (formerly of AI, Australia), the own country rule arose from the Cold War emphasis on impartiality and the security of prisoners of conscience AI worked for. Groups had to work on three prisoners of conscience, one from the communist bloc, one from the West, and one from neither, and the own country rule was designed to demonstrate that AI members were not partial (e-mail correspondence, 11 September 2002). This distinction made progressively less sense, as did (by extension) the Cold War justification for the own country rule.

[19] Winston, "Assessing the Effectiveness of International Human Rights NGOs," 32.

[20] Ibid.

[21] A close Chinese friend of mine who joined AI as an Oxford graduate student was disappointed when she was told she could not do research on China, and she let her membership lapse after the violent suppression of the spring 1989 student-led movement in Beijing since her main reason for joining AI was her concern for the rights situation in her own country.

may have carried the disadvantage that lack of local knowledge impeded accurate diagnosis of the main human rights problems and ways of dealing with them.

In response to such practical problems, AI has recently softened its own country rule. But there may also be the recognition that the ethic of international solidarity needs to come to grips with manifestations of the particular. Securing people's vital human interests may require special attention to their particular circumstances and needs that locals are best able to understand (and research). Moreover, there may not be any reason to foreclose claims on behalf of "critical patriotism"—one characteristic of the true patriot may be the special concern to criticize one's own country when things go wrong. If special concern for the human rights abuses of one's country need not preclude concern for human rights abuses in other countries, and may sometimes be the stepping stone for such concerns, then there may be a case for relaxing the blanket ban on investigating abuses of rights in one's own country.

Habitat's experience in Fiji and Papua New Guinea provides another example of institutional learning. Habitat initially insisted that its projects be structured according to Western-style democratically elected rotating local boards, but this conflicted with the chiefly system that oversees local matters. Because Habitat's methodology insulted the local chief and was anathema to the villagers, its projects were relatively ineffective. In response to such experiences, Habitat created a broader regional organizational structure with a network of subcommittees or satellite branches that respect the local chiefly tradition, a strategy that seems to be resulting in increased cooperation and sustainability.[22]

These examples point to the possibility of a culturally sensitive response to conflicts with local norms, meaning that the INGO revises the moral principles underpinning its work along with the practices that flow therefrom. This response has the advantage of allowing for institutional learning in response to moral input from non-Western cultures. But it can lead to demoralization and a sense of betrayal among founding members and defenders of the old faith, as well as fund-raising problems in Western countries that prioritize liberal values.

The Challenge of Dealing with Global Poverty

Many human rights INGOs begin with a particular focus and then feel pressure to expand their concerns so as to deal with the broader, under-

---

[22] Steven Weir, "Transformational Development as the Key to Housing Rights" (revised version), paper presented at the New York workshop (on file with author).

lying forces that give rise to the particular problem they are addressing. For example, Oxfam, as the name suggests, began as a famine relief organization. The organization gradually came to believe, however, that it was not enough to relieve the immediate suffering of those caught up in a famine situation. It was equally or more important to address the underlying conditions that gave rise to situations where people found themselves in desperate need for food. Consequently, much of Oxfam's work today deals with problems of economic and social development. The two largest human rights INGOs—Amnesty International and Human Rights Watch (HRW)—have also decided to expand their concerns to include work in the areas of human rights violations stemming from global poverty. As we will see, however, the challenge of dealing with global poverty does not come without cost. No organization can do everything, and if an organization fails to focus on concrete tasks where it can actually make a difference, its activities may be scattered and ineffective. This section reviews the debates within and between human rights organizations, particularly Amnesty International and Human Rights Watch, over the extent to which social, economic, and cultural rights should be a focus of concern in their work.

Amnesty International

Amnesty International is the oldest and largest human rights INGO. AI had traditionally concentrated exclusively on violations of civil and political (CP) rights.[23] In 2001 it officially expanded its mission to include social, economic, and cultural (ESC) rights within its ambit of concern. This was not a simple decision for the organization. It followed lengthy internal discussions, in which members raised a number of objections to the change.

According to Curt Goering, deputy executive director of Amnesty International USA, the objections included a number of overlapping concerns, many of which were tied to the impact of the change on the effectiveness of the organization.[24] Some feared that expanding the mandate to include ESC rights would cause the organization to lose its clear focus and make its work too diffuse. They pointed out that there was still a lot

---

[23] Indeed, it traditionally was concerned only with human rights violations by states, but in the 1990s it expanded this to include violations by nonstate actors. For a useful report on the extent to which international law creates obligations on companies to respect human rights, see *Beyond Voluntarism: Human Rights and the Developing International Legal Obligations of Companies* (Versoix, Switzerland: International Council on Human Rights Policy, 2002).

[24] Curt Goering, "Amnesty International and Economic, Social and Cultural Rights," adapted from remarks of Curt Goering at the New York workshop (on file with author).

of work to be done in existing areas of concern. Some worried that the inclusion of ESC rights in AI's mandate would blur what had been a clear organizational identity and jeopardize AI's hard-won reputation for consistency, credibility, and impartiality. Also, there was the worry it could undermine the unity and cohesion of the movement because they felt that there was not the same degree of consensus within the membership of AI and within the wider public about the moral status of ESC rights as there was about the moral status of CP rights, in part because it is often much harder to establish standards for ESC rights or to determine what constitutes a violation of them. Still another concern was that the organization did not have the expertise to address issues of ESC rights and that, if AI attempted to acquire the necessary expertise, this would lead to an undesirable shift in power away from the membership toward the professional staff.

Despite these powerful objections, AI did decide to expand its mission to include ESC rights. Why? According to Goering, three lines of argument played a particularly important role in identifying the advantages of an expanded mandate and in overcoming the objections to change.

First, the focus on civil and political rights had sometimes led to misguided priorities that implicitly downplayed or ignored the sometimes more serious areas of human suffering. Goering mentions two cases: One example frequently cited in internal debates was Sudan, where in 1994 the government engaged in massive displacement of local populations and destruction of their crops and food reserves. It was difficult to explain why AI treated the shooting and torture of a few victims as human rights violations and the manufactured starvation of thousands as background. Another example was Afghanistan. The warring factions opposed to the government imposed a total road blockade on Kabul in 1996. AI denounced the indiscriminate killings from daily bombings but said little about the starvation resulting from the blockade. Goering says: "As one of my colleagues wrote, 'We were seen to be suddenly irrelevant and our inaction at a time when everyone else was shouting left a scar on our work in Afghanistan and on AI's credibility for that matter, for a very long time. We still hear echoes of AI having no interest in the real suffering of the people.' "[25]

[25] Ibid., 6. Another example illustrating the misguided set of priorities resulting from AI's previously limited mandate was AI's refusal to condemn or oppose apartheid per se on the grounds that the organization should remain neutral with respect to political ideologies, and its refusal to support the sanctions and divestment movement on the grounds that it should remain neutral on these questions. See Winston, "Assessing the Effectiveness of International Human Rights NGOs," 34. This example (and others, such as when the International Red Cross did not speak out against Nazi concentration camps because of its policy of neutrality) raises the larger issue of the costs of "neutrality." For more discussion, see Bell and Carens, "The Ethical Dilemmas of International Human Rights and Humanitarian NGOs," 317–20.

Second, there was strong support for an expansion of AI's mandate among its branches in the "South."[26] As Goering notes,

> As an international human rights organization, AI has taken important steps over the past several years to become a truly multicultural organization. Yet, the focus of its work—the selection of which categories of human rights violations to actively research and campaign against—reflected, some felt, a "Northern" preference for civil and political rights, instead of ESC rights. Many people and NGOs in the "Global South" and a growing number in the "North" felt that AI's narrow mandate with its limited serious work on violations of ESC rights was a barrier to inclusion of people whose views on this issue differed from the prevailing "Northern consensus." And for an organization that strived to be truly international, the civil and political focus was also seen as a barrier to the development of AI's structure and membership in the South. This was seen to undermine AI's credibility in general with important audiences.[27]

One might add that AI's use of rights language to understand and address problems of poverty and ill health in the South may increase the likelihood that international organizations, Northern governments, and Northern-based foundations will take action to remedy these problems.[28] As Michael Ignatieff put it, "the rights argument is a way to leverage money to fulfill this obligation."[29]

Third, AI responded to the argument that its CP focus was biased toward male concerns. To quote Goering once again: "Some noted that women's experience of human rights is often different to men's: property rights and reproductive rights, and the rights to health, education and nutrition were some of these areas. In addition, by maintaining the distinction, AI limited its opportunities for cooperation with other civil society and human rights groups at a time when coalition work was becoming ever more critical in advancing a human rights agenda."[30]

---

[26] Interestingly, the U.S. branch of AI—its biggest in terms of resources and members—generally supported the expansion of AI's mandate. This reflects the large normative gap between human rights activists in the United States and their government (supported perhaps by the dominant view of human rights as equivalent to CP rights in American society at large).

[27] Goering, "AI and ESC Rights," 7n. 26. AI's response to this concern is another example of "changing the principles and practices of the human rights INGO," discussed above.

[28] The "North" refers here to relatively wealthy industrialized countries, most of which are located in the Northern Hemisphere (but not all: for example, Australia would be considered part of the "Northern" camp). The "South" refers here to relatively poor countries that often receive development aid, most of which are based in the Southern Hemisphere (but not all: for example, China and India would be considered part of the "Southern" camp).

[29] Quoted in "Righting Wrongs: Special Report on Human Rights," *The Economist*, 18 August 2001, 19.

[30] Goering, "AI and ESC Rights," 7n. 26.

In the end, the vast majority of AI members found the arguments for expanding the formal mission of the organization to include ESC rights more persuasive than the arguments for the status quo. But expanding the formal mission does not eliminate the tensions reflected in this debate; it simply moves them to another forum, namely, the question of how best to promote ESC rights. This was illustrated by the contribution to the conference from Kenneth Roth, executive director of Human Rights Watch, the second largest human rights organization.

Human Rights Watch

Like AI, HRW had traditionally focused exclusively on civil and political rights, and like AI it expanded its concerns to include ESC rights, but it made this change earlier (in the early 1990s) and without the same amount of internal debate. As Roth presents it, Aryeh Neier, the previous director of HRW, had been opposed to ESC rights on philosophical grounds. When Neier left, Roth, as new director, put forward the view that HRW should rest its basic conception of human rights on the international covenants (which clearly include ESC rights) and should gradually expand its concerns to include work in the area of ESC rights when the organization could be effective in doing so. The board of HRW agreed to this proposal.

Effectiveness is the key here. In Roth's view, international human rights organizations like HRW (as distinct from national and local ones) tend to be most effective when they employ the methodology that he calls "shaming": investigating, documenting, and publicizing behavior by states (and some nonstate actors) that conflicts with widely accepted public moral expectations. As Roth puts it,

> In my view, the most productive way for international human rights organizations like Human Rights Watch to address ESC rights is by building on the power of our methodology. The essence of that methodology . . . is not the ability to mobilize people in the streets, to engage in litigation, to press for broad national plans to revitalize ESC rights, or to provide technical assistance. Rather, the core of our methodology is our ability to investigate, expose, and shame. We are at our most effective when we can hold governmental (or, in some cases, nongovernmental) conduct up to a disapproving public.[31]

[31] Kenneth Roth, "International Human Rights Organizations and Economic, Social, and Cultural Rights: A Practical Defense," revised version of paper presented at the New York workshop (on file with the author), 3. This section also draws on several e-mail exchanges between Roth, Joseph H. Carens, and myself in September and October 2002.

For the shaming methodology to work, Roth says, "clarity is needed around three issues: violation, violator, remedy. That is, we must be able to show persuasively that a particular state of affairs amounts to a violation of human rights standards, that a particular violator is principally responsible, and that there is a widely accepted remedy for the violation."[32] Roth argues that these requirements can often be met, even when dealing with ESC rights. He cites a number of examples from HRW's own work in the area and states explicitly that cases like the ones in Sudan and Afghanistan, which Goering cited as reasons for AI to expand its focus of concern, could be addressed with this shaming methodology, and that HRW has often done so.

In some circumstances in which ESC rights are involved, however, Roth thinks that the three preconditions of effective shaming cannot be met, and in those circumstances international human rights organizations should cede the field to local and national NGOs because the INGOs will not be able to have any significant impact on the problem. If people lack adequate food or health care, for example, one can say that their human rights are not being respected, but unless one can trace these lacks to the arbitrary or discriminatory actions of a government, intergovernmental organization, or organized nongovernmental actor such as a corporation or a rebel group, it will not be possible to use the shaming methodology to bring about change. Roth puts it this way:

> [G]iven that respect for ESC rights often requires the reallocation of resources, the people who have the clearest standing to insist on a particular allocation are usually the residents of the country in question. Outsiders such as international human rights organizations are certainly free to have a say in such matters, but in an imperfect world in which the fulfillment of one ESC right is often at the expense of another, their voice has less legitimacy in insisting on a particular tradeoff than does that of the country's residents. Why should outsiders be listened to when they counsel, for example, that less be spent on health care and more on education—or even that less be spent on roads, bridges or other infrastructure deemed important for long-term economic development, and more on immediate needs?[33]

Roth is careful to point out that his argument applies only to international human rights organizations working in countries away from their organizational base, not to local and national NGOs, which often employ other methodologies besides shaming and have clearer standing to speak out about the proper direction of politically contested national

[32] Ibid., 4.
[33] Ibid., 2.

policies in their own states.[34] Roth specifies that his argument does not apply to INGOs addressing the domestic or foreign policy of their home governments, where they have standing comparable to that of a local human rights group.[35]

It is striking how many of the concerns that appeared in the internal AI debate as reasons not to expand AI's interests to include ESC rights reappear here as reasons to limit the scope of the activities of international human rights organizations. In both cases we find a concern about the effectiveness of the organization's work being undermined by overreaching. There are the same worries about a lack of normative consensus on principles, a lack of clarity about standards, the absence of expertise, the depletion of moral capital, the loss of focus, and there is the same sense that the organization will waste scarce resources unless it sticks at what it is good at and leaves certain problems and issues to others.

In many ways, the reactions to Roth's line of argument at the workshops mirrored the reactions to the arguments in favor of limiting Amnesty's concerns to civil and political rights. The critics did not accept Roth's view that there is such a tight link between the effectiveness of international human rights organizations and the methodology of shaming. What Roth saw as pragmatic, they saw as unduly cautious and conservative. They feared that restricting the activities of international human rights organizations in the way Roth recommended might impede rather than contribute to the development of the international human rights movement and might fail to address the most important human rights issues of our times.

One set of objections, advanced by Larry Cox, senior program officer of the Ford Foundation's Human Rights and International Cooperation Unit, among others, focused on the implications of Roth's approach for relationships between international human rights organizations based in the North and local and national NGOs based in the South. The main concern was that giving the shaming methodology the strong priority that Roth advocated would make it more difficult for international human rights organizations to establish cooperative links with Southern human rights organizations.[36] In the same vein, Bonny Ibhawoh of Brock

---

[34] In an exchange with Leonard S. Rubenstein (executive director of Physicians for Human Rights), Roth explicitly allows for the possibility that there are various ways to promote ESC rights, such as public mobilization, standard setting, litigation, and technical assistance, but he argues that it is nonetheless important to focus on the question of when shaming is effective "given the number of organizations that are interested in using a shaming methodology—and given Human Rights Watch's own parochial interest in when this methodology works." Roth, "Response to Leonard S. Rubenstein," *Human Rights Quarterly*, vol. 26, no. 4 (November 2004), 1.

[35] Roth, "International Human Rights Organizations," 4–5.

[36] Larry Cox, comment made at New York workshop.

University argues that INGOs should learn from organizations in the South that have successfully used new methodologies for advocacy of economic rights, such as education and mass mobilization: "rather than argue that ESC rights are 'not doable' the focus should be on fashioning new tools for the task ahead."[37]

Amnesty International, it is worth noting, does not see itself as exclusively a "shaming" organization. As Goering put the point,

> It is true, of course, that a substantial portion of our work is documenting abuses and campaigning to stop them, and public exposure plays an important role in such situations. But AI is more than that. Our members around the world are active from within, helping to build a domestic human rights constituency and to strengthen civil society. Much energy at the local, regional, and national levels is aimed at promoting human rights education among the public, in the school system, working constructively with, training and lobbying home governments to incorporate human rights standards in penal codes and constitutions. There are also many situations where we engage with targets (governments and/or non-state actors) behind the scenes and, as long as progress is being made, are content to conduct "quiet diplomacy."[38]

The "quiet diplomacy" approach has affinities with the approach of human rights organizations like the Danish Institute for Human Rights, which are discussed below. Such organizations collaborate with governments and semiofficial NGOs in areas of common ground (such as women's rights in China) and explicitly refrain from open critique or shaming tactics in areas of controversy.

One problem with relying on shaming is that people in the South often understandably resent any apparent claim of moral superiority from the North, given the role of the North, past and present, in the South. If international human rights organizations spend their energies in the South on exposing the moral failings of those in the South, this is apt to be experienced as carrying with it a tone of moral superiority, even if the failings are real, there is no intention to claim moral superiority, and the same INGOs also criticize Northern states (as HRW, for example, clearly does). Equally important, as Roth's critics at the workshop argued, if

---

[37] Bonny Ibhawoh, "Human Rights INGOs, the North/South Gap and the Challenge of Legitimacy," paper presented at Hong Kong workshop (on file with author).

[38] E-mail communication with Curt Goering, 25 September 2002. AI is also actively involved in work with the United Nations, and since the early 1990s it has extended its spectrum of UN activities by adding activities in implementing policies (and reducing its traditional approach as agenda setter). See Kerstin Martens, "An Appraisal of Amnesty's International's Work at the United Nations: Established Areas of Activities and Shifting Priorities since the 1990s," *Human Rights Quarterly*, vol. 26, no. 4 (November 2004), 7.

human rights NGOs in the South rely primarily on methods other than shaming in their work (and Roth himself says that this may be appropriate for them), they will have less basis for cooperative work with international human rights organizations that focus exclusively on shaming activities in the South than with ones that take a broader approach to their human rights work there. This could undermine the sense that there is a genuinely *international* human rights movement in which participants in both the North and the South share common projects and common agendas.

Roth replied to this line of criticism by pointing to the example of HRW's work on the dalits: "The HRW shaming report on India launched the national coalition for dalit rights: It took HRW's careful, systematic work to establish the credibility of this issue, thus making it far easier for activists to organize around it." Such debates point to the need to distinguish between the conditions under which shaming facilitates and those under which it impedes cooperation with Southern NGOs.[39]

The second set of objections to Roth's approach was concerned with the danger that a focus on what international human rights organizations can do well might draw attention away from what is really important. If the most severe and extensive violations of human rights stem not from the misbehavior of authoritarian rulers but from the global maldistribution of wealth and power and from structural features of the international political and economic systems, then to limit the activities of international human rights organizations to problems where there are clear standards, a clear culprit, and a clear remedy may be to render the organizations irrelevant to the most important struggles for justice today.[40] Bonny Ibhawoh, for example, points to studies that

[39] In contexts (such as India) where some local/regional/national human rights NGOs are themselves openly at odds with their own governments and allowed to function unimpeded (for political and cultural reasons), NGOs might welcome intervention by international organizations such as HRW. But in less-than-democratic political contexts (such as China), it is quite likely that shaming tactics would reduce the likelihood of establishing cooperative links with local/regional/national human rights organizations because such organizations may conclude that the disadvantages of links with international "shamers" outweigh the advantages. (The discussion of "collaborators" below spells out some of the advantages and disadvantages of confrontational tactics.) Cultural differences may also reduce the likelihood of establishing links with non-Western INGOs. In relatively democratic East Asian countries such as Japan and Korea, for example, open confrontation is considered to be in bad taste, even if the shamer may be correct in terms of substance, and this may limit possibilities of cooperation with shaming organizations such as HRW.

[40] It is important not to overstate this. Clearly the genocide in Rwanda was a great evil that could have been stopped without transforming the international system. On the other hand, as Roth notes, the shaming methodology was ineffective in this case despite its obvious relevance.

draw links between the operations of international financial institutions and transnational corporations and human rights abuses in Third World countries, and he argues that Western-based INGOs should pay more attention to the negative impact of economic globalization on economic rights in the South.[41] Again, Goering indicated that one of the reasons AI expanded its mandate was its sense that its narrower approach was preventing it from confronting the most urgent human rights issues.

In a subsequent exchange with Roth, Neera Chandhoke of the University of New Delhi did not put forward such radical critiques of Roth's methodology. Chandhoke argues that HRW can and should critique violations of economic rights in particular states, including violations of economic rights stemming from an unfair distribution of resources, without abandoning its dual commitments to shaming and effectiveness. For example, Chandhoke notes that the right to health care can be violated by a government that fails to fulfill its obligations through an act of omission rather than open discrimination or arbitrary policy making. Such violations can lead to the same loss of human life as deliberate violations of rights—say, if health care is commercialized and poor people can't afford to get treated for illness—and ought to fall under the purview of human rights INGOs.[42] Chandhoke recognizes that remedying such violations may indeed require the redistribution of resources, but she responds to Roth's worry about effectiveness by noting that human rights INGOs may well have the power to effect change in such cases. Human rights movements based in the West "do happen to exert an inordinate amount of influence on the way human rights movements based in the South do or do not privilege rights." An INGO that shames a government for failing to fulfill its obligations to secure economic rights

---

[41] Bonny Ibhawoh, "Human Rights INGOs, the North/South Gap and the Challenge of Legitimacy," paper presented at Hong Kong conference (on file with author).

[42] In some cases, HRW's policy of focusing on arbitrary or discriminatory governmental action or inaction can actually make things worse. As Leonard S. Rubenstein notes, "looking at arbitrariness may even distract attention from violations against the worst-off members of society. Chronic indifference to core obligations, for example, should generate urgent attention, but the absence of action to provide a particular core service may not seem arbitrary. Suppose a government operates a health clinic program that is arbitrary in restricting hours of operation in a manner that prevents working parents from bringing their children to the clinic. To be sure, this is a violation of the Covenant, but how does it compare to a decision to have no child immunization program? The lens of an arbitrariness standard invited attention to obvious problems that may not be the most serious ones." Rubenstein, "How International Human Rights Organizations Can Advance Economic, Social, and Cultural Rights: A Response to Kenneth Roth," *Human Rights Quarterly*, vol. 26, no. 4 (November 2004), 7.

and calls on it to redistribute resources to remedy this problem can help to shape the agenda of local NGOs. It can also muster public opinion internationally and put moral pressure on the government in a way that relatively poorly funded and less visible local NGOs cannot. Roth, in other words, may be underestimating the power of his organization to effect change in some contexts: "he just does not take cognizance of the power of INGOs to highlight some rights and underplay or even demote others."[43]

In his written reply to Chandhoke's paper, Roth says that he agrees with the substance of Chandhoke's main theoretical propositions, but that they fail to challenge HRW's existing methodology. He reaffirms that empirical claim that shaming organizations could not successfully press for redistribution in foreign lands, such as calling for resources to be redirected to help secure the right to healthcare in another country.[44] Once again, however, Roth may be unduly cautious. Naming and shaming tactics by foreign entities have been successfully deployed to promote the right of education in some poor countries,[45] and they may also be effective to promote the right to health care.

Such reflections point to the need for more contextual judgments. In some contexts, the naming and shaming approach may be counterproductive, and in others the approach may be under-utilized. If the aim is to promote economic rights in foreign lands, the human rights INGO should be willing to deploy a variety of approaches, or at least be willing to recognize that one particular approach may not be the "one size fits all" solution to the problem of global poverty.[46]

[43] Neera Chandhoke, "The Status of Social and Economic Rights," paper presented at Hong Kong conference (on file with author).

[44] Kenneth Roth, "Response to the Critique of Neera Chandhoke," paper presented at Hong Kong conference (on file with author).

[45] See Katarina Tomasevki, "Unasked Questions about Economic, Social, and Cultural Rights from the Experience of the Special Rapporteur on the Right of Education (1998–2004): A Response to Kenneth Roth, Leonard S. Rubenstein, and Mary Robinson," *Human Rights Quarterly*, vol. 27, no. 2 (May 2005).

[46] INGO representatives had been asked to discuss the advantages and disadvantages of their selected approaches, but Roth's discussion generated heated responses by otherwise likeminded workshop participants because of his insistence on the virtues of HRW's approach and sensitivity to criticisms of that approach (in contrast to Curt Goering's forthright discussion of Amnesty's internal debates regarding the pros and cons of different approaches.) In her short reply to Roth's reply, Chandhoke also alludes to the importance of striking the right tone for productive debate: "It is almost as if HRW refuses to listen to persons located within the very constituency that the organization works for and caters to. And this saddens me for it negates the very notion of dialogue, thereby rendering both the practitioner and the theorist of human rights poorer in understanding as well as sympathy for each other." Neera Chandhoke, "A Final Response to Kenneth Roth," ms. on file with author.

THE CHALLENGE OF DEALING WITH STATES THAT
RESTRICT THE ACTIVITIES OF INGOS

Human rights INGOs grapple with the question of whether or not to collaborate with governments in order to help remedy human rights violations. Different organizations adopt different strategies, but we can distinguish two basic stances: collaboration and criticism.

The Collaborators

Some organizations focus on the necessity of working with governments, even less-than-democratic governments,[47] such as that of China, to achieve any improvement in human rights or any success in pursuing humanitarian goals. It is obvious that such governments do not welcome critical perspectives from outside forces (not to mention inside forces), which puts human rights INGOs in a difficult position. Nonetheless, organizations such as the Ford Foundation and the Danish Institute for Human Rights (DIHR) are actively involved in human rights projects in China and other countries with less-than-democratic governments.

In China, the Ford Foundation has been establishing and developing grant-making activities in areas such as judicial reforms, legal aid, and constitutional law research. Such projects are explicitly designed to promote greater awareness and respect for individual rights and concern for the worst-off groups in society. Effective implementation of these projects is premised upon successful collaboration with government officials and institutions, notwithstanding appearances. One review of Ford Foundation projects observed:

> For instance, the Center for the Protection of the Weak at Wuhan University would not have been able to begin its operations without the Foundation's funding. However, the mission of the center has been largely in line with the official rhetoric of protecting the interests of the weaker members of the society. In addition, all the major government figures are honorary members of the center. Although one may categorize the center as an NGO,

---

[47] The term "less-than-democratic" is meant not to be a euphemism to cover up an unpleasant reality but rather to suggest a continuum of regime types. The term "authoritarian" is more common to lump together all governments not elected by means of competitive elections, but this term has the drawback of reinforcing the tendency in the West to dichotomize regimes into "good" Western liberal democracies and "bad" authoritarian others.

it is hardly the kind of NGO which resists or confronts the government that one would see elsewhere.[48]

This analyst argues that collaboration with government officials is necessary given the political context because working with truly autonomous NGOs would incur the government's suspicion and "jeopardize the Foundation's existing relatively good rapport with governmental organizations."[49] The presupposition is presumably that official collaboration is an important way for the foundation to advance the causes of human rights and social justice in China.[50]

The Danish Institute for Human Rights adopts a similar cooperative approach. This government-funded agency (its largest funder is the Royal Danish Ministry of Foreign Affairs) has been funding and supporting various human rights projects in China,[51] including a program concerned with the prevention of the use of torture and ill treatment by police in the pretrial phase, another program designed to train Chinese legal scholars and practitioners in European law and practice, a human rights center in a provincial capital, a project providing legal aid to women, and a death penalty study. As with the Ford Foundation, the activities of the DIHR require active collaboration with the government sector: "In authoritarian states, where the local NGOs might be few or nonexistent within certain sectors, cooperation with governments might be the only option."[52] It would be a mistake, the DIHR implies, always to view less-than-democratic governments as evil perpetrators of human rights abuses.[53] Sometimes, government officials are sincerely committed to improving the rights situation in selected areas. Where human rights violations do occur, this may be "due to institutional inertia rather than to active state-willed perpetration of violations." It could also be due to lack of technical skills and know-how, and the government might welcome INGO aid in this respect.

---

[48] Song Bing, "A Review of Selected Judicial-Reform Projects Funded by the Ford Foundation," report on file with author, May 2001, 24.

[49] Ibid.

[50] There has been increased tolerance for genuinely independent NGOs in China of late (e.g., the Women's Migrant Center in Beijing), so there may be more alternatives to collaboration with official organizations now (early 2006).

[51] The choice of country is partly motivated by the practical concerns of the Danish government: "An official Danish goal of opening Chinese markets complements the need to meet concerns raised by human rights activists and NGOs in the South." Birgit Lindsnaes, Hans-Otto Sano, and Hatla Thelle, "An Assessment of Success Stories, Trade Offs, and Failures," paper presented at New York workshop (on file with author), 6.

[52] Ibid., 10.

[53] It would also be a mistake to think that democratic governments are necessarily less inclined to human rights abuses. The recent U.S. experience in Iraq suggests that the human rights records of democratic governments is less than impeccable. It is also possible that democratic rights can actually worsen the human rights situation of some groups (see chapter 7).

One important issue regards terminology. In China, human rights concerns need not be expressed in terms of the language of human rights: "The Chinese side [wishes] to downplay the human rights discourse and instead speaks of citizen's rights or rights of special groups like suspects, women, retired persons, etc. To speak of someone's legal rights is also non-controversial in China, while human rights for some reason is tinged with power politics, colonial exploitation, and often prompts a very nationalistic response." In such cases, the DIHR avoids "conflict of 'formalities,'" as "the problem is more technical than substantial, and we have not had any strong confrontations from either side."[54] Sophia Woodman, formerly of Human Rights in China, makes a similar point. Drawing on interviews with representatives of INGO donors as well as Chinese recipients of INGO aid, Woodman notes that hostility and suspicion in the Chinese bureaucracy to foreign cooperation regarding matters of human rights remain strong. Woodman argues that problems can be avoided by dropping the language of human rights and democracy for more "politically correct" terms like the rule of law and governance.[55] The problem, however, is that Western INGOs can face pressure from their own constituents and donors if they adopt this tactic. For example, the Canadian International Development Agency (CIDA) had originally planned to drop the term "human rights and democratic development" from the new country development policy framework now under preparation and refer only to "good governance," the goal of which would be to "support Chinese efforts to increase rule of law as a means to uphold the rights of its women and men." After the proposed change met with an outcry from Canadian NGOs, CIDA backed down.[56]

In sum, "the successful cases demonstrate that it is indeed possible to obtain very good results even in authoritarian regimes."[57] But success may require compromises that Western backers of INGOs will object to.

The Critics

There are other disadvantages linked to partnership with less-than-democratic governments. The most obvious is that human rights organizations

---

[54] Ibid., 8–9.

[55] Of course, the politically correct labels can change over time. During the 1997 Jiang–Clinton summit, the Chinese side rejected the term "rule of law," but both sides managed to achieve substantial cooperation by using the (then) neutral term, "legal cooperation." Peerenboom, "Human Rights and Rule of Law," 905n. 307.

[56] Sophia Woodman, "Driving without a Map: Implementing Legal Projects in China Aimed at Improving Human Rights," paper presented at Hong Kong conference (revised version, on file with author).

[57] Lindsnaes, Sano, and Thelle, "An Assessment of Success Stories," 13.

working in China often choose to "avoid politically sensitive issues" such as labor rights,[58] press freedom, and the political rights of dissidents[59] and "avoid politically sensitive places" such as Tibet and Xinjiang.[60]

Another potential disadvantage is that human rights INGOs that co-operate with less-than-democratic governments may grant moral legitimacy to those governments, thus postponing the day of reckoning.[61] The authors of a report titled "Promoting Human Rights in China" express their doubts regarding those who favor engaging the Chinese government on human rights issues: "In general the Chinese government has succeeded in taking control of standard setting for engagement programs and has shaped these programs so that their impact on human rights practices is slight. . . . In some cases the dialogue process has become a substitute for more critical approaches that could generate real pressure for change."[62] One has only to recall how many corporations and governments opposed policies of disinvestment and other economic sanctions against the apartheid regime in South Africa, arguing instead for policies of constructive engagement. In retrospect it seems clear that constructive engagement was far less effective than sanctions in assisting the transition to a new South Africa. This is not to imply that the current Chinese government ranks on the same scale of injustice as the former apartheid regime,[63] but similar worries may arise.[64]

Another disadvantage of collaboration was raised by Sophia Woodman. Her Chinese informants were virtually unanimous in asserting that

---

[58] The substance of what is politically correct also changes over time. In the space of two or three years, it has become politically correct to deal with labor rights, and such organizations as UNESCO are now openly organizing exhibitions to raise awareness of the rights of migrant workers (see "Together with Migrants," UNESCO Office Beijing, 2004) and funding such NGOs as the Women's Migrant Center in Beijing.

[59] Note, however, that one organization—John Kamm's Dui Hua [Dialogue] Foundation—has had remarkable success in securing the release of dissidents from Chinese jails by engaging and cooperating with Chinese political authorities.

[60] Lindsnaes, Sano, and Thelle, "Human Rights in Action," 9.

[61] If the "day of reckoning"—meaning a Soviet-style collapse of the government—seems imminent, this would provide another reason to refrain from collaboration. Even if the central level seems on the verge of collapse, however, there may still be reason to collaborate with well-intentioned and relatively "clean" local officials.

[62] See "Promoting Human Rights in China," Report of the China Human Rights Strategy Study Group, November 2001, 21,

[63] At a certain point of "evilness," collaboration becomes indefensible. Brian Joseph suggests that this can occur when the country in question is entirely nondemocratic (as opposed to less than democratic) and the rights violations that take place are immediate, gross, and clearly the fault of the government (e-mail communication, 26 September 2002).

[64] On the other hand, the authors of the DIHR paper argue that the "partnership approach" may eventually allow for institutional problems of governance to be addressed: "A step-by-step method of implementation where the aim during the first phases is to create a foundation of cooperation and trust within what is sometimes a limited scope of activities, while during the subsequent phases more emphasis is put on broadening the scope

international pressure has played an important role in contributing to human rights concessions by the Chinese government, and consequently the "engagers" should be wary of collaborative projects that undermine international pressure.[65] Kenneth Roth of HRW made a similar point. The DIHR argues for an international "division of labor," with organizations such as AI and HRW adopting a confrontational approach and playing the role of documenting violations and lobbying for international criticism while "engagers" such as the DIHR and similar organizations cooperate with the government on long-term rights projects.[66] Roth pointed out, however, that there are trade-offs because less-than-democratic governments can use their cooperation with the "engagers" as evidence that their policies on human rights are not so bad and are getting better, thus weakening the force of criticisms put forward by other organizations.

It is inevitable, of course, that any human rights reforms or humanitarian efforts will be trumpeted for public relations purposes, and INGOs must always try to determine whether the substantive merits of the changes are worth the public relations advantage that the targets of their efforts will obtain with a particular reform. This problem emerges with nonstate actors as well. For example, Morton Winston reports that Shell responded to plans for demonstrations by several groups, including Friends of the Earth and the Nigerian group MOSOP, at the 1997 Shell Annual General Meeting by announcing the day before that it had agreed with AI and Pax Christi to adopt human rights principles in its business code.[67] Presumably AI and Pax Christi made the judgment that the substantive commitments that Shell made were significant enough to justify giving the company the opportunity to use their names to deflect the criticisms of the other groups.

The Challenge of Fund-Raising

The need to raise funds has also generated debates within human rights and humanitarian INGOs.[68] The source of funding and the means employed to raise funds both raise ethical questions.

---

of interaction, thus creating a foundation for more far-reaching institutional changes." An example is the Helsinki and OSCE processes that started with dialogue at the political level in 1975, a dialogue that "probably had a decisive influence on Gorbachev's Glasnost policy" (Lindsnaes, Sano, and Thelle, "Human Rights in Action," 12, 3).

[65] Woodman, "Driving without a Map."

[66] Lindsnaes, Sano, and Thelle "An Assessment of Success Stories," 11.

[67] Morton Winston, "NGO Strategies for Promoting Corporate Responsibility," ms., 2002, 24.

[68] Another morally and practically relevant issue is the extent to which local (Southern) NGOs have to compromise in order to obtain funding and support from wealthy Northern INGOs. See Mona Younis, "An Imperfect Process: Funding Human Rights—A Case Study,"

Conflicts over Sources

One important area of controversy is the issue of government funding for INGOs. Many INGOs do accept government funds, and the main advantage, of course, is that they can carry out their projects without wasting too much time and money on fundraising efforts. This raises questions regarding their independence, however: "Many of the largest and most respectable INGOs of today (such as Save the Children and Oxfam) were born and raised in opposition to government policy and vested interests at the time. But can this role continue when Northern NGOs are becoming more and more dependent on government support?"[69] The contrast between CARE and Oxfam America is instructive. Both organizations provide emergency and development aid in the South, but the comparison ends there. CARE relies on large, regular grants from the U.S. government, is not critical of U.S. public efforts, and handles numerous contracts on behalf of the U.S. government.[70] Oxfam America "neither solicits nor accepts funding from governments. . . . This policy allows Oxfam America to act with conviction and integrity when encouraging governments, IGOs, and international financial institutions to adopt policies that support long-term development (and criticizing them if they do not)."[71]

---

paper presented at New York workshop (on file with author), and Clifford Bob, "Merchants of Morality," *Foreign Policy*, March/April 2002. Sometimes just the presence of INGOs can hamper the fund-raising efforts of local NGOs: In postauthoritarian states such as South Africa and Nigeria, the influx of better funded INGOs in the late 1990s was seen as undermining the local human rights NGOs because there was concern that the better known INGOs would get funds for local projects that would otherwise have gone to the NGOs. See Bonny Ibhawoh, "Human Rights INGOs, the North/South Gap and the Challenge of Legitimacy," paper presented at Hong Kong conference (on file with author).

[69] David Hulme and Michael Edwards, "Too Close to the Powerful, Too Far from the Powerless," in *NGOs, States and Donors: Too Close for Comfort?*, ed. David Hulme and Michael Edwards (Houndmills: Macmillan, 1997), 280. According to Brian Joseph, however, the relevant issue is not government funding per se, because organizations that rely on one or two big private donors are also susceptible to pressure. He argues that the number and diversity of sources is often more important than the original source of the funds (e-mail communication, 26 September 2002).

[70] Claude E. Welch, Jr., "Conclusion," in *NGOs and Human Rights*," ed. Claude E. Welch, Jr. (Philadelphia: University of Pennsylvania Press, 2001), 270. In coalition-occupied Iraq, however, the Bush administration imposed so many constraints on INGOs that accepted USAID funding that several INGOs, including CARE, made the difficult decision not to seek USAID funding. Lyal Sunga, "Dilemmas Facing INGOs in Coalition-Occupied Iraq," paper presented at Hong Kong workshop (on file with author).

[71] Scott, "Evaluating Development-Oriented NGOs," 209. On the other hand, Oxfam Canada receives about half of its funding from CIDA, an agency of the Canadian government concerned with economic development in poor countries. This may reflect different judgments about the policies and politics of the respective governments.

The recent experience of the Danish Institute for Human Rights further illustrates the disadvantages of dependence on government funds. Governments can force agendas onto reluctant human rights organizations. In one case, the DCHR found it "necessary to refrain from a rather promising cooperation project on the protection of social and economic rights that was based on a Chinese initiative, because the Danish Ministry of Foreign Affairs did not count this as a human rights project."[72]

Similar concerns may arise in the case of funding from international organizations that are composed of national governments. One human rights organization that prefers to remain anonymous works in Nepal as consultants for the United Nations Development Programme (UNDP), but they cannot criticize the Nepalese government to the extent they would like because the relatively conservative UNDP (dependent on good relations with the Nepalese government, one of its constituent members) might be reluctant to use its services, which would affect the finances of the organization.[73]

The INGOs that rely more on confrontational approaches have been particularly wary of dependence on government funding. Amnesty's founder, Peter Benenson, was forced to resign in 1967 following accusations that he had British government funds to help finance AI's relief operations in Rhodesia,[74] and the organization has since shied away from government funding.[75] Today, AI shows the heaviest reliance on membership dues and individual contributions among major INGOs. Human Rights Watch, for its part, has an absolute prohibition on ac-

---

[72] Lindsnaes, Sano, and Thelle, "An Assessment of Success Stories," 10. One might not have been surprised if the American government had similarly pressured a government-funded human rights organization, but it is interesting to note the governmental bias toward the protection of civil and political rights even in social democratic West European states such as Denmark.

[73] Such dilemmas can be partly resolved by collection action by human rights and humanitarian organizations that allows them to speak out and leaves particular organizations less open to retaliation: "A group of around 25 German NGOs, working exclusively for Nepal, have expressed their deep concern over the current political and 'unresolved arguments' between the government and the Maoists, further calling for peace and 'concentration on the well-being of the people' to resolve all existing differences" (KOL report, 6 June 2002).

[74] William Korey, NGOs and the Universal Declaration of Human Rights: A Curious Grapevine (New York: Palgrave, 1998), 167. At the same time, the revelation that the International Commission of Jurists, headed by AI Cochair Sean MacBride, had received funding from the CIA early in its history "threatened to torpedo both organizations." Claude Welch, Jr., "Amnesty International and Human Rights Watch," in NGOs and Human Rights, ed. Claude E. Welch, Jr. (Philadelphia: University of Pennsylvania Press, 2001), 92.

[75] To be precise, AI does not accept money from governments for its research or campaigning work, but some of its smaller sections have occasionally accepted very limited amounts for human rights education programs (e-mail from Curt Goering, 27 October 2002).

cepting funds either directly or indirectly from governments. As Widney Brown explains, "this prohibition is aimed at avoiding even the appearance of undue government influence on any choices or investigations made by HRW and to avoid the inference that the organization is implicitly endorsing a government as not being a human right violator."[76]

Conflicts over Means

There have also been vigorous debates over the legitimacy of means employed for raising funds from the public at large. INGOs reliant on public support must choose between dubious but effective fund-raising tactics that enhance their capacity to do work on behalf of human rights and "appropriate" methods that limit fund-raising success and constrain its ability to do good. Betty Plewes and Rieky Stuart of Oxfam Canada condemn the "pornography of poverty," vivid images of helpless, passive poor and starving Third World peoples that are used by Northern NGOs to raise money from the public for their development work. Emotional appeals of this sort based on notions of guilt and charity have been relatively effective at raising funds:

> Last year in Canada the five largest NGOs (mainly child sponsorship organizations) raised over $300 million from private donations. . . . [Child sponsorship organizations] tell us that these images of misery and passive victimization generate much more in donations than alternatives they have tested, and that it is vital to raise large amounts of money in order to be able to carry out their relief and development work.[77]

Such images, however, convey other, more destructive images and can undermine NGOs' efforts to create a broader understanding of the underlying structures causing poverty and injustice: "These images portray people as helpless victims, dependent, and unable to take action and convey a sense that development problems can only be solved by Northern charity. They ignore Northern complicity in creating inequality. At

---

[76] Widney Brown, "Human Rights Watch: An Overview," in *NGOs and Human Rights,* ed. Claude E. Welch, Jr. (Philadelphia: University of Pennsylvania press, 2001), 78.

[77] Betty Plewes and Rieky Stuart, "The Pornography of Poverty: A Cautionary Fundraising Tale," 1, paper presented at Hong Kong workshop (on file with author). In the long term, however, such images may not be as effective. Their impact may diminish with repetition, and more and more graphic images would be needed to generate the same shock effect (just as Hollywood movies and video games need to get more and more violent to generate the same shock effect), and eventually this whole process may lead to donor fatigue. As David Keen puts it, "If the only thing you get is negative stories, you become inured and people seem less human—they are either emaciated victims or violent and evil. This erodes our ability, willingness or interest in helping [them]" (quoted in ibid., 4).

the very least they convey a limited picture of life in Southern countries. At their worse they reinforce racist stereotypes."[78]

In view of such critiques of charity-based approaches, Oxfam Canada favors justice-based strategies that "focus on the claiming of rights by marginalized individuals or groups through changes of skills, organizational capacity, control of resources, law, policy, or practice"[79] and opposes fund-raising tactics that conflict with this framework, notwithstanding the costs. It therefore rejects pornography of poverty images and uses positive images ("the smiling children, the women smiling as they operate their new village pump, the smiling nurse vaccinating plump healthy children") and clever or ironic images, such as its award-winning ad during the OJ Simpson trial that used only text to compare the amount of media coverage of that event with the much smaller coverage of the Rwanda genocide taking place at the same time.[80]

Similar debates took place at AI, but with a different outcome. The national office of AI in Australia had heated debates within the organization and with the advertising agency commissioned to assist with fund raising over whether to use pictures of torture victims. AI had refused to use such pictures because it was felt they exploit the victims (who probably didn't agree to being used in such images), that it "feels bad," and that AI should appeal to people's better nature. Eventually AI reversed its policy, and the ad agency (working pro bono, it should be said) did use such pictures in fund raising activities. This likely had a positive effect on fund raising (though it is difficult to disentangle cause and effect) and increased AI's capacity to do its work on behalf of human rights.[81]

IMPLICATIONS FOR INGOs IN EAST ASIA

This chapter has drawn on dialogue sessions between high-level representatives of human rights INGOs and academics with an interest in human rights. Based on these dialogues, I have discussed four ethical challenges that are commonly experienced by INGO representatives during the course of their work: (1) the challenge of cultural conflict; (2) the challenge of dealing with global poverty; (3) the challenge of dealing with states that restrict the activities of INGOs; and (4) the ethical challenge of fund raising.

These ethical challenges often overlap in practice, and I do not claim to have presented an exhaustive list of the ethical challenges encountered

---

[78] Ibid., 1.
[79] Stuart, "Ethics in Action," 9
[80] Plewes and Stuart, "Money Talks," 8.
[81] I owe thanks to Andre Frankovits for this information.

by human rights INGOs. The main purpose of this chapter has been to distinguish between and thus clarify the advantages and disadvantages associated with various responses to ethical challenges commonly encountered by human rights INGOs operating in the Asian region and elsewhere. Such an effort will hopefully allow INGOs to learn from each other's experience, avoid past mistakes (e.g., due to insufficient awareness and anticipation of the disadvantages associated with particular responses to ethical dilemmas), and increase the probability that human rights goals can be successfully implemented.

Let me end with some normative reflections that have implications for INGOs operating in the East Asian region.[82] It is fruitless to search for universally right or wrong answers to the kinds of ethical challenges identified in this chapter; there are better or worse ways of dealing with these challenges that will depend on the context. No strategy will be cost-free, and the main task will be to select the strategy with the most advantages and the fewest disadvantages, something that can only be done with those intimately familiar with the details of the particular case. Normative views, however, may help to determine outcomes in truly hard cases, that is, when the advantages and disadvantages of different approaches seem comparable and/or epistemological uncertainty renders different comparisons near impossible. Regarding the conflict between Westcentric human rights norms and local cultural norms, for example, the absence of a truly international human rights regime[83] speaks in favor of erring on the side of culturally sensitive approaches. To the extent that different cultures express values worth of respect, they should not be trumped by a highly contestable Westcentric rights regime. There may also be good pragmatic reasons for representatives of Western-based INGOs to defer to local cultural outlooks in hard cases because more interventionist approaches can decrease the likelihood of successful implementation of projects. In China, for example, the legacy of Western intervention has left a deep and lasting effect on Chinese collective memory, and Western-based INGOs not sufficiently sensitive to the "victim mentality"[84] may run into resistance.

Another potential contribution of normative theory lies in the possibility that there are dilemmas that representatives of human rights INGOs *ought* to experience but fail to do so due to lack of awareness of, or insufficient emphasis on, relevant moral principles. The philosopher Thomas Pogge put forward the following moral principle governing INGO conduct: "Other things being equal, an INGO should choose

---

[82] This section draws on my introduction to *Ethics in Action*.

[83] See the final section of chapter 3.

[84] See Zhou Qi, "Conflicts over Human Rights between China and the US," *Human Rights Quarterly*, vol. 27, no. 1 (February 2005), 8 (Internet version).

among candidate projects on the basis of the cost effectiveness of each project, defined as its moral value divided by its cost. Here a project's moral value is the harm protection it achieves, that is, the sum of the moral values of the harm reductions (and increases) this project would bring about for the individual persons it affects."[85] Given the empirical fact that severe poverty is the most pressing human rights problem in the contemporary world, Pogge argues that INGOs have an obligation to concentrate their limited funds in places that allow for the cost-effective reduction of severe poverty. Since efficiency tends to be higher in countries with better government policies and/or a higher incidence of poverty, this would mean concentrating funds in a few countries: Pogge names India, Bangladesh, Ethiopia, and Uganda as likely worthy candidates of INGO aid. By implication, INGOs that seek to spread their aid over many developing countries out of some misguided ideal of distributive justice are making decisions that are preventing fewer deaths and other harms than they might. INGOs that spend lots of time and money cultivating relationships with government officials in China to promote civil rights in that country are using scarce resources that should have been spent saving lives elsewhere (assuming that more bang for the buck in terms of harm prevention could have been achieved, say, by helping the victims of the 2005 earthquake in Kashmir). INGOs that seek to promote dialogue with Southern NGOs that is not maximally conducive to the cost-effective allocation of funds designed to alleviate severe poverty are wasting precious time and resources. INGOs that have moral qualms about using "exploitative" images of poverty to raise funds may be needlessly limiting their capacity to prevent harm.[86] And INGOs that divert funds to help some badly off people in conflict zones where it is expensive to protect them are preventing fewer deaths than if they had focused their efforts on helping (more) badly off people in peaceful countries who could have been cheaply protected from harm. Pogge does note that INGOs funded by citizens of rich countries might have a special responsibility to avert harms caused by the policies of their own governments, but he argues that the North is so deeply implicated in causing the South's predicament that it is impossible to distinguish between harms that rich countries are, and harms they are not, materially involved in causing. In this context, INGOs need to direct their aid (only) toward the most cost-effective harm protection projects.

[85] Thomas Pogge, "Moral Priorities for International Human Rights NGOs," paper presented at Hong Kong workshop (on file with author).

[86] The Pogge principle may also lead to the conclusion that INGOs with a track record of inefficiency should simply hand over their funds to more efficient INGOs (or even to business enterprises, if it turns out that business investment is the best long-term way to deal with poverty reduction, as some free-market economists argue).

Not surprisingly, Pogge's views generated a storm of controversy at the workshops. Joseph Carens articulates some of these objections to Pogge's view.[87] Pogge's reluctance to turn his mind to the actual experiences of INGOs, Carens argues, leads to an important mistake in his moral analysis. Carens notes that few INGOs would disagree with Pogge's argument that INGOs have responsibilities both to the poor and oppressed abroad and to the contributors on whose behalf they set priorities. The problem is, "[w]hat if the contributors' own views of their moral responsibilities—the ones they want the INGOs to carry out—lead to different priorities from the ones that flow from Pogge's principle? Should the INGOs adopt Pogge's priorities or those of their contributors?" Carens responds that even if we assume (contrary to the experience at the workshops) that the INGOs are convinced by Pogge's argument, they could not justifiably override the views of contributors that cannot be so convinced. One reason is practical: "if an INGO were to persist in a course that its contributors regarded as significantly different from the one which they thought they were supporting, the INGO would lose its contributors and so soon would have no funds to spend." The second reason is moral: "The people running the INGOs are not morally free to follow their own moral views (by hypothesis here, Pogge's principle) and to disregard those of their contributors, precisely because of the trustee relationship between INGOs and contributors to which Pogge has drawn our attention."

If Pogge had paid more attention to the actual workings of INGOs, he would not have assumed that contributors do not have enough information to make any judgments about what the priorities of the INGOs ought to be. In the real world, there are many different kinds of INGOs with different missions and priorities, and, when they seek contributions, the INGOs describe their particular histories and commitments. Most contributors would be able to learn enough from conventional fund-raising materials to distinguish among the basic orientations of the various INGOs, and they are likely to contribute only if they share the organization's basic moral views and established priorities.[88]

It could be, of course, that both contributors and the organizations are

[87] Joseph H. Carens, "The Problem of Doing Good in a World That Isn't: Reflections on the Ethical Challenges Facing INGOs," paper presented at Hong Kong workshop (on file with author).

[88] INGOs, of course, would prefer the unrestricted gift that allows them to spend as they see fit, but "ever since donors learned that the American Red Cross planned to set aside for other uses more than $200 million donated for families of the Sept. 11 attacks, they have increasingly insisted on earmarking or restricting their gifts." Stephanie Strom, "Giving for a Cause, and That Cause Only," *The New York Times*, 5 January 2005.

wrong, that they should be the using moral standard put forward by Pogge for assessing INGO work. Carens, however, argues for an approach that incorporates a recognition of the plurality of moral views without succumbing to relativism. He notes that INGOs generally refrain from open criticism of each other, and that this mutual forbearance lies at least partly in the recognition "that there are many different ways of doing good in the world, and that all of them deserve respect." Not all ways need to be viewed as equally morally valuable, but many pass a morally permissible standard "in the sense that it sets a minimum threshold for the justification of the activities of INGOs." Carens says that he personally agrees with Pogge's view that the most urgent moral task is to reduce harm caused by severe poverty along with the implication that INGOs focusing on severe poverty are doing the most morally valuable work, but "that does not mean that I see the work of human rights INGOs that do not focus on severe poverty as unimportant or, worse still, as morally unacceptable."

Even if we need to respect the basic organizational mission of INGOs that pass a morally permissible standard, Carens argues that Pogge's principle could still provide guidance to INGOs on how to set priorities in spending their money on specific projects. If an INGO must choose between two projects, it should choose the one that does more good. This might well lead INGOs to place less emphasis on geographical diversity of projects, but Carens notes that few, if any, INGO participants at the workshops really confronted the challenge that they should restrict the geographical scope of their projects to places where they can do the most good. In this sense, INGOs might benefit from deeper engagement with the views of a moral theorist.

Let me apply some of these insights to the East Asian context. It is clear that not all human rights INGOs are free to follow the "Pogge principle" as they see fit. As Carens argues, they must honor the trustee relationship with their donors: Oxfam USA raised millions of dollars by requesting funds on the Internet to help victims of the Asian tsunami, and they should not divert these funds to other projects, even if they can get more bang for the buck elsewhere.[89] In other contexts, however, INGOs do raise funds under the general umbrella of human rights work, and they have more moral discretion regarding the use of those funds. If the moral imperative, as Pogge argues, is the cost-effective reduction of severe poverty, then Human Rights Watch, for example, might not be

---

[89] This is not simply a theoretical argument. Relief agencies were remarkably successful at raising funds for the victims of the Asian tsunami, to the point that organizations such as UNICEF and Oxfam had to publicly call on donors to stop giving money for this cause.

making optimal use of its resources by researching and publicizing deviations of Western-style electoral democracy in wealthy Hong Kong.[90] Even organizations with more limited mandates, such as Habitat for Humanity, might benefit from another look at the Pogge principle. Habitat is constrained by the mandate to focus on housing and provide an equitable distribution of homeowner ethnicity, with the implication that scarce resources may not be optimally utilized in ethnically polarized countries like Sri Lanka that require constant monitoring to ensure that Habitat's aims are not overly compromised.

It is worth noting two problems with the Pogge principle not discussed at the aforementioned workshops. First, it seems to imply that human beings should be nothing but altruistic, utility-maximizing machines, that personal experiences and relationships do not have any special moral value. But this view is drastically at odds with ordinary moral intuitions. Ding Ziling, the mother of a university student killed on June 4, 1989, has been actively (fruitlessly, thus far) campaigning for the Chinese government to reverse its official verdict on the June 4 killings. It would seem strange for an outsider to criticize Ms. Ding on the grounds that she could do more good by, say, collaborating with the government on poverty reduction programs.[91]

Second, Pogge's principle may not be as generally applicable as he suggests. Just as agreement over abstract human rights principles like the right to life soon dissolve into disagreement when rights are interpreted and implemented in concrete contexts, so Pogge's principle may prove to be controversial when it is brought down to earth. More specifically, Pogge's discussion of harm may be subject to the same sorts of ambiguities that mark debates about John Stuart Mill's harm principle: Is harm just physical, or does psychological suffering (like fear in war time) also count? Pogge's interpretation of his own principle, with the focus on severe poverty, seems to be based on a physical conception of harm, with material deprivation leading to death viewed as the most serious kind of harm. But an Islamic fundamentalist, for example, might consider the harm resulting from moral laxity in liberal Western countries to be far more serious than material deprivation in predominantly Islamic countries. Having said that, East Asian countries with a Confucian heritage may be particularly receptive to Pogge's view. The emphasis on the harm

[90] See http://www.hrw.org/english/docs/2004/09/09/china9325.htm. This particular report was immediately denounced by the Hong Kong and mainland Chinese governments. Even "liberals" in Hong Kong were somewhat embarrassed by the exaggerated polemics about the "climate of fear," and few, if any, local critics of the government made use of the report.

[91] From a Confucian standpoint that values family ties over public obligations in cases of conflict, the outsider's criticism would be immoral as well as strange.

caused by hunger resonates with traditional cultural outlooks that prioritize the government's obligation to feed the people.[92] Hence, human rights INGOs that follow the Pogge principle would be showing cultural respect. In China, considerations of effectiveness also speak in favor of the Pogge principle. The government is likely to welcome collaboration with INGOs that work on economic rights, whereas INGOs that intervene on behalf of civil and political rights will find it much more difficult to implement their ideals.[93] Given the empirical finding that wealth is the best predictor of rights performance in Asia,[94] it could also be argued that focusing on poverty reduction and economic development is the most effective long-term way to secure other rights, including civil and political rights. In other words, human rights groups that target severe poverty in China will likely be able to do more good relative to those with other priorities.

Part I of the book has focused on East Asian debates related to human rights, drawing implications for political thought and practice in East Asia that vary from Western-style approaches to human rights. The next part turns to another main plank of liberal democracy: rule by the people. Democratic ideas were completely absent from Confucianism prior to the nineteenth century. It does not follow, however, that Confucianism and democracy must inevitably clash. Nor does it mean that Confucian values must be subordinated to Western-style democratic ideas. As we will see, Confucian values can shape "rule by the people" in ways that may be appropriate for the modern world.

[92] See chapters 2 and 9. The contemporary "Marxist" emphasis on the right to subsistence can be seen as an extension of the traditional Confucian view.

[93] Sun Zhe of Fudan University argues that INGOs should give economic and social rights more priority in China, though he does allow for the possibility that political rights can be invoked in such areas as criticizing the Chinese government's widespread use of administrative detention. Sun Zhe, "Normative Compliance and Hard Bargaining: China's Strategies and Tactics in Response to International Human Rights Criticism," paper presented at the Hong Kong workshop, on file with author.

[94] See Peerenboom, "Show Me the Money," and Peerenboom, *China Modernizes: Threat to the West or Model to the Rest* (Oxford: Oxford University Press, forthcoming).

PART TWO

Democracy for an East Asian Context

5

What's Wrong with Active Citizenship?
A Comparison of Physical Education
in Ancient Greece and Ancient China

IMMANUEL KANT famously argued that "the problem of setting up a state can be solved even by a nation of devils."[1] So long as the institutions are just, the self-seeking inclinations of individuals will be neutralized or eliminated. Today, however, it is widely recognized that democratic institutions are not sufficient for stable and effective democratic government. If people are narrowly self-interested and circumvent civic responsibilities whenever they have the opportunity to do so—evading taxes, refraining from voting, avoiding jury duty, deserting from the battlefield—democratic institutions will not last long or produce desirable results, no matter how beautifully they are designed. Hence, much political theorizing of late has been devoted to "democratic education," the kind of education that will shape future citizens with the motivation and ability to participate in democratic rule.[2]

The origin of democratic education can be traced to ancient Athens. The main purpose of the Athenian educational system was to prepare future citizens for the rough-and-tumble arena of democratic politics. Physical education, perhaps surprisingly, was also designed (at least partly) to produce citizens actively participating in the democratic process. This might seem like a good thing. A comparison with physical education in ancient China, however, may cast doubt upon the virtues of democratic-inspired physical education as well as the ideal of active citizenship more generally.

---

[1] Immanuel Kant, "Perpetual Peace," in *Kant: Political Writings*, ed. Hans Reiss and trans. H. B. Nisbet (Cambridge: Cambridge University Press, 1991), 112.

[2] See, e.g., Amy Gutmann, *Democratic Education* (Princeton: Princeton University Press, 1999); Stephen Macedo, *Diversity and Distrust: Civic Education in a Multicultural Democracy* (Cambridge: Harvard University Press, 2000); Rob Reich, *Bridging Liberalism and Multiculturalism in Modern Education* (Chicago: Chicago University Press, 2002); Amitai Etzioni, *The Spirit of Community: Rights, Responsibilities, and the Communitarian Agenda* (New York: Crown Publishers, 1993), chap. 3; William A. Galston, *Liberal Purposes: Goods, Virtues, and Diversity in the Liberal State* (Cambridge: Cambridge University Press, 1991), chap. 11.

In both ancient Greece (c. 7th–4th century B.C.E.)[3] and the Warring States period in ancient "China"[4] (c. 500–221 B.C.E.),[5] small states[6] engaged in intense military competition, fighting for either survival or expansion of territory. In such contexts, there was naturally much emphasis on the training of soldiers. One might have expected state-sponsored physical education—designed to toughen bodies and (as Aristotle puts it) to "foster the virtue of courage"[7]—to develop as a by-product of the need to train soldiers. This need would be particularly acute in cultures like ancient Greece and the late Warring States that made wide use of amateur soldiers. Yet the historical record[8] shows that ancient Greek states placed far more emphasis on physical education than did their counterparts in ancient China. Greek states actively promoted physical education and interstate sporting competitions, and these features of political life were taken for granted in the works of Greek philosophers; yet physical education had hardly any political importance in ancient China. What accounts for this difference? This chapter will attempt to shed light on this question. The first part outlines the practice and philosophy of physical education in ancient Greece and ancient China and asks why the two ancient civilizations should be compared in this respect. The next part discusses the political differences between ancient Greece and ancient China that help to explain the different outcomes regarding state-sponsored physical education. The main argument is that the Greek emphasis on citizenship underpinned the Greek states' emphasis on physi-

[3] My main concern is the period characterized by small, autonomous, and politically dynamic city-states in ancient Greece. This period ends roughly with Alexander the Great's victory over the Greek city-states (c. 335 B.C.E.).

[4] I use quotes because the pre-Qin states cannot be described as the culturally unified state of China (*Zhongguo*, 中國). The cultural unity of China owes much to the destruction of local records by the first emperor in 213 B.C.E., a deliberate act of policy aimed at extinguishing local loyalties (Mark Elvin, *The Pattern of the Chinese Past* [Stanford: Stanford University Press, 1973], 21–22), though the process of cultural assimilation of non-Sinitic peoples via war and conquest had begun earlier, as far back as the Spring and Autumn period. For stylistic reasons, I drop the quotes around China from here on.

[5] The point at which Chinese states clearly existed, and functioned as an interstate system, begins with the effective elimination of Zhou power in 771 B.C.E. The date for the transition between the Spring and Autumn and Warring States periods is a matter of controversy. The year 403 B.C.E. is the officially recognized date for the tripartite division of Jin, although this had taken effect much earlier. A very rough starting date of 500 B.C.E. is sufficient for my purposes.

[6] While small by today's standards, states in ancient China were larger than Greek city-states.

[7] Aristotle, *The Politics*, 1337b 1, ed. and trans. Ernest Barker (London: Oxford University Press, 1946), 335.

[8] In the case of ancient China, unfortunately, the historical record is relatively limited. Most of it comes from an elite theoretical stratum (court advice and its dissents), and there are few private documents, secular state papers, or ritual texts.

cal education,[9] and the corresponding lack of emphasis on citizenship in ancient China helps to explain why the training of soldiers did not translate into more general state concern for physical education.[10] The chapter ends with some normative reflections on the implications of state-sponsored physical education for contemporary East Asian societies, drawing some more general lessons about the problems associated with the ideal of active citizenship.

Two Ancient Civilizations

Physical education involves training in physical fitness and in skills requiring or promoting such fitness.[11] It may also involve competitive activities that require physical strength and/or skills and that are played by teams or individuals according to prescribed rules.

Physical Education in Ancient Greece

Ancient Greece is widely viewed, and rightly so, as the birthplace of systematic, state-sponsored physical education programs. Modern scholars of physical education point to Homer's masterpieces, *The Iliad* and *The Odyssey*, as proof of the early emphasis on physical education.[12] In both works, the ancient Greek system of physical education may be studied through the authors' depictions of recreational sports, welcoming ceremonies, and funeral games.[13] In subsequent periods, state-sponsored physical education developed further in Greek city-states. This was a pan-

---

[9] The Greek practice of citizenship may also have helped to generate other innovations. G.E.R. Lloyd argues that the development of generalized skepticism and of critical inquiry directed at fundamental issues in science (and philosophy) can most likely be explained by the social and political context of ancient Greece, namely, the experience of radical debate and confrontation in small-scale, face-to-face societies. Lloyd, *Magic, Reason and Experience: Studies in the Origin and Development of Greek Science* (London: Gerald Duckworth, 1999), 232.

[10] An earlier version of this chapter was coauthored with Paik Wooyeal. E. Bruce Brooks provided detailed comments on an earlier draft, and all references to his ideas, unless otherwise noted, are drawn from those comments (on file with the author).

[11] Britannica CD 2000 Deluxe Edition, "Physical Education."

[12] See Robert A. Mechikoff and Steven G. A. Estes, *A History and Philosophy of Sport and Physical Education*, 3rd ed (New York: McGraw-Hill, 2002), 48; and Mark Golden, *Sport and Society in Ancient Greece* (Cambridge: Cambridge University Press, 1998), 88–95; Kim Dongkyu, *The World History of Physical Education* (Kyungsan: Young Nam University Press, 1999), 95–98.

[13] See Homer, *The Iliad*, trans. Martin Hammond (London: Penguin Books, 1987), chap. 4, 8; and Homer, *The Odyssey*, trans. E. V. Rieu (London: Penguin Books, 1991), chap. 23.

Hellenic phenomenon, and the ancient Greeks held physical education in higher esteem than most societies—to be unfit was unacceptable.

The Greek states' role in sponsoring physical education most famously took the form of state-sponsored international competitions such as the Olympic Games.[14] Olympic athletes, who trained and competed naked,[15] were admired and idealized by Greek citizens, and their "godlike" physical abilities provided the prototype for others to follow. There were no team competitions,[16] and the whole system was geared to a "winner-take-all" mentality: as Stephen Miller explains, "Every event pitted man against man, one on one. In addition, there was no prize for second place. One man won, and everyone else lost."[17] Winners were regarded as having attained the excellence of gods and goddesses. The respect for the winners of sporting competitions is well illustrated by Plutarch, who

---

[14] There were four major sporting competitions: the Olympic Games, the Pythian Games, the Isthmian Games, and the Nemean Games (see Golden, *Sport and Society in Ancient Greece*, 10–11). These competitions had diverse games that were identical with physical education subjects in the gymnasium.

[15] Women were excluded from the Olympic Games, with the exception of chariot-and horse-race events where the owner and not the jockey was honored as victor. The first such female victor was Cynisca of Sparta, who won a four-horse chariot race at Olympia ca. 390 B.C.E. Xenophon and Plutarch recounted an anecdote with the lesson that Cynisca's victory "is not an example of manly valor, but of wealth," apparently to reinforce the perception that females were not capable of *arête* (excellence) and fame in the public, political sphere. See Thomas F. Scanlon, *Eros & Greek Athletics* (Oxford: Oxford University Press, 2002), 21–22. There were separate foot-racing competitions for women, who would "run in the following manner: their hair hangs loose, a *chiton* [tunic] reaches to a little above the knee, and the right shoulder is bared as far as the breast." Pausanias, quoted in Stephen G. Miller, *Ancient Greek Olympics* (New Haven: Yale University Press, 2004), 155. Before any comparisons are drawn with the sexual antics of Janet Jackson, it is worth noting that all participants were virgins, and the games were meant to be "celebrations by maidens of their transitional, prenuptial status between the 'wildness' of adolescence of the past and the 'tameness' to come with marriage." Scanlon, *Eros and Greek Athletics*, 323; see also Golden, *Sport and Society in Ancient Greece*, 125–30.

[16] The emergence of team sports dates from the latter part of the nineteenth century. As Michael Mandelbaum explains, "baseball, football, and basketball reflect the great changes that distinguish the modern from the traditional world: equality in the organization of society, cooperation and competition in the operation of the economy, and formal laws governing both. Team sports reflect these changes more vividly than do the longer-established individual sports." Mandelbaum, *The Meaning of Sports: Why Americans Watch Baseball, Football, and Basketball and What They See When They Do* (New York: Public Affairs, 2004), 26.

[17] Miller, *Ancient Greek Athletics*, 19. Jean-François Doré traces the origins of the sports cliché, "Winning isn't everything, it's the only thing,' to its Greek roots. Doré, *Y en aura pas d'facile: Dix clichés du sport et leurs racines philosophiques* [There Won't be Any Easy Ones: Ten Sports Clichés and Their Philosophical Roots] (Montréal: Leméac, 2003), 90–94.

points to an example from Sparta:[18] an Olympic Games winner chose "the right to a place in the unit defending the king in battles against our enemies"[19] over a large sum of money.

Such games are only part of the picture of state-sponsored physical education, however. Greek states actively promoted physical education as a matter of domestic policy. The content of state-sponsored physical competition typically included boxing, running, wrestling, javelin, discus, and ball games. Let us turn to an account of state-sponsored physical education in the two most influential city-states, Athens and Sparta.

In ancient Athens, state-sponsored physical education began at the age of seven. The male children of citizens were educated in two educational institutions—the Didaskaleion (Dadiscaleum) for intellectual disciplines such as literature, rhetoric, poetry, music, and mathematics, and the Palaistra (Palestra) for physical education. From seven to eleven, students in the Palaistra learned simple dance and sporting games, and from twelve or thirteen they were trained in more rigorous physical disciplines such as the high jump, running, wrestling, javelin throwing, and discus throwing (the five sports of the pentahalon). They also learned gymnastics and dance with music.

At approximately sixteen years old, young boys moved to the gymnasium (gymnasion in ancient Greek) for further physical education and intellectual disciplines such as philosophy and social communication. The literal meaning of gymnasium was "school for naked exercise." This facility was a large room used for physical education and training for sporting competitions such as the Olympic Games. It was equipped with most facilities necessary for these activities, including the main training place, the contesting place, changing rooms, a bath, and a shrine for gods.[20] The gymnasium was a public institution, primarily funded and managed by the state[21] and supervised by its chief, the gymnasiarch, who was elected by the city council and ruled according to the

---

[18] Even critics of Sparta's emphasis on physical fitness do not question the goal of Olympic glory. For example, Aristotle criticizes the Spartans for excessive early physical training on the grounds that this actually reduces, rather than increases, the likelihood of Olympic victories: "The bad effects of excessive early training are strikingly evident. In the lists of Olympic victors there are only two or three cases of the same person having won in the men's events who had previously won in the boys'; and the reason is that early training, and the compulsory exercises which it involved, had resulted in loss of energy. Aristotle, *The Politics* of Aristotle, 1339a 8.

[19] Plutarch, *Plutarch's Lives*, Lycurgus 82.

[20] See Golden, *Sport and Society in Ancient Greece*, 47.

[21] Every important Greek city had at least one publicly funded gymnasium, which illustrates the significance of physical education in ancient Greece.

gymnasium law.[22] Following training in the gymnasium, young men spent two years, from eighteen to twenty, doing a course of compulsory military training.

In ancient Sparta, state-sponsored physical education was even more intense than in Athens. The selection process actually began from birth—a council of elders inspected the physical quality of all the offspring of male citizens and took weak bodies away to "Apothetae," Mount Taygetos.[23] At the age of seven, boys were conscripted to military service and remained until the age of fifty. The Paidonomus (the person selected as the best citizen in Sparta) and the Eiren (the twenty-year-old director of the military company composed of four boys' platoons) taught them such diverse physical activities as running, gymnastics, javelin and discus throwing, wrestling, swimming, ball games, music, and dancing. The recruits slept on a primitive barracks floor.[24] At the age of twelve, they were expected to find their food by themselves, which occasionally involved quasi-legalized theft. At the age of twenty, they began to take part in real wars, normally full-time until the age of thirty. Unlike their Athenian counterpart, the Spartans' education did not normally involve intellectual discipline, and Spartan physical education took place in relatively "Spartan" gymnasia and palaestrae. One unique feature of Spartan physical education is that women were also brought to the gymnasia and taught the same subjects and engaged in the same physical activities, although they stayed at home during their education and their program ended at the age of twenty, when they began their married life.[25]

[22] The gymnasiarch was elected among men between thirty and sixty years old and was expected to carry out the gymnasiarchal law of Zeus, Ge, Helios, Apollo, Hercules, and Hermes. Kim Joo-Hwa. "A Sport Archeological Study on the Gymnasiarchal Law of Beroea," *Korean Journal of Physical Education History* 6 (Seoul: Korean Forum of History Physical Education, 2000).

[23] See Mechikoff and Estes, *A History and Philosophy of Sport and Physical Education*, 51. On the practice of infanticide in ancient Greece, see Martha L. Edwards, "The Cultural Context of Deformity in the Ancient Greek World: 'Let There Be a Law That No Deformed Child Shall Be Reared,'" *The Ancient History Bulletin*, vol. 10, nos. 3–4 (1996), 79–92.

[24] See Kim, *The World History of Physical Education*, 99.

[25] According to Plutarch, physical education for women in Sparta was also justified in terms of its benefits for childbearing: "Lykourgos exercised the bodies of the virgins with footraces and wrestling and throwing the *diskos* and the *akon* [javelin] so that their offspring might spring from strong roots in strong bodies, and so that they might be patient and strong in childbirth and struggle well and easily with its pains. He removed all softness, daintiness, and effeminacy from them and accustomed the girls no less than the boys to parade in the nude and to dance and sing at certain religious festivals in the presence of young men as spectators" (quoted in Miller, *Ancient Greek Athletics*, 154). Scanlon more pithily expresses the aim of physical education for women in Sparta: "The whole educative process aims at the acquisition of beauty for real, practical aims in service of the state. Whereas boys become good soldiers, girls become mothers who produce good warriors" (Scanlon, *Eros & Greek Athletics*, 127).

Few, if any, philosophers in ancient Greece questioned the need for state-sponsored physical education and the highly competitive, victory-oriented nature of athletics. Both Plato and Aristotle affirmed the importance of physical education in their suggested educational programs. Plato was an implacable critic of Athenian-style society and politics, but his defense of physical education in *The Republic* does not differ widely from the actual practice of Athenian society at the time. He argues that people must be carefully trained in physical education "from childhood onwards" (403d).[26] From the ages of eighteen to twenty, young men (and women; see book 5) are meant do a course of compulsory military training (410c). Aristotle, for his part, argues, "there is now general agreement about the necessity of physical training, and about the way in which it ought to be given" (*The Politics*, 1338 b 8). As against the Spartan practice, he favors light exercises before the age of puberty (1338 b 1), followed by more rigorous exercises. In his treatise on the Constitution of Athens, Aristotle describes—with apparent approval—the military training of Athenian youth from eighteen to twenty.[27]

Physical Education in Ancient China

There are few detailed records on state-sponsored physical education in ancient China, but works such as *Records of the Historian* (*Shiji* 史記; c. 1st century B.C.E.),[28] *History of the Han Dynasty* (*Hanshu* 漢書; c. 1st century C.E.), and Sunzi's *The Art of War* (*Sunzi bingfa* 孫子兵法; c. 5th–4th century B.C.E.)[29] offer some indications of the practice. During the Western Zhou period (1111–771 B.C.E.), schools were established for the sons of aristocrats in important cities, such as the capital of the Zhou state. In this period, physical activities were taught in schools in spring and summer, and

---

[26] Plato, however, argued (in apparent contrast to the dominant Athenian justification) that the point of physical education should not be to develop the body as an end in itself, but rather that the cultivation of the body should be seen as another means to develop the soul (*The Republic*, 410c). Still, Plato was known to enjoy athletic competitions in ways that were more than cerebral, as when he "shared a tent at Olympia with some men he did not know, nor did they know him. He so gained their affection with his comradery, eating with them simply and passing the days with all of them that the strangers felt fortunate to have met this man" (Aelian, quoted in Miller, *Ancient Greek Athletics*, 119).

[27] See *The Politics of Aristotle*, appendix 4, 384.

[28] The *Shiji* is a "universal" history of the known world covering the period from the earliest times (the era of the mythical "Yellow Emperor") to the reign of Emperor Han Wudi (156–87 B.C.E.).

[29] The *Sunzi bingfa* is often regarded as the oldest military treatise in the world, but it was compiled over a long period of time, and its exact dating is a matter of great controversy. See *The Art of War*, trans. Ralph D. Sawyer, 157–62.

literary education was taught in autumn and winter.[30] These schools primarily taught the six arts (六藝), namely, ritual (禮), music (樂), archery (射), charioteering (御), reading (書), and mathematics (數). Ritual and music were regarded as cultural education, writing and mathematics as literary education, and archery and charioteering as physical education. A boy during the Zhou dynasty was expected to learn the *Six Books* (*Liushu* 六書) and mathematics while living at the school, music, poetry, and dance at the age of thirteen, and dance, archery, and charioteering at the age of fifteen.[31] Also, the basic condition for government officials in the Zhou dynasty is that they should excel at performing musical instruments as well as archery, charioteering, recording, and calculating.[32] Physical education in the Zhou was at least partly designed to train soldiers, but this did not translate (unlike the Greeks) into glorification of physical prowess on the battlefield. As H. G. Creel puts it, "Warfare was regarded, in Western Zhou, as a task, important and necessary but on the whole, insofar as the sources indicate, rather distasteful. . . . A boastful tone concerning military exploits is exceedingly rare in Western Zhou."[33]

This educational system remained more or less intact during the Eastern Zhou period, but the third part of this system—physical education—began to disappear from public education shortly thereafter. This seems counterintuitive because the Warring States period required the use of trained soldiers due to the furious wars between states at the time, and one might have expected state-sponsored physical education to become more, rather than less, prominent during this period.[34] Sunzi's *The Art of*

---

[30] See *Shiji*, King Wen section (文王世家). The *Shiji*, however, presents a controversial account of history. The *Shiji* may be projecting later ideals into the early Zhou for the purpose of providing a linear account of Chinese history (with the ideal situation represented as the actual past situation).

[31] See The Book of Rites (*Liji*).

[32] Kim, *The World History of Physical Education*, 44.

[33] H. G. Creel, *The Origin of Statecraft in China* (Chicago: University of Chicago Press, 1970), 256–57, 255. Creel contrasts the less-than-positive Chinese attitude toward military matters with the Western Roman Empire's glorification of warfare, but a similar contrast can be drawn with the ancient Greeks.

[34] Note, however, that this claim rests on the assumption that the *Shiji* accurately describes the past. According to E. Bruce Brooks, it is possible, if not likely, that such practices never existed in the mythical Zhou. If his suggestion is correct, this would also explain the apparently counterintuitive phenomenon described in the previous sentence (i.e., it would not be the case that physical education became less prominent in the Warring States period because it would not have been prominent in the Zhou period either). In any case, I do not need to defend the historical argument that state-sponsored physical education actually declined in importance during the Warring States period. What matters for our purpose—what needs to be explained—is that state-sponsored physical education was surprisingly deemphasized during the Warring States period, particularly in comparison to ancient Greek societies that were also engaged in incessant warfare and similarly depended on trained soldiers from the lower classes.

War alludes to military training, but this is usually discussed in terms of (a) securing the obedience of the men and (b) drilling them in executing maneuvers not from verbal commands but from long-distance drum or other signals. The "concubines of Wu" story[35] was invented during the Han dynasty, but the military practice described in this story stays wholly within the above lines. According to E. Bruce Brooks, the story could be read as an argument that it is possible to achieve results with an army whose soldiers possess no particular strength or other physical prowess, as prompt and disciplined maneuver is the only crucial element. Individual feats of strength or daring are generally discouraged[36] (consider the contrast with *The Illiad*, which depicts the exploits of personal prowess of different warriors). The only physical action that gets repeated mention in the military texts is squatting, which puts special strain on certain muscles; there is hardly anything on physical conditioning or weapons drills.

Intellectual education, of course, flourished during this period. Many schools of thought (*zhuzibaijia*, 諸子百家), including Confucianism, Daoism, and Mohism, proposed diverse ethical and political philosophies.[37] Each school of great thinkers recruited its students and pursued its own rigorous intellectual curriculum, but arguments for state-sponsored physical education are few and far between. In the case of Confucianism, there was a political shift from a military stance to a strong antiwar position, as reflected in the famous passage of *The Analects*: "Duke Ling of Wei asked Confucius about military formations. Confucius replied, 'I have heard something about the use of ritual vessels, but I have never studied military matters.' The next day he left the state."[38] The transition in Confucianism from a more physically active ideal to a more cerebral one—the more bookish kind of cultivation

[35] The commander-in-chief of Wu (吳) executed two of the king's most beloved concubine-commanders, who had disobeyed orders during military practice. The female soldiers were subsequently punctilious in following orders, and the harsh discipline led to military victory.

[36] Confucius's father furthered his career by means of great individual feats since he was a great weightlifter as well as a military commander. See Brooks and Brooks, *The Original Analects*, 268. But by the mid to late Warring States period, individual prowess came into disrepute because mass coordination was the basis of the new army. In Sunzi's *The Art of War*, the prowess ethic of the warrior had been completely replaced by the colder skills of the operations manager and intelligence chief. See Brooks's website, http://www.umass.edu/wsp/dummies/sundz/index.html.

[37] This period's intellectual legacy has dominated the philosophical, political, and social debates of East Asia to this day, much as ancient Greek philosophy has influenced Western thinking.

[38] Ames and Rosemont, *The Analects of Confucius*, 15.1 (modified). Here and elsewhere, the translations of classical Chinese have been modified to my own style and vocabulary.

represented by the classical curriculum—seems to have occurred during the Warring States period.[39] By the time of Mencius (i.e., the late Warring States period), the ideal of the exemplary person or Gentleman (*junzi*, 君子) no longer included a physical component.

However, the third leading thinker of Confucianism, Xunzi (c. 313–238 B.C.E.) did mention the physical tests used to select crack warriors in Wei:

> The Head of Wei employs fixed standards in selecting his martial soldiers. They must be able to wear the three types of personal armor, wield the twelve-stone crossbow, carry a quiver with 50 arrows on their back with a halberd placed on top of them, wear a helmet, suspend a sword from their girdle, and carry three days provisions on a forced march of a hundred *li* by noon. If they succeed in all these tests, then their family is given an exemption from certain taxes and special benefits for farmlands and buildings.[40]

The "tough-minded" Xunzi, however, downplays the ultimate importance of such tests and affirms the importance of moral education, even for soldiers. He argues, in a vein similar to "tender-minded" Mencius,[41] that the key to military victory is for soldiers to "possess the fundamental principles required for order: honoring their superiors, contentedly conforming with the regulations, and being disciplined to the utmost. If one of the feudal lords had the capacity to grasp the subtle and mysterious essence of it through true discipline, then he would become ascendant and threaten the others."[42]

The evidence for interstate physical competitions in ancient China is even more scant. Athletic performances and competitions did take place in ancient China, perhaps dating to the Warring States period.[43] In cases of heavenly sacrifices, people gathered, ate and drank with music and dance, and pursued athletic arts (*jiyi*, 技藝), including primitive

---

[39] According to the periodization of *The Analects* in *The Original Analects*, this would not have been the historical Confucius because *The Analects* was written over a period of time, and only the earliest layers come close to representing the historical Confucius. Brooks's theory about the transmission of *The Analects* remains controversial, however.

[40] *Xunzi*, trans. Knoblock, vol. 2, 15.1d, 222–23.

[41] William James contrasted the "tough-minded" Xunzi with the "tender-minded" Mencius. But see chapter 2 of this book for an interpretation of a not-so-tender Mencius.

[42] *Xunzi*, 15.d, 223–24.

[43] Benny Josef Peiser reviews the evidence for competitive sporting competitions in early China, but he argues that it is difficult to establish the precise chronology because most modern publications that trace the origins of Chinese sports such as archery, wrestling, charioteering, and soccer rely on mythological traditions and legends that have been revealed as unhistorical fabrications. Peiser, "Western Theories about the Origins of Sport in Ancient China," http://www2.umist.ac.uk/sport/peiser2.html, visited 13 November 2002, esp. 2.

wrestling (*jiaodi*, 角抵), miniature archery (*touhu*, 投壺), and an early form of soccer (*cuju*, 蹴鞠). *Cuju* in particular may have been used for military training in the Warring States period.[44] The noble classes took part in these festivals, as did common people, who engaged in some sporting competitions for the entertainment of royal and/or noble classes. The *Chunqiu Zuozhuan*, a chronicle covering the Spring and Autumn period (c. 722–481 B.C.E.), describes one physical competition between two rulers:

> The ruler of Jin was feasting with Duke Jing of Qi, and Xun Wu was master of ceremonies. When they played the game of throwing arrows into jars the ruler of Jin started first. Then Xun Wu said, "There is spirit like that of the Huai River. There is meat like a high hill. My ruler throws into the jar. He will lead the princes of all." The Duke of Jin succeeded. Then, holding up an arrow, Duke Jing of Qi said, "There is spirit like that of the Sheng River. There is meat like a wide plain. My throw is successful. My power overwhelms yours."[45]

Still, such festivals and competitions did not translate into anything like regularized Greek-style interstate sporting competitions. They seem to have been relatively ad hoc, designed partly to encourage the physical fitness of soldiers, and did not have nearly the same political import as their ancient Greek counterparts, the Olympic Games. Sports were usually noncompetitive, and when competition took place, it typically involved group rather than individual competition (wrestling is an exception). This principle was made to apply even to archery, where one might expect individual competition to be the rule. As Derk Bodde explains, "the contests were highly stylized, with the participants carrying out their successive movements to the accompaniment of music, almost as if taking part in a ballet. Elegance was apparently judged to be as important as the actual skill in hitting the mark. A significant feature was that the competition was between teams, not individuals. The shooting was done in alternate succession, first by a member of one team and then by a corresponding member of the other, until all had their chance."[46]

---

[44] See Kim, *The World History of Physical Education*, 48, and Mark Edward Lewis, *Sanctioned Violence in Early China* (Albany: State University of New York, 1990), 146–48.

[45] Yang Bojun, ed. *Chun qiu zuo zhuan* [Annotation on Spring and Autumn Zuo Zhuan], vol. 4 (Beijing: Zhonghua shuju, 1981), 1332–33.

[46] Derk Bodde, *Chinese Thought, Society, and Science: The Intellectual and Social Background of Science and Technology in Pre-modern China* (Honolulu: University of Hawaii Press, 1991), 293. Bodde does note that this account of archery in pre-imperial China draws on later sources and may have been idealized to some extent.

To the extent that physical activity was organized, in short, it was typically valued for its contribution to the morality of the group as a whole, not the physical well-being of individual participants. It is likely, however, that much physical education took place in the nonpolitical, "private"[47] realm. Ancient Chinese medicine was based on the belief that good health depended on the unobstructed flow of energy or *qi* (氣). It was held that moderate movement could help to circulate *qi* and that this kind of physical training could provide health benefits. The idea of *qi* proved to be influential in the development of martial arts, breathing exercises, and sexual practices. While this points to concern with the cultivation and preservation of the body,[48] the important point for our purposes is that these activities were not systematically promoted by the state as beneficial for people at large, in contrast to the Greek states' concern with promoting physical education for all citizens.

WHY COMPARE STATE-SPONSORED PHYSICAL EDUCATION IN THE TWO ANCIENT CIVILIZATIONS?

The justification for focusing on state-sponsored physical education in ancient Greece is obvious—ancient Greek states exhibited a concern for sponsoring physical education and sporting competitions that may have been unparalleled in world history, and the legacy of this concern is still evident today.[49] But why compare this with ancient China? Why not compare ancient Greece with ancient Rome,[50] or the Islamic world, or early modern Europe, where concern with training soldiers for warfare did not give rise to Greek-style political concern for physical education and international sporting competitions? The comparison with China may smack of the Orientalist tendency to write works on why the Chinese did not have democracy, science, capitalism, human rights, the rule

[47] I use quotes because classical Chinese philosophy did not distinguish between the private and the public. The "private" realm of the family, for Confucian thinkers, has political implications (see chap. 6, n. 28). The point here is that systematic physical education was not considered to be an important task of the state in ancient China, beyond training for soldiers.

[48] Note, however, that the use of the term "body" may be misleading in the ancient Chinese context. See David L. Hall and Roger T. Ames, *Thinking through Confucius* (Albany: State University of New York Press, 1987), 20.

[49] But for an account of the significant differences between ancient Greek athletics and modern-day sports, see Scanlon, *Eros & Greek Athletics*, 330–31.

[50] Derk Bodde does draw an interesting comparison between organized sports in ancient Greece and ancient Rome: in Rome, the prime purpose of organized sports was the amusement of the spectator rather than the physical and moral well-being of the participant (as in Greece). Bodde, *Chinese Thought, Society and Science*, 301.

of law, or whatever feature of Western civilization we decide everybody should have had. China would seem to be cast yet again as the "Great Other," fundamentally different from and by implication inferior to Western civilization.

My response is not to deny that revealing comparisons can also be drawn with other civilizations. The focus on the Warring States period in ancient China is justified partly because it shares important similarities with ancient Greece. The international context was similar: small states engaged in frequent warfare, and consequently there was great concern for the training of soldiers. Moreover, the intellectual context was similar: there were great philosophical debates about the nature of education, society, and government that set many of the parameters for subsequent debates in the respective civilizations. Yet in the case of China these similarities did not translate into substantial concern for state-sponsored physical education and international sporting competitions. Moreover, philosophical debates in ancient China tended to focus on intellectual education rather than physical education; the major schools concerned with the relationship between state and society had much to say about the role of the state in promoting moral and intellectual education, but it usually ends there. In short, it is worthwhile trying to understand why similar international conditions did not give rise to similar practices regarding state-sponsored physical education and international sporting competitions, or at least to arguments for such practices among Chinese philosophers.

Another reason to compare the two civilizations is normative, but not in the Orientalist sense of affirming the superiority of the West over the mysterious "Other." The aim here is not to praise ancient Greece for its "success" at developing state-sponsored physical education and international sporting competitions and criticize ancient China for its "failure" do so. Quite the opposite, in fact: my view is that the Greek legacy in this respect can and should be open to critique and, conversely, that there is much to learn from the ancient Chinese view on physical education that regards it primarily as a "private" matter rather than the state's concern. Moreover, as I will suggest in the conclusion, the Greek emphasis on state-sponsored sporting competitions points to larger problems with the ideal of active citizenship, with the implication that modern societies (particularly family-centered East Asian societies) should be wary about drawing inspiration from this ideal.

Let me now turn to the main argument. Why did state-sponsored physical education develop to such an extent, and assume such political importance, in ancient Greece, as compared to ancient China? There may be many reasons, but I focus on the political conditions and outlooks that underpinned the philosophy and practice of state-sponsored physical education and international sporting competitions in ancient Greece, followed by an explanation of why these factors were lacking in ancient China.

POLITICAL COMPETITION AND SPORTS COMPETITION

Ancient Greece

The city-states of ancient Greece had diverse political systems. To borrow Aristotle's classification, the main types were democracies, oligarchies, and aristocracies. These types were unstable and often changed according to the city-states' domestic and international context. Notwithstanding these political differences, the ancient Greeks also believed that Greece is one pan-Hellenic community. The Greek historian Herodotus (c. 484–425 B.C.E.) defined the Hellenic body or unity as a community of race, a community of language,[51] a community of religion, and a community of manners. These four features maintained the ancient Greek universal identity and pan-Hellenic worldview. This process of common identity formation can be illustrated with the case of religion. Each city-state had its own cast of gods and goddesses, but their purposes and characters were similar, and they gradually became integrated as pan-Hellenic gods and goddesses, such as Zeus, Apollo, Poseidon, and Aphrodite. The merging process of religion can be seen by the fact that the rebuilding of the pan-Hellenic sanctuary between the sixth and fourth centuries B.C.E. was funded by many city-states from Asia Minor to the Italian peninsula.[52] This sense of commonality or ethnic solidarity encouraged the formation of pan-Hellenic confederacies or leagues and may eventually have placed ethical limits on the pursuit of intra-Greek warfare.[53]

Still, this did not translate, at the level of either principle or political practice, into the pursuit of a unified empire. States formed temporary alliances for defense or offense against common enemies, domestic or

---

[51] But different regions spoke different dialects: see http://crystalinks.com/greeklanguage .html.

[52] See A. Jarde, *The Formation of The Greek People* (London: Routledge, 1996), 239.

[53] For example, Plato argued that inter-Greek fighting should be regarded as "civil strife" rather than "warfare," with the implication that "[O]ur citizens ought to behave in this [relatively humane] way to their enemies; though when they are fighting barbarians they should treat them as the Greeks now treat each other [i.e., brutally]." "Then let us lay it down as a law for our Guardians, that they are neither to ravage land nor burn houses." Plato, *The Republic*, 2nd ed., trans. Desmond Lee (London: Penguin Books, 1987), 471b–c. Of course, Plato was recommending rather than describing, and whether or not cultural commonality actually limited the conduct of intra-Greek warfare is a separate question.

international, but even powerful city-states like Sparta or Athens did not accomplish, or even aspire to, unification of the Greek world.[54]

The main reason for opposition to political unity lay in the concept of citizenship, which most (possibly all) city-states possessed. According to Aristotle, "it has become clear who a citizen is: as soon as a man becomes entitled to participate in office, deliberative or judicial, we deem him to be a citizen of that state; and a number of such persons large enough to secure a self-sufficient life we may, by and large, call a state."[55] Citizenship is the qualification and the duty to participate in discussion of the congress or the senate and to participate in decision making of the *polis*'s most important matters, including war and peace. However, as Aristotle shows in *The Politics*, the degree of citizens' political participation relied upon each city-state's political system or polity, and the aforementioned definition of citizenship is most compatible with democracy, which is the polity where the ruling are also the ruled.[56] Athens, of course, best instantiated the ideal of citizenship. But even Sparta, with property qualifications and therefore relatively few citizens[57] (compared to Athens), allowed for equal political participation among them.[58]

Due to the importance of citizenship, most city-states placed strict limits on the number of citizens and excluded foreigners from political participation. Although movement between city-states in ancient Greece was relatively free, most city-states rarely granted citizenship to foreigners and kept to the principle of citizenship based on both parents' citizenship. Once again, the philosophers echoed the need to maintain small states, even in an ideal Republic: " 'I suggest, therefore,' I said, 'that our Rulers might use this as the best standard for determining the size of our state and the amount of territory it needs and beyond which it should not expand.' 'What standard?' 'The state should, I think,' I replied, 'be allowed to grow so long as growth is compatible with unity, but no further.' "[59]

[54] The Pan-Hellenic league was more of a confederacy of independent states.

[55] Aristotle, *The Politics*, 1275b.

[56] Ibid., 1275a–b.

[57] Land became concentrated in fewer and fewer hands in Sparta, which led to a decline in the number of citizens. In 480 B.C.E. about 7,000 Spartans owned enough land to qualify as citizens; by 371 B.C.E. it had fallen to a couple of thousand, and by the third century B.C.E. to just a few hundred (I am grateful to Ian Morris for this information). According to Aristotle, poor Spartan citizens who could not contribute their quota to common meals were debarred from sharing in constitutional rights (ibid., 1271a).

[58] On the practice of deliberation in oligarchies, see Lloyd, *Magic, Reason and Experience*, 261.

[59] Plato, *The Republic*, 423b. In *The Laws*, Plato argued that the number of households in the state should be limited to 5,040 (737e ff). Aristotle argued that the state should not be too large because the citizens of a state must know one another's characters in order to give decisions in matters of disputed rights and to distribute the offices of government according to the merit of candidates (*The Politics*, 1326b 13).

The benefits associated with citizenship and the exclusivity of citizenship all worked to strengthen civic pride. Citizens believed that they
needed to maintain their political independence to maintain their citizenship, and consequently they fought hard against any threats to their independence. Changes to military training and practice also strengthened citizenship and civic pride. Until the eighth century B.C.E., the ancient Greek
military system was composed of heavy-armed (charioteering) aristocratic soldiers as its main force, and light-armed normal soldiers as its assistant force.[60] After the seventh century B.C.E., this system underwent
rapid change, most importantly, the introduction of hoplite, heavy-armed
infantry, which was composed of most classes. Hoplite warfare "implied
a new degree of cohesive fighting"[61] and presumed a strong sense of mutual trust among those holding the shields. In 594 B.C.E. the great Athenian reformer Solon created a new military system that imposed on every
citizen the duty to serve either in the heavy armed infantry or in the cav-
alry (for the wealthy who could afford to buy their own horses) and light
armed infantry as assistant forces. In 508 B.C.E. the regional-tied tribes
were established, and this further reinforced the new military system
based on common citizens. Every able-bodied citizen was expected to
participate in military service, and this only began to change when merce-
nary soldiers were hired in the fourth century B.C.E. Other Greek city-
states' military systems were similar to those of Athens.

Needless to say, these developments further reinforced the psychological, if not physical, boundaries between Greek city-states. Even as an
ideal, the citizens of city-states did not typically aspire to political unification among all Greek city-states[62] or formal annexation of non-Greek
speakers. The result was that city-states accepted the fact of co-existence,
whether peaceful or not.

State-sponsored sporting competitions between Greek city-states
were ways of expressing this ideal of *political difference within cultural
unity*. These competitions were meant to reflect the idea of pan-Hellenic
solidarity (illustrated most famously by the fact that interstate military

---

[60] Homer's *The Iliad* and *The Odyssey* show this military composition, with two great
charioteering soldiers (Alexandros and Menalaos) engaging in a one-on-one fight. (Homer,
The Iliad, Book 3: 325–70, 49–50). These works are retrospective, however, and may not
accurately reflect chariot warfare at the time.

[61] Simon Hornblower, "Creation and Development of Democratic Institutions in Ancient Greece," in *Democracy: The Unfinished Journey 508 BC to AD 1993*, ed. John Dunn
(Oxford: Oxford University Press, 1993), 4.

[62] This is not to deny that there were internal attempts at unification, but these did not
succeed. Pericles famously summoned every city-state's delegate to Athens for the purpose
of launching a Pan-Hellenic league based on the Athenian political system, but other city-
states rejected this overture. "Unification" was only achieved by the force of an outside
power, monarchical Macedonia.

conflicts were temporarily suspended during the Olympic Games[63]), but they were also opportunities to display the power of each city-state. Victory in athletic competitions, that is, was evidence of the state's strength and prosperity. Athletes were supposed to be motivated by patriotism and explicitly instructed to compete against athletes of other city-states: the general Pelopidas, for example, encouraged young Theban citizens "to challenge and wrestle with the Spartans" in their exercises, with the philosopher general Epaminondas inflaming them.[64] Material incentives were also invoked, without any twentieth-century qualms about amateur sports: Solon of Athens introduced a law to grant the winner of the Olympic games at Olympia 500 drachmas (equivalent to 500 lambs) and the winner of Isthmian Games at Corinth 100 drachmas.[65] In some cases, success in sporting competitions was the surest road to fame.[66] As Homer put it, "It is only right that you should be an athlete, for nothing makes a man so famous during his lifetime as what he can achieve with his hands and feet."[67]

Ancient China

The Warring States period was characterized by endless conflicts between competing states, but the states themselves were far less politically diverse[68] than their ancient Greek counterparts. All states were monarchies of some form or other,[69] and there is no evidence that they attempted

[63] There were, however, some violations of truces: see Miller, *Ancient Greek Athletics*, 219–92.

[64] See Plutarch, *Plutarch's Lives*, trans. John Driden and rev. Arthur Hugh Clough (London: Dent, 1921), Pelopidas, 438.

[65] As with contemporary athletes like Darryl Strawberry, however, "when they retire money quickly becomes a problem for them and they soon run through their funds until they have less than they started before their careers" (Galen, quoted in Miller, *Ancient Greek Athletics*, 210). In Athens, fortunately (for the athletes), each victory was also rewarded with one meal for the rest of the athlete's life, with multiple meals for multiple winners (ibid., 213).

[66] See Plutarch, *Plutarch's Lives*, Solon, 136.

[67] See Homer, *The Odyssey*, Book 8, 145–50, 110. The Phaeacian people insulted Odysseus since he refrained from demonstrating his physical ability while young competitors were racing, wrestling, jumping, throwing, and boxing in front of him. But he eventually overwhelmed those people by throwing a discus far beyond anybody else. On the ancient Greek valuation of athletic glory, see also Homer, *The Iliad*, Book 23 (Funeral Games for Patroklos).

[68] These states may have been as culturally diverse as Greek states in the Spring and Autumn era, but a process of cultural assimilation took place (including the suppression of non-Sinitic populations in the state of Lu). The increasing cultural homogeneity may partly explain (along with other factors, such as the massive resource expansion program) the growing commitment to the ideal of unification during the Warring States period.

[69] I am using the term "monarch" in the Aristotelian sense. The formal title "king" was reserved for the successor Zhou rulers.

other systems such as oligarchy or democracy. Moreover, the relatively strong states aspired to take over the rest, and this was often justified by the idea that unification that would put an end to the period of disunity and chaos.[70] As the historian Ge Jianxiong argues, "The Spring and Autumn and the Warring States period is not the process of division, but the process of integration of the highly separated political entities."[71] Other scholars argue that the balance of power politics was predominant during much of the Warring States period.[72] Still, at the very least it seems clear that states began to compete for world empire toward the end of the Warring States period. From 325 B.C.E. onward, according to E. Bruce Brooks, there was a strong sense among the governmental elites that unity achieved through conquest was the future, leaving open such details as who would be in charge of it and who would provide the master plan for it.[73] As a result of this process, the dozens of feudal states (in the Western Zhou period) gradually merged, and the multistate period was finally put to an end by the conquests of the Qin state that established the first Chinese dynasty. The Qin dynasty (221–206 B.C.E.) was significantly larger than the Western Zhou (the earlier unitary "Chinese" state that was more of an ideal than a physical reality).

The "logic of unification" was reflected in the dominant political philosophies of the time. Most notably, Legalists such as Han Fei Zi[74] argued for militarily powerful states that could control their population by means of harsh laws and punishments and successfully pursue

[70] The independent Chinese states had a cultural memory of single overlordship, namely, the Zhou situation, which could be invoked (and mythologized) as the Golden Age of peace and harmony. The Warring States thinkers, regardless of their political orientation, all drew on this memory to advocate the ideal of unified rule. Yuri Pines, "'The One That Pervades the All' in Ancient Chinese Political Thought: The Origins of the 'Great Unity' Paradigm," *T'oung Pao*, vol. 86 (2000), 280. In contrast, the earlier unified Greek phase of history, namely, Mycenaean history, was effectively blotted out in subsequent Greek history.

[71] Ge Jianxiong, *Putianzhixia* [The World under Heaven] (Jilin: Jilin jiaoyu chubanshe, 1989), 37.

[72] See Mark Edward Lewis, "Warring States Political History," in *The Cambridge History of Ancient China: From the Origins of Civilization to 221 B.C.*, ed. Michael Loewe and Edward L. Shaughnessy (Cambridge: Cambridge University Press, 1999).

[73] See also Victoria Tin-Bor Hui's paper, "Rethinking the Hobbesian Metaphor for International Politics: Comparing the Hobbesianess of the Ancient Chinese and Early Modern European Systems." Hui argues that Qin's eventual domination of other states can be explained by the relative strength of coercive mechanisms vis-à-vis countervailing mechanisms in the processes of international competition. Where coercive capabilities are more limited, as in Early Modern Europe, attempts at domination are less likely to be successful.

[74] Note, however, that the dating of the Han Fei Zi is a matter of controversy, and much of it may have been composed under the aegis of (later) Han political theorists.

wars of conquest abroad. These political realists were partly reacting to Confucian criticisms of wars of conquest.[75] Even Confucian "idealists," however, did not object to the ideal of unification; rather, they objected to the means employed. As Joseph Chan explains:

> The Confucian school of thought, as represented by Confucius, Mencius, and Xunzi, was particularly important in idealizing the order of "*tian xia*" [literally: the world under Heaven], carrying much critical, ethical import . . . the Confucian conception of "*tian xia*" refers to an ideal moral and political order admitting of no territorial boundary—the whole world to be governed by a sage according to the principles of rites (*li*, 禮) and virtues (*de*, 德). This ideal transcends the narrowness of states.[76]

This unified order, however, was to be achieved by means of "moral power," not coercion or punitive laws.[77] In short, the hope of merging all states into one giant empire with unlimited territorial boundaries was shared by defenders and critics of military expansionism alike,[78] particularly toward the end of the Warring States period. It would have been difficult, if not impossible, to officially recognize political competition between states with fixed boundaries that could underpin interstate sporting competitions like the Olympic Games, even if such competitions had been proposed. The political diversity and "logic of balance" that characterized the ancient Greek city-state system were far less prominent in the interstate system of the Warring States period.

The same is true of the other Greek component—the ideal of citizenship—that played the role of curbing the ideal, if not the practice, of unificationism in ancient Greece. None of the three elements of citizenship—equality, exclusivity, and patriotism—of Greek citizenship was widely practiced or defended in the Warring States period. Most societies were rigidly hierarchical "clan-law" (*zongfa*, 宗法) feudal societies, where the patriarch of a clan or extended family had almost complete

---

[75] See chapter 2.

[76] Joseph Chan, "Territorial Boundaries and Confucianism," in *Boundaries, Ownership, and Autonomy*, ed. David Miller and Sohail H. Hashmi (Princeton: Princeton University Press, 2001), 96. This is not to deny, however, that classical Confucians also provided practical, morally informed guidance in a nonideal political world of competing states (see chapter 2).

[77] See, e.g., *The Analects of Confucius*, 12.19, 16.1, and *The Works of Mencius*, 1A.6, 4A.4, 4A.10. 4A.14.

[78] Lao Zi's description of the ideal state—"Make your state small, make your people few"—is the obvious exception. Quoted in Roger T. Ames, *The Art of Rulership: A Study of Chinese Political Thought* (Albany: State University of New York Press, 1994), 6. See also A. C. Graham, *Disputers of the Tao: Philosophical Argument in Ancient China* (La Salle, IL: Open Court, 1989), 69–70.

authority over the members of the family.[79] Confucian critics of these societies did not argue for political participation by equal citizens; rather, the dominant Confucian view was that political legitimacy comes from the "Mandate of Heaven" (*tian ming*, 天命), an all-pervading cosmic power that secures the moral and physical order of the universe and passes judgment on the performance of rulers.[80] The workings of "Heaven" were to be partly determined by the ruler's success at providing benefits for the people—the idea of *minben* (民本)—but the people are still being ruled, unlike the ancient Greek citizen who partakes of both ruling and being ruled.[81]

Nor were Warring States societies as exclusive as Greek city-states. Unlike the ancient Greek citizens who had to protect their citizenship from others by limiting their population and excluding foreigners from political membership (they could of course be enslaved or employed as *metics* or migrant workers), these societies actively accepted and incorporated neighboring ethnic groups during the unification process. The ruling minorities were usually eager to strengthen their states' power by merging land and expanding population for more prosperous agricultural economics.

Once again, dominant political ideals reinforced this process. The idea of *tian xia*, as noted previously, meant that there are no political boundaries in an ideal world. It meant openness to other people. In contrast to the Greek restrictions on membership, anybody could be a member of the political community since the political ideal of "One Family under Heaven" (*tian xia yi jia*, 天下一家) could cover the family, the state, and the world. It also meant that one should strive to be an exemplary person regardless of the context: as *The Analects of Confucius* puts it, "Fan Chi inquired about benevolence, and the Master replied, 'At home be deferential, in handling public affairs be respectful, and loyal in your relationships. Even if you were to go and live among the Yi and Di barbarians, you could not do without such

[79] Some early Warring States societies, however, did have the functional equivalents of constraints on the power of the state—see Victoria Tin-Bor Hui, "The Emergence and Demise of Nascent Constitutional Rights: Comparing Ancient China and Early Modern Europe," *Journal of Political Philosophy*, vol. 9, no. 4 (2001). Moreover, some societies did allow for social mobility—e.g., low-ranking persons (other than slaves) could aspire to landownership, through social merit rather than paterfamilial decree.

[80] On the contrast between *tianming* and liberal democratic values, see Shi Yuankang, "Tianming yu zhengdangxing" (The Mandate of Heaven and Political Legitimacy), in *Zhengzhi lilun zai Zhongguo* (Political Theory in China), ed. Joseph Chan and Lo Manto (Hong Kong: Oxford University Press, 2001).

[81] Note that there were also non-Confucian ideas regarding the workings of Heaven in the Warring States period. Mencian ideas of Heaven are discussed here because they are closest to—yet still far apart from—the Greek idea of democracy.

an attitude.'"[82] The Greek idea that foreigners were somehow incapable of achieving human potential (and therefore could be treated worse than members of one's own ethnic group)[83] was largely absent from Warring States ethical thought.

Another feature of Greek citizenship—patriotism, or attachment to one's own geographically based political community—may not have been as prominent in Warring States societies (relative to ancient Greek states). No doubt many statesmen and soldiers were motivated by patriotic sentiments. Many commoners, however, were conscripted into service or served for instrumental reasons such as social advancement. It is interesting to note that Legalist thinkers such as Han Fei Zi—concerned primarily with devising means to strengthen the state—did not even pretend that patriotic sentiments could be manufactured. Confucian scholars, for their part, were explicitly critical that one should be attached to a particular place or political community: "The Master said, 'A scholar-apprentice who is attached to a settled home is not worthy of the name.'"[84] Instead, an exemplary person or Gentleman (*junzi*, 君子) should seek out virtuous rulers: "The Master said, 'Exemplary persons cherish virtuous rule; petty persons cherish their (native) land.'"[85] But what if the exemplary person cannot find a state that is actually governed by benevolence (*ren*, 仁) and moral power (*de*, 德)? The Confucian solution is to move to a state governed by a potentially virtuous ruler who is willing to listen to and put into practice ideas about good government.[86] If the standard account of Confucius's life is correct,[87] that is precisely what Confucius himself tried to do, thus setting an example for all subsequent Confucians.

Interestingly, changes in the military system that parallel transformations in ancient Greece led to opposite effects. During the Spring and Autumn period, the aristocracy was the main military force and was educated[88] in archery, charioteering, and other physical skills. In the War-

---

[82] *The Analects of Confucius*, trans. Ames and Rosemont, 13:19 (modified).

[83] Even moral universalists such as Plato defended such ideas (see note 53).

[84] *The Analects of Confucius*, trans. Ames and Rosemont, 14.2 (modified; Ames and Rosemont translate 居 *ju* more controversially as "wordly comforts" rather than "settled home"). See the discussion in Edward Shils, "Reflections on Civil Society and Civility in the Chinese Intellectual Tradition," in *Confucian Traditions in East Asian Modernity*, ed. Tu Wei-ming (Cambridge: Harvard University Press, 1996), 70.

[85] *The Analects of Confucius*, trans. Ames and Rosemont, 4.11 (modified). See also 4.1, 15.10, 18.2.

[86] Ibid., 18.3, 18.4; see also Mencius, 7A.32.

[87] E. Bruce Brooks has cast doubt on this standard account (see note 39), but whatever the historical facts, this ideal served to inspire subsequent Confucians (including Mencius, who moved from state to state, looking for opportunities to put his political ideals into practice).

[88] The elite military class was most likely self-educated in these skills (as opposed to being educated by the state).

ring States period, as in ancient Greece, the main force became the infantry, which was composed primarily of common people,[89] and the importance of the aristocracy in the military system decreased. As Mark Edward Lewis notes, "As for the composition of the armies, the infantry army marked the end of the dominance of the warrior nobility and the shift to a state based on the service of the peasant household."[90] Unlike ancient Greece, however, the equalization of soldiers did not occur: "However, the new pattern of service generated its own forms of social ranking, a hierarchy based on military service."[91] The *junzi*, or "exemplary persons," began to shun military service, if not express outright disdain, and the peasant infantry did not view compulsory military service as a source of pride.[92] Whereas the "democratization" of military service in ancient Greece meant that both aristocrats and common people engaged in soldiering for the state and this had the effect of increasing group solidarity, in ancient China the obligations of military service were pushed from the aristocrats onto lower classes, and this contributed, if anything, to further the stratification of society.[93]

In short, the key elements of ancient Greek citizenship that reinforced the patriotism in ancient Greek city-states and helped to inspire athletes in state-sponsored sporting competitions were either marginalized, absent, or explicitly challenged by practices and values in Warring States societies.

[89] The chariot had many defects as a fighting machine, according to H. G. Creel (*The Origin of Statecraft in China*, 262–71), which may help to explain the transition to infantry. See also Ralph D. Sawyer, *The Seven Military Classics of Ancient China* (Boulder: Westview Press, 1993), 364–65.

[90] Mark Edward Lewis, "Warring States Political History," in *The Cambridge History of Ancient China: From the Origins of Civilization to 221 B.C*, 621 (Lewis actually dates the infantry army transition to the Spring and Autumn period). In the same vein, David A. Graff notes that "the aristocratic chariot warfare of the seventh century B.C. was profoundly different from the conflicts waged by disciplined mass armies of infantry four centuries later." Graff, *Medieval Chinese Warfare, 300–900* (London: Routledge, 2002), 17. However, E. Bruce Brooks argues that we do not have enough evidence to speak of "the end of the dominance" of the warrior elite (more likely, the class or its social successors continued to provide the officer corps, and the expansion of the army, not the totality of the army, was made up of infantry of lower social status).

[91] Lewis, "Warring States Political History," 621.

[92] While military service could leave to social advancement under certain states' rules, this would be an instrumental reason for valuing military service, which is not the same as being motivated by patriotism and civic pride (as in the Greek case).

[93] In the early Warring States period, military service did arguably lead to quasi-citizenship status for the lower social orders. By the mid–Warring States period, however, the growth of autocratic states meant that there was no need for social negotiation and states could simply compel obedience, with attendant (negative) implications for the "social benefits" of military service.

COMMERCIAL SOCIETIES, LEISURE TIME,
AND THE PURSUIT OF PHYSICAL EXCELLENCE

Ancient Greece

The natural environment of ancient Greece did not readily lend itself to agriculture. The farmable land was scarce and surrounded by high mountains. The ancient Greeks thus began to search for economic alternatives to agriculture and marine commerce gradually assumed prominence in the economy of many Greek city-states. As Paul Millet states, "Trade was vital for the survival of every Greek polis."[94] When the population of states increased, the city-states did not adopt the ancient Chinese strategy of increasing agricultural capability by such means as double cropping and the use of more protein-rich plants; rather, they increased their grain imports and/or exported their citizens to colonies. By the middle of the fifth century B.C.E., the priority of marine commerce over agriculture was firmly established.[95] According to Jean Hatzfeld, "it can be estimated that about two-thirds [of the four million people who constituted the Hellenic world] lived near the sea—in eastern Sicily, Greater Greece, the gulfs of Corinth and Athens, the Cyclades, and the western shores of Asia Minor. Henceforth the economic history of Greece was to be that of her great ports: Athens, Syracuse, Rhodes, Delos, Alexandria, and Byzantium."[96] Their trade involved exchanges based on elaborate banking systems and standardized weights and measures. In times of peace, the relations between the city-states were chiefly commercial and in principle, trade was free.[97] With the development of commerce and economic prosperity, Greek citizens came to be exempted from agricultural labor.[98]

Moreover, male citizens also came to be freed from obligations to the

[94] Paul Millett, "The Economy," in *Classical Greece*, ed. Robin Osborne (Oxford: Oxford University Press, 2000), 39.

[95] Proximity to the sea also led to the development of marine warfare in ancient Greece (absent from ancient China), which in turn made the knowledge of swimming necessary for Athenians. The ability to swim well was a reason for ethnic pride, and the image of drowning enemies recurs in celebrations of victory Edith Hall, "Drowning by Nomes: The Greeks, Swimming, and Timotheus' Persians," in *The Birth of European Identity: The Europe-Asia Contrast in Greek Thought 490–322 B.C.*, ed. H. A. Khan, Nottingham Classical Literature Studies, vol. 2 (Nottingham: University of Nottingham, 1994), 44. Greek literature, however, says very little about swimming as such, most likely because it was never formally performed at public games in ancient Greece (ibid., 52).

[96] Jean Hatzfeld, *History of Ancient Greece* (New York: W. W. Norton, 1966), 121.

[97] Jarde, *The Formation of the Greek People*, 253.

[98] Slaves from the hinterlands ensured that most Greek citizens did not have to do the hard labor themselves.

oikos or household, which was seen as playing a secondary role vis-à-vis the polis or state. The realm of the household was the realm of need, where people engaged in labor to secure the basic necessities for survival. It was relevant for the public realm only to the extent that it provided the conditions for male household heads to engage in the activities of the polis. As Hannah Arendt put it, "Historically, it is very likely that the rise of the city-state and the public realm occurred at the expense of the private realm of family and household."[99]

Most male citizens therefore focused on activity in the public or political sphere, the realm of the good life. In the best of Greek times, Tracy Strong notes, "the state is the arena where people compete, both physically as in games, and, more importantly, publicly through argument."[100] Greeks viewed such competitions as allowing for human self-realization as well as bringing glory to the state.

Ancient China

The economic conditions that provided "freedom from necessity"[101] for substantial numbers were not present in China. Agriculture, not commerce, was the primary mode of production.[102] The fertile plains of China allowed for production of food and other material necessities. When production was insufficient due to increase of population, states sought to merge with neighboring lands. The great economic question in China was how to control flooding (especially from the Yellow River) and the consequent need for large-scale irrigation projects that required massive labor force mobilization. Success at this endeavor may also have contributed to political power—according to the *Shiji, Annals of the Xia Dynasty* section (*Xiabenji* 夏本記) and *Mencius* (3a:4), King Yu succeeded Shun due to his success in flood control.[103] In this type of political economy, large numbers of people were engaged in production, and it would have been difficult if not impossible for the idea of equal citizens with leisure time to develop.

Given this context, moreover, there were few if any reasons to make a distinction between the political, public realm (the state) and the private, economic realm of necessity (the household). The Greek idea that large

---

[99] Hannah Arendt, *The Human Condition* (New York: Doubleday, 1959), 27.

[100] Tracy B. Strong, *Friedrich Nietzsche and the Politics of Transfiguration*, expanded ed. (Berkeley: University of California Press, 1988), 194.

[101] Karl Marx, *Capital,* vol. 3, *in The Marx-Engels Reader*, ed. Robert Tucker (New York: W. W. Norton, 1978), 441.

[102] See Fung Yu-Lan and Derk Bodde, *A Short History of Chinese Philosophy* (New York: Macmillan, 1961), 25–27.

[103] Once again, these sources are controversial, and this particular story may be a myth.

numbers should be freed from the obligation to produce so that they would have sufficient leisure time to engage in the activities of citizenship was quite simply not a consideration. In the Warring States period, soldiers were not citizens but were typically farmers who also served as soldiers when called upon to do so. The Qin state, for example, established a peasant militia designed to build up a "rich country and strong army" (*fuguo qiangbing*, 富國強兵).[104] According to Mencius, even emperors were originally producers:[105] "Shun rose from among his channeled fields. Fu Yue was called to office from the midst of his building frames; Jiao Ge from his fish and salt; Kuanyi Wu from the hands of his jailer; Sun-shu Ao from [his retreat by] the seashore; and Bolixi from the market place."[106]

To the extent that economic and military obligations to the state were challenged, this came not from the idea that the "best and brightest" should be freed from the realm of necessity, but rather from the idea that family obligations were sometimes of prime importance. Confucian classics are replete with pronouncements and aphorisms concerning the importance of the family and the obligations attached to it, and those obligations could outweigh all other obligations, including one's obligation to obey the law (see, e.g., *The Analects*, 13.18). The family was not seen as a necessary condition for the good life, it was the good life.[107] Here the contrast with ancient Greek views is at its starkest.[108]

The point here is that the ancient Chinese, from the lower to the upper classes, did not have sufficient leisure time (freedom from economic and family obligations) to develop the idea of state responsibility for physical

[104] See Hui, "The Emergence and Demise of Nascent Constitutional Rights," 383. This was succeeded in the Han dynasty (202 B.C.E.–220 C.E.), Qin's successor, as "a farm cultivated by the militia (*tun tian zhi*, 屯田制)." (In Qin, when peasants were conscripted, they abandoned their farming activities and needed to obtain food from others, but under the new system, soldiers in remote areas also grew their own food.)

[105] Historical evidence for this claim is lacking, however.

[106] *Mencius*, 6B.15. Mencius, however, opposed the idea that rulers were expected to continue to engage in production once they assumed their political posts: "There are those who use their minds and there are those who used their muscles. The former rule; the latter are ruled. Those who rule are supported by those who are ruled" (3A.4). The context for this famous passage clearly shows that Mencius was trying to counter the view that "a good and wise ruler shares the work of tilling the land with his people" (ibid.), but unfortunately Mencius has been read to argue for a strict division of labor between intellectuals and peasants (a view that was explicitly challenged to disastrous effect during the Cultural Revolution).

[107] To be more precise, the family was seen as an important (and necessary) part of the good life.

[108] See Hahm Chaibong, "The Family vs. the Individual: The Politics of Marriage Laws in Korea," in *Confucianism for the Modern World*, ed. Daniel A. Bell and Hahm Chaibong (New York: Cambridge University Press, 2003), 337–42.

education as part of citizenship. Nor did the Chinese need to develop state-sponsored physical education designed to perfect the human body and promote excellence in state-sponsored sporting competitions. The fact that most people—including soldiers—were engaged in material production meant that they were already quite fit, and there may have been less of a need to develop a separate program of physical education designed to improve the level of fitness of soldiers (compared, once again, to ancient Greek citizen-soldiers, who typically did not engage in material production to the same extent and would not have been sufficiently fit for warfare without a separate program of physical education).

Implications for Contemporary East Asian Societies

The main aim of this chapter has been to solve an apparent puzzle. An important impetus for the development of systematic state-sponsored programs of physical education in ancient Greece lies in the fact that these programs were necessary to train soldiers and raise their overall level of fitness. The societies of the Warring States period were also characterized by small states engaged in frequent warfare and competition for material and territorial advantage, and states also promoted the training of soldiers. Yet this did not translate into state-sponsored physical education and sporting competitions to nearly the same extent. What accounts for the divergent outcomes? This chapter pointed to the relative importance of citizenship in ancient Greek states and its marginalization in the ancient Chinese context. More specifically, two factors were crucial:

1. In ancient Greece, the citizens of diverse polities fought hard to maintain their political independence, though the sense of cultural commonality allowed for international events such as sporting competitions that provided the forums for the expression of the "political difference within cultural unity" principle. In ancient China, the "logic of dominance" (especially toward the end of the Warring States period) and the principle of *tian xia* meant that there were powerful political and ideological forces in favor of unification, and it would have been difficult, if not impossible, to justify or sanction territorial boundaries between autonomous states that could engage in peaceful international competitions such as the Olympic Games.
2. In ancient Greece, the material surplus of largely commercial societies (along with material production by slaves and *metics*) and freedom from family obligations provided sufficient leisure time for a class of male citizens to perfect their human bodies and train for physical excellence. Moreover, separate physical education programs were necessary to raise the level of fitness of citizens-soldiers. In ancient China, the largely agri-

cultural political economies, and obligations to the family, did not provide sufficient leisure time for large numbers; even the rulers were occasionally expected to contribute to productive activities and family obligations. Moreover, the fact that large numbers engaged in agricultural production meant that the overall level of fitness was relatively high and there may have been less of a need (compared to ancient Greece) to raise the level of fitness of soldiers, even when commoners were called upon to do the fighting.

Given the lack of firsthand evidence and the paucity of the historical record, there is inevitably an element of speculation in our findings. Moreover, this thesis is not meant to deny that religious and philosophical differences between the two ancient civilizations also bear on the question of the development of state-sponsored physical education and international sporting competitions. Rather, the argument is that political differences played an important role in explaining the differing outcomes and the possibility that other factors may also have been important is not precluded.[109]

Let me end with some normative reflections. What seems to be most attractive about the Greek emphasis on state-sponsored physical education and sporting competitions is its tight connection with democratic citizenship. Stephen G. Miller, for example, argues that "perhaps the most important contribution of [ancient Greek athletics is] its creation of the concept of equality before the law, *isonomia*, the foundation on which democracy is based." Everyone was treated as an equal in athletic competitions, and the winners were determined according to objective criteria, with social and economic position playing no role whatsoever. This sort of equality, according to Miller, was most compatible with democratic rule, as suggested by the fact that the depiction of nude athletic scenes in Attic vase paintings "parallels the rise and fall of Athenian democracy."[110] But the idea of a meritocracy of (male) physical prowess is also compatible with nondemocratic forms of rule, in both theory and practice: contemporary (nondemocratic) China, for example, se-

---

[109] Thomas F. Scanlon has written a fascinating book on the religious and erotic dimensions of physical education in ancient Greece (*Eros & Greek Athletics*).These dimensions were not entirely separate from the political function of state-sponsored physical education— more often than not, they helped to reinforce the political function. For example, Scanlon notes that the gymnasium was the setting for institutionalized (legitimate) pederasty, and that such bonding served the purpose of the state by strengthening bonds in society at large. Those who wanted to "atomize" political society and destroy these bonds therefore attempted to close gymnasia. As Scanlon puts it, these "hotbeds of pederastic bonding" were threatening to tyrants because they could give rise to coup attempts: one "famous example of tyrannical repression of gymnasia is that of Aristodemus of Cymae (died 524) who, seeking to discourage a 'noble and manly spirit,'" closed all gymnasia and forced all youths reared in the city to dress and wear long hair in the fashion of girls" (ibid., 268).

[110] Miller, *Ancient Greek Athletics*, 232, 233.

lects the best country's best athletes from a young age according to objective criteria and makes them undergo rigorous state-sponsored physical education.

Moreover, the Greek practice of state-sponsored physical education rests on a conception of active citizenship that may be less defensible in contemporary societies. The Greek ideal of citizenship is tightly linked to the glorification of warfare and underpins a highly competitive mode of life, including macho pride in athletic rivalry. The Greek ideal can also serve to justify quasi-totalitarian control over everyday life. Even such seemingly innocuous activities as sports and physical exercise are monopolized by the state and made to serve its militaristic purposes. To the extent that modern-day societies ought to place less emphasis on military glory, this should be a cause for concern.

Conversely, the Confucian view that physical activity should be tied to the pursuit of nonmilitaristic virtues and that the test of success should be its contribution to moral and intellectual development rather than victory in international sporting competitions and warfare may be an ideal worth pursuing. This ideal, moreover, is not entirely unrealistic in contemporary societies. Mencius's account of the archer's psychological reaction to "failure"—"an archer makes sure his stance is correct before letting fly the arrow, and if he fails to hit the mark, he does not hold it against the victor. He simply seeks the cause within himself"[111]—is not dissimilar to the tennis player who graciously shakes the winner's hand after the game and pursues a rigorous self-improvement program afterwards. Confucius's account of gentleman-archer—"Exemplary persons are not competitive, but they must still compete in archery. Greeting and making way for each other, the archers ascend the hall, and returning they drink a salute. Even during competition, they are exemplary persons"[112]—echoes the rituals of sumo wrestlers.

Olympic Games in the contemporary era, unfortunately, still emphasize victory for the sake of glorifying the state.[113] States have capitalized

---

[111] *Mencius*, trans. D. C. Lau, 2A.7.

[112] *The Analects of Confucius*, trans. Ames and Rosemont, 3.7 (modified).

[113] Other contemporary sporting events can more indirectly serve the state's purposes, including glorification of war. On the parallels between American football and war, see Mandelbaum, *The Meaning of Sports*, 128–43. Mandelbaum notes that President Theodore Roosevelt "was an enthusiastic supporter of the game of football. He and other champions of war and empire in 1898 considered football valuable because it fostered precisely the qualities of character necessary for success on the battlefield, which he, like many others of his era, regarded as the supreme and necessary test of men and nations" (143). One recent exemplar was NFL player Pat Tilman, who gave up his sports career to fight for the United States in Afghanistan, where he died a "war hero" killed by "friendly fire." It is not a coincidence that professional football games in the United States open with solemn national anthems and are often characterized displays of military might and visits by war leaders and presidents.

on international sporting competitions to mobilize support for policies and obedience to rulers—a trend that was manifest in Athens in 2004 and is likely to continue in China itself for the 2008 Olympic Games. Perhaps social critics can point to political "misuses" and (re)call attention to Confucian athletic ideals. This is not to imply that the state should not seek to promote the physical fitness of citizens and soldiers. Beyond that, however, physical education and sporting competitions should not be politicized or used to trump up patriotic pride; Confucian ideals of physical education are best realized without state coercion, not to mention the pressures of corporate sponsors who exercise their own form of power.

But do these reflections on the militaristic foundation of Greek-style physical education and sporting competitions really cast doubt on the ideal of active citizenship? Contemporary defenders of civic republicanism argue that the ideal of active citizenship can be detached from the particular context of the Greek city-state and applied in contemporary liberal democratic societies. The republican conception of citizenship, as David Miller puts it, "takes the liberal conception of citizenship as a set of rights, and adds to it the idea that a citizen must be someone who thinks and behaves in a certain way. A citizen identifies with the political community to which he or she belongs, and is committed to promoting the common good through active participation in its political life."[114] Such an ideal involves replacing the city-state with the political nation as the communal attachment for humans to cherish and nourish, as well as abstracting from other "contingent" features of the Greek context such as the exploitation of slaves, women, and noncitizens. The contemporary civic republican might add that the ancient Greek practice of state-sponsored physical education designed to produce heroic soldiers can also be separated from the ideal of active citizenship.

Let us assume, for the sake of argument, that the ideal of active citizenship can be implemented in the context of the modern nation-state without its problematic ancient Greek "contingent" features.[115] Even if it is realistic, it may not be desirable. The problem is that nationalist republican citizenship threatens to overwhelm all our other communal commitments, particularly ties to the family. Republicans argue that

---

[114] David Miller, *Citizenship and National Identity* (Cambridge: Polity Press, 2000), 53.

[115] I have argued elsewhere that the ideal of republican citizenship (as formulated by David Miller) is not realistic in contemporary liberal democratic societies because there is an apparently insurmountable gap between the ideal and "actually existing" modern liberal states, and contemporary republicans do not provide any plausible mechanisms for overcoming this gap. Bell, "Is Republican Citizenship Appropriate for the Modern World?" in *Forms of Justice: Critical Perspectives on David Miller's Political Philosophy*, ed. Daniel A. Bell and Avner de-Shalit (Lanham, MD: Rowman and Littlefield, 2003).

active participation in politics is the key to the good life,[116] but is it really appropriate to condemn those who abstain from politics because they are committed, first and foremost, to family life? The republican tradition will likely seem problematic for members of modern-day liberal Western societies for whom, in Charles Taylor's words, "the affirmation of ordinary life" has assumed greater importance.[117] In East Asian societies with a Confucian heritage, where the good of the family has been regarded as the key to the good life for more than two millennia,[118] the republican tradition is so far removed from people's self-understanding that it is a complete nonstarter.[119] Most people have devoted their time and energy to family and other "local" obligations, with political decision making left to an educated, public-spirited elite.[120] Elite politics does not

[116] There is an alternative strand of republicanism that values freedom from nondomination above all and takes the main goal of the state to be the promotion of this ideal. See Philip Pettit, *Republicanism: A Theory of Freedom and Government* (Oxford: Clarendon Press, 1997). This version of republicanism is explicitly critical of the idea that the good of the state lies in active, democratic citizenship (ibid., 8) and draws on an alternative republican tradition inspired mainly by late seventeenth- and eighteenth-century English and American thinkers. These two versions of republicanism share little more than a common label, and my arguments directed against Miller's republicanism do not necessarily bear on those put forward by Pettit. Let me just make one brief observation regarding Pettit's version of republicanism. It may be appealing in Western countries, but the emphasis on assertion and open contestation will not resonate as much in East Asian cultures that value harmony, humility, and deference.

[117] See Charles Taylor, *Sources of the Self: The Making of the Modern Identity* (Cambridge: Harvard University Press, 1989), part 3.

[118] I do not mean to deny that the ideal of family life has been challenged in Chinese history: the Cultural Revolution, most obviously, sought to substitute attachment to the family with attachment to the state. But such experiences have proven to be short-lived (ten years, in the case of the Cultural Revolution, short by Chinese historical standards) and have been subsequently regarded as temporary periods of collective insanity.

[119] Nor do I mean to deny that some East Asian intellectuals have put forward political ideals similar to republican ideals of active citizenship: Sun Yat-sen, for example, defended democracy on the grounds that it can help to energize the people and mobilize their force for the sake of building up the nation's economic and social power. Sun, *Selected Writings of Sun Yat-sen*, ed. J. L. Wei, R. H. Myers, and D. G. Gillin (Stanford: Hoover Institution Press, 1994), 130–31. Such ideals owed more to the desire to build up the nation so that it could stand up to foreign imperialists than to the desire to restore Athenian-like active citizenship. More pertinently, the republican ideal was never implemented, and it was abandoned as an ideal once it turned out that Leninist/Legalist centralism was a more efficient way to build up national power.

[120] It is interesting to note that Li Qiang, one of China's leading political theorists, has written an essay that praises republicanism for its emphasis on "aristocratic" decision making that checks popular will ("The Lessons of Western Classical Republicanism for Constitutional Democracy in China," paper presented at the International Conference on Justice, Community, and Democracy, Tsinghua University, Beijing, 14–17 October 2003). Contemporary Anglo-American political theorists such as David Miller and Michael Sandel appeal to this tradition for the opposite reason, viz., to empower the people against an elite.

rule out democratic participation by ordinary citizens, but democracy will take "minimal" forms, not much more demanding than visiting the voting booth every few years. The following chapter points to the Confucian underpinnings of elite politics in East Asia and sketches an ideal that reconciles minimal democracy with elite politics and helps to remedy some of the flaws of "actually existing" elite rule.

6

Taking Elitism Seriously: Democracy with Confucian Characteristics

IN THE EYES of Singapore elder statesman Lee Kuan Yew, a "Confucianist view of order between subject and ruler helps in the rapid transformation of society . . . in other words, you fit yourself into society—the exact opposite of the American rights of the individual."[1] A modern Confucian society ruled by wise and virtuous elites, that is, can provide the benefits of rapid economic growth and social peace, but it must sacrifice the democratic political rights that make government so difficult in the West. A leading American political scientist, Samuel Huntington, puts it more bluntly: a Confucian democracy is a "contradiction in terms."[2] For a society reflecting on its political future, the possibilities seem to come down to two options: either Western democracy or Confucian authoritarianism.[3]

Let us instead imagine that Western and Confucian political values need not be fundamentally incompatible. It is rather tempting, in fact, to conceive of the possibility of reconciling the Confucian emphasis on rule by wise and virtuous elites with the democratic values of popular participation, accountability, and transparency. But this is easier said than done. What are the political institutions of a modern Confucian democracy? Either elected politicians rule, or an educated elite rules, but how can both rule in the same society? This chapter proposes an answer to this dilemma: a bicameral legislature with a democratically elected lower house and an upper house composed of representatives selected on the basis of competitive examinations.[4] But first let me develop the argument that modern democratic regimes have an interest in accommodating elite rule.

[1] Quoted in *The Economist*, 9 December 1995, 12.

[2] Quoted in Sor-Hoon Tan, *Confucian Democracy: A Deweyean Construction* (Albany: State University of New York Press, 2003), 6.

[3] For more positive assessments of the compatibility of Confucian and democratic values, see ibid.; Brooke A. Ackerly, "Is Liberalism the Only Way toward Democracy?" *Political Theory*, vol. 33, no. 4 (August 2005), 547–76; and Shaun O'Dwyer, "Democracy and Confucian Values," *Philosophy East and West*, vol. 53, no. 1 (January 2003), 39–63. The above sources lack detailed institutional prescriptions, and that is what I have tried to provide in this chapter.

[4] I have put forward this proposal in earlier essays, the latest incarnation of which appeared as chapter 5 of my book, *East Meets West*. However, I have substantially revised my views, and the current version is meant to override any areas of conflict. I have also updated the proposal: my essay in *East Meets West* was set in the year 2007, on the assumption that there would be a constitutional convention in China by that date where such proposals could be discussed, and I freely confess that my view was wildly optimistic!

POLITICAL ELITISM AND DEMOCRACY: TWO IMPORTANT VALUES

A Confucian Tradition of Respect for a Ruling Educated Elite

A basic assumption of Confucian ethics of special relevance to those successful in a meritocratic educational system is that the highest human good lies in public service:

> Zilu asked about exemplary persons. The master replied, "They cultivate themselves in order to be respectful." "Is that all?" asked Zilu. "They cultivate themselves in order to bring peace to their peers." "Is that all?" asked Zilu. "They cultivate themselves in order to bring peace to the common people. Even a Yao or a Shun [exemplary rulers of the past] would find such a task daunting."[5]

In contrast to Plato's philosopher rulers, burdened with the task of public duty among unenlightened "cave-dwellers," and to Aristotle's idea that intellectual contemplation is the highest pleasure, and to "the prophets of Israel and the West, who appear to be more free standing and less professionally committed to such secular functions,"[6] Confucius's superior individuals achieve complete self-realization in their public vocation.[7]

Only ethical and intellectual elites have a vocation to lead society, it is important to note, as the bulk of persons are not thought capable of exercising such initiative.[8] Confucius does speak of "teaching" the people,[9] but Benjamin Schwartz points out that what they are taught "is presumably no more than the rudiments of family relationships. They are hardly in a position to achieve the extensive cultivation required for the achievement of full self-realization, and it is obvious that only those in public service can do anything substantial to order human society."[10]

---

[5] *The Analects of Confucius*, trans. Ames and Rosemont, 14.42 (modified).

[6] Wm. Theodore de Bary, "The Trouble with Confucianism," *Institute of East Asian Philosophies (Singapore) Public Lecture Series*, no. 13 (1989), 16.

[7] Two books have cast doubt on the idea that Confucius himself valued public-spirited service as life's highest goal: Brooks and Brooks, *The Original Analects:* and Robert Eno, *The Confucian Creation of Heaven* (Albany: State University of New York Press, 1990), esp. chap. 2. Whatever the truth of these (controversial) arguments, what matters here is that the public-spirited service message has been the dominant interpretation of Confucianism transmitted over the past two thousand years. The importance of public service is reflected in the particularities of the Chinese language: for example, the term *guanyin* 官癮 means "strong desire for public office."

[8] See *The Analects of Confucius*, 8.9, 12.19, and 16.9.

[9] Ibid., 13.9.

[10] Benjamin Schwartz, "Some Polarities in Confucian Thought," in *Confucianism in Action*, ed. D. Nevinson (Stanford: Stanford University Press, 1960), 53. On the different ethics for scholars and for ordinary people, see Kwang-Kuo Hwang, "The Deep Structure of Confucianism: A Social Psychological Approach," *Asian Philosophy*, vol. 11, no. 3 (2001), 179–204.

In short, only those who acquire knowledge and virtue ought to participate in government, and the common people are not presumed to possess the capacities necessary for substantial political participation. This brand of political elitism does not differentiate Confucianism from, say, Plato's views in *The Republic*. But Confucian societies *institutionalized* a stable mechanism capable of producing at least on occasion what was widely seen as a "government of the best and brightest": China's famous two-thousand-year-old meritocratic civil service examination system. Entry to the civil service through competitive examination was open to all males, with a few exceptions, and those who eventually succeeded in passing (often having to undertake half a lifetime to do so) were thought to be in sole possession of the moral and intellectual qualities necessary for public service. Put differently, scholar-officials proved their ability by succeeding in a fair and open examination system, as opposed to merely arguing in favor of their superior virtue in political theory texts, universities, churches, and so on, and consequently they were granted uncommon (by Western standards)[11] amounts of legitimacy, respect, and authority.[12] There are countless stories in Chinese folklore about talented and hard-working young men from poor rural villages who "made it" to the Beijing bureaucracy via successful examinations.

Contemporary Manifestations of Confucian Meritocracy in East Asia

According to Tu Wei-ming, "the Confucian scholar-official mentality still functions in the psychocultural construct of East Asian societies."[13]

---

[11] Also by the standards of some Asian societies that have not been influenced by Confucianism. For example, the Hmong are known to hold bureaucrats in low esteem, as expressed in the proverb, "To see a tiger is to die; to see an official is to become destitute" (quoted in Fadiman, *The Spirit Catches You and You Fall Down*, 184).

[12] In the Yuan dynasty (ruled by Mongols, who showed their "civility" by reestablishing the civil service examination system), even Buddhist monks had to "prove" their worth by passing examinations that tested for knowledge of texts. This led to a protest by a Chan (Zen) master who adhered to the view that religious truths could not be tested in words and that it is impossible to state who has the final authority to interpret scripture. Wm. Theodore de Bary explains how both sides reached a compromise: "In a face-saving formula that one would think could only come out of a comic opera, or perhaps from the wildly whimsical Ming novel, *A Journey to the West* [or perhaps from a contemporary university prone to grade inflation], it was agreed that 'the examination would take place, but no candidates would fail.'" de Bary, *Nobility and Civility: Asian Ideals of Leadership and the Common Good* (Cambridge: Harvard University Press, 2004), 55.

[13] Tu, *Confucian Traditions in East Asian Modernity*, 7.

This is not to deny that the Chinese Communist Party did its best to eradicate the Confucian political value of rule by intellectual elites during the Cultural Revolution.[14] For ten years, politics was driven by the slogan "better red than expert," although ideology began to take a back seat to considerations of talent and expertise with the advent of economic reform. Communist Party leaders are now more likely to be Tsinghua graduates than old revolutionary cadres. Most parents dream of sending their kids to the top universities,[15] and even such seemingly "trivial" debates as revising the appointment system for young professors at Beijing University generate intense public interest.[16] The competitive examination system is rigorously implemented at all levels of education, from primary school[17] to university,[18] including doctoral

[14] The Chinese Communist Party may have been inspired by the Legalist tradition of antipathy to intellectuals. On the continuity between PRC official Marxism-Leninism-Maoism and the Legalist (and Legalized Confucianism) autocratic tradition in China, see Zhengyuan Fu, *Autocratic Tradition and Chinese Politics* (Cambridge: Cambridge University Press, 1993). Others have argued that Maoist ideology and practice owed much to Confucianism, whatever the official rhetoric (see de Bary, *Nobility and Civility*, 211–16). Whatever the truth of these interpretations, there is no doubt that Confucian studies are now back in official favor. For example, the government has provided substantial funding for a Confucian institute in Qufu (Confucius's hometown). The institute has been visited by Jiang Zemin and other Communist Party leaders, and it has two rather contrasting exhibits: a collection of Mao badges, and a photographic account of Confucian studies around the world (information gathered during my own visit and lecture at this institute, February 2005).

[15] Of course, the same may be true in non-Confucian societies such as the United States. What really differentiates societies with a Confucian heritage is that all classes of society (not just the educated bourgeoisie) expose their children to a rigorous work and educational ethic at home and school. One anecdote: our regular taxi driver in Beijing reads the Confucius's *Analects* during her breaks and makes her ten-year-old child memorize two passages per day.

[16] Xu Jilin, "Yi ci bu zijue de minzhu shijian: Beida gaige yu shangyixing minzhu" [A Democratic Practice That Wasn't Self-Consciously Implemented], paper presented at the International Conference on Deliberative Democracy and Chinese Practice of Participatory and Deliberative Institutions, 18–21 November 2004, Hangzhou, China. An English version of this paper will be published as "Reforming Peking University: A Window into Deliberative Democracy?" in *The Search for Deliberative Democracy in China*, ed. Ethan J. Leib and Baogang He (New York: Palgrave Macmillan, 2006). Xu argues that the extensive public debate regarding the proposed Beijing University appointment system reform was an urban form of deliberative democracy in China (most papers at this conference discussed deliberative democracy in rural settings).

[17] My son currently (early 2006) attends the public primary school attached to Tsinghua University, and I was vividly made aware of the importance of the examination system when I was called in, along with the parents of my son's classmates, to sit in class (at my son's desk) and review the midterm examination, question by question. I hadn't felt so nervous in about thirty years!

[18] The whole country is mobilized for the university entrance examinations. My colleagues with university-age children let me know several weeks beforehand that they

studies.[19] Those who want to join the civil service also have to take competitive exams.[20]

Contemporary manifestations of Confucian political elitism are perhaps more evident in East Asian societies fortunate enough not to have experienced a full-scale "cultural revolution." In Japan, for example, the top candidates of the nationwide preuniversity examination system enter the Law Faculty at Tokyo University, and upon graduation they obtain posts with the most prestigious government ministries.[21] The political system then empowers them to make most of their nation's policy, and they effectively answer to no one, including the nation's elected politicians.[22] In Korea, the system is not dissimilar, with Seoul National University's law faculty as the stepping-stone to important government posts. In Singapore, the top graduates from the National University compete not for prime jobs in the private sector but rather for the best

---

would not be available for academic seminars because they had to help their children prepare for the examinations. During examination week (8–10 June 2005), there was no construction work around examination sites, and the government even provided emergency vehicles for students unlucky enough to be stuck in Beijing's notorious traffic jams.

[19] The prospective doctoral candidate in political theory at Beijing University needs to pass examinations in political theory, English, and Marxism, and slots are allocated strictly in accordance with examination performance. It might seem like a rigid system, but the alternatives may be worse: one political theorist friend told me that without this system, he would face pressure from colleagues, administrators, and political cadres to relax the admission criteria for their children. Now he can just point to the examination system and tell them, "*meiyou banfa*" (there's no way [I can help]).

[20] Examinations are also administered in a surprisingly (for a Westerner) wide range of activities in everyday life in China. Three examples: (1) I had to pass an exam to have the right to swim in the deep end of the Tsinghua University swimming pool; (2) the management of several Beijing restaurants administers English-language exams to waitresses and waiters, and their salary is pegged to their examination scores; and (3) senior management in a Goldman Sachs joint venture had to pass an exam to participate in China's securities market.

[21] The debates at the time of the Meiji Restoration and the early twentieth century set the tone for subsequent political developments. Even staunch defenders of parliamentary democracy, such as Yoshino Sakuzo, insisted on "the essential leadership of an educated (not a social) elite, and the need for such leaders both to exemplify and to inculcate in the people at large the public virtues essential to the workings of any government, on any level" (de Bary, *Nobility and Civility*, 186).

[22] I do not mean to imply that the phenomenon of powerful civil servants overriding the wishes of elected politicians is distinctive to the East Asian region (though it may be more prevalent there than elsewhere). This kind of phenomenon in the UK context was famously satirized in the television show "Yes, Minister." The show itself, interestingly enough, influenced reality and made politicians more suspicious of the maneuverings of civil servants. One high-ranking Canadian civil servant told me that in conversation with an elected member of the Cabinet, he inadvertently said, "Yes, Minister." The minister angrily replied, "Don't you play that one on me!" (conversation with high-ranking Canadian civil servant during Canadian Prime Minister Paul Martin's visit to Beijing, 21 January 2005).

posts in the civil service. Those who scored highest on their "A levels" are given government scholarships to study abroad at top American and British universities, and when they return to Singapore they are almost immediately given responsible positions in the public sector. As a condition of having accepted the scholarship, they are under a legal obligation to work for the government for a minimum of six years. In Hong Kong, the top graduates compete to be "administrative officers" (AOs) in the civil service, high-paying posts that provide opportunities for rapid upward mobility within the bureaucracy.

The Importance of Rule by an Educated Elite in Modern Societies

It can be argued more generally that the "rule of the wise" is distinctly appropriate for "knowledge-based" contemporary societies. Economic, political, and legal issues have become so complex that most elected leaders—not to mention ordinary citizens—cannot even begin to make sound and effective judgments. The sheer complexity of public affairs, in other words, means that a substantial amount of decision-making power must be placed in the hands of an intellectually agile elite, almost as a functional requirement of modern political societies. More than ever before, there is a pressing need for "brains" in government.

But not just any kind of brain. Today's decision makers must also show an ability to adapt quickly to new circumstances in a rapidly changing modern world. Far from being narrow, highly specialized experts, policy makers should be sufficiently wide-ranging and innovative to propose and implement original solutions to new problems. This is recognized by some East Asian political systems. In Japan, top law graduates from Tokyo University are appointed to make political decisions not in law, but rather in such fields as finance and international affairs. The assumption seems to be that "the best and the brightest" can learn on the job, transferring their brain power from one area to another.[23] In Singapore, the ruling People's Action Party favors high-level officials and ministers who have a "helicopter view," meaning that they can detach themselves from nitty-gritty policy details to focus on the big picture, put issues in their overall social and political context, and anticipate the likely impact of a changing environment. In Hong Kong, the AOs are generalists, and they change departments every five years or so. The assumption is that they need to be broad-minded and wide-ranging, spotting new trends in different areas and adapting to new situations.

---

[23] The institutional origins of the preference for generalists can be traced to the Meiji era (late nineteenth century). See Ezra Vogel, "Japan: Adaptive Communitarianism," in *Ideology and National Competitiveness: An Analysis of Nine Countries*, ed. George C. Lodge and Ezra F. Vogel, (Boston: Harvard Business School Press, 1987), 150–53.

The political systems of Western countries also recognize the need to identify wise and broad-minded decision makers. In France, students compete for entry to the Ecole Nationale d'Administration, and successful graduates are subsequently empowered to make decisions in the political and business worlds, often moving back and forth between the private and the public sectors. In the United States, however, it is mainly prestigious (and high-paying) firms in the private sector that draw on academically successful individuals with the ability to move from one domain to another and to develop the required skills on the job. The leading business consultancy firm, McKenzie and Co., offers jobs to all Rhodes Scholars who apply, no experience necessary. Once employed, consultants at McKenzie use their talent to help resolve different kinds of problems in the business world. Investment firms like Goldman Sachs hire Ph.D.s from top universities in fields completely unrelated to banking (e.g., physics), once again on the assumption that real talent is not narrow but rather transferable from one domain to another.

Economic and political decisions in the modern world can sometimes cause serious long-term damage to the environment and the economic prospects of future generations, so political rulers must also consider the long-term consequences of present-day decisions. This may entail limiting the power of elected politicians beholden to particular constituencies and strengthening the autonomy of unelected decision makers.[24] In the United States, the Federal Reserve Board, composed largely of successful academics, has a greater say in managing the macro economy than either the president or Congress. This secretive institution is explicitly insulated against interference by elected politicians, on the grounds that it must have the power to take tough economic decisions that benefit the country in the long run. For example, the Fed sometimes increases interest rates so as to ward off inflation, even if this means increasing unemployment. A more responsive central bank may not be able to act against the wishes of politicians who might find it in their interest to combat unemployment, whatever the long-term consequences. There seems to be an implicit understanding that elite, unresponsive decision making is essential to the successful conduct of monetary policy, and that most elected politicians have

---

[24] The forging of bureaucratic autonomy need not grow at the expense of democratic participation in the early stages, but eventually bureaucratic agencies develop reputations that allow them to act against the initial preferences of elected politicians. On the U.S. case, see Daniel P. Carpenter, *The Forging of Bureaucratic Autonomy: Reputations, Networks, and Policy Innovation in Executive Agencies* (Princeton: Princeton University Press, 2001).

neither the competence nor the political will to make sound economic decisions.[25]

It is also important to protect unpopular individuals and vulnerable minorities from the decisions of democratic majorities,[26] which may mean empowering an educated elite to look after their interests. One antidemocratic device is the constitutional Bill of Rights enforced by nonelected judges holding final powers of review. The U.S. Supreme Court, for example, has the power to override the decisions of elected politicians said to violate the U.S. Constitution.[27]

Political decision makers, needless to say, must also show a certain moral sensibility. They should be public-spirited and sensitive to the effects on their decisions on those who bear the consequences. This includes not just citizens, but also noncitizens affected by particular policies, such as

[25] See, e.g., John Cassidy, "Fleeing the Fed," *The New Yorker*, 19 February 1996, 45–46. The title of this article refers to Alan Blinder, who is supposed to have "fled the Fed" due to differences over the lack of transparency and accountability at the central bank, but it is interesting to note that Blinder himself has since written an article extolling the virtues of the Fed and arguing for the need to extend such "apolitical" decision-making bodies to other domains. Blinder, "Is Government Too Political?" *Foreign Affairs* vol. 76, no. 4 (November/December 1997). At the other extreme, an editorial in the Mexican newspaper *La Jornada* praises the Uruguayan people for overturning, by means of a popular referendum, a law that would have allowed for privatization of the oil sector. "Uruguay: No a la Privatizadores," *La Jornada*, 8 December 2003, 2. Are "the people" really capable of making informed decisions regarding the costs and benefits of privatizing the oil industry?

[26] In Hong Kong, even leaders of the prodemocracy camp worry that "full" democracy (i.e., the introduction of universal suffrage) may result in fewer protections for (unpopular) minorities such as gay groups. Keith Bradsher, "As China Considers Hong Kong Democracy, Advocates Are Split," *The New York Times*, 6 April 2004, A9.

[27] Ronald Dworkin argues that the "antimajoritarian" Supreme Court *is* democratic (as opposed to acting as a constraint on the decisions of elected majorities), not simply because the people have the ultimate power of being able to override a court decision by amending the Constitution, but also because people realize that the majority needs to be restrained in certain circumstances and so support the Supreme Court and its role as constitutional watchdog. Dworkin, *Freedom's Law* (Cambridge: Harvard University Press, 1996). Dworkin can make this move because he defines democracy not as decision making by elected politicians but rather as decision making that treats "all members of the community, as individuals, with equal concern and respect," but he provides no reason(s) to support the claim that this "alternate account of the aim of democracy . . . demands much the same structure of government as the majoritarian premise does" (17). If less-than-democratic institutions composed of unelected decision makers can feasibly do a better job at treating people with equal concern and respect compared to political institutions composed of elected politicians, then Dworkin should endorse the former. In my view, Dworkin should state that he is really talking about justice, not democracy, and that he would favor more constraints on the powers of democratically elected politicians if this can achieve the end of securing more justice. Admittedly, such an argument would be politically counterproductive in the antielitist American context.

farmers in Third World countries impoverished by agricultural subsidies in rich countries. Taking into account the interests of noncitizens is problematic for decision makers who owe their political lives to particular constituents.

To sum up, political decision makers in contemporary societies should be intelligent, adaptable, long-term minded, and public-spirited—traits not all that different from the traditional virtues of Confucian exemplary persons. Of course, one key difference with traditional Confucian ideas about exemplary persons is that women should not be excluded, de jure or de facto, from political posts in modern societies.[28]

The Need for Democracy

Just as modern societies need to empower "the wise," there is an equally profound need to institutionalize the democratic virtues of accountability,

---

[28] Another key difference is that traditional Confucian views prioritized family obligations over public ones in cases of conflict, for ordinary persons as well as public officials. Confucius (in)famously argued that the care owed to elderly parents could justify breaking the law: "The Duke of She told Confucius, 'In my country there is a man called Upright Kung. When his father stole a sheep, he bore witness against him.' Confucius said, 'In my country, the upright men are different from this. A father covers up for his son, and a son covers for his father. Uprightness lies in this.'" The Analects of Confucius, trans. Arthur Waley (London: Allen & Unwin, 1938), 13.18 (modified). But this may just mean that the family members should not be forced to incriminate each other, which is not very different from the "Western-style" immunity that protects spouses from testifying against each other in court (though the Confucian justification would appeal to the central value of filial piety rather than intimacy, and the Confucian immunity would refer primarily to the relationship between adult children and their elderly parents rather than between spouses). Mencius's idea of an exemplary ruler showing care for his murderous father may be more problematic: "He would have secretly carried the old man on his back and fled to the edge of the Sea and lived there happily, completely forgetting about the Empire" (7A.35; I have modified the translation in D. C. Lau's Mencius: Volume One). But this advice is not meant to be taken literally (there are more efficient modes of transport than carrying a person on one's back). Perhaps Mencius meant to say that public officials should resign from their posts if close family members have committed serious crimes (for one thing, they would lose much of their moral authority, and governing would be more difficult). I have argued elsewhere that the Confucian view regarding the priority of family over public responsibilities may in fact have some advantages compared to the (opposite) liberal view in "Does Liberal Justice Really Work? A Critical Perspective on the Liberal Aspiration to Prioritize Public over Private Commitments," translated into Chinese by Zhang Qixian, in Gong si lingyu xin tao: Dongya yu xifang guandian zhi bijiao [Exploring the New Relationship between the Public and the Private: East Asian Perspectives in Comparison with Western Views], ed. Jiang Yihua and Huang Junjie (Taipei: Taida chuban zhongxin, 2005), 243–78. In any case, what's clear is that the central preoccupation of Confucian political theory has been the tension between obligations to the family and the state, not between the sacred and the secular. See Hahm Chaibong, "The Ironies of Confucianism," Journal of Democracy, vol. 15, no. 3 (July 2004), 4 (Internet version).

transparency, and equal political participation. Recent incidents in Japan, for example, have exposed the dangers of granting excessive power to unelected bureaucrats. The Ministry of Finance has been accused of prolonging, if not causing, Japan's crippling economic crisis in the 1990s.[29] Bureaucrats at the Health Ministry resisted allowing imports of sterilized blood until 1985, well after they had been told of the risks of HIV contamination. As a result, several hundred Japanese hemophiliacs died from AIDS.[30]

The drawbacks of "Confucian authoritarianism" are even more evident in Singapore. Singapore is nominally democratic, but opposition candidates face retaliation in the form of bankruptcy, humiliation, and exile, with the result that few qualified individuals dare to contest the ruling People's Action Party (PAP) at election time. In between elections, the government employs harsh measures against professionals and religious organizations critical of its policies. The predictable consequence is a pervasive atmosphere of fear in the country, as well as implicit encouragement for antisocial, narrowly self-interested behavior.[31]

Even societies that secure civil liberties, however, may benefit from political participation in the form of universal suffrage. Consider the case of Hong Kong. In 1985 the government of Hong Kong decided to institute elections for a number of seats in order to represent more authoritatively the views of the Hong Kong people, but it disparaged the idea of direct elections by universal suffrage on the grounds that it might lead to political instability at a crucial time. The solution was to award the largest block of seats in the legislative assembly to functional constituencies based on various interest groups, primarily business groups and professional associations. This system, however, is severely flawed. Most functional constituency representatives are explicitly instructed to serve their interest groups rather than vote for the common good, with the result that the richest and most privileged sectors of the community have a disproportionate influence over the political process.[32] Functional constituency representatives from the business sector explicitly question the value of direct elections on the grounds that prodemocracy politicians would stand up for workers' rights and turn Hong Kong into a welfare state, with the consequence that businesspeople "will simply leave and

[29] See Peter Hartcher, *The Ministry: How Japan's Most Powerful Institution Endangers World Markets* (Boston: Harvard Business School Press, 1998).

[30] See Sheryl WuDunn, "Japan's Bureaucrats Fumble Away the Traditional Center of Power," *International Herald Tribune*, 7 May 1996, 4.

[31] See my book, *East Meets West*, part II.

[32] See Norman Miners, *The Government and Politics of Hong Hong*, 5th ed. (Hong Kong: Oxford University Press, 1995), 111–17.

pick another place to do business."[33] Not surprisingly, functional constituencies never did gain much legitimacy in the population at large. Polls show that most Hong Kongers want the right to vote, and political parties that favor extending the franchise tend to fare well given the opportunity to compete for seats in the legislative assembly.[34]

Modern societies, in short, face the challenge of combining dual commitments to democracy and decision making by talented and public-spirited elites. More specifically in the East Asian context, societies must try to reconcile rule by "Confucian" exemplary persons with democratic values and practices.

INSTITUTIONALIZING CONFUCIAN DEMOCRACY

Voting for the Wise?

A Western democrat might favor letting "the people" decide. The idea here is that ordinary citizens can be trusted to make sensible choices as to capable rulers. If people want "Confucian" political rulers of talent and integrity, they will vote for them at election time.

The problem with this view, however, is that politicians often get elected by pandering to the short-term interests of the populace. In industrialized countries, voters frequently vote with their pocketbooks, even if they impose economic burdens on their children and grandchildren.[35] In poor countries, it may be easier to get elected by promising to provide the conditions for rapid economic development, regardless of the ecological costs for future generations. Politicians will thus feel

[33] James Tien (representative of the Hong Kong General Chamber of Commerce in the legislature), quoted in Jimmy Cheung, "Firms May Baulk at Direct Elections, Warns James Tien," South China Morning Post, 4 August 2003, A3.

[34] On 4 December 2005, about eighty thousand people took to the streets in a peaceful demonstration for universal suffrage.

[35] I do not mean to imply that "actually existing majorities" inevitably get their economic preferences realized via the democratic process because the rich tend to have disproportionate influence, particularly in democratic systems that do not place substantial restrictions on campaign finance. An oft-expressed cynical view is that the U.S. political system should be described as "one dollar, one vote" rather than "one person, one vote." In fact, this view may not be sufficiently cynical because the cost of being elected to high electoral office in the United States is often higher than one dollar per vote. The giant gap between the ideal and the reality of representative democracy helps to explain why the U.S. Congress—in principle, the most representative of political institutions—scores at the bottom of most surveys asking Americans which institutions they most respect, whereas the Supreme Court, the armed forces, and the Federal Reserve system (all appointed rather than elected bodies) score highest. Fareed Zakaria, The Future of Freedom: Illiberal Democracy at Home and Abroad (New York: W.W. Norton, 2003), 248.

constrained by the need to accommodate the interests of particular, present-day constituencies even if it conflicts with their view of common good.

Perhaps the situation is different in East Asia. Ordinary people seem to have imbibed the Confucian ethic of respect and deference toward educated elites, which may lead one to expect that voters will choose talented and public-spirited politicians. In China, there is a long tradition of student-led protests for political change that have inspired mass followings: the latest example is the May–June 1989 prodemocracy movement in Beijing, where more than one million ordinary citizens participated in a protest led and organized by students from China's most prestigious universities. The fact that candidates for national political office in Singapore, South Korea, and Taiwan often flaunt their educational qualifications, apparently with the hope that people are more inclined vote for a ruler with a Ph.D. from a prestigious university, also suggests that East Asians place special emphasis upon educational achievements as a qualification for ruling. Overall, however, the situation in East Asia is not encouraging. In Japan, voters appear to be swayed primarily by short-term material benefits, and most political talent finds its way to the bureaucracy rather than the legislature. In Taiwan, voters appear to be swayed by emotional appeals to parochial forms of identity (see the following chapter). In Korea, regional identities carry more electoral weight than substantive policy differences. Even supposing that voters are motivated by a desire to identify "Confucian" political rulers, they may not be able to identify such men and women during the course of a free-for-all political fest held every four or five years. In the case of China, even political dissidents "have expressed only horror at a democratic formula that would give equal voting rights to peasants."[36] The assumption seems to be that China's problems—overpopulation, pollution, increasing economic inequality, a risk of civil war—are so severe that many reformers are nervous about granting too much power to relatively uneducated rural people.

In short, political rulers chosen on the basis of Western-style democratic elections may lack both the motivation and the competence to make sound political judgments.

---

[36] Vivienne Shue, "China: Transition Postponed?" *Problems of Communism*, vol. 41, nos. 1–2 (January–April 1992), 163. In a survey of proposals for political reform in China, Andrew Nathan notes that he is "not aware of any proposal to move to one-man-one-vote." The possibility of a farmer-dominated legislature has led some reformers to endorse the current system of malapportionment, which favors urban over rural voters. "China's Constitutionalist Option," *Journal of Democracy*, vol. 7, no. 4 (October 1996), 48.

Huang Zongxi's Proposal for a Parliament of Scholar-Officials

Huang Zongxi, a seventeenth-century Confucian scholar, proposed a different mechanism for choosing political rulers with "Confucian" virtues. Huang's book, *Waiting for the Dawn: A Plan for the Prince*, is a radical attack on despotic government. As Huang put it in chapter 1, "In ancient times, the people were considered the master, and the ruler was the tenant. The ruler spent his whole life working for the people. Now the ruler is the master, and the people are tenants. That no one can find peace and happiness anywhere is all on account of the ruler."[37]

The dynastic system, in Huang's view, was not to be reformed merely by finding a virtuous ruler of exemplary character with the will to implement good policies. Unlike most Confucians, Huang argued for specific laws and institutions designed to curb imperial power, such as the establishment of a strong prime minister and relatively powerful ministers.

Huang's proposal to strengthen the political role of the schools for the training of Confucian scholar-officials is particularly relevant. Schools of all levels, in Huang's view, should serve as forums for open public discussion. He noted that during the Eastern Han (25–220), scholars at the Imperial College, the top school for the training of scholar-officials, engaged in outspoken discussion of important issues without fear of those in power, and the highest officials were anxious to avoid their censure. Moreover, Huang proposed that the rector of the Imperial College, to be chosen from among the great scholars of the day, should be equal in importance to the prime minister, and that once a month the emperor should visit the Imperial College, along with the prime minister and some ministers. The emperor was to sit among the ranks of the students while the rector questioned him on the administration of the country.[38] The primary function of the system, in short, would be to hold rulers accountable to what Theodore de Bary terms a "Parliament of Scholars."[39]

Huang also proposed to revise the Confucian examination system for selecting scholar-officials. He condemned the examinations of his day for rewarding superficiality and plagiarism, thus failing to identify scholars of "real talent."[40] Examinations, in Huang's view, should test both the

---

[37] Huang Zongxi, *Waiting for the Dawn: A Plan for the Prince*, trans. Wm. Theodore de Bary (New York: Columbia University Press, 1993), 92 (modified).

[38] Ibid., 107.

[39] Ibid., 83.

[40] Huang was not the first to condemn superficial learning. Xunzi (c. 310–219 B.C.E.) contrasted true learning with those who "only learn diverse (disordered) facts and mechanically follow the Odes and Documents." *Xunzi*, trans. Knoblock, 1.12 (modified).

capacity to memorize the classics and subsequent commentaries as well as the capacity for independent thought: "After listing one by one what is said by the various Han and Sung scholars, the candidate should conclude with his own opinion, there being no necessity for blind acceptance of one authority's word."[41]

Whether or not Huang's proposal for a parliament of scholar-officials holds the promise of empowering scholars of "real talent," the main problem is that it still deprives ordinary people of any voice in politics.[42] In other words, Huang defends politics *for* the people, but he fails even to recognize the need for politics *by* the people.[43]

A Proposal for a Modern Confucian Democracy

A modern-day "Confucian democrat" is therefore confronted with the dilemma that while Western-style democratic institutions do not fully accommodate concerns for the "rule of the wise," the "Parliament of Scholar-Officials" idea goes too far in the elitist direction by failing to incorporate any form of political decision making by the people. The compromise solution may seem obvious at this point: a bicameral legislature, with a democratically elected lower house and a "Confucian" upper

---

[41] Huang, *Waiting for the Dawn*, 113.

[42] Confucian thinkers began to consider the possibility of politics "by the people" only in the late nineteenth century. Since then, however, they have consistently campaigned for giving common people some form of a political voice. See Wang Juntao, "Confucian Democrats in Chinese History."

[43] The same criticism can be made of Sun Yat-sen's proposed constitution of five separate powers, which includes an independent branch responsible for setting civil service examinations. Under Sun's proposed scheme, all public officials, including those elected to the legislature, "must pass examinations before assuming office" (*Selected Writings of Sun Yat-sen*, 49). Sun hoped to avoid "the corruption and laxity of American politics," where "those endowed with eloquence ingratiated themselves with the public and won elections, while those who had learning and ideals but lacked eloquence were ignored," but the effect would be to exclude from political power elected politicians who fail examinations, no matter how popular they may be. It is difficult to imagine that a government that excludes the people's chosen leaders could achieve much legitimacy in the eyes of the people (consider a situation where someone elected with 80 percent of the vote but who fails examinations is replaced by a successful examination candidate who received only 20 percent of the vote). Joseph Chan has suggested (without explicitly defending) a model that might remedy this flaw: individuals who want to run for elections need to sit for an exam, and they would be required to publish their results in their campaign materials. Chan, "Democracy and Meritocracy: Toward a Confucian Perspective," ms. on file with author, 18. This would allow people to vote for candidates who may not be intellectually impressive (in the United States, where politicians seem to "dumb down" to attract electoral support, a low score on a political entrance exam could actually be an advantage).

house composed of representatives selected on the basis of competitive examinations.[44] The British House of Commons is an obvious example of a democratic lower house, but the ideal of a Confucian upper house has yet to be implemented, so I will try to articulate some preliminary thoughts on the subject.

First, it is important to specify the context for a Confucian upper house. The proposal is a nonstarter in societies without a tradition of respect for meritocratically chosen scholar-officials. Given an American tradition of popular resentment against "pointy-headed" intellectuals, for example, it is difficult to imagine that a proposal for a meritocratically selected upper house could ever achieve much popular legitimacy in the United States (not to mention the constitutional impediments).[45] A cultural base of support for a meritocratically selected upper house also seems to be lacking in the United Kingdom—an English tradition of deference to one's "betters" seems to have been tainted with notions of property and class privilege.

The cultural terrain is relatively favorable in Confucian-influenced East Asia. The idea of respect for rule by an educated elite, to repeat, is a

[44] I have critically evaluated some alternative proposals for combining democracy with a concern for the "rule of the wise" in my book, *East Meets West*, 289–307. More recently, Jiang Qing has put forward an interesting proposal for a tricameral legislature that includes representation for Confucian elites, elites entrusted with the task of cultural continuity, and people's representatives. Jiang, *Shengming xinyang yu wangdao zhengzhi: Rujia wenhua de xiandai jiazhi* [Life, Belief, and the Kingly Way of Politics: Cultural Confucianism's Contemporary Value] (Taipei: Yang zheng tang wenhua shiye gufen youxian gongsi, 2004), 312–17. However, Jiang's proposal requires that all three houses agree upon bills before they are passed, without any provision for prioritizing or dealing with gridlock, with the likely result that few laws would get enacted. Edward P. H. Woo, *In Search of an Ideal Political Order & an Understanding of Different Political Cultures* (Hong Kong: Novelty Publishers, 2002) has argued for another proposal to choose virtuous leaders within the confines of one-party rule, but it will likely have the same legitimacy problems as the current political system. Another possibility was informally put forward by a leading Chinese dissident, who said that China should reinstitute the monarchy as part of a constitutional monarchical democracy (he told me that China's biggest mistake in the twentieth century was abolishing the monarchy). But this proposal would not address the need for talent in government, and from a practical point of view it is difficult to bring back the magic of the monarchy once it has been abolished.

[45] Daniel Bell (the distinguished American sociologist) has proposed what may be the closest approximation of a meritocratically selected house for the American context. Bell's idea is to impose terms limits on members of Congress and then group the "retirees" into a third chamber, the "House of Counselors." The retirees would be financially rewarded and would be ready and able to act for the common good without worrying about getting reelected. Bell, "The Old War: After Ideology, Corruption," *The New Republic*, 23 and 30 August 1993, 20–21. The House of Counselors, however, may still be composed of some mediocre people whose sole qualification is that they succeeded in getting elected to Congress by pandering to the short-term interests of "the people," and it may be difficult to shed old habits.

dominant strand of Confucian political culture.[46] Competitive examinations for scholar-officials did often serve as a vehicle for upward mobility (and downward mobility, for established families that could not produce successful offspring),[47] and successful candidates have attracted a large measure of respect among the population at large. In East Asian countries, a meritocratic upper house may well be viewed as a plausible alternative to the political status quo. I will henceforth limit my discussion to the case of China, though the proposal may also be considered in other East Asian societies.

Let me add a few words about terminology. I will call the upper house the Xianshiyuan (賢士院). This Chinese term can be translated roughly as House of Virtue and Talent, but it sounds ridiculous in English, as do other possible English ways of referring to the upper house.[48] The translation problem illustrates the context-bound nature of this proposal: there is no way that a political institution composed of intellectual elites can seem remotely plausible (or desirable) in English.[49] Hence, I will stick to the Chinese term "Xianshiyuan," which does not have pejorative connotations in Chinese. This term will also serve to remind English readers

[46] I do not mean to imply that this cultural tradition is uniquely Confucian: it could be argued that the French tradition of social respect and political empowerment of intellectuals is similar (though recent political events in France show that there has been growing resentment against elite rule: see David. A. Bell, "Paris Dispatch: Class Conflict," *The New Republic Online*, 6 June 2005, http://www.tnr.com/doc.mhtml?i=w050531&s=bell060105).

[47] See He Huai Hong, "Rujia de pingdeng guan jiqi zhiduhua" [Confucianism's Equality and Its Institutionalization], paper presented at the conference on Confucianism and Human Rights, Beijing University, June 1998. For an argument that Confucian-style meritocracy reflects an aspect of equality, see A. T. Nuyen, "Confucianism and the Idea of Equality," *Asian Philosophy*, vol. 11, no. 2 (2001), 61–71.

[48] I have developed the idea for a Xianshiyuan in previous works, and I now regret using the English term "House of Scholars," which made it sound as though I was defending a political institution composed of professional academics (anybody who passes the exam can be a deputy; it need not be an academic). I considered other English-language labels—the Confucian House, the House of Merit, the Senate of Intellectuals—but they all sounded nearly as ridiculous. In my contribution to a book on deliberative democracy in China ("Deliberative Democracy with Chinese Characteristics: A Comment on He Baogang's Research," in *The Search for Deliberative Democracy in China*), I have used the term "deliberative chamber," but this term does not connote the Confucian-inspired aspect of the political institution. Finally, I concluded that it's better to use the Chinese term "Xianshiyuan" (I thank Song Bing for this suggestion).

[49] Consider the difference between the Chinese and English versions of a recent petition signed by hundreds of academics to protest curbs on the freedom of speech in Hong Kong (May 2004). The Chinese version begins "*Women shi yi qun zhishifenzi . . .*," which translates literally as "We are a group of intellectuals." The English version, however, begins "We, the undersigned . . ." In Chinese, the idea of intellectuals being specially committed to high moral principles does not seem problematic, and intellectual social critics can proudly affirm their status qua intellectuals.

that the Xianshiyuan is not meant to be transplanted to predominantly English-speaking societies.

A Xianshiyuan for the Twenty-first Century

Members of the Xianshiyuan would be selected on the basis of competitive examinations. Examinations employed to select civil servants in East Asian countries can be used as the basis for Xianshiyuan examinations, but they should be improved. As Huang Zongxi argued, examinations should test for both memorization and independent thought. Essay questions can be used to test for the latter capacity, and blind grading can help to ensure a fair and impartial grading process. The ability to score well in examinations points to the ability to manage stress, an essential trait for decision makers dealing with crisis situations. The examinations would need to be further tailored to identify the desired traits of political actors. This may involve testing for economic and political knowledge of the contemporary world as well as problem-solving ability, but exams should also test for knowledge of philosophy and literature that have inspired great leaders of the past.[50] It would also be important to test for problem-solving ability[51] and to include one or two essay questions on ethics to help filter out political demagogues[52] and brilliant but morally insensitive technocrats.[53] In any case, there is no need to design an examination from scratch: as mentioned, the

[50] On the importance of literature for leaders, see Robert D. Kaplan, *Warrior Politics: Why Leadership Demands a Pagan Ethos* (New York: Vintage Books, 2003), 39.

[51] The examination system for the Canadian Foreign Service previously tested only for breadth of knowledge, but it has recently been revised to test for problem-solving ability. This change of examination content has led to the development of two cultures within the Canadian Foreign Service, a group of academics who succeeded on the basis of their extensive knowledge, and a group of pragmatists who succeeded on the basis of their problem-solving abilities (conversation with Kim Henrie-Lafontaine of the Canadian Foreign Service in Beijing, 12 January 2005).

[52] One way of filtering out political demagogues is to ask for the ability to argue forcefully on behalf of two sides of the same public-policy controversy, as in the examinations for AO candidates in Hong Kong. This approach would not filter out clever Sophists (or lawyers), but it would filter out Hitler, Mao, et al., who seem congenitally incapable of understanding, much less articulating, opposing arguments. For more details on the content and form of the examinations, see Bell, *East Meets West*, 308–16.

[53] For example, the "best and brightest" (to borrow David Halberstam's ironic term) were chosen by President Kennedy to lead the fight against communism, and they provided the intellectual "vision" for the Vietnam War. That the best and brightest performed so disastrously (three million Vietnamese died in what they call the American War, including two million civilians) is a reason to worry about vesting too much political power in the hands of an intellectual elite. Note, however, that deputies in the Xianshiyuan would be greater in number than Kennedy's hand-picked elite, and most deliberations would be open and subject to public scrutiny, so the potentially disastrous plans of a handful of morally insensitive intellectuals, even if they pass the examinations, are less likely to be approved.

examination committee can draw from past and present civil service examinations in East Asia and elsewhere,[54] as well as ideas for improving actually existing exams.[55]

Needless to say, the examination process is a highly imperfect mechanism for selecting decision makers of talent and integrity. But arguably this procedure is more effective than other methods of political selection currently on offer,[56] including democratic elections. The social and economic achievements of East Asian societies in the post–World War II era can be explained at least in part by the sound policy choices of civil servants selected on the basis of competitive examinations.

The worry about giving too much power to young and inexperienced people can be addressed by imposing a minimum age requirement of thirty-five or forty years for the examinations. Once representatives are selected, they can choose an area of specialization (the top candidates get first choice), such as economic policy or foreign affairs, followed by work under the guidance of the previous batch of deputies for a transition period of a year or two in order to develop a certain degree of expertise.

It may also be a necessary to ensure representation by diverse groups in society, particularly in multiethnic societies where minority groups

---

[54] For an interesting comparison of the Singaporean system of civil servant selection and the imperial examination system (*keju*, 科舉) system of late imperial China, see Kris Su Hui Teo, "Singapore's Civil Service: A System of Life-Long Examinations," ms. on file with author.

[55] In Singapore and Japan, for example, there have been lively debates on the question of how to test for creativity in exams. One recent reform along these lines in Singapore is to present the examination candidate with several scenarios and many different factors, and then ask him or her to determine which ones are more important (conversation with Kris Su Hui Teo, October 2004).

[56] John S. Dryzek has argued for random selection as a procedure for the selection of political talent: "I would suggest that the evidence from the very high quality of lay citizen deliberation as revealed in consensus conferences, citizen's juries, planning cells, and deliberative opinion polls points to the possibility of an upper house composed of ordinary citizens selected at random from the population who would serve for perhaps one year at a time. Such a proposal was advanced by the think tank Demos in the context of recent British debates about reform of the House of Lords." Dryzek, "Deliberative Democracy in Different Places," in *The Search for Deliberative Democracy in China*. In the contemporary Chinese context, however, random selection would mean that the Xianshiyuan would most likely be composed of relatively uneducated farmers from the countryside (given that they constitute the majority of the population). And it would take a rather giant leap of faith to believe that they are as likely to engage in high-quality deliberations as representatives chosen by competitive examinations. In any case, Dryzek's proposal is a nonstarter in the Chinese context. There is no history of random selection as a procedure for selecting decision makers in China, and the risk-averse Chinese are not about to embark on such an untested experiment for selecting representatives that are supposed to deliberate about such issues as whether or not to go to war. In contrast, the examination system has proven itself as a means of selecting political talent in East Asia and consequently commands a great deal of social legitimacy, and political proposals for reform that appeal to the examination system are more likely to be taken seriously.

are more likely to trust representatives of their own group. This concern can be met by guaranteeing a certain number of seats to minority groups and by modifying examination content to suit the cultural particularities of different groups (for example, the examination for Tibetan representatives can include a component on Buddhism and the Tibetan language). The Xianshiyuan proposal is also compatible with granting substantial self-administration to minority areas and with federal arrangements that would allow provinces to manage their own affairs in particular areas.

In the absence of an electoral mechanism, it is important to ensure that members of the Xianshiyuan be held accountable for abuses of power. A term limit for members may therefore need to be imposed, but it should be long enough (say, seven or eight years) to give them enough time to learn about politics and to work for the common good in effective ways.[57] The risk of corruption can also be minimized by means of open and televised political deliberations in the Xianshiyuan transmitted directly to the public (with the exception of debates concerning national security) and by a free press with the right to investigate and publicize incidents of corruption. Deputies should also be paid handsome salaries to reduce the incentive for corruption, and stiff penalties for corrupt behavior can serve as an additional deterrent.

To promote high-quality deliberations, the Xianshiyuan should be relatively small in scale (several hundred seats at the most).[58] Members engaged in deliberations will presumably be motivated by conceptions of

[57] Term limits may also have the consequence of promoting justifiable decentralization. That is, deputies bound by term limits may be more likely to ensure that decisions at the local level are not usurped by national political institutions (in contrast to relatively power-hungry bureaucrats with life-time tenure and ambitious politicians concerned about the next elections).

[58] It is interesting to note that there have been successful local experiments with deliberative institutions in China. See He Baogang, "Participation and Deliberative Institutions in China," in *The Search for Deliberative Institutions in China*. In this paper, He does not argue that experiments dealing with relatively straightforward local issues (e.g., determining the salaries of local cadres) should be tried at the national level. There are obvious practical impediments to extending deliberative democracy from the local to the national level, including the power of capitalist economic interests, the secrecy required for national security policy and time-sensitive economic policy (e.g., the setting of interest rates), the empirical complexity of modern-day decision making, as well as the sheer impracticability of getting the large bulk of citizens involved in the decision-making process. Deliberative democracy at the national level will also face cultural obstacles in East Asian societies with political traditions that value decision making by a wise and public-spirited elite. But it may not be realistic to expect that the ideals of deliberative democracy can inform the decision-making process of meritocratically chosen political elites, and constitutional designers can help to structure the Xianshiyuan so that it facilitates deliberation.

the common good (as opposed to democratically elected politicians who are often constrained by the need to accommodate the interests of particular constituencies).[59] High salaries can minimize the need to pander to the rich and powerful, and perhaps members can be further insulated from political pressure by means of laws barring them from joining political parties and receiving contributions from interest groups (similar to the mechanisms that help to ensure the integrity of federal judges in the United States). In any case, these issues can be ironed out during the course of deliberations at an actual constitutional convention.[60]

The Problem of Conflict between the Democratic House and the Xianshiyuan

The Xianshiyuan can decide on policies by means of a majority vote following open and public deliberations on the relevant topic. But what if "meritocratic" majorities in the Xianshiyuan disagree with democratic majorities in the lower house? The problem of gridlock can be addressed by means of constitutional mechanisms regulating the relationship between the two houses of government. The "Confucian" solution might be to strengthen the Xianshiyuan, for example, by means of a constitutional formula providing supermajorities in the upper house with the right to override majorities in the lower house. The head of government and important ministers could be chosen from the Xianshiyuan. Most significant legislation would emanate from the Xianshiyuan, with the lower house serving primarily as a check on its power.

The "democratic" solution would be to empower the lower house, with the Xianshiyuan playing the relatively minor role of revising legislation passed on from the lower house, pointing out flaws and proposing small amendments like the British House of Lords. The head of government could come from the lower house, though the ceremonial head of state could come from the Xianshiyuan.[61]

---

[59] I do not mean to suggest that deputies of the Xianshiyuan will necessarily converge on the same interpretation of the common good. In the case of conflicts between interpretations of the common good, deputies can vote on the alternatives, and decisions can be taken on the basis of majority rule.

[60] Another important issue is the need to regulate the relationship between the Xianshiyuan and the highest court of the land. Tom Ginsburg has argued that Supreme Courts in Confucian-influenced East Asia tend to defer to the preferences of the highest political authority. Ginsburg, "Confucian Constitutionalism? The Case of Constitutional Review in Korea and Taiwan," *Law & Social Inquiry*, vol. 27, no. 2 (Fall 2002), 792. The Xianshiyuan, expected to deal more explicitly in policy matters, can be more active in this respect.

[61] One virtue of the British political system is that ordinary people can invest their emotions into reverence for a relatively powerless head of state while being more critical in

The next section will argue that a relatively weak Xianshiyuan may be more feasible, and the following section is an argument that a strong Xianshiyuan may be more desirable.

The Question of Feasibility

The current Chinese political system is not stable for the long term. Even Chinese Communists have labeled the current system the "preliminary stage of socialism," implying that the political status quo is transitional. At the moment, less-than-democratic rule may be justified because it allows for rapid economic development, which benefits the large majority of people in the medium to long term. Since the bulk of people may not be willing to put up with the hardship required for providing the foundations of economic development (particularly the highly disruptive, East Asian–style economic development),[62] some constraints on majority rule may be necessary. The question is, what comes after economic development? Surprisingly, perhaps, there is general agreement regarding the political end point, namely, that voting rights are likely to be extended to the people and that some form of multiparty democracy will take root. There are disputes over timing (will it take ten years or fifty years?) and mechanisms (will it be elite led or mass led, violent or peaceful?), but the large bulk of China observers, including leaders of the Communist Party, seem to believe that democratic opening is almost inevitable. There are many reasons for thinking that China will democratize eventually, but perhaps the most compelling one is that the right to vote has emerged as an important symbol of political recognition in modern societies, a way of letting people know that the government recognizes each citizen as a

---

their evaluation of the prime minister with real political power (in contrast to the U.S. presidential system, where the head of state is also the country's most powerful political decision maker). So the symbolic head of state can be chosen from the Xianshiyuan; perhaps it can be the eldest member or the deputy with the highest grade on the entry exam.

[62] Consider the fact that the industrial take-off in England led to an average growth rate of only 1 percent between 1660 and 1760, rising to nearly 3 percent (and never higher) in the midnineteenth century. In this period, Michael Mann notes that the high-growth areas like Manchester became the "hell on earth" so graphically described in Engels' 1844 work *The Condition of the Working Class*, and that "most of the English themselves barely benefited at all for another hundred years." Mann, "The Sources of Social Power: Explaining the Great Divergence between Europe and China," lecture delivered at Beijing University, 21 September 2004. The process of industrialization has been much faster in East Asia due to higher growth rates, but the short-term costs to the large majority have also been correspondingly higher (I'm reminded of a joke that economic reforms since the 1980s have helped the Chinese people, with the exception of workers, farmers, and women). One hopes that the time lag before the large bulk of East Asians benefit from industrialization will also be correspondingly shorter.

valued member of society. Any political system that denies its people the symbolic ritual of free and fair competitive elections—even if the people's views have minimal impact on actual policies—is likely to lack political legitimacy, and it is hard to believe that China will prove to be the exception.[63]

If China's top politicians are democratically elected, a constitutionally weak Xianshiyuan is the most likely scenario. But a Xianshiyuan with minimal constitutional powers could still play a politically significant role in China. The country would have a group of talented and disinterested individuals ready to act for the common good, for example, by sitting on commissions and independent bodies that evaluate policy and advise the government. Moreover, viewpoints by members of the Xianshiyuan may attract substantial social support in a society with a tradition of respect for meritocratically chosen officials. Democratically elected politicians in the lower house who systematically disregard policy recommendations of the Xianshiyuan may thus find it harder to get reelected.

But is there any reason to expect that the Xianshiyuan, even as a weak upper house, is likely to be chosen in constitutional deliberations on China's future? The Xianshiyuan is, of course, an ideal that has yet to be

---

[63] According to survey data, the majority of the public in China (and other East Asian countries) endorse the position that democracy has faults but is still better than other forms of government. Russell J. Dalton and Doh Chull Shin, "Democratic Aspirations and Democratic Ideals: Citizen Orientation toward Democracy in East Asia," 25 September 2003 (http://www.worldvaluessurvey.org/library/index.html, visited 19 May 2005). The alternatives presented in this survey, however, were limited and rather unattractive (the choices were "having experts, not government, make decisions according to what they think is best for the country," "having a strong leader who does not bother with Parliament and elections," "having the army rule," and "having a democratic political system"). I suspect there would be less support for democracy in China if respondents were asked to choose between democratic rule with low economic growth and one-party, nontotalitarian rule with high economic growth, between rule by democratically elected uneducated politicians and rule by meritocratically chosen exemplary persons (*junzi*, 君子), or between nondemocratic rule with social order and democratic rule with chaos. Another survey found that 59 percent of East Asians prefer democracy (http://www.globalbarometer.org), but here too the alternatives (e.g., technocratic rule) were not as desirable as they might have been. Even when East Asians prefer democracy, as Randall Peerenboom notes, "they prefer majoritarian or nonliberal variants to liberal democracy. Nearly two-thirds of Koreans agreed with the statement that 'If we have political leaders who are morally upright, we can let them decide anything,' 40% believed that 'the government should decide whether certain ideas should be allowed to be discussed in society,' while 47% believe that 'if people have too many different ways of thinking, society will be chaotic.'" Peerenboom, "Human Rights and Rule of Law," Georgetown Journal of International Law, 867n.195; quoting survey data by Chongmin Park and Doh Chull Shin. Such surveys also have more general problems, such as the difficulty of measuring the strength of preferences and their effect on behavior, the difficulty of distinguishing between informed and uninformed preferences, and the difficulty of translating moral and political concepts into different languages.

implemented. It is difficult to predict if it will ever see the light of day, and it might seem foolish to speculate. Still, it is worth offering some thoughts about feasibility, if only to prevent misunderstandings and misuses.[64] One argument for feasibility is that the Xianshiyuan resonates with traditional political culture, as noted above. Let me suggest two other arguments that increase the likelihood of implementation.

A constitutional convention may produce various interest groups in favor of the Xianshiyuan proposal. Women's groups may endorse examinations that will have the effect of increasing the proportion of women in the political process. Labor groups concerned about the possibility that a democratically elected legislature will be captured by big-business interests may also go along. Intellectuals frustrated with the debased character of democratic political discourse may support institutionalizing meritocratic rule. Even democrats may be tempted by the idea of institutionalizing an element of traditional culture. It is humiliating for a people, particularly if they identify with an old and proud civilization, to jettison the past as a whole, to be told that nothing valuable can be found in their national history. People may go along with Western-style democracy if it delivers material benefits and provides social peace, but what if democratic progress does not go according to plan? When things go wrong, the temptation will be to turn to a strongman who promises to restore national pride with "traditional" authoritarian political institutions.[65] But this scenario can be avoided if a democratic system incorporates an element of traditional political culture, as citizens may bear with the system even in difficult times. In a Chinese context, prodemocracy forces may come to appreciate the notion that the Xianshiyuan can stabilize the democratic system.

Another practical argument for the Xianshiyuan is that it can be

[64] Marx's ideal of communism easily lent itself to misuse because he said so little about it. Had he written more than a few cryptic lines about postcapitalist society, the gap between the ideal of communism and actually existing communist regimes would have been more obvious, and power-hungry dictators may have found it more difficult to justify their most egregious practices.

[65] By 2003 democracy failed to bring prosperity in Russia, disenchantment had set in, and no more than 10 percent of the people continued to favor democracy. As a result, there was widespread support for President Vladimir V. Putin, who moved Russia in an autocratic direction. Richard Pipes, "On Democracy in Russia: It's Not a Pretty Picture," *The New York Times*, 3 June 2003, B8. Similar developments may be occurring in Latin America: a United Nations survey of 19,000 Latin Americans in eighteen countries in April 2004 found that a majority would choose a dictator over an elected leader if that provided economic benefits. Juan Forero, "Latin America Graft and Poverty Trying Patience with Democracy," *The New York Times*, 24 June 2004, A1. Popular support for president Hugo Chavez, the less-than-democratic populist leader of Venuzuela, suggests that these preferences also affect the political reality.

grafted onto an existing political institution without dramatic change. The Chinese People's Political Consultative Conference (CPPCC) is designed to provide political consultation on major state policies and important issues concerning the well-being of the people.[66] In practice, it has been criticized for being a showcase sinecure composed of ineffective political appointees. Still, it has included leading intellectuals such as Liang Shuming, the Confucian traditionalist who continued to participate even after he was publicly chastised by Mao himself.[67] Recently, the CPPCC has assumed greater prominence under the leadership of Li Ruihan.[68] The mainland Chinese press openly discusses proposals for reforming the CPPCC, such as allowing it to play a more political role supervising other organs of government and reducing the number of deputies to facilitate deliberation.[69] The main problem, perhaps, is the one least discussed: the fact that appointees owe their loyalty to the party that appoints them and thus are not likely to deviate too far from the official line. If "the key to democratic supervision lies in developing democracy, letting everyone air his or her views freely, and creating conditions and opportunities for everyone to speak his or her own mind, tell the truth and air different views,"[70] as an official document puts it, then deputies selected by examinations, owing their loyalty only to what they think is best for the country (and humanity at large), are far more likely to do what the CPPCC is supposed to do. The best way to increase the legitimacy and efficacy of the CPPCC would be to convert it into a Xianshiyuan with meritocratically selected deputies.

In short, it may not be entirely unrealistic to assume that China's democratic system will institutionalize a constitutionally subordinate upper house. The Xianshiyuan would resonate with traditional political culture, it could be supported by interest groups at a constitutional convention, and it could be readily adapted from an existing political institution. It would be Chinese-style democracy: rule by the people with Confucian characteristics.

[66] www.china.org.cn/english/archiveen/27750.htm (visited 11 July 2003).

[67] See Guy S. Alitto, *The Last Confucian: Liang Shu-ming and the Chinese Dilemma of Modernity*, 2nd ed. (Berkeley: University of California Press, 1986).

[68] Lowell Dittmer, "Chinese Leadership Succession to the Fourth Generation," in *China After Jiang*, ed. Gang Lin and Xiaobo Hu (Washington, D.C.: Woodrow Wilson Center Press, 2003), 15.

[69] See, e.g., "Zhuanjia huyu zhengxie jinxing tizhi gaige" [Experts Appeal for Carrying Out Structural Reform of the CPPCC], 21 *Shiji huanqiu baodao*, 5 March 2003 (http://www.sina.com.cn/c/2003–03-05/1510934116.shtml, visited 23 May 2005).

[70] General Affairs Office of the CPPCC National Committee, *The Chinese People's Political Consultative Conference* (Beijing: Foreign Languages Press, 2004), 181.

A Nonauthoritarian Alternative to "Rule by the People"

But what if "China's democratic future" fails to materialize? The future is impossible to predict with certainty, and it could well be that founding mothers and fathers get cold feet when it comes down to turning over the world's most populous country to "the people." Would China then be condemned to autocratic one-party rule or violent civil war? One alternative, of course, is meritocratic rule: a society governed by deputies selected by competitive examinations. Such a political system need not be "authoritarian," in the sense that people have no voice and their civil rights are severely restricted. Consider the following scenario: A referendum is held, and a majority supports the idea of a strong Xianshiyuan. At the national level, the top decision makers are chosen by free and fair competitive examinations, and deputies engage in substantial deliberation before taking decisions. The national democratic legislature's main function is to transmit the people's (relatively uninformed) preferences to the Xianshiyuan. At provincial, township, city, and village levels, the top decision makers are chosen by means of competitive elections, and decisions are taken in deliberative forums. The freedom of the press is basically secure, and there are many opportunities to raise objections and present grievances to deputies in the Xianshiyuan. Most debates in the Xianshiyuan are televised and transmitted to the public on the web. In this scenario, meritocratic rule would not be "authoritarian," but neither would it be compatible with "minimal democracy." It would mean marginalizing, at the highest political levels, government officials chosen by means of the people's vote. At the very least, majorities in the Xianshiyuan would have power to override those of deputies in the lower democratic house in cases of conflict.

Should meritocratic rule be viewed as less than ideal? Put differently, does it have any merit relative to "rule by the people"? The best defense of a strong Xianshiyuan is that it is more likely to enact policies that benefit not just current majorities or minorities with the financial means to get their way, but also potential citizens, actual and potential members of minority groups, and foreigners. Imagine, for example, that deputies of the two houses had to deliberate about family planning. Most farmers oppose governmental limits on the number of children, partly due to the deeply held rural preference for siring male children. Those views would probably dominate the lower house—the large majority of Chinese still live in the countryside—and the democrats may well vote to repeal governmental attempts at limiting the number of children, whatever the long-term demographic consequences. But the *Xianshiyuan*—dominated by intellectuals, most of whom understand the need for some sort of family planning[71]—would probably oppose the lower house.[72]

Intellectuals in the Xianshiyuan are also likely to act against the widely shared preferences of urban voters. At the moment, for example, urban dwellers seem to aspire to the "American" dream of owning a car, and few democratically elected deputies are likely to counteract such views (just as few U.S. politicians openly favor raising taxes on gasoline). The Xianshiyuan, in contrast, is likely to be more sensitive to the negative effects of widespread car ownership (pollution, traffic jams, increased dependence on oil, etc.) and to favor more stringent curbs on the sale of cars and more state funding for public transport.[73] In economic policy, it may be similarly reckless to depend on the people's choices. It is quite likely, for example, that submitting to the rigors of the World Trade Organization regime will lead to growing poverty and social unrest in the short term, as inefficient farmers and workers in state-run enterprises lose their jobs. The hope is that economic benefits will eventually pay off when unemployed workers find decent jobs in the growing private sector, but democratically elected politicians are not likely to be so patient.[74] The Xianshiyuan, in contrast, is more likely to take a long-term view.[75]

[71] Even critics of China's population control policy point to the need for some sort of planning. For example, Wang Feng argues that the negative consequences of China's one-child policy now outweigh the good consequences, and he argues instead for a two-child policy. Wang Feng, "Can China Afford to Continue Its One-Child Policy?" *Asia Pacific Issues: Analysis from the East-West Center*, no. 77 (March 2005), 1–12. Some constraints on sex selection may also be justifiable—if it were entirely up to farmers, they would likely favor male births.

[72] There may be similar differences between the two houses regarding the merits of the *hukou* (household registration system that restricts the residency rights of people): the majority of rural residents may favor repealing the system, even if it leads to floods of migrants to cities and hence to unwelcome consequences such as overcrowding and social unrest (see chapter 11 for discussion of the pros and cons of the *hukou* system).

[73] The nondemocratic colonial government of Hong Kong and the less-than-democratic government of Singapore both implemented curbs on car consumption and funded excellent public-transport systems that have minimized traffic jams and made the two cities models of energy conservation. I hope that cities like Beijing will follow suit, but this will require going against the wishes of most people, who seem to aspire to car ownership.

[74] As Jack Snyder explains, "statistical evidence suggests that new democracies are inclined on average to become more protectionist. Though some groups gain from increased trade, others may lose from it. If the average voter suffers in the short run from increased exposure to foreign competition, a backlash against free trade may develop. Nationalist politicians may then be able to win support for a program of protectionism or even of seizing foreign markets through imperial expansionism. This may be a particular danger in new democracies, where elites can take advantage of their media monopolies or their power to set agendas to determine what information and options voters consider." Snyder, *From Voting to Violence: Democratization and Nationalist Conflict* (New York: W. W. Norton, 2000), 342–43.

[75] In the following chapter, I suggest that there will be substantial popular support for war against Taiwan if Taiwan declares formal independence: here, too, the intellectuals in

In short, Chinese intellectuals (i.e., those likely to be deputies in the Xianshiyuan) are often swimming against the mainstream. Of course, a more open political system could change things. The people would have many channels to make their preferences known via the democratic lower house, substate democratic legislatures, deliberative forums, the Internet, newspapers, and polls, as well as more traditional mechanisms such as remonstrance and petitioning. Perhaps substantial numbers would change their views following open debate. But if actually existing majorities continue to be motivated by narrow economic interests or crude expressions of emotion (as seems to be the case in "advanced" democracies), then deputies from the Xianshiyuan should be able to knock some sense into "the people." At the very least, the Xianshiyuan should be able to temper the people's worst excesses without having to worry about payback at election time.

The more serious objection to the idea of a strong Xianshiyuan is that it may not be realistic. For one thing, it is difficult to imagine political leader(s) with the motivation to strive hard for strong meritocratic rule. In newly established democratic political systems, the leading critics of the ancien régime tend to be rewarded with top political posts once their ideas are implemented: consider the Mandelas, Havels, and Walesas of our time. The same goes for newly established authoritarian systems: consider the Parks and Pinochets of our time. In a meritocratic system, however, the odds of such political returns are minimal. Even the most brilliant and virtuous founding fathers and mothers cannot be certain of scoring top grades in an examination system with one billion candidates. So they would have to actively promote a new system without the realistic hope of being rewarded with the highest levers of state power. The founders would have to fade away from the political limelight once they get their way. It would take, in other words, truly altruistic constitutional founders to devote time and energy to this cause.

Even if the system is established, it may not be stable. The people's patience with rule by meritocratically selected elites, no matter how deeply embedded the tradition, will run out if the Xianshiyuan systematically overrides the people's wishes. So the deputies of the Xianshiyuan would not be able to deviate too far from popular attitudes without affecting the legitimacy of the institution. The Xianshiyuan would have to tread a very fine line between respecting the popular will (in which case it could make itself redundant) and disrespecting it (in which case it could trigger violent opposition).

---

the Xianshiyuan are more likely to be cautious, just as American intellectuals were generally opposed to the decision to rush into the invasion of Iraq without more international support.

The next two chapters are less speculative. There is an obvious tension between democracy, understood as majority rule, and minority rights: the majority can choose to oppress or marginalize minority groups. In chapter 7, I argue that actually existing East Asian less-than-democratic regimes can do a better job at protecting the legitimate interests of minority groups (compared to democracies), which is an important reason for being cautious about calls for democracy in the region. Chapter 8 focuses on the topic of democratic education, drawing on my own experience to show that well-intentioned plans to promote democratic deliberation in and out of the classroom can exacerbate tensions with minority students unless special measures are taken to take into account of their interests. In both chapters, I point to some proposals that may be particularly appropriate for multicultural societies in East Asia.

7

Is Democracy the "Least Bad" System
for Minority Groups?

TAIWAN IS an apparent democratic success story. In 2000 the election of presidential candidate Chen Shui-bian represented the first democratic transition of power in Chinese history. In 2004 Chen was reelected in a bitterly fought contest, further institutionalizing democratic rule in Taiwan.[1] Today the press is free, there are almost daily manifestations of the freedom of assembly, and it is almost inconceivable to imagine that Taiwan could revert back to the "bad old days" of authoritarian rule under the Kuomintang (KMT).

On the face of it, Taiwan should serve as a positive model for democratic reform in mainland China. Yet few mainland intellectuals turn to Taiwan for inspiration. Quite the opposite, in fact. Even—especially— mainland Chinese democratic reformers with personal experience in Taiwan and full awareness of political developments there condemn the politics of postdemocratic Taiwan. At one recent conference on democratic deliberation in China, for example, Ethan J. Leib reports that "not a single Chinese participant had anything good to say about a country/territory that China treats as its own, and which has successfully democratized. . . . The unanimous disrespect afforded Taiwan at the conference by mainland Chinese democratic reformers was a bit hard to digest."[2] What might explain this "bizarre" (as Leib puts it) phenomenon?

---

[1] Chen Shui-bian's reelection was preceded by an "assassination attempt" on himself and his vice-presidential candidate Annette Lu, and the sympathy vote seems to have swung the election in his favor. The opposition parties suspected that the assassination attempt was deliberately staged for precisely this purpose. At first, the accusation sounded preposterous to me, until I learned about the Chinese expression *kurouji*, 苦肉計, meaning the "ruse of self-injury." This ruse, first discussed in the Han dynasty work *Three Kingdoms*, has frequently been deployed in Chinese history to attract sympathy and win the confidence of the enemy, and the expression is well known to contemporary Chinese (thus helping to explain the skeptical response to the assassination attempt among members of the opposition). A source with good connections to the ruling Democratic Progress Party (DPP) subsequently told me that the assassination attempt was in fact staged.

[2] Ethan J. Leib, "The Chinese Communist Party and Deliberative Democracy," *Journal of Public Deliberation*, vol. 1, no. 1 (2005), http://services.bepress.com/jpd/vol1/iss1/art1. I participated in the same conference (held in Hangzhou, November 2004) and can confirm Leib's impression.

First, a bit of history. The sharpest divide in Taiwan over the last fifty years has been that between the Taiwanese and the mainlanders who came to Taiwan with the KMT. More than one million mainlanders came to Taiwan, and they proceeded to establish political dominance over the native Taiwanese (approximately 85 percent of the population). In 1947 the KMT brutally put down an uprising by native Taiwanese, and it did not permit political opposition for the next four decades. The KMT denied that it officially discriminated against the native Taiwanese, but it often used provincial origins as a criterion for decisions on political inclusion or exclusion.[3]

Not surprisingly, political favoritism for the mainlanders generated resentment among the native Taiwanese, and provincial origin was made into a political cause following political liberalization in the late 1980s. The opposition movement identified the Taiwanese as the oppressed and the mainlanders as the oppressors, and this became the main source of political conflict. The KMT responded by opening itself up to native Taiwanese, particularly under the leadership of the native Taiwanese President Lee Teng-hui.[4] Nonetheless, the opposition Democratic Progress Party (DPP), supported almost exclusively by native Taiwanese and committed to the cause of political independence, made steady inroads into the corridors of power, culminating in Chen Shui-bian's election to the presidency in mid-2000 and reelection in early 2004. Today the political atmosphere has become sharply polarized,[5] and it is the mainlanders who complain about limited political opportunities.[6]

It is not just a question of competition for political power, however. The ruling DPP has identified Chinese culture and Mandarin Chinese with the mainland KMT arrivals, and it has sought to reduce, if not eliminate, Chinese culture and Mandarin Chinese from public and cultural

[3] The KMT did, however, reserve certain political posts for native Taiwanese. The mayorships of Taipei and Kaohsiung (Gaoxiong), for example, were traditionally reserved for native Taiwanese. Ge Yong Guang, *Wenhua duoyuanzhuyi yu guojia zhenghe* [Cultural Pluralism and National Integration] (Taipei: Zhengzhong shuju, 1991), 173.

[4] Lee has since left the KMT and started his own political party that is even more straightforwardly proindependence than the Democratic Progress Party. He has campaigned wearing Japanese clothing as a show of attachment to Taiwan's Japanese cultural and colonial legacy.

[5] Such polarization can have negative effects on academic discourse. Academics are more reluctant to express their own views on cross-strait relations for fear of being viewed as a member of one of the "camps." An article by Perry Anderson on the topic received lots of attention in Taiwan because academics could hide behind his views to express their own: only a foreigner, I was told, could raise certain politically sensitive topics (interview with Taiwanese academic, December 2004).

[6] See, e.g., Chang Maukei, "Toward an Understanding of the Sheng-chi Wen-ti in Taiwan," in *Ethnicity in Taiwan*, ed. Chen Chung-min, Chuang Ying-chang, and Huang Shumin (Taipei: Institute of Ethnology, Academia Sinica, 1994), 98.

discourse by such means as deemphasizing Chinese history in schools and challenging the use of pinyin (the alphabetic system of writing used in mainland China) and street signs named after Chinese provinces.[7] In its place, the DPP has been promoting the local Taiwanese culture[8] and the Taiwanese language/dialect.[9] Partly, this can be viewed as an understandable reaction to the suppression of Taiwanese culture and language/dialect under the KMT.[10] But the DPP has veered into extremes that no one except the most sympathetic insider would view favorably.[11] Consider the following examples:

- Minister of Foreign Affairs Chen Tang-shan openly criticized the Singapore government's opposition to Taiwanese independence with the insulting words, "Singapore, a little snot [bi shi, 鼻屎] of a country, is really just kissing China's ass [pai ma pi, 拍馬屁]." He was using the local Taiwanese dialect/language, thinking that only the domestic audience could understand him in what he considered to be the national language. But the minister apparently forgot that 70 percent of Singaporeans also trace their ancestry to the same part of China and speak the same dialect/language![12] Thus the insult was readily understandable by Singaporeans, and needless to say the minister's comment did not improve relations between the two countries.
- Minister of Education Tu Cheng-sheng has suggested cutting the proportion of classical Chinese in high schools by 20 percent, with the

[7] As far as I know, the DPP has yet to call for the repatriation of China's cultural treasures. The KMT took treasures from China's Forbidden City when it left mainland China for Taiwan; today, they are housed in Taipei's Palace Museum (Gugong in Chinese, the same characters used to refer to the Forbidden City). If the DPP really wants to treat China as a foreign country, then it would have a moral obligation to return the treasures to the mother country.

[8] See, e.g., Yunxiang Yan, "Managed Globalization: State Power and Transition in China," in *Many Globalizations: Cultural Diversity in the Contemporary World*, ed. Peter L. Berger and Samuel P. Huntington (New York: Oxford University Press, 2002), 57–58.

[9] I do not mean to take sides in the dispute concerning what constitutes a dialect and what constitutes a language. Linguists tell the joke that a language is a dialect with an army.

[10] On the denigration of Taiwanese language and culture under KMT rule, see Thomas B. Gold, "Identity and Symbolic Power in Taiwan," *Asia Program Special Report*, Woodrow Wilson International Center for Scholars, no. 114 (August 2003), 2.

[11] "Insider" here refers to hard-core members of the DPP. Notwithstanding majority support for the view that Taiwan should be seen as an independent and separate political entity from the mainland, only one-fourth of Taiwanese view the Taiwanese culture as different from Chinese culture. T. Y. Wang, "Double-Renunciation: Could This Be the Solution for Cross-Strait Conflict?" paper presented at the 2005 Annual Meeting of the American Political Science Association, 4.

[12] Zheng Hong Sheng, "Taiwan de dalu xiangxiang" [Taiwan's Imagination of the Mainland], *Du shu*, January 2005, 43. This essay, written by a Taiwanese and published in

possibility of further reductions in the future.[13] This proposal has been criticized by most high school teachers and university professors. One of Tu's supporters, a famous novelist in Taiwan, has written an article in defense of this policy. He explains that Taiwan's education system needs a "cultural revolution," and he condemns defenders of classical Chinese for being lazy, arrogant, and "enslaved" [nu hua, 奴化] by Chinese education.[14] He also argues that it's more worthwhile to read popular Taiwanese poetry than classical Tang dynasty poetry because the former expresses the people's everyday life as well as opposition to foreign control.[15]

• The DPP announced a new high school curriculum after it took power. The history curriculum proposed to draw a line at 1500 partly because "the major events that happened in China after the sixteenth century were mostly the result of the interaction with other countries or foreign forces."[16]

At this point, the "unanimous disrespect" of mainland Chinese intellectuals regarding Taiwanese-style democracy might not seem so "bizarre."[17] If Taiwanese-style democracy involves breaking up their

---

an influential mainland Chinese periodical, is a frank historical account of the different factors that have contributed to cultural estrangement between Taiwan and the mainland. The author concludes with a brief plea for retrieving a common Chinese tradition, but he does not propose any concrete steps for doing so (e.g., regarding the educational curriculum). Given the deep differences between Taiwanese and mainland Chinese identities laid out in the essay, one wonders how realistic the recommendation may be.

[13] The same minister has been condemned in mainland Chinese publications for his attempt to rewrite history in ways that diminish the contributions of the mainlanders and positively reevaluate the Japanese colonial legacy. One Taiwanese academic writing in a mainland Chinese newspaper notes that thirty million Chinese, including 650,000 Taiwanese, sacrificed their lives in the anti-Japanese war and then rhetorically asks the minister, "Have the Chinese not suffered enough?" Yu Gong Li, "Tu Zhengshen de lishiguan quefa le shenme" [What Does Tu Zhengshen's Historical Consciousness Lack?"], Guangming ribao, 10 November 2004. Another proindependence politician, Shu Ching Chiang, (deliberately?) inflamed Chinese sentiments by visiting the infamous Yasukuni Shrine, the symbolic center of unrepentant Japanese militarism in Asia. Norimitsu Onishi, "Symbol at the Heart of a Troubled History: Japanese Struggle Bitterly over Shrine," International Herald Tribune, 23 June 2005, 1, 8.

[14] A political theorist in Taiwan tells me that parents have organized informal study sessions so that their children can learn the Chinese classics, which are being cut from schools. So much for the laziness argument.

[15] Yang Qingchu, "Guowen, you ji ke Taiwan benguo benwen" [How Much Material Taught in Taiwan's Literature Course Is Taiwanese?], Ziyou shibao, 2 January 2005.

[16] Bi-yu Chang, "From Taiwanisation to De-sinification: Culture Construction in Taiwan since the 1990s," China Perspectives," no. 56 (November–December 2004), 41 n. 53.

[17] One prominent Chinese liberal political theorist (with personal experience in Taiwan) noted that Taiwanese theorists take great interest in the works of the German theorist (and

country and attacks on their cherished identities, no wonder Chinese intellectuals otherwise sympathetic to political reform condemn the model.[18]

Unfortunately, the Taiwan model—democratization leading to ethnic polarization and marginalization of the minority group and its culture—may not be unique. In fact, it may be an expression of a profound tension between democracy and minority rights that has taken more violent forms elsewhere. Ethnic warfare in the postcommunist states has led many observers to conclude that democratization often conflicts with minority rights.[19] In ethnically plural societies, the majority group can decide to oppress minority groups democratically.[20] Serbia's treatment of the Kosovo Albanians is an obvious example. It is also dismaying to note that the typical mechanisms for dealing with group conflict in Western democracies—such as federalism and consociationalism—may not be workable in the absence of a deeply rooted culture of mutual respect and tolerance between groups. In societies with intense levels of hatred and mutual mistrust, dominant groups may not be willing to subordinate their interests under the framework of a constitutional system designed to protect minority groups. In the worst cases, only military intervention and subsequent occupation by third parties can keep the peace and (hopefully) protect the interests of minority groups.

One typical response to the failings of democracy is to invoke Winston Churchill's (apocryphal?) quip that democracy is the worst possible system, except for all the others. Whatever the "short-term" problems of transitions to democratic rule, democracy is the "least bad" medium- to long-term solution to good government. Even forceful critics of pro-democracy intervention such as Amy Chua claim that "the best political hope for [developing and postsocialist] countries lies in some form of

---

Nazi supporter) Carl Schmitt because of his point that states need to draw a sharp distinction between friends and enemies. He was asked at an open seminar, "Who's the enemy?" and he responded "We are."

[18] There are other factors that help to explain the more critical attitude toward democracy in China. The U.S. invasion of Iraq, for one thing, has cast doubt on the desirability of U.S.-style democracy. It is interesting to note that state television in China provided live, relatively unbiased coverage of the 2004 U.S. presidential election. In the past, such elections would have been either ignored or deliberately cast in a negative light to show the inadequacies of U.S.-style democracy. It seems that the CCP now has less to fear from the example of U.S.-style democracy.

[19] Ted Gurr, "Communal Conflicts and Global Security," Current History, vol. 94, no. 592 (May 1995), 212–17.

[20] See, e.g., Chua, World on Fire; Jack Snyder, From Voting to Violence: Democratization and Nationalist Conflict (New York: W. W. Norton, 2000); and Zakaria, The Future of Freedom.

democracy."[21] But is democracy really the least bad system for protecting minority groups? Should we rule out of court the possibility that nondemocratic forms of government can better protect the legitimate interests of minority groups for now and the foreseeable future?

The post–World War II experience of modernizing East and Southeast Asian countries casts doubt on the prodemocracy hypothesis. While the debate on "Asian values" has largely focused on the alleged benefits of East Asian–style authoritarianism for rapid economic development and social stability, some less-than-democratic political systems in the region can also be defended on the grounds that they help to secure the interests of minority groups—and that democratization can be detrimental to those interests, no matter how well the "transition" is managed.

In this chapter, I will discuss one specific way that democracy can harm minority interests, namely, that it tends to promote a form of nation building centered on the culture of the majority group. I will also try to argue, pointing to actual examples from the East Asian region, that these problems need not arise to the same extent in less-than-democratic political settings. My argument will be directed specifically at Will Kymlicka's argument that less-than-democratic states do not have any comparative advantages for minority groups in the East Asian context. In the final section, I draw implications for outside prodemocracy forces and return to the example of China's relationship with Taiwan.

SOME DEFINITIONS

First, however, let me begin by defining the relevant terms. Democracy will be defined in the "minimal" sense as free and fair competitive elections under universal franchise for occupants of those posts where actual policy decisions are made.[22] Democracy thus understood is a procedure for the filling of political offices through periodic, free, and fair elections. Such elections are only possible if there is some measure of freedom of speech, assembly, and press, and if opposition candidates and parties can criticize incumbents without fear of retaliation.[23] This

[21] Chua, *World on Fire*, 263. In the same vein, Jack Snyder concludes his book with the following comment: "Democracy is not instant. If it came in a bottle, everyone would have it. But for the patient and persistent, the wait will be worthwhile" (Snyder, *From Voting to Violence*, 353).

[22] See, e.g., Andrew Nathan, "Chinese Democracy: The Lessons of Failure," *Journal of Contemporary China*, no. 4 (1993), 3.

[23] Samuel Huntington, "American Democracy in Relation to Asia," in *Democracy and Capitalism: Asian and American Perspectives*, ed. Robert Bartley et al. (Singapore: Institute of Southeast Asian Studies, 1993), 28.

definition is provided in most international rights documents,[24] and it is the least controversial definition available. More importantly (for my purposes), this definition of democracy is helpful for identifying the tension between democracy and minority rights.[25] The standard definitions of minority groups in multiethnic societies are more problematic, however. Political thinkers tend to define ethnocultural groups in terms of language, race, or religion. Vernon Van Dyke, for example, defines an ethnic community as "a group of persons, predominantly of common descent, who think of themselves as collectively possessing a separate identity based on race or on shared characteristics, usually language and religion."[26] If the aim is to identify vulnerable minority groups, however, definitions in terms of shared language, race, or religion may have the effect of unjustifiably rewarding some groups and denying the legitimate aspirations of others.

It is instructive to look at some examples from China. According to the Chinese government, there are fifty-five ethnic minorities in the country, amounting to more than 8 percent of the population. These officially recognized minorities are labeled as such by virtue of being "non-Han," meaning they do not use the Chinese script or bear all the physical characteristics of the Han Chinese. Leading experts on the subject, such as June Teufel Dreyer and Colin Mackerras, also operate with the government's definition of a minority group.[27]

Contrary to popular belief, the Chinese government does recognize in principle that minority groups are entitled to special status in the Chinese political system. For example, the National People's Congress in 1984 passed the Law on Regional Autonomy for Minority Nationalities, which allows for self-administration in Tibet and other "minority regions." Self-administration in practice, needless to say, does not always amount to much. But some tangible benefits are in fact granted to officially recognized minority groups. The most significant privileges include

permission to have more children (except in urban areas, minorities are generally not bound by the one-child policy), pay fewer taxes, obtain better

---

[24] See, e.g., article 25 of the International Covenant on Civil and Political Rights.

[25] It is possible to define democracy in such a way that secures minority rights in its very definition (as Western liberal democrats may prefer), but such terminological sleights of hand simply mask conflicts between the majoritarian tendencies of democracy and minority rights in the real world.

[26] Vernon Van Dyke, "The Individual, the State, and Ethnic Communities in Political Theory," in *The Rights of Minority Cultures*, ed. Will Kymlicka (Oxford: Oxford University Press, 1995), 32.

[27] June Teufel Dreyer, *China's Forty Millions: Minority Nationalities and National Integration in the People's Republic of China* (Cambridge: Harvard University Press, 1976); Colin Mackerras, *China's Minorities: Integration and Modernization in the Twentieth-Century* (Hong Kong: Oxford University Press, 1994).

(albeit Chinese-language) education for their children, have greater access to public office, speak and learn their native languages, worship and practice their religion (often including practices such as shamanism that are still banned among the Han), and express their cultural differences through the arts and popular culture.[28]

Indeed, as Dru Gladney puts it, "one might even say it has become popular to be 'ethnic' in today's China."[29]

The problem, however, is that, under the current system, benefits may accrue to individuals and groups *not* in need of special protection. For example, members of minority groups from economically privileged backgrounds can get admitted to universities with lower marks.[30] Not surprisingly, the children of mixed marriages between Han and minority members usually choose minority rather than Han status. Whole countries and districts have applied for autonomous minority status on the basis of extremely slender evidence, such as the discovery of non-Han names in genealogies of several generations' depth.

At the same time, restricting the definition of minority groups to shared language or ethnicity can conceal minority groups from political view—and so play into the hands of conservative majorities intent on denying legitimate aspirations for economic and political benefits. As Emily Honig explains, the prejudice against Subei people is comparable to that experienced by African Americans in the United States.[31] Unlike most African Americans, however, the Subei people are not physically distinct from the rest of the Shanghainese population, almost all of whom are Han Chinese. Rather, they are defined as Subei by virtue of being individuals whose families were originally poverty-stricken refugees from Jiangsu province. The political result is that Subei people do not benefit

[28] Dru C. Gladney, "Ethnic Identity in China: The Rising Politics of Cultural Difference," in *Democratization and Identity: Regimes and Ethnicity in East and Southeast Asia*, ed. Susan J. Henders (Lanham, MD: Lexington Books, 2004), 141.

[29] Gladney argues that foreign policy and economic considerations (rather than incipient democratization) largely explain the "rising politics of cultural difference" in China. Ibid., 141–45.

[30] For example, Tibetans can enter universities with lower examination points (210 for liberal arts and 170 for sciences) than their Han counterparts (250 for admission). He Baogang, "Minority Rights with Chinese Characteristics," in *Multiculturalism in Asia*, ed. Will Kymlicka and He Baogang (Oxford: Oxford University Press, 2005). This phenomenon leads to a certain amount of resentment among Han students, not entirely dissimilar to the kind of resentment that some U.S. whites feel in response to economically privileged beneficiaries of affirmative action programs in U.S. universities. Even more resentment, however, is generated by the practice of lowering the barriers of entry for Beijing residents to Beijing University and Tsinghua University (in Beijing), the two most prestigious universities in China: in effect, affirmative action for the privileged.

[31] Emily Honig, *Creating Chinese Ethnicity: Subei People in Shanghai, 1850–1980* (New Haven: Yale University Press, 1992), 2–3.

from the official Chinese policy of positive discrimination and special political representation for minority groups.

Consider as well the case of the Burakumin (literally, the people of the hamlets) in Japan. The Burakumin—numbering almost three million— speak Japanese and are ethnically indistinguishable from other Japanese. Most consider themselves to be ethnically Japanese,[32] and they enjoy the same legal rights as their fellow citizens. Nonetheless, they are widely considered to be descendants of a less human "race" than the stock that fathered the Japanese nation as a whole. Burakumin, according to the early twentieth-century popular notion, have "one rib-bone lacking; they have one dog's bone in them; they have distorted sexual organs; they have defective excretory systems; if they walk in moonlight their neck will not cast shadows; and, they being animals, dirt does not stick to their fee when they walk barefooted."[33] Still today, they are often re-garded as hereditary outcasts and are the victims of various social prac-tices that serve to keep them sexually and socially apart from Japanese society.[34] The majority live in impoverished ghettos known as *buraku*, and other Japanese shun contact with them as much as possible and carefully check the pedigrees of prospective sons-in-law or daughters-in-law to make sure they do not carry the taint of "blood."[35] Yet the usual definition of minority groups in terms of shared language or race al-lowed the Japanese government to declare to the United Nations in 1980 that there are no discriminated minorities in Japan.[36]

Similar problems arise if we consider the development of a distinctive Taiwanese identity defined primarily by a common experience with free market institutions, (more recently) a relatively democratic form of gov-ernment, and historical experience with non-Chinese rule, rather than by shared language or ethnicity. Any prospect for a fair and workable

[32] John Lie, "The Politics of Recognition in Contemporary Japan," in *Democratization and Identity*, ed. Susan J. Henders (Lanham, MD: Lexington Books, 2004), 128.

[33] Quoted in ibid., 122.

[34] George de Vos and Hiroshi Wagatsuma, "Introduction," in *Japan's Invisible Race: Caste in Culture and Personality*, ed. de Vos and Wagatsuma (Berkeley: University of Cali-fornia Press, 1967), xx.

[35] Robert C. Christopher, *The Japanese Mind* (Tokyo: Charles E. Tuttle, 1983), 50.

[36] Alastair McLauchlan, "Introduction," in Suchiro Kitaguchi, *An Introduction to the Buraku Issue: Questions and Answers*, trans. Alastair McLauchlan (Richmond, Surrey: Japan Library, 1993), 3. In other ways, however, the Japanese government does recognize the *buraku* problem—the Law on Special Measures for *Buraku* Improvement Projects, in-tended to improve the housing, health, and education of the Burakumin, was passed in 1969 and remained in force until 1997. Much remains to be done, however—the Funda-mental Law for *Buraku* Liberation (first drafted in 1985) "has still not come to pass, yet it is this law which, perhaps more than any of the others, would set the platform for what could become a practical implementation of government assurances over the last decade that Buraku problems must be addressed and solved" (ibid., 6).

political arrangement with the People's Republic of China cannot ignore the fact that many Taiwanese now think of themselves as sufficiently distinct to seek some form of self-administration, if not complete independence. But this is a nonissue if one accepts the official Chinese view that the Taiwanese are not a distinct cultural grouping. And defining minority groups in terms of language or ethnicity leads one to endorse the official view.[37] In the same vein, it is difficult to make sense of the political conflicts within Taiwan itself by relying on the standard definition of what constitutes a cultural group. While there is a linguistic dimension to this conflict[38] (many mainlanders are unable to converse in the language/dialect commonly used by native Taiwanese), provincial origin, as noted earlier, is the main line of demarcation between the two groups.

In short, the standard definition of ethnocultural groups cannot adequately shed light on the nature of group conflicts in some East Asian societies. Nor can it identify all the vulnerable groups in need of special political protection. Once again, this suggests the need to define group identity in terms not restricted to language or race. But it is equally important to control for the opposite problem of an overly elastic definition of ethnocultural identity. Amy Chua argues that majority ethnic groups almost invariably target market dominant minority groups when democracy increases the political power of the impoverished majority. Whatever the plausibility of this argument at the multination state level,[39] Chua overstates her case by extending the majority/minority dynamic "upwards" to refer to regional conflicts in the Middle East and global conflicts between wealthy Americans and poor Third World peoples, and "downward" to refer to conflicts between groups (or the absence of conflicts) in U.S. inner cities and semiautonomous cities such as Hong Kong.[40] Chua's overly elastic definition of an ethnocultural group

[37] It is worth nothing, however, that in a different context even the Chinese government concedes that minority groups with legitimate aspirations for autonomy need not be defined in terms of language or ethnicity. In the case of Hong Kong, the Chinese government has officially implemented a "one country, two systems" political proposal for postcolonial rule. What defines group particularity in this case is shared attachment to the rule of law, civil rights, and experience with a capitalist economic system and other legacies of colonialism, not shared language or ethnicity. The case of Macau is similar.

[38] See Henning Kloter, "Language Policy in the KMT and DPP eras," *China Perspectives*, no. 56 (November–December 2004), 56–63.

[39] Chua does recognize that there are various "exceptions," such as China (*World on Fire*, 177–78).

[40] In the case of Hong Kong, Chua argues that the lack of a market-dominant minority helps to explain its economic success relative to neighboring Southeast Asian countries

thus leads to the conflation of different kinds of conflicts between majorities and minorities that have different combinations of economic, political, and cultural causes and require different kinds of remedies.

It is important, then, to limit the definition of ethnocultural groups so that it refers only to groups that view themselves and/or are viewed by others as partaking of a joint identity based on some sort of fellow feeling and extended kinship rather than shared economic characteristics or shared lifestyle activities like sports or entertainment. This definition is broad enough to allow for common characteristics other than race, language, or religion yet narrow enough to exclude class identification as the key variable. The details will have to be filled in by particular accounts of political conflict that are sensitive to the actual history and self-understanding of minority groups.

Democracy and Nation Building

Let us now turn to the main source of tension between democracy and minority rights[41]—the need for democratic states to promote nation building centered on the majority culture. The nineteenth-century political thinker John Stuart Mill laid the intellectual foundations for this view. According to Mill, democracy is "next to impossible in a country made up of different nationalities. Among a people without fellow-feeling, especially if they read and speak different languages, the united public opinion, necessary to the working of representative government, cannot exist."[42] In other words, democratic deliberation requires mutual trust and understanding, and this can only be provided by a shared language and a common national identity. Mill recognized, however, that the boundaries of governments do not always coincide with those of cultural groups: "There are parts even of Europe, in which different nationalities are so locally intermingled, that it is not practicable for them to be under separate

---

(ibid., 178). The English minority, however, has been economically dominant relative to most Chinese Hong Kongers, and according to Chua's theory, the majority group should have targeted the English (and the English-speaking minority) after the relative empowerment of the Chinese in posthandover Hong Kong, which didn't happen. It could be argued that more electoral democracy would have led to this result, but this is quite unlikely, judging by the fact that the "prodemocracy" parties campaigned largely on an anti-Beijing rule rather than an anti-English platform.

[41] There are other tensions not discussed in this chapter. For example, democracy can fail to protect (and may actually harm) the interests of foreign resident workers (see chapter 11).

[42] John Stuart Mill, "Considerations on Representative Government," in *Three Essays*, ed. Richard Wollheim (Oxford: Oxford University Press, 1975), 382.

government."[43] In such cases, Mill argued that minority groups can and should be absorbed into the culture of the relatively "civilized" group:

> Experience proves, that it is possible and desirable for one nationality to merge and be absorbed into another: and when it was originally an inferior and more backward portion of the human race, the absorption is greatly to its advantage. Nobody can suppose that it is not more beneficial to a Breton, or a Basque of French Navarre, to be brought into the current of the ideas and feelings of a highly civilized and cultivated people—to be a member of the French nationality, admitted on equal terms to all the privileges of French citizenship, sharing the advantages of French protection, and the dignity and prestige of French power—than to sulk on his own rocks, the half-savage relic of past times, revolving in his own little mental orbit, without participation or interest in the general movement of the world.[44]

The experience of the twentieth century, needless to say, points to different lessons. Far from being content with "being brought into the current of ideas and feelings of a highly civilized and cultivated people," minority groups have typically sought to assert their distinctive identities in various ways. Some contemporary liberals have responded by recognizing the need to protect minority rights against the tendencies of absorption into the dominant national culture.

Will Kymlicka is perhaps the most prominent contemporary liberal defender of minority rights. He argues that justice requires equality between ethnocultural groups in a state. But since minority groups may be particularly vulnerable to the economic, political, or military power of the majority, this can justify special political protections for minority groups. In a series of lectures delivered in Japan in 1998, Kymlicka argues for the universal applicability of his theory.[45]

Minorities in non-Western states, he claims, need the same sorts of protections against majority power that minorities in Western states need.[46] Kymlicka's key argument for this claim is that modern nation-states must engage in nation-building programs centered on the majority

---

[43] Ibid., 384.

[44] Ibid., 385.

[45] More precisely, Kymlicka argues that his account of justice *between* ethnocultural groups (requiring equality between groups, which can justify special protection for vulnerable minority groups) is applicable in the East Asian context. He recognizes that the part of his theory dealing with justice *within* groups—individual members of minority groups should have the freedom to question and revise group traditions and practices—may presume a conception of the importance of freedom and autonomy that is not shared in East Asia. Will Kymlicka, "The Future of the Nation-State," *Fifth Kobe Lectures*, December 1998, 3.

[46] Ibid., 6.

culture, and these programs pose grave threats to minority interests and identities. He notes that

> historically, virtually all liberal democracies have, at one point or another, attempted to diffuse a single societal culture throughout all of their territory. They have all engaged in this process of "nation-building"—that is, a process of promoting a common language, and a sense of common membership in, and equal access to, the social institutions based on that language. Decisions regarding official languages, core curriculum in education, and the requirements for acquiring citizenship, all were made with the express intention of diffusing a particular culture throughout society, and of promoting a particular national identity based on participation in that societal culture.[47]

Nation building of this sort is essential because only the existence of a national identity centered on a common language can motivate and mobilize citizens to act for common political goals. But these goals need not be liberal, thus explaining why nation building has been so ubiquitous. Nationalism can be used to promote liberal goals such as democratization and equality of opportunity, but it can also be used to promote illiberal goals such as chauvinism and unjust conquest. Thus, it is not surprising

> that the model of the "nation-state" has been adopted by many non-Western countries as well, which have embarked on their own nation-building programs. In Asia, as in the West, nation-building has appealed to both democratic reformers and authoritarian conservatives, since it can be used to mobilize people behind a wide range of political projects. And Asian governments have often used the same tools of nation-building as Western governments: regulating the language and content of education and public services; establishing a national media; controlling immigration and naturalization.[48]

Nation building poses a distinctive threat to minority interests because it tends to be centered on the majority culture, with special emphasis on the language of the majority. In a democratic system, political leaders must be sensitive to majority preferences, and thus the language and culture of the majority group tend to be the only feasible basis of nation building. Given the danger that majority nation building poses for minority interests, Kymlicka suggests a variety of measures such as language rights to protect vulnerable minorities.

But why should we expect the same dynamic of politically, economically, and culturally favored majority groups versus oppressed minorities in East Asia's less-than-democratic states? In such states, it may be easier for politi-

---

[47] Ibid., 11.
[48] Ibid., 12.

cal elites to suppress majority nationalism. Although political leaders may have to construct a common national identity to promote goals such as political stability and economic development, they are not as constrained by the majority culture (in comparison with democratic states) if political leaders decide that the majority's culture conflicts with the state's goals.

Consider the case of Singapore. In 1965 Singapore was expelled from the Malaysian federation and forced to be independent. At the time, nation building was perhaps Singapore's greatest challenge. As founding father Lee Kuan Yew put it, "[We had] to build a nation from scratch."[49] This was not made easy by the fact that Singapore was, and is, an ethnically plural society—77 percent Chinese, 14 percent Malay, and 8 percent Indian—and that the various groups were literally at war with each other in the early 1960s. The Malay minority in particular posed a challenge to the creation of national unity in Singapore because its members were more inclined to side with Malays in the surrounding states than with the majority Chinese. Thus, the ruling People's Action Party (PAP) felt it could not create a new identity by appealing to Chinese culture. Instead, it attempted to combat all forms of ethnic parochialism by fostering the growth of a new Singaporean identity that would underpin security and prosperity. For example, the government broke up ethnic enclaves by moving people into ethnically mixed public housing blocs and marginalized ethnic Chinese clan associations.[50] It also promoted the use of English, which involved overriding the wishes of all groups, including the majority Chinese. Lee is quite explicit that Singapore's nation-building exercise was incompatible with majority rule:

> Supposing we had chosen Chinese or tried to sponsor Chinese, how would we make a living? How would we fit ourselves into the region and into the world? We could not have made a living. But the Chinese then would have wanted it. And if we had taken the vote, we would have had to follow that policy. So when people say, "Oh, ask the people!", it's childish rubbish. We are leaders. We know the consequences. . . . They say people can think for themselves? Do you honestly believe that the chap who can't pass primary six knows the consequences of his choice when he answers a question viscerally, on language, culture and religion? But we knew the consequences. We would starve, we would have race riots. We would disintegrate.[51]

[49] Lee Kuan Yew, *The Singapore Story* (Singapore: Prentice Hall, 1994), 9.

[50] Eugene K. B. Tan, "Re-engaging Chineseness: Political, Economic and Cultural Imperatives of Nation-Building in Singapore," *The China Quarterly*, vol. 175 (September 2003), 756.

[51] Quoted in Han Fook Kwang, Warren Fernandez, and Sumiko Tan, *Lew Kuan Yew: The Man and His Ideas* (Singapore: Times Editions, 1998), 134. It is worth noting that native tongues (including Chinese) were not entirely suppressed, as they could still be taught as second languages. As Lee explains, "We needed a common language. We solved this by

In the same vein, other less-than-democratic states in Southeast Asia suppressed manifestations of majority culture in the interests of promoting a form of nation building relatively conducive to political stability and economic development. Indonesia has approximately 180 million Muslims—more than any other country—yet President Suharto managed to suppress political manifestations of Islam during his thirty-four-year reign (1965–1998). Suharto proclaimed a vague philosophy termed *Pancasila* that was originally formulated by his predecessor, Sukarno. *Pancasila* was defended "as a moderate, middle-of-the-road ideology, somewhere between Communist ideology on the Left and Islamic theocracy on the Right,"[52] and all religious and political groups were required to pledge adherence to it. Whatever the drawbacks of this approach, it succeeded in suppressing ethnic and religious conflict and allowed for political stability and economic development.

Malaysia has been relatively democratic,[53] and it cannot suppress political manifestations of Islam to the same extent. Still, Prime Minister Mahathir Mohamad, the ruler of Malaysia from 1981 to 2003, placed some restrictions on public religious activity that would have been impossible to justify in more democratic states.[54] The freedom of the press was severely restricted on the grounds that it was necessary to preserve social stability in a communally divided society.[55] Moreover, Mahathir often used the bully pulpit to criticize manifestations of Islam deemed to be incompatible with economic modernization. In 1994 the Malaysian government made explicit the limits of religious expression that threaten his political program by banning Al Arqam, a relatively "fundamentalist" Islamic group, and arresting its leader Ashaari Mohammed. This arrest was carried out in accordance with a ruling from the National Fatwa Council and justified on religious grounds,[56] though

---

encouraging everyone to learn two languages, English and the mother tongue as the second language. English is not any group's mother tongue, so no one gained any advantage." Lee Kuan Yew, "For Third World Leaders: Hope or Despair?" *Collins International Fellowship Lecture*, John F. Kennedy School of Government, Harvard University, 17 October 2000, 5. This statement is somewhat misleading, however, because Lee and other "founding fathers" were largely educated in English and therefore felt most at ease in the English language, so their cohorts did in fact gain an advantage by the promotion of English as the main language of Singapore.

[52] Clark Neher and Ross Marlay, *Democracy and Development in Southeast Asia* (Boulder: Westview Press, 1995), 80.

[53] Compared to Suharto's Indonesia, not to the present regime in that country.

[54] A reminder that the term "democracy" here refers to free and fair competitive elections, along with the associated freedoms of the press and association.

[55] Neher and Marlay, *Democracy and Development*, 80.

[56] According to Abdullahi An-Na'im, however, the Malaysian government's decision to ban the group was not in accordance with the essence of Islam. See An-Na'im, "The

the government was probably more concerned by the political threat posed by Al Arqam's growing popularity[57] and its multimillion-dollar business empire.

From the standpoint of the minority group, another "advantage" of a less-than-democratic political system is that it might be easier for members of minority groups to strike bargains with political elites that suit the interests of both parties—and subsequently to suppress protests by the majority group. The Chinese minority in Suharto's Indonesia is a case in point. President Suharto acquired power in murky circumstances that included a race pogrom against those of Chinese ancestry in the mid-1960s. For the next three decades, the Chinese minority—roughly 3 percent of the population—was constrained from expressing its cultural identity. Public manifestations of Chinese festivals were banned, the Chinese language could not be taught in schools, and Chinese-language newspapers (with the exception of one small publication issued by the army) were forbidden. However, the Chinese were among the main beneficiaries of state-led economic development.[58] Suharto built his own family's wealth through connections with wealthy Chinese business leaders, and Chinese tycoons were granted substantial economic benefits in return. Indonesia's nontycoon Chinese minority, described as "a small prosperous class socially situated between traditional nobles and common peasants,"[59] also reaped economic benefits from Suharto's regime. By the late 1990s the Chinese minority controlled more than half of the country's wealth (some estimates range as high as 70 percent).

Elections in Malaysia have been more vigorously contested,[60] but the political process has been tightened of late. The ruling National Front's (BN) electoral advantage has been guaranteed by its control of the press and its deep pockets. After the 1986 elections, Mahathir purged his political party of dissidents and invoked the Internal Security Act to arrest critics of the government.[61] In 1999 Mahathir's deputy prime minister, Anwar Ibrahim, was sacked and jailed on dubious charges.

Cultural Mediation of Human Rights: The Al-Arqam Case in Malaysia," in *The East Asian Challenge for Human Rights*, ed. Joanne R. Bauer and Daniel A. Bell (New York: Cambridge University Press, 1999).

[57] It could be argued that Al-Arqam was a minority group in conflict with the majority of Muslims, but part of the problem (from the government's viewpoint) was precisely that this group was gaining in popularity and could conceivably have become the majority had it not been banned.

[58] Amy Freedman, *Political Participation and Ethnic Minorities: Chinese Overseas in Malaysia, Indonesia, and the United States* (New York: Routledge, 2000), 186.

[59] Neher and Marlay, *Democracy and Development*, 87.

[60] Once again, the comparison is with Suharto's Indonesia.

[61] Neher and Marlay, *Democracy and Development*, 105.

The Chinese minority—roughly 29 percent of the population—has also been marginalized from the political process. Prior to the 1969 race riots, Malay politicians needed to rely on Chinese political support to help thwart the Communist insurgency and to consolidate financial strength. Since then, however, there has been less of a need to reach out to the Chinese community. The BN has imposed several constraints on political participation by the Chinese minority, most notably by using its power to create new electoral districts in rural areas where Malays are the majority. As Amy Freedman notes, "This marginalizes the Chinese in two ways: first, it violates the principle of one person one vote, or the notion that all votes have equal weight. Second, it serves to keep the number of Chinese elected officials to a minimum because it is not likely that the BN would run a Chinese candidate in a rural Malay district."[62]

Notwithstanding the less-than-democratic political system, however, the Chinese business community has continued to prosper by becoming closely tied with state development goals. Chinese businesses, which were once family and community centered, rely increasingly on state or public financing. As a result, Malay political elites have become increasingly involved in Chinese business enterprises,[63] though the Chinese still control the largest share of Malaysia's capital. This mutually beneficial arrangement has been in place for over two decades.

In short, the experience of the Chinese minority groups in the less-than-democratic states of Indonesia and Malaysia shows that members of minority groups can rely on personal networking for economic benefits. So long as political elites find it to their advantage to maintain mutually beneficial arrangements with members of minority groups, the latter can benefit from less-than-democratic arrangements. Of course, the economic dominance of minority groups often leads to resentment among the majority culture. But the political elites of less-than-democratic states need not be as responsive to majority preferences, and they can rely on coercion and direct or indirect control of the media to suppress threats to political stability.

To be fair, Kymlicka does recognize the possibility that less-than-democratic states are less prone to nation-building centered on the majority culture, along with the implication that minority groups are not as

---

[62] Freedman, *Political Participation*, 188.

[63] The increasing participation of the Malays is also the product of the New Economic Policy (implemented in 1971) that granted special privileges to Malays in business ownership, investment incentives, and employment quotas. From 1971 to 1991 Malay ownership of Malaysia's capital increased from 3 to 20 percent (Neher and Marlay, *Democracy and Development*, 100). Not surprisingly, this affirmative action–style policy has generated some resentment among the relatively well-off Chinese minority, as when university quotas often mean that bright Chinese students must leave their homeland to get a tertiary education.

vulnerable to injustice in less-than-democratic states. But he develops three responses to this kind of objection.

First, he says that countries like Singapore are "the exception, rather than the rule. Most authoritarian regimes in Asia, like most authoritarian regimes in the West, have engaged in majority nation building: consider Burma/Myanmar, China, or the Philippines under Marcos."[64] In the case of China, however, the concept of Han nationality (*Han minzu*) was invented and promoted by early twentieth-century democratic reformers. Sun Yat-sen, leader of the republican movement, popularized the idea that there were "Five Peoples of China"—the majority Han and four minorities—and the authoritarian Communists expanded the number of minority groups to fifty-five after they took power.[65] In prewar Japan, according to John Lie, distinctive ethnic groups were officially recognized by the imperial government. The establishment of democracy after World War II, however, had the effect of replacing an inclusionary idea of citizenship with "an exclusionary one that was narrowly restricted to ethnic Japanese."[66] If the focus is Southeast Asia, the "exceptions" include Indonesia, Malaysia, and Singapore, which together constitute the majority of the population in the region.[67]

The presence of several exceptions is sufficient reason to cast doubt on efforts to democratize countries in the region. The possibility that democratization can worsen the situation of vulnerable minorities in Southeast Asia—even if "most authoritarian regimes" do not fall in this category—should be a reason for caution.[68] At the very least, foreign governments, international agencies, and nongovernmental organizations need to be well acquainted with local circumstances to assess the likely impact of democratization on particular minority groups and to consider what political processes, institutional arrangements, and norms would best promote minority rights.

Kymlicka's second response is to call into question the assumption that nation-building occurred in response to populist pressures in democratic countries:

> It may be true that authoritarian regimes can, in principle, ignore populist pressures more readily than democracies. But it is a mistake, I think, to sup-

---

[64] Kymlicka, "The Future of the Nation-State," 13.

[65] Gladney, "Ethnic Identity in China," 137.

[66] John Lie, "Politics of Recognition," 118. Lie writes that "[t]he establishment of a 'true' democracy is, ironically, one of the sources of monoethnic Japan," but the irony would not arise if one begins with the theoretical assumption that democracies are more likely to promote nation-building centered on the culture of the majority group.

[67] One might also ask how Kymlicka distinguishes between exceptions and rules.

[68] Even a single exception should lead to caution in that particular country, and (to a lesser extent) in other countries with similar characteristics.

pose that nation-building policies in the West were adopted in response to populist pressure. Even in Western democracies, nation-building almost always began as an elite-initiated project, which only later became a matter of passion for the masses. Far from being the result of majoritarian preferences, nation-building policies were initially adopted by elites precisely in order to create a cohesive sense of "nationhood" amongst the masses, which could then be mobilized in pursuit of various public objectives. And, as I've noted, this need to mobilize citizens applies to all modern states—it applies as much to authoritarian regimes as to democracies, and as much to Asian countries as to Western countries.[69]

Kymlicka, however, is referring primarily to the experience of nineteenth-century Europe. John Stuart Mill and other nineteenth-century liberals viewed nation building primarily as a civilizing mission, as a way of uniting various groups by the language and culture "of a highly civilized and cultivated" people. Liberals worried about "half-savage relic[s] of past times" that impeded the spread of Enlightenment values, and the task was to unify peoples in a state dominated by one of the "civilized" languages (English, French, German, or Italian). Thus, Kymlicka is correct to note that nation building was not the result of "majoritarian preferences"—in the *nineteenth* century. But elites could initiate these projects precisely (or at least partly) because European countries were not fully democratic. In nineteenth-century England, women and non–property holders did not have the right to vote, and even liberals such as Mill argued for qualifications to the one-person, one-vote principle (such as granting extra votes to the educated).[70]

In contemporary democracies, however, it would be relatively difficult to initiate and maintain nation-building projects that run counter to the majority culture. Even if nation-building projects do not result directly from majoritarian preferences, those preferences would serve as an important constraint upon feasible nation-building projects. Less-than-democratic Asian states, in contrast, do not face these constraints to the same extent.

This hypothesis can be supported with the experience of nation building following "twentieth-century-style" democratization. In the postcommunist states of Eastern Europe, perhaps the most obvious political development was a resurgence of nation-building that explicitly drew on the language and culture of the majority group. Majority-centered nation-building may not have been the direct result of majority preferences, but political leaders did find that invoking the majority culture was

[69] Kymlicka, "The Future of the Nation-State," 13.
[70] Mill, "Representative Government," chap. 8.

the most effective way of mobilizing "the masses." It is difficult to imagine that, say, a democratically elected leader inspired by Lee Kuan Yew could have successfully suppressed the Serbian language in Yugoslavia's schools in favor of an external "neutral" language such as English.

Recent democratization in East Asia has also led to nation-building centered on the language and culture of the majority.[71] In Indonesia, the collapse of Suharto's rule has been followed by a resurgence of Islam in politics and society. Abdurrahman Wahid, leader of the country's largest Islamic group (Nahdlatul Ulama), was elected president in 1999 (he was subsequently impeached in July 2001). Wahid's group had played an important social and educational role in Suharto's Indonesia, but it had eschewed competitive politics.[72] Relatively "fundamentalist" Islamic groups have been at the forefront of the proindependence movement in Aceh, and open conflict between Muslims and Christians has broken out in the Muluka islands, leading to thousands of deaths.

Even in Taiwan, which has avoided such violence, political liberalization in the late 1980s has led to the growth of an independence movement almost entirely supported by the native Taiwanese. As noted earlier, the Taiwanese dialect has been promoted in schools, and the educational curriculum has been revised to place more emphasis on Taiwan's distinctive culture and history (as opposed to the history of mainland China).

In short, democratization in contemporary societies has typically been accompanied by nation-building policies centered on the culture of the majority group. While political leaders may not have been directly responding to majority preferences, they realized that appealing to the majority culture was the most effective way of promoting various nation-building projects (not to mention cementing their own grip on power). Given that nation building is more likely to be centered on the majority culture in democratic states, minority groups may be particularly vulnerable during democratization, and advocates of democracy need to take this factor in account.

Kymlicka's third response to the claim that less-than-democratic Asian states can better protect minority groups is to question the assumption that these states can resolve—as opposed to postpone—ethnic conflict. But the experience of at least some Asian states suggests otherwise. In Singapore, the various ethnic groups engaged in bloody communal violence in the early to mid 1960s. Since then, however, various nation-building measures, centered on the promotion of the English language,

---

[71] See, e.g., Jacques Bertrand, "Democratization and Religious and Nationalist Conflict in Post-Suharto Indonesia," in *Democratization and Identity*, ed. Susan J. Henders (Lanham, MD: Lexington Books, 2004).

[72] Neher and Marlay, *Democracy and Development*, 84.

seem to have reduced tensions between ethnic groups.[73] No doubt economic development has also played a role, but development occurred at least partly because the PAP succeeded in promoting the use of the English language and checking ethnic conflict.

In Hong Kong, the British colonial authorities also suppressed majority culture by encouraging the use of English in primary and secondary schools (and suppressing the Cantonese language, spoken by 97 percent of Hong Kongers). Whatever the advantages of this approach, it is now argued that Cantonese-language education would be a more effective medium of instruction for most Hong Kong students.[74] In response, the government has been trying to limit the number of English-language schools and to promote the use of Cantonese in local schools, but many parents object because they want their children to be educated in English.[75] In this sense, the British colonial authorities were too successful in promoting the use of English in schools.

Still, it must be conceded that measures to limit ethnic conflict in less-than-democratic societies do not always succeed. In the worst cases, they can exacerbate conflict, because tensions are allowed to build up and can explode when the political system opens up. But this is yet another reason to be cautious about democratization! In Taiwan, as noted above, the roles have been reversed, and now the mainland Chinese minority feels victimized by discriminatory practices. From the perspective of the local Taiwanese, the special benefits granted to this minority group could not be justified. But arguably the pendulum has swung too far the other way. As noted earlier, the government has been promoting policies designed to wipe out the Chinese heritage identified with the KMT mainland arrivals.

[73] In fact, the PAP may have been too successful for its own good. The main justification for less-than-democratic rule has been the need to preserve political stability in an ethnically volatile social and political context. But the PAP's strong-arm measures are less justified now that the various groups are less likely (compared to the 1960s) to engage in communal violence. A cynical view is that the PAP has been deliberately refanning the flames of ethnic conflict (e.g., by proposing ethnic based welfare schemes and filling the pages of local newspapers with horror stories of ethnic conflict from around the world) to further justify constraints on democracy. Luckily for the PAP, the September 11 terrorist attacks, along with the capture of Islamic "fundamentalists" planning a terrorist attack in Singapore shortly thereafter, provided more plausible justifications for maintaining the tight security apparatus underpinning less-than-democratic rule.

[74] Lin Fengmei, "Zhongwen zuoda kaosheng chengji jiao jia" [Answering Exam Questions in Chinese Leads to Better Grades], *Ming pao*, 4 November 2000.

[75] Parents object because they believe that English-language skills increase the likelihood of landing high-paying jobs, but Ruth Hayhoe, former head of Hong Kong's Institute of Education, argues that even English-language skills can be improved if courses other than English are carried out in Cantonese because English-language education tends to demoralize students and negatively affects their performance in school, including English classes (conversation with Ruth Hayhoe).

In civil society too, there has been an upsurge in intolerance: for example, local Taiwanese oppose the use of Mandarin in public demonstrations, insisting that speakers articulate their demands exclusively in the
local Taiwanese dialect.[76]
More worrisome, the explosion of ethnic conflict in Indonesia since
political liberalization has exposed deep fault-lines. In the spring of 1998,
long-bottled up antagonism against the relatively wealthy Chinese minority finally resurfaced. Riots destroyed Sino-Indonesian property throughout Indonesia, hundreds were killed in Jakarta's Chinatown, and an un-
known number of Chinese women were raped and abused by roving
bands of thugs.[77] Subsequent democratization does seem to have benefited the Chinese minority to a certain extent—cultural symbols such as
dragon dances and open celebration of the Lunar New Year are allowed
for the first time in years—but "parliament has done almost nothing to
address a stack of anti-discriminatory bills and abolish 62 laws seen as
racist."[78] From the perspective of minority groups, the post-Suharto developments illustrate the risk of depending on personal relationships
with unpopular leaders for protection. But they also suggest the need to
consider the likely impact of democratization on minority groups.[79] If
harsh measures to suppress ethnic conflict in less-than-democratic societies have not reduced tensions, this is yet another reason to worry about
the potential impact of democratization.
In sum, nation-building centered on the majority culture in democratic
states may pose distinctive threats to vulnerable minority groups.[80] This

[76] Chang Maukei, "Taiwan de zhengzhi zhuanxin yu zhengzhi de 'zuqunhua' guocheng"
[The Political Transformation of Taiwan and the Emergence of Politically Significant Ethnic Identity], *Jiaoshou luntan zhuankan*, no. 4 (1997), 52.
[77] Freedman, *Political Participation*, xii.
[78] Dini Djalal, "Empty Party Promises," *Far Eastern Economic Review*, 30 November
2000.
[79] It is worth keeping in mind the broad definition of an ethnocultural group noted
above. If the definition of an ethnocultural group is restricted to language and/or race, the
Indonesian Chinese may not count as a minority. The harsh measures to curb the expression of Chinese identity under Suharto's rule did "succeed" (to a large extent) in assimi-
lating the Chinese into the Indonesian language and culture. But in the minds of many
Indonesians, they were still "Chinese," and, rich or poor, they were targeted by ethnic
pogroms in 1998.
[80] Note that my critique has been directed at Kymlicka's argument to the contrary, but I
have not specifically questioned Kymlicka's view that justice requires equality between ethnocultural groups in the state. I challenge such views in chapter 11, where I argue that inequality between groups may be justified if it benefits the least well-off minority groups
and/or inequality creates opportunities for relatively deprived groups in other societies to
improve their lives. For an account of Confucian-style minority rights that differs from
Kymlicka's theory, see He Baogang, "Confucianism versus Liberalism over Minority
Rights: A Critical Response to Will Kymlicka," in *The Journal of Chinese Philosophy*, vol.
31, no. 1 (March 2004), 103–23.

claim should not be too controversial; on reflection, I suspect that most people will accept the weak prodemocracy thesis that democracy is generally advantageous for majorities and sometimes for minorities, but that it may also hinder legitimate minority rights, depending on the context. It only challenges the strong thesis that democracy guarantees minority rights (with a few minor exceptions that should not affect public policy). To the extent that only academics defend the strong thesis, it may not be worth worrying about. However, it remains possible that outside prodemocracy forces act on the strong prodemocracy thesis, perhaps causing real harm to minority groups, so let me say something about the policy implications of the weak prodemocracy thesis.

IMPLICATIONS FOR OUTSIDE PRODEMOCRACY FORCES

Democracy as it is usually understood tends to benefit most members of a political community.[81] Sometimes it also benefits minority groups who can mobilize and voice their interests in the political system. In some contexts, however, democracy can be detrimental to the interests of minority groups. I have tried to show, by pointing to the experience of several modernizing East Asian countries, that democracy may pose special dangers to vulnerable ethnocultural minority groups because nation-building projects centered on the majority culture can marginalize or eliminate expressions of minority traditions and languages.

I have also tried to show that some minority groups in less-than-democratic states of East Asia may benefit from constraints on democracy. The state can promote a form of nation-building that does not privilege the culture of the majority group, and minority groups can strike deals with political elites in a way that might not be possible in relatively democratic states. Also, political elites in less-than-democratic states may find it easier to resist pressure from the local population to enact policies detrimental to the interests of vulnerable minority groups.

In other words, democratization in East Asian states may *worsen* the situation of minority groups. This would not really undermine the practical case for democracy in those states where military dictators rely on systematic terror and totalitarian means to govern most people. There is no doubt, for example, that Burma would have been better off had the

---

[81] If democratization leads to social chaos and economic decline, however, then even the majority may not benefit: Fareed Zakaria praises Suharto, who had achieved order, secularism, and economic growth (whatever his flaws), and he writes: "Gradual political reform rather than wholesale revolution would have been preferable, certainly for the average Indonesian, who one assumes was the intended beneficiary of Western policies." Zakaria, *The Future of Freedom*, 8.

military junta respected the majority will favoring Aung San Sun Kyi in the 1988 election, and it seems beside the point, if not politically dangerous, to point out that judgments regarding the benefits of democracy need to be balanced against the actual and potential costs for minority groups. But the modernizing, less-than-democratic states of East Asia often do relatively well at providing political goods like economic growth, political stability, and personal freedom—goods that benefit "the many"—and the fact that minority groups can also benefit from "Asian-style" constraints on democracy is an extra reason for caution.

Once again, I do not mean to suggest that democratization in an Asian context necessarily harms minority groups. In some cases, minority groups will benefit from the goods traditionally associated with democracy, such as more opportunities for political participation and greater respect for civil liberties. Still, the real possibility that democratization may harm minority groups means that outside prodemocracy forces (international organizations, Western governments, human rights INGOs, etc.) need to investigate the local reality to determine the likely effects of democratization. If it turns out that democracy is likely to be detrimental to minority groups, then outside prodemocracy forces should also pay special attention to measures designed to protect the legitimate interests of minority groups (e.g., giving extra funds to local NGOs that struggle for minority rights).[82] The aim, in other words, would be to minimize, if not eliminate, the negative effects of democratization on minority groups. In the worst cases, however, it could be that democratization would result in serious harm to minority groups, no matter what is done from the outside. This might require outside prodemocracy forces to admit that democracy may not be appropriate in that particular context. In such cases, they should pack up their bags and return in more propitious times.

These are not simply theoretical soundings for caution. At this moment (early 2006), China seems to fit the model of the modernizing, less-than-democratic East Asian state: it provides economic growth, personal freedom, and political stability, while denying the right of the majority to exercise substantial power at the national level. The mainland's relationship with Taiwan is an obvious source of contention, but its record with the

---

[82] It is important, needless to say, to weigh the advantages of such policy proposals against their disadvantages. If it turns out that promoting minority group rights would only marginally benefit the relevant group(s) but have the effect of unnecessarily politicizing ethnicity and undermining the chance of establishing cross-cutting ties between members of different groups in the political community, then such proposals may not be desirable. For some thoughtful policy suggestions that attempt to balance the interests of disadvantaged minority groups with the need for cross-cutting social and political ties (to avert nationalist conflict) during the process of democratization, see Snyder, *From Voting to Violence*, chap. 7.

Taiwanese minority is not straightforwardly problematic. Of course, there is the threat of war if Taiwan declares formal independence. Beyond this constraint, however, the mainland is prepared to grant wide autonomy to Taiwan, including the right to have its own military force (I do not know of an analogous situation elsewhere). Moreover, the mainland Chinese state has been actively cultivating Taiwanese businessmen as part of its effort to deepen ties between Taiwan and the mainland, with the result that there has been a huge boom in trade between Taiwan and the mainland.

Let us then consider the likely effect of Western-style democratization on China's relationship with Taiwan. This may well be the one policy area where we can confidently say that the Communist Party leadership reflects the wishes of the people. If Taiwan declares formal independence, there would be substantial popular support for war against Taiwan, even if it means tens of thousands of casualties.[83] If Taiwan does not declare formal independence, skillful Chinese politicians could easily mobilize people's passions against separatist tendencies in Taiwan. The free press would expose and publicize the de-Sinification discourse in Taiwan, further increasing the people's anger. So taking a hard-line stance on Taiwan would be the ticket to political power in the mainland (as opposed to the current CCP leadership, which derives its legitimacy primarily from its capacity to deliver economic goods). And the willingness to act on this hard-line stance is likely to increase the popularity of elected politicians in the mainland, just as President Putin has profited from his bloody war against Chechnya. In short, democracy in China may well increase the likelihood of war with Taiwan.[84] To the extent that the majority of Taiwanese view themselves as a distinct ethnocultural group, such an eventuality would represent an obvious setback for anybody who cares about the interests of minority groups.

[83] In the event of a transition to democracy in China, Bruce Gilley speculates that a Taiwan leader could promise to support the democratic reformers in China and not declare independence in return for a promise that the future Chinese state would recognize Taiwan's autonomy and drop threats of war. Gilley, *China's Democratic Future*, 145, 237–39. This is wishful thinking, and it would be reckless to base one's policies on the hope of such an outcome. One political theorist in Taiwan told me that if China drops its threat of war, it is almost certain that Taiwan would declare formal independence. This scholar—the son of a mainlander, who is considered to be "pro-KMT" and is sharply critical of the de-Sinification policies of the DPP—told me that even he would support independence for Taiwan if there were no threat of warfare from the mainland.

[84] Of course, other factors may have the same effect. For example, if the economic situation suddenly deteriorates in mainland China, hawkish factions within the CCP (that previously derived its legitimacy primarily from its capacity to deliver the economic goods) could provoke hostilities with Taiwan so as to generate support at home.

Once again, I do not mean to deny that Western-style democracy would bring benefits to the majority of newly empowered citizens. But if the choice is between less-than-democratic political arrangements that provide some benefits to the majority as well as some protection for minority groups and Western-style democracy that may lead to violence and insecurity for minorities, then prodemocracy reformers may need to refocus their energies elsewhere.

In modern-day multicultural societies, in short, the challenge is to secure the kind of social cohesion that underpins stable and peaceful societies. Democracy has an unfortunate tendency to favor the interests of the majority, and special measures must be taken to ensure that minority groups are not harmed or made to feel alienated from the political system. As we will see in the following chapter, this finding also has implications for educational policy. Just as democratic arrangements benefiting the majority can be harmful to minorities, so an educational curriculum designed to prepare democratic citizens for political participation can exacerbate tensions with minority students if serious efforts are not made to consider their interests. Rather than point to nondemocratic alternatives, however, I will try to make a case for the possibility and desirability of curricula more likely to ensure that diverse ethnic groups in multicultural East Asian societies respect each other and feel some sort of identification with the larger political community.

8

Democratic Education in a Multicultural Context:
Lessons from Singapore

THE PREVIOUS chapter pointed to an important flaw of Western-style democracy, conceived in the minimal sense of free and fair competitive elections along with the freedoms that make such elections meaningful. If the people are not inclined to tolerance and peace, then democracy won't be sufficient for good government. And if people are too passive, they can easily be misled by political (and military) leaders into supporting policies that harm particular groups in their polity, if not electoral democracy itself (as in the extreme case of the Nazis who were brought into power by means of elections). The quality of the people, in other words, matters, and political thinkers need to consider the question of how best to educate the people so that they express desirable political virtues and help to sustain free and fair political institutions. It is widely recognized today that the educational system is crucial for the purpose of cultivating democratic virtues.

One of the teaching methods designed to improve democratic virtues is public recognition of the intellectual contributions of different groups, including those historically marginalized. Failing to recognize those contributions, as Amy Gutmann puts it, "morally damages democracy by conveying a false impression that members of these groups have not contributed significantly to making . . . politics what it is today."[1] In the East Asian context—particularly those societies that have been subject to Western imperialism—this means reaching beyond the works of Great White European Males to include works by Asian thinkers that may resonate more with the interests and backgrounds of the students. The aim is not so much to transmit specific moral content from particular traditions as to identify significant contributions by authors of scholarly traditions that students take pride in and that seem to address their concerns, thus increasing the students' desire to learn and participate in

---

[1] Gutmann, *Democratic Education*, 305. Gutmann writes with the American context in mind. For an interesting account of the battles over history textbooks in India between quasi-fascist Hindu nationalists (who aim to demonize the contributions of Muslims in Indian history) and leftist democrats (who try to show the positive contributions of Hindus and Muslims), see William Dalrymple, "India: The War over History," *The New York Review of Books*, 7 April 2005, 62–65.

classroom discussion, and, it is hoped, improving their ability to participate intelligently as adults in the political processes that shape their society.

The argument is supported with my own experience teaching political theory at the National University of Singapore. I had hoped that giving greater recognition to Asian thinkers such as Han Fei Zi and Confucius would generate more interest among students and improve their desire to participate in classroom discussion as well as, ultimately, the politics of their community. It turns out that things were more complicated than I had anticipated. First, however, it is worth saying something about the political context.[2]

SINGAPORE'S POLITICAL HISTORY

Singapore is a small tropical island roughly the size of Brooklyn; its current population is nearly four million. In the early nineteenth century, Singapore was colonized by the British, who tried to turn the island into an important trading center. This effort was partly successful, and the territory attracted migrants from China, India, and the surrounding Malay-Islamic archipelago. The British granted internal self-government to Singapore in 1959. But the ruling People's Action Party, led by Lee Kuan Yew, had doubts about the economic viability of a small, independent island without any natural resources and fought hard to join a federation with the surrounding territories. In 1963 Singapore, Malaya, Sarawak, and North Borneo formed a new federation—Malaysia. After two years, however, Singapore was expelled from Malaysia and forced to be independent. The expulsion was partly due to ethnic differences— mutual mistrust between the predominantly Chinese Singaporeans and their predominantly Muslim Malay neighbors. Disputes over economic policy and personality clashes between the leaders of Singapore and Malaya also played a role.

Lee Kuan Yew famously wept in public when he announced the separation. Singapore did not have any difficulty in winning international acceptance of its independence, but the economic and security challenges lying ahead seemed insurmountable. To deal with the former, the PAP— although nominally socialist—adopted the strategy of opening its country to foreign investment. As Lee explains,

> Of course, the prevailing theory was that multinationals were exploiters of
> cheap labor and cheap raw materials and would suck [us] dry. We had no

---

[2] The next three sections draw upon my article, "Teaching in a Multicultural Context: Lessons from Singapore," *Dissent* (Spring 2000), 9–16.

raw materials for them to exploit. All we had was labor. Nobody else wanted to exploit labor. So why not, if they want to exploit our labor? They're welcome to it. And we found out that whether or not they exploited us, we were learning how to do a job from them, which we would never have learnt.[3]

This innovative strategy has underpinned Singapore's rapid economic development since the 1960s.[4] Even "communist" countries like China now follow the Singaporean model of reliance on multinational corporations to import capital, provide employment, and build up management skills.[5]

Singapore did have a model—Israel—in meeting its security challenges. As a small country surrounded by large, potentially hostile, and predominantly Muslim neighbors, Singapore looked to Israel for guidance. As Lee put it, "We intend to fight for our stake in this part of the world, and [to] anybody who thinks they can push us around, I say: over my dead body. . . . We opted for the Israeli fashion, for in our situation we think it might be necessary not only to train every boy but also every girl to be a disciplined and effective digit in defense of their country."[6] Lee's government invited a group of Israeli military advisers to provide covert training of Singapore's defense force, and in 1967 Singapore introduced an Israeli-style policy of compulsory military national service (but only for adult males). The PAP also launched a massive nation-building exercise designed to forge a common identity—one that would motivate patriotic soldiers to face harm and danger on the nation's behalf.

Nation building, however, was perhaps Singapore's greatest challenge. As Lee puts it, "[We had] to build a nation from scratch."[7] This was not made easy by the fact that Singapore was, and is, an ethnically plural society—77 percent Chinese, 14 percent Malay, and 8 percent Indian—

---

[3] Quoted in Han, Fernandez, and Tan, *Lee Kuan Yew*, 109.

[4] Dr. Goh Keng Swee, then deputy prime minister of Singapore, has been widely credited as the architect of Singapore's economic success. See Tilak Doshi and Peter Coclanis, "The Economic Architect: Goh Keng Swee," in *Lee's Lieutenants: Singapore's Old Guard*, ed. Lam Peng Er and Kevin Y. L. Tan (St. Leonards, Australia: Allen & Unwin, 1999).

[5] I do not mean to imply that this model is fundamentally incompatible with communism. It can be argued that Mao misinterpreted Marx's idea of communism, and that Marx himself would have recognized the (short-to medium-term) necessity of capitalist reform programs. See my article, "From Mao to Jiang: China's Transition to Communism," *Dissent* (Summer 1999), 20–23.

[6] Quoted in Christopher Tremewan, *The Political Economy of Social Control in Singapore* (Houndsmills: Macmillan/St. Antony's College, 1994), 107–8. Another feature learned from Israel was the practice of building pedestrian overpasses, the idea being to force people to do physical exercise and thus stay fit for warfare, if need be (conversation with Singaporean official, March 2003).

[7] Lee, *The Singapore Story*, 9.

and the various groups were literally at war with each other in the early 1960s. The Malay minority in particular posed a challenge to the creation of national unity in Singapore because its members were more inclined to side with Malays in the surrounding states than with the majority Chinese. Thus, the PAP felt it could not create a new identity by appealing to Chinese culture. Instead, it attempted to combat all forms of ethnic parochialism by fostering the growth of a new Singaporean identity that would underpin security and prosperity. For example, the government broke up ethnic enclaves by moving people into ethnically mixed public housing blocs. It also promoted the use of English, which involved overriding the wishes of all groups, including the majority Chinese. Lee is quite explicit that Singapore's nation-building exercise was incompatible with democracy because the Chinese majority would have preferred to promote Chinese as the official language.[8]

Ethnic attachments, however, proved to be more resilient than expected. Lee now recognizes the excessive chutzpah of his early days: "It was as well that we did not realize how daunting were the problems of building a nation out of peoples of totally different races, languages, religions and cultures. I would be appalled if I [were] asked to start off all over again . . . with the heavy knowledge of the almost irreconcilable divisions which were to open up."[9] The PAP eventually gave up on the aim of replacing ethnic identity with a new Singaporean identity.[10] Instead, it now seeks to accommodate the fact of ethnic pluralism in various ways, such as promoting ethnic-based welfare groups. The primary language of education is still English, but the various groups also receive education in the various "mother-tongues"—Mandarin for the Chinese, Malay for the Malay Muslims, and Tamil for the Indians.[11] In the late 1980s the government also promoted religious education in secondary schools, with different religions corresponding roughly to the different ethnic groups.[12]

---

[8] See chapter 7.

[9] Quoted in Jon Quah, "Government Policies and Nation Building," in *In Search of Singapore's National Values*, ed. J. Quah (Singapore: Institute of Policy Studies, 1990), 83.

[10] Rapid economic development in China and Southeast Asia provided an economic incentive for renewed emphasis on Asian languages and cultures. On the Chinese case, see Tan, "Re-engaging Chineseness."

[11] Lee Kuan Yew has since recognized that the bilingual policy was too demanding, especially for the Chinese who spoke English at home, and the teaching method will move away from memorization of characters and put emphasis on oral communication and fun applications of the language. In a speech to Parliament, Lee compared the difficulties of bilingualism in Singapore with the failure of Pierre Trudeau's dream to make Canada into a fully bilingual country (e-mail communication with Gary Bell, 28 November 2004).

[12] This policy was abandoned after some fundamentalist Christian teachers encouraged children to enroll in the Christian curriculum, which upset some parents and, the government argued, exacerbated ethnic tensions.

One might have been led to expect that the renewed emphasis on ethnicity be accompanied by a certain degree of political opening, as in the case of Taiwan (discussed in the previous chapter). To the extent that the earlier promotion of English and the breaking up of ethnic enclaves relied on autocratic measures, the new respect for the cultural traditions of ethnic groups could have allowed for greater political participation by groups that feel more pride in their community. As it turns out, however, the PAP has not loosened its grip on national politics.[13] Any challenges to its political dominance are harshly met, with responses ranging from job sackings, public humiliation, and bankruptcy to forced exile.[14] Even the PAP's measures to promote ethnic pride have been designed in such a way as to solidify its grip on political power. For example, the PAP implemented a system of guaranteeing a seat for minority candidates in multiseat constituencies—termed the Group Representation Constituency (GRC) system—that also includes a great deal of gerrymandering. The political motivation was made more explicit shortly before the 1997 election when the ruling PAP increased the size of GRCs from four to six seats without increasing minority representation. The number of constituencies with a single candidate was effectively cut from twenty-one to nine, and the fragmented opposition found it more difficult to field so many team candidates, correspondingly reducing their prospects at election time. In short, the renewed pride in ethnicity has not been accompanied by substantial opening of the democratic process.

[13] One Singaporean academic who prefers to remain anonymous (for obvious reasons) told me that the real stumbling block to political liberalization is Lee Kuan Yew himself, and that the system will likely open up after his death. A more pessimistic view regarding the likelihood of political liberalization is put forward by science fiction writer Yann Quero: he imagines a world in 2143 where Singapore, under the leadership of an enlightened despot, remains the world's only functioning state. Yann Quero, *Le Procès de l'Homme Blanc* (La Courneuve: Editions Arkuiris, 2005).

[14] See my book, *East Meets West*, chaps. 3 and 4. In chapter 4 I argue that the PAP's ruthless measures make Singaporeans more individualistic than they would otherwise be, and that there are good communitarian reasons for favoring more democracy in Singapore because the freedom of association and the right to run for the opposition without fear of retaliation are more likely to make people care about the good of others beyond their immediate circle of family and friends. I first put forward this communtarian justification for democracy in a Singaporean publication ("What Communitarianism Is," *Trends* [a monthly publication of the Institute for Southeast Asian Studies, Singapore], 27–28 March 1993, i, iv), an argument that was explicitly quoted by opposition figure Dr. Chee Soon Juan in his first book, *Dare to Change: An Alternative Vision for Singapore* (Singapore: Singapore Democratic Party, 1994). Dr. Chee was a friend and colleague at the National University of Singapore who was sacked from his job on trumped up charges shortly after he joined the opposition Singapore Democratic Party. Not surprisingly, my contract at the National University of Singapore was not renewed in 1994.

Racism in the Classroom?

In 1991 I was offered a job teaching political theory at the National University of Singapore. The lectures were to be given in English, but it was obvious that university authorities—following the general political trend in Singapore—were leaning toward a renewed emphasis on ethnic pride and heritage. I was not given any explicit guidance in this respect,[15] but I took this to mean that I should give greater recognition to Asian "civilizations" in the course curriculum. I also took this to mean that I could try to draw on Asian thinkers for the purpose of increasing a sense of student ownership of the curriculum, thus increasing the desire to participate in classroom discussion and, I hoped, in politics at large (of course I did not make this aim explicit).

It was not difficult to increase the proportion of Asian material. I had replaced an expatriate who relied solely on Western sources to teach a large (more than three hundred students) first-year "Introduction to Political Theory" course. He began the course with some arguments for realpolitik, drawing on Machiavelli's *Prince* to make his points. This seemed like a good starting point for the course. I would begin with the theme of "Politics without Morality," and then move on to various thinkers who argued for different combinations of morality and politics. Instead of Machiavelli, however, I decided to draw on the ancient Chinese thinker Han Fei Zi (c. 280–233 B.C.E.). Han Fei was a profoundly cynical—and very witty—proponent of realpolitik. He wrote a political handbook for power-hungry rulers, supporting his advice with colorful examples that occasionally went beyond the bounds of good taste:

> If the ruler reveals what he dislikes, his ministers will be careful to disguise their motives; if he shows what he likes, his ministers will feign abilities they do not have. . . . Because Duke Huan of Ch'i was jealous and loved his ladies in waiting, Shu-tiao [a minister] castrated himself in order to be put in charge of the harem; because the duke was fond of unusual food, Yi-ya steamed his son's head and offered it to the duke. Because Tzu-k'uai of Yen admired worthy men, Tzu-chih insisted that he would not accept the throne

---

[15] I was, however, given explicit guidance in other respects. I had to submit my reading list to the head of department. I was informed not to teach J. S. Mill's *On Liberty* and that I should teach more communitarianism instead (naturally this made me want to do the opposite). I was also requested not to teach Mill's *The Subjection of Women* to first-year students in political theory on the grounds that female students might get "radical" ideas about equality that they might try to implement at home, with the result that the students' grandmothers will complain to the university about the radical education they were getting in our department. A local colleague subsequently informed me not to take the process too seriously—simply agree with the head of department and change the syllabus later.

even if it were offered to him. . . . Hence, Tzu-chih, by playing the part of the worthy, was able to snatch power from his sovereign; Shu-tiao and Yi-ya, by catering to the ruler's desires, were able to invade his authority. . . . What caused this? It is an example of the calamity that comes when the ruler reveals his feelings to his ministers. As far as the feelings of the ministers go, they do not necessarily love their ruler; they serve him only in the hope of substantial gain. Now if the ruler of men does not hide his feelings and conceal his motives, but instead gives his ministers a foothold by which they may invade his rights, then they will have no difficulty in doing what [those ministers] did.[16]

Even—especially—loved ones cannot be trusted:

> It is hazardous for the ruler of men to trust others, for he who trusts others will be controlled by others. . . . A man at fifty has not yet lost interest in sex, and yet at thirty a woman's beauty has already faded. If a woman whose beauty has faded waits upon a man still occupied by thoughts of sex, then she will be spurned and disfavored, and her son will stand little chance of succeeding to the throne. This is why consorts and concubines long for the early death of the ruler. . . . The ruler must not fail to keep close watch on those who might profit by his death. Though the sun and moon are surrounded by halos, the real danger to them comes from within. Prepare as you may against those who hate you, calamity will come to you from those you love.[17]

Han Fei had special contempt for Confucian political thinkers who stressed tolerance and moral education. He did not deny that light rule had its place in a Golden Age of social harmony and material abundance. But in his own day—the Warring States period—such policies would lead to disaster, and Confucians were naively drawing inappropriate lessons from accidental features of past societies:[18]

> [T]he sage does not try to practice the ways of antiquity or to abide by a fixed standard, but examines the affairs of the age and takes what precautions are necessary. There was a farmer of Sung who tilled the land, and in his field was a stump. One day a rabbit, racing across the field, bumped into the stump, broke its neck, and died. Thereupon the farmer laid aside his plow and took up watch beside the stump, hoping that he would get another rabbit in the same way. But he got no more rabbits, and instead became the laughing stock of Sung. Those who think they can take the ways

[16] *Basic Writings of Mo Tzu, Hsun Tzu, and Han Fei Tzu*, trans. Burton Watson (New York: Columbia University Press, 1967), 33–34.

[17] Ibid., 85–86.

[18] This critique may not be fair. Even the relatively "idealistic" Mencius distinguished between prescriptions for ideal societies and those appropriate for less-than-ideal societies (see chapter 2 of this book).

of ancient kings and use them to govern the people of today all belong in the category of stump-watchers![19]

In his own period, Han Fei argued that state power needed to be strengthened by means of harsh laws and punishments. His aim was nothing less than total state control, and he stressed over and over again that moral considerations should not get in the way. Not surprisingly, rulers were quite receptive to this sort of advice, starting with the ruthless king of Qin who ascended to the throne in 246 B.C.E. and drew on Han Fei's advice to conquer and rule all of China under the title of First Emperor of the Qin dynasty. Following Han Fei's recommendation, the king of Qin also buried several hundred Confucian scholars alive with their books. This dynasty was short-lived, but Han Fei's influence persisted. It would only be a slight exaggeration to describe subsequent Chinese imperial history as a constant struggle between Han Fei's realpolitik and Confucian morality.

So it seemed reasonable to begin my political theory course with a leading Chinese political thinker who was both more straightforwardly Machiavellian and more politically influential than Machiavelli himself. It also seemed reasonable to use Chinese characters from Han Fei's original text during the lectures, which most students could understand. In the next part of the course, on "Morality without Politics," I discussed the views of anarchist thinkers who argued against all forms of state coercion on the grounds that human beings were potentially rational and self-regulating. Mikhail Bakunin was an obvious choice, but I made an effort to discuss the views of Chinese Daoist thinkers as well. In the last part of the course, on "Morality and Politics," I discussed the views of political thinkers who argued that the state was necessary, but that its policies should be informed and constrained by moral ideals. I drew on Aristotle and Mill, but I also discussed the views of Confucius. I hoped that students would appreciate my attempts to incorporate more Asian viewpoints in the course syllabus.

Shortly before my last lecture, a student slipped a letter signed X under my office door. It was not friendly. The student accused me of racism—more specifically, of glorifying Chinese thinkers and denigrating the cultural contributions of Singapore's minority groups. On the face of it, this was an absurd accusation—what could a newly arrived Canadian academic with no previous ties to the country possibly gain from taking sides in local culture wars? X, who had a fertile imagination, suggested possible motives. Either I was trying to curry favor with my departmental head (a PAP parliamentarian of ethnic Chinese descent) or I was trying to help my Chinese wife climb within the PAP political establishment

[19] *Basic Writings of Mo Tzu, Hsun Tzu, and Han Fei Tzu*, 97.

(my wife did work for a government think-tank, but she did not have any political aspirations). To support the claim of a pro-Chinese bias, X argued that all my accounts of Chinese thinkers were positive. Furthermore, I cast minority groups in a negative light—for example, I referred to Indians as "barbarians." I was dumbfounded by the latter accusation, until I realized that X must have been referring to my lectures on John Stuart Mill. Like most nineteenth-century European liberals, Mill had nothing but contempt for non-Western civilizations. He justified "civilizing missions" to uplift what he called "barbarians" in India,[20] apparently oblivious to the ugly reality of European imperialism (notwithstanding—or perhaps because of—the fact that he worked for the East India Company).

During my lectures on Mill, I had assumed that his views on imperialism were so obviously repugnant—especially in an Asian context!—that there was no need to condemn them explicitly. I realized that I may have made one or two ironical references to "barbarians" and that the irony may not have been obvious to all students. I did, however, use scare quotes around the word "barbarians" in my lecture notes. Apparently all this was missed, and X believed that I was endorsing Mill's views.

Because I could not respond personally to X's letter, I brought it to class, read parts of it out loud, and clarified my motives to the whole class. I made a distinction between presenting and defending arguments. I stated my own (critical) views on Mill's defense of European imperialism. I further explained that I did not mean to endorse all the arguments of Chinese thinkers discussed in class—for example, I didn't agree with Han Fei's advice that Confucian scholars should be liquidated. I added that it was difficult to construe my presentation of Han Fei's ideas—for example, his claim that a minister would try to climb up the political ladder by steaming his son's head for an emperor who was fond of unusual food—as an attempt to glorify Chinese political thinkers. I also responded to the speculations about my hidden political agenda.

By the time I had finished, many students were laughing, apparently amused by the absurdity of the accusations and my dry responses. Still, I noticed—for the first time—that several male students of Indian descent were grouped together at the back of the class. They were not laughing.

When I showed X's letter to a senior Singaporean colleague, he pointed out that I was partly to blame because I had only discussed the contributions of Chinese thinkers. The point is not whether or not I actually endorsed their arguments; merely presenting them in class showed that

[20] See, e.g., chapters 2 and 3 of J. S. Mill's *Considerations on Representative Government*.

I took them seriously. And by excluding the contributions of Muslim and Indian thinkers from the curriculum, I was implicitly sending the message that their views were unimportant and uninteresting—or at least, that is how it would be seen by Malay and Indian students. My use of Chinese characters in class further contributed to the alienation of minority students, since they would not be able to follow.

INCLUSIVE MULTICULTURALISM

The lesson was clear—I needed to expand my curriculum to include the contributions of Muslim and Indian thinkers. The following year I decided to spend more time on the "Politics without Morality" section of the course. I investigated the contributions of Indian and Muslim thinkers, and to my surprise I learned that there were influential Machiavellian thinkers in the Indian and Islamic traditions as well—once again, long before Machiavelli's time.

Kautilya's *Arthasastra* (fourth-century B.C.E.) is arguably the most famous political treatise in ancient Indian philosophy. Kautilya, a minister of the first Mauryan empire, relied on the historical and comparative method to draw lessons for the establishment, operation, and expansion of the machinery of government. He favored a centralized system of administration with the king at the top of a hierarchy and an extensive use of spies to guarantee internal security. The section on foreign policy is particularly Machiavellian. The ruler should do his best to expand his territory, without moral or religious constraints. Quite the opposite—he should go out of his way to prey on people's superstitious beliefs to further his own ends. Consider the following list of tactics for assassinating an enemy ruler:

> [He may] be killed by mechanical contrivances of the kind described below, when, out of piety, he comes to worship on the occasion of a festival or a frequently visited temple:
>
> 1. by releasing a mechanism causing a wall or a stone to fall on him after he has entered the temple;
> 2. by letting loose a shower of stones from an upper storey;
> 3. by dislodging a door on him;
> 4. by dropping a beam fixed at one end on him;
> 5. by firing weapons concealed in the image of the deity at him;
> 6. by poisoning the cowdung spread on the floor or the water used for sprinkling in the places where he stays, sits or moves about;
> 7. by poisoning the flowers and incense offered to him;
> 8. by making him inhale [inside the temple] poisonous fumes concealed by fragrances; or

9. by causing him to fall in a spiked pit by the release of a trap door in the floor under his bed or seat.[21]

To fulfill my self-imposed Islamic "quota," I selected Ibn Khaldun (1332–1406).[22] Like the other Machiavellians, Khaldun led an active political life in turbulent times. He withdrew from the "real world" in his forties and settled down to write *The Muqaddimah*, or "Introduction to World History." This descriptive, sociological work—Khaldun is often referred to as the founder of modern sociology—covers a range of topics. Volume 1 focuses on political themes, and Khaldun drew on history and his own political experience to make his points. His approach contrasts with al-Farabi's account of the ideal Islamic city-state. Khaldun argued that the political thinker should describe what is, understand it, and draw lessons on the basis of history. According to Khaldun, *asabiyah* (group feeling), the tribal loyalty that makes the individual devote himself to the tribe, is the key to political power. The stronger the attachment to the group, the more the tribe is capable of fighting and conquering others: "It should be known that since . . . desert life no doubt is the reason for bravery, savage groups are braver than others. They are, therefore, better able to achieve superiority and to take away the things that are in the hands of other nations."[23] Rulers should be well acquainted with *asabiyah* and rely on nomads to increase their power. They should make use of religion to unify nomads and form a solid front against the world. Eventually, however, nomadic conquerors will succumb to the temptations of luxurious city life, and that is the beginning of the end. The once brave nomads become soft, flabby, and docile to outsiders, and the dynasty eventually falls to new tribes bound by strong *asabiyah*. This cyclical process, Khaldun argues, is socially necessary, and moral ideals are powerless to stop it.

So I included Kautilya and Khaldun in the course syllabus. I began with a Machiavellian checklist, suggesting that Machiavellian political thinkers have ideas about genre (they write practical handbooks for rulers), the ends of politics (maintenance and expansion of state power), the means of politics (expediency, not morality), human nature (prone to corruption and untrustworthy), and international relations (states pursue

[21] Kautilya, *Arthasastra*, ed. and trans. L. N. Rangarajan (New Delhi: Penguin Books, 1987), 532.

[22] I have recently been informed that the "Mirror of Princes" literature may be more directly relevant for the purpose of identifying realpolitik outlooks in Islamic political thought.

[23] Ibn Khaldun, *The Muqaddimah: An Introduction to History, Vol. 1*, trans. Franz Rosenthal (London: Routledge & Kegan Paul, 1958), 282.

naked self-interest in an anarchical world). I then surveyed the four thinkers from the various traditions (including Machiavelli). I concluded that Han Fei Zi was the most consistent Machiavellian—he scored a perfect five out of five on the Machiavellian checklist—and poor Machiavelli came in last place.

This time, I did not get any hate mail. In fact, I dare say immodestly that the course was quite successful, judging by the lively discussion in tutorial groups and the subsequent course evaluations. As far as I could tell, no one felt left out. Students seemed to be more motivated to learn about scholarly contributions from traditions that they took pride in—notwithstanding the fact that the political thinkers surveyed often held unsavory views. Moreover, several students told me that they enjoyed learning about thinkers from other traditions, and that this actually contributed to interethnic harmony. To the extent that ethnic tension was still being used as an excuse by the PAP for maintaining autocratic measures, I also felt I was doing my little bit to encourage democratic reform.

The lesson I would like to draw is obvious: It is fine to draw on students' cultural traditions for the sake of increasing their willingness to deliberate in and out of the classroom, but a teacher should make an effort to design a curriculum that draws on the scholarly contributions of all ethnic groups in the class. More generally, multicultural education should draw on the traditions of all ethnic groups in society. From the pedagogical point of view, this has the advantage of enhancing positive feelings about the contributions of the students' own ethnic groups, thus developing individual self-esteem among members of all groups and improving their academic performance.[24] From the political point of view, an inclusive curriculum has the advantage of encouraging mutual learning and understanding, and thus strengthening the links between the various ethnic groups in society. Put differently, if individuals feel that their "own" tradition is not being slighted, they are more likely to engage with "other" traditions. The paradoxical effect of drawing on the scholarly contributions of (all) ethnic groups is to break down the barriers between them and reinforce the desire to coexist peacefully and participate in the political life of the same society. Fully inclusive education of this sort can therefore contribute to the social cohesion that underpins "rule by the people" in the modern world.

---

[24] On the link between cultural pride, individual self-esteem, and improved academic performance, see Walter Feinberg, *Common Schools/Uncommon Identities: National Unity and Cultural Difference* (New Haven: Yale University Press, 1998), 127–28, 133–34, 139.

BEYOND SINGAPORE?

Of course, one should be cautious about exporting this "lesson" to other teaching contexts. For one thing, it may only apply to introductory classes in the social sciences and the humanities (more advanced classes tend to be relatively specialized, and the cultural background of contributors does not matter as much in the natural sciences). Moreover, Singapore is perhaps a unique case, where there are three clearly defined ethnic groups, each of which takes pride in its own cultural heritage (and is encouraged to do so by the government). In other societies, it may not always be easy to draw a line between the different ethnic groups (even in Singapore, there are overlapping categories, such as Indian Muslims and Euroasians).[25] Some classrooms may be so diverse that it may not be feasible to include the scholarly contributions of all ethnic groups.[26] There may be a fear that the principle of ethnic inclusiveness will lead to petty disputes about how much time should be spent on each tradition (in my case, I gave equal time to each group, and the majority Chinese students did not complain). It is also conceivable that learning about another group's tradition will promote conflict rather than mutual understanding.

[25] Chua Beng Huat argues that the Singapore government's "ethnic" policies tend to "flatten" or "homogenize" ethnic, linguistic, and religious differences within each ethnic category and have led to significant cultural costs both to the individuals and to the smaller ethnic groups that were amalgamated into each umbrella ethnic group: see Chua, "The Cost of Membership in Ascribed Community," in *Multiculturalism in Asia: Theoretical Perspectives*, ed. Will Kymlicka and Baogang He (Oxford: Oxford University Press, 2005).

[26] What about the opposite situation, viz., the classroom is ethnically homogenous? In my experience, the "right" pedagogical approach depends on the context. In Hong Kong, I taught political theory to classrooms composed entirely of Cantonese-speaking Chinese students, and I usually began with Chinese authors, then discussing writers from other traditions. In Beijing, however, there is greater curiosity about Western thinkers (and there seems to be an assumption that Western professors should teach Western material), so I usually begin with Western thinkers before moving on to Chinese and other material. Ideally, my view is that classrooms composed of students from diverse ethnic/cultural backgrounds are preferable to more homogenous ones (so long as the multicultural context allows for mutual learning). Being exposed to other cultures often leads people to question "the way things are done at home" and helps them learn from other ways (i.e., it allows for moral and political progress). There are also economic advantages: individuals able to navigate between different cultures have competitive advantages relative to those intimately familiar with only one culture. One way of meeting the challenge of promoting in-depth learning of other cultures in homogenous settings is to establish regular exchanges with students from other societies so that classrooms are composed of students from different backgrounds. In Hong Kong and mainland Chinese universities, there are increasing numbers of foreign exchange programs, but there is still a long way to go.

Notwithstanding these caveats, I still believe that the principle of ethnic inclusiveness in the educational curriculum may be relevant for other multicultural contexts—and that this does not necessarily involve compromising on Great Works. Let me try to respond to some key objections.

First, a critic may note that some ethnic groups do not feel the kind of attachment to "their" tradition that would motivate further study and the desire to participate in discussion. In Singapore, the various groups may be fully conscious of their ethnic heritage, but the situation is different in other immigrant societies. For example, second-or third-generation immigrants in the United States or Canada may not identify with the cultural background and scholarly achievements of their blood ancestors. In such a context, there would be no point in applying the principle of ethnic inclusiveness in the educational curriculum.

But is this an accurate diagnosis of the situation in North America? Some long-established, settled communities—Will Kymlicka calls them "national minorities"[27]—do in fact identify with, and take pride in, the scholarly contributions of their ancestors. The Québécois, for example, might be more motivated to study the works of French thinkers. During my undergraduate days at Montreal's McGill University in the early 1980s, the political theory curriculum revolved almost entirely among Anglophone and German thinkers (with the exception of a few lectures on Rousseau in the Introduction to Political Theory course). In retrospect, one can wonder about the effect of this curriculum on the large number (over 30 percent) of Francophone students at McGill. Perhaps some would have appreciated the opportunity to learn more about French political thinkers (I must confess I did not personally notice this lacuna at the time, perhaps because I am "only" half Francophone). Another potential benefit of exposure to French political thinkers is that Anglophone students could have developed a better understanding of French political culture—and who knows, this may have led to a rapprochement of the "two solitudes."[28]

This argument for multicultural education does not apply only to national minorities. Even second- or third-generation children of immigrants who willingly left their homelands sometimes identify with the contributions of their ancestors. Consider the large numbers of students of Chinese descent at the University of Toronto and the University of British Columbia. They often converse in Cantonese and Mandarin and retain a preference for Chinese food, and it is quite likely that they are interested in other parts of Chinese culture. Courses that include material

[27] Will Kymlicka, *Multicultural Citizenship* (Oxford: Clarendon Press, 1995).
[28] See Hugh MacLennan, *Two Solitudes* (New York: Duell, Sloan and Pearce, 1945).

from Chinese thinkers may well attract and interest such students—and
sensitize other students to the contributions of Chinese civilization.

Opponents of multiculturalism may reply that there is a risk of unintentionally creating or reinforcing boundaries between students. Instead
of "natural" assimilation into the majority culture, the children of immigrants will learn to identify with the culture of their ancestors, which can
lead to conflicts with the majority culture that might otherwise be prevented. In North America, however, the forces of assimilation are so
strong that learning about the contributions of immigrant cultures in a
few high school and university courses will not prevent the ultimate
"victory" of mainstream culture. The potential benefits of multicultural
education—motivating minority and immigrant students and improving
mutual understanding—far outweigh the risks.

Yet another objection from the opponent of multicultural education is
that the teacher should simply teach the most intellectually stimulating
Great Works whatever their origin or context, as opposed to taking into
account of such political considerations as the promotion of democratic
deliberative skills and social harmony. The choice is not between teaching the cultural traditions of the majority and those of all groups, but
rather between politically neutral teaching and politicizing the classroom. But this idea of politically neutral teaching is dubious in the social
sciences and the humanities. It may be possible to teach students who
are completely passive and unreflective about the political implications
of what they're learning, and to teach the material so that students remain in this "vegetative" state, but such a teaching strategy is itself a political choice, and not one that teachers who care about the cultivation
of democratic virtues would endorse. The choice of teaching material
(along with the way of teaching it) inevitably sends political messages to
the students, and claims of political neutrality are either self-deluding or
disingenuous. So it is best to be consciously aware of the likely political
implications of various possibilities, and to structure the curriculum in
ways that accord with the most politically desirable possibilities. If it is
possible to draw on intellectually stimulating material while also communicating politically desirable messages, then that is the way to go.

The next set of objections comes from the opposite direction: that my
suggested approach is *insufficiently* sensitive to multicultural considerations. One objection is that I was not consistently applying my own principle of ethnic inclusiveness in ways that cast doubt on the principle itself. As Theresa Man Ling Lee puts it, "[T]his whole notion of teaching
by way of ethnic representation is fundamentally flawed in principle. It is
a view based on the centrality of Western culture and I may add, it is
also the white professor's perspective. For if Bell were to be consistent,
the [Western] 'Great Works' should never have been represented in the

curriculum in the first place given the ethnic makeup of the classroom."[29] Lee's criticism leads me to reformulate the "ethnic inclusiveness" principle. The principle should not be that the teaching curriculum is determined *exclusively* by the ethnic composition of the classroom. The point is rather that the teaching curriculum should be *at least partly* drawn from the ethnic composition of the classroom so that no one group feels slighted and unwilling to participate in class discussion (and the polity more generally). Once the aim is achieved, then one can draw on whatever Great Works are most likely to stimulate the intellect and the desire (and capacity) to participate in informed discussion.

Still, it may seem that I was still privileging Western sources in ways that denigrate non-Western traditions:

> Perhaps even more disturbing is the fact that Bell used the West as the baseline for comparison in that course. For example, in the "Politics Without Morality" section of the course, he juxtaposed thinkers from the four respective traditions by way of a "Machiavellian checklist." . . . Apparently "Han Fei was the most consistent Machiavellian" and "poor Machiavelli came in last place." But why should these non-Western thinkers be judged by Machiavellian standards, especially since they all predated Machiavelli?[30]

But the point was not to judge the non-Western thinkers by means of *normatively defensible* Machiavellian standards. My own view is that Machiavellian standards themselves are deeply problematic from a moral point of view. Moreover, I used the term "Machiavellian" because of its widespread use in the English language. I tried to explain what this term typically means in its contemporary everyday usage and then concluded that Han Fei's ideas more consistently meet what we mean by (nonmoral) Machiavellian standards, joking that the Anglophone world would be using the term "Han Feizian" had Westerners been more aware of the history of non-Western political theory and practice. Far from being "Westcentric," I was trying to cast doubt on the "originality" of Machiavelli (as Isaiah Berlin put it) and to show the value of looking at non-Western sources.

Another objection along the lines that there's a need for more multicultural education is that Singapore-style political multiculturalism, as

[29] Theresa Man Ling Lee, "Intercultural Teaching in Higher Education," *Intercultural Education*, vol. 16, no. 3 (August 2005), 208.

[30] Ibid., 208–9. The main aim of Theresa Man Ling Lee's article is to argue for "intercultural teaching" as a means of promoting critical thinking (my approach is criticized because it seems inconsistent with this aim), not to argue for the thesis that Western material is not worth teaching. Western material "constitutes the bulk of [her] teaching" in Lee's own political theory classes (e-mail sent to author, 16 December 2004).

well as the kind of educational multiculturalism I am defending here, is limited to the good of ethnic groups. But shouldn't the multicultural course curriculum also include the contributions of nonethnic groups, such as gays, the deaf, and the blind? Truly inclusive multiculturalism would depend, I suppose, upon the extent to which the target group identifies with a distinct scholarly tradition and the availability of relevant scholarly sources in that tradition. Even in the absence of relevant scholarly sources, however, there may still be reasons to tailor one's teaching with the sensitivities of the group in mind. One of my keenest and most able students in Singapore was blind from birth. Once, during the course of a lecture on Plato's *Republic*, I discussed Plato's simile of the cave. I explained how (according to Plato) people within the cave were "completely blind," "living in the dark," and it was only outside the cave that they "saw the light," that is, grasped eternal truths. I noticed that my blind student seemed less than pleased. I surmised that either he was not satisfied with my choice of words or he was taking Plato's simile too literally, and perhaps he thought he was really missing out on something philosophically interesting. So I apologized for my use of "sight-centric" language. I also made an exception to my usual teaching strategy of presenting arguments in their best possible "light" and refraining from explicitly taking sides in scholarly disputes.[31] I provided several explicit arguments against Plato's theory of forms, and I said that in my view, it is best to stay "in the cave" (or, at least, in the "cave system") rather than try to philosophize from outside of any social and political context. All that seemed to help a bit.

Another set of objections question the aspiration to combine an emphasis on Great Works from diverse traditions with the aim of cultivating democratic virtues in and out of the classroom. It may be possible to draw upon "Machiavellians" from different traditions because a certain kind of political toughmindedness can be found in many different cultures. Non-Western traditions, however, lack strong contributions on many other topics, and then it will not be possible to tailor the curriculum to mirror the ethnic composition of the classroom in such cases.

---

[31] The idea is to allow students to discuss and come to their own conclusions, as they might do in political debate outside the classroom. But for a critique of this teaching strategy, see Avner de-Shalit, "Can't You Do Something about It? Teaching Political Philosophy and Academic Neutrality," paper presented at Stanford University's political theory discussion group, November 2003. If the dispute regards a flagrant injustice in contemporary society, particularly if that injustice is being carried out by members of one's political community and is the subject of everyday debate, then I agree with de-Shalit that political philosophers can and should make their views known in the classroom. Otherwise, I would be inclined not to make my own views too explicit.

And if the aim is to cultivate democratic virtues, then it might be best to teach more directly about democracy, and a teacher planning a high school civics course on democratic government or a university course on democratic theory could not avoid Eurocentrism. It remains a fact that the history of democracy and of democratic theory is largely, if not exclusively, a Western history.

But is it really a fact? In East Asia, for example, there are countless debates about the sources of democratic ideas within Confucianism, Islam, and so on. The practice of competitive elections for selecting rulers may have been invented in the West, but not all the values informing and justifying democratic elections are distinctly European (for example, Mencius argues that the ruler must gain the trust of the population).[32] Of course there are substantial differences between the West and the "rest,"[33] but this too can be a topic of interest. Moreover, most non-Western societies have been in contact with Western liberal democratic ideas for over a century, and this has produced some fascinating debates over the pros and cons of Western-style democracy in this or that context. For example, early twentieth-century Chinese intellectuals wrote at length about the implications of Western-style democracy in a Chinese context.[34] In principle, there is no reason why such works cannot be part of the curriculum for a course on democratic theory. There may, however, be political constraints: in mainland China, it may be too sensitive to spend too much time teaching such material (whereas I'm free to teach such Western material as J. S. Mill's *On Liberty*).[35] But this only points to the normative/political importance of teaching Chinese works to students of ethnic Chinese descent.

Needless to say, I do not mean to rule out the possibility that Great Works on particular topics may be lacking in some particular traditions. But it is difficult to know this in advance, prior to investigating the actual traditions. When I was made aware of the need to include the con-

[32] See *The Works of Mencius* (e.g., 5A.5).

[33] These differences typically manifest themselves in disputes over the centrality and/or social/political relevance of particular values in particular traditions; if one digs deep enough, it is usually possible to find someone who has said something similar to what somebody said in another tradition. Nonliterate cultures would seem to be an exception, but contemporary archeologists rely on such techniques as pollen and charcoal analysis to uncover the ways of life and beliefs of such cultures (I thank Kathleen Morrison for this information), so even this difference may be questioned.

[34] See, e.g., the discussions in Edmund S. K. Fung, *In Search of Chinese Democracy* (Cambridge: Cambridge University Press, 2000); and Andrew J. Nathan, *Chinese Democracy* (London: I. B. Tauris, 1986).

[35] On the political and cultural challenges of teaching political theory in China, see my essay "Teaching Political Theory in Beijing," *Dissent* (Spring 2006), 9–17.

tributions of Muslim and Indian civilizations in Singapore, I had no idea that great political thinkers in those traditions had developed arguments that could be compared in interesting ways to Machiavelli's ideas. But once I looked into it, I was pleasantly surprised. The same may be true of democratic theory, and, I suspect, of other areas in political theory.

Avner de-Shalit has questioned the whole idea of teaching Great Works to students of political theory. If the aim is to teach political theory so that it promotes democratic citizenship, they should not learn political thought as stories about great philosophers and what they wrote:

> [This way of teaching] causes students, especially high-school students and first-year undergraduates, to assume that the great texts of philosophy were produced by very special, unique people—the great philosophers—and that they (the students) could never theorize about these questions. . . . Thus, students often just repeat what these scholars wrote, without critically examining the texts. Moreover, when asked to apply the philosophical methods they have studied and to philosophize or theorize about a certain issue, they balk at the task, thinking "who am I to say something about that issue?" . . . [This approach] is detrimental to these students' potential as good citizens. If being a good citizen involves being reflective and critical about politics, and entails developing critical faculties, then teaching the history of ideas in the way just described will not help make these students good citizens. Those who teach political philosophy in this way may mean well, but it is suggested here that they ascertain whether their students feel dwarfed by the stature they ascribe to philosophers, and so devalue their own abilities as thinkers and theoreticians, thus as critical citizens.[36]

Rather than teach the history of ideas as the history of scholars, de-Shalit suggests teaching it as the history of issues and questions, with greater emphasis on popular sources such as newspaper articles.

But the unhappy outcomes de-Shalit describes depend partly on the kinds of Great Works taught in class. If the texts are written by Great Thinkers from "foreign" traditions, the students are less likely to engage with them and more likely to treat them as artifacts to worship (or show blind hostility to), without critically engaging with them. On the other hand, if the students learn texts written by Great Thinkers from cultural traditions that they identify with and take pride in, the students are less likely to come to the conclusion, "Who am I say something about that issue?" The ideas will be treated as a kind of family argument that one can and should take part in. And if the students also learn ideas written by

---

[36] Avner de-Shalit, *Power to the People: Teaching Political Philosophy in Skeptical Times* (Lanham, MD: Lexington Press, 2006), 105–6.

Great Thinkers from other traditions, they can compare the ideas, thinking about similarities and differences, and reflect critically about them.

Having said that, I think de-Shalit places too much emphasis on the cultivation of critical skills. From a pedagogical point of view, the development of critical thinking should not be viewed as the only aim. Improving understanding of the material is equally important, and it's best to start off with the ideas of Great Thinkers that set the questions and problems (if not boundaries) for subsequent debate. From a political point of view, what matters is not just developing one's views and criticizing those of others, but also tolerating and respecting the views of others (particularly those of vulnerable groups and minorities). So the desire to participate in political discussion should be accompanied by a certain humility and acceptance of one's own limitations. For this purpose, the teaching of Great Works, along with the concomitant recognition that the student's own ideas could never really match those of the Masters, may be useful.

Such observations will be deeply controversial in Western societies that devalue the virtue of humility: as Amy Gutmann puts it, "[a] participatory approach gives priority to cultivating self-esteem and social commitment over humility and order, a priority presumed by the democratic goal of educating citizens willing and able to participate in politics."[37] The low priority placed on the virtue of humility is related to the deeply rooted anti-elitism—meaning lack of deference to, if not hostility toward, the views of educated intellectuals—in societies such as the United States. The idea that everyone's political beliefs matter equally—or at least, that there are no qualitative differences between the views of "the many" and "the few" with the talent and opportunity to be educated—is widely shared.[38] Translated into educational policy, it means that students should be made to think that there are no qualitative differences between their capacities and those of Great Thinkers regarding their capacities to think about politics,[39] so that they are well prepared to critically reflect upon

[37] Gutmann, *Democratic Education*, 90. Gutmann does go on to say that this priority is not absolute: "it should be overridden when disorder and arrogance are so great as to threaten the very enterprise of education within schools." Gutmann adds a footnote, noting that even the most self-consciously democratic of schools have such safety rules as not allowing kids under a certain age to possess matches or knives. The barriers to disorder and arrogance seem very low indeed!

[38] This idea is not limited to political beliefs; it may apply to beliefs in general. As David Wong points out (drawing on the ideas of Samuel Fleischacker), "we in the West have given precedence to our interests in 'egalitarian knowledge' (wanting and believing that people have roughly equal access to the truth) and in prediction and control of this-wordly objects" (Wong, "Comparative Philosophy: Chinese and Western").

[39] I do not mean to imply that this view necessarily translates into de-Shalit's proposal that political theory should not be taught as the history of the texts of Great Thinkers. John Rawls, for example, taught the history of texts on the assumption that "in the great

and assert their (legitimate) interests in the rough and tumble of democratic politics. Some students (and citizens) may seem too quick to assert their own views without spending enough time to grasp the material, but it will be a price worth paying. And there will be a rather giant gap between the ideal and the reality—it is no coincidence that ideal forms of democratic deliberation seem to be practiced almost exclusively in the graduate seminars of the country's most prestigious educational institutions—but this too will be a price worth paying.

In East Asian societies, however, the idea that only a selected few have the talent to play a substantial role in their society's political life is not nearly as controversial. And the idea that even (especially) the "selected ones" should display the virtue of humility as they participate in politics is even less controversial.[40] Translated into educational policy, it means teaching the works of the Great Masters that set the terms for subsequent debate will not be viewed as a controversial starting off point.[41] The point may be to educate students so that they are willing and able to participate in politics, but democratic education should be done in ways

---

texts of our tradition we find the efforts of the best minds to come to terms with many of the hardest questions about how we are to live our lives." Editor's foreword (Barbara Herman), in John Rawls, *Lectures on the History of Moral Philosophy* (Cambridge: Harvard University Press, 2000), xi. Nor do I mean to imply that Avner de-Shalit himself is anything less than humble: in fact, he is a dear friend, and one of the most humble people I have ever met. What I do mean to imply is that de-Shalit's objection to the teaching of the texts of Great Thinkers resonates in a Western culture that emphasizes our interest in "egalitarian knowledge" and would be regarded as highly eccentric in an East Asian context that does not similarly prioritize that interest.

[40] As *The Zhongyong* [The Doctrine of the Mean] puts it, "Thus, when occupying a high station, [the exemplary person] is not arrogant" (twenty-seventh chapter). *The Zhongyong* is the last of the four classic books (to be read following *The Great Learning*, *The Analects of Confucius*, and *The Works of Mencius*) that were tested in the imperial examinations from the Song dynasty onward. In the history of Western thought, the concept of humility has been "closely associated with the following terms: the *low, inferior, ignoble, base, and vulgar.*" Mark Button, "A Monkish Kind of Virtue? For and Against Humility," *Political Theory*, vol. 33, no. 6 (December 2005), 841. Button goes on to provide a defense of humility as an ethos of civil attentivenesss, but it appears to be a virtue for democratic citizens (ibid., 856–61). What may be distinctive about the Confucian approach is that humility is a virtue for *political leaders*.

[41] This chapter has focused on the question of *what* to teach. I have argued elsewhere that the question of *how* to teach the material should also vary from context to context (Liberal Education versus Confucian Education: A (Fictitious) Debate on Teaching the Humanities in East Asia," ms. on file with the author). For example, the aggressive exchange of ideas and the shaming of interlocutors characteristic of the Socratic method (see Rob Reich, "Confucian about the Socratic Method: Socratic Paradoxes and Contemporary Invocations of Socrates," ms. on file with the author) is less likely to produce beneficial results (improved knowledge, greater willingness to participate in political debate, etc.) in an East Asian context that prizes humility and harmony.

that reinforce, rather than challenge, the virtue of humility (and commitment to social order). And it will be seen as the natural course of things if such an education happens to take place largely in the society's most prestigious educational institutions.

I would like to close this section on democracy in an East Asian context. I hope it is clear by now that whatever form of democracy takes root in East Asian societies will have "elitist" characteristics. This does not rule out participation by the people, but such participation will be minimal at best and constrained by the views of educated elites. Rather than challenge such arrangements on the basis of inappropriate (and often hypocritical) "anti-elitist" beliefs from liberal Western societies, the question should be how best to organize political and educational life so that educated elites make decisions that produce desirable results.

Note, however, that elitism can take different forms. In East Asia, there may be widespread acceptance of elitism grounded in differences of education and social status, but there is far less acceptance of elitism grounded in differences of material wealth that are taken for granted in some Western countries. An average American would never dream of bowing to an aged person yet might not seem deeply perturbed by the gross inequalities of income in the United States. In Japan, by contrast, extensive hierarchies of status and education coexist with a society that has the most equal distribution of wealth in the industrialized world. The next section will turn to the third plank of liberal democracy—capitalism—and show how such features as the concern for material equality have shaped the capitalist economy in ways that differ from Western-style capitalism (Anglo-American capitalism in particular). As elsewhere, I will argue that some of these variations on Western-style liberal democracy may be normatively justifiable, and I will suggest ways that they be made even more so.

PART THREE

Capitalism for an East Asian Context

9

Culture and Egalitarian Development: Confucian Constraints on Property Rights

EAST ASIAN states such as Japan and Korea have been widely praised for the combination of rapid economic development with increasingly egalitarian distributions of income. Even China, with its increasing inequality over the decade or so,[1] has done a near miraculous job of lifting millions of people out of poverty.[2] There are, of course, many economic and political reasons that help to explain East Asia's economic achievements. However, policy decisions may have also been influenced by traditional philosophical outlooks. It would be foolish to posit a direct causal link between the sayings of Confucius and Mencius and policy outcomes, but it would be equally foolish to reject the possibility that philosophical resources may have affected economic decision making as well as people's motivation to act in accordance with (or defy) the government's policies. This chapter will point to the Confucian underpinnings of some economic policies in East Asia that have contributed to egalitarian development.

[1] Contemporary Chinese intellectuals refer to the "Latin-Americanization" (*Lameihua*) of China. According to the CIA *World Fact Book*, however, China is much less unequal than Brazil and Mexico and a little less unequal than the United States (http://www.cia .gov/cia/publications/factbook/fields/2172.html, visited 27 December 2005).

[2] In the past twenty-six years, the absolute poor population in rural areas has dropped from 250 million to 26.1 million. China Human Development Report 2005 (www.undp. org.cn/downloads/nhdr2005/05chapter1.pdf, 1, visited 6 January 2006). Between 1996 and 2002, however, the proportion of poorest people increased. See Wing Thye Woo et al., "The Poverty Challenge for China in the New Millenium" (www.econ.ucdavis.edu/fac ulty/woo/1%20Oct%2004.Woo.China%20Poverty.pdf, visited 6 January 2006). In other words, over 200 million people were lifted out of poverty, but the proportion of the "worst-off" people increased: from a Rawlsian perpective (inequality is justified only if it benefits the worst-off) there has been an increase in economic injustice in China, but from a utilitarian perspective there has been an increase in justice. A moral judgment may also depend on one's patriotic allegiances. There has been an increase in inequality in Hong Kong over the past two decades, partly because the manufacturing sector has relocated to southern Guangdong province (thus underpinning the economic boom in that region). From the perspective of a Hong Kong patriot, that might be bad news, but it would be good news from the perspective of a Chinese patriot (because the relocation of the manufacturing sector to southern China has probably benefited more Chinese than the number of relatively well-off Hong Kong people who were disadvantaged).

The earliest Confucian critics opposed heavy-handed government control. Confucius himself stressed rule by moral example and informal rituals rather than coercive punishments. Mencius extended this bias against state intervention to the economic realm. He suggested that anything beyond a taxation level of 10 percent is "unjust" (3B.8).[3] Minimal taxation would also have desirable economic consequences: "Tend the fields of grain and flax well, tax their yield lightly, and the people will be prosperous" (7A.23, Dobson).[4] The government, he added, should refrain from fixing the prices of goods under exchange. Since people understand that different things have different value, the prices of goods should be primarily determined by means of people's judgment of the worth of goods: "That things are unequal is part of their nature. Some are worth twice or five times, ten or a hundred times, even a thousand and ten thousand times, more than others. If you reduce them to the same level, it will only bring confusion to the whole world. If a roughly finished shoe sells at the same price as a finely finished one, who would make the latter?" (3A.4; Lau, modified).[5] Nor should the state levy import duties: "If there is inspection but no taxation at the borders, then travelers in the whole world will be pleased, and they will be willing to go by way of your roads" (2A.5; Lau, modified). Mencius, in short, argues that restrictions on trade and high taxes result in the demoralization and the pauperization of the people.[6] Open economic policies, put positively, will attract commerce and improve the material conditions of people.

Mencius did not have much luck translating his ideas into practice, but his views eventually had practical consequences. As early as the Han dynasty (202 B.C.E.–9 C.E.), Chinese rulers began to heed Confucian warnings about the negative effects of state intervention in the economy. The "Debate on Salt and Iron" records a dispute on economic policy between Confucian literati and Legalist officials that took place in 81 B.C.E. The Confucians favored abolishing government monopolies in the vital industries of iron, salt, liquor, and coinage of money, on the grounds that

---

[3] Elsewhere, Mencius suggests that the level of taxation depends on the context (6B.10).

[4] The translator of Mencius is indicated following the quoted package. I indicate my own modifications with the word "modified." If no translator is noted, it is my own translation.

[5] Judging from the context of this passage, Mencius raises this example to oppose the "way of Xu Zi," an emperor who did his best to level all differences of status and hierarchy (e.g., by sharing the work of tilling with his people). Just as prices of goods will (should) vary with their quality, so people's roles should vary according to their quality. For our purposes, it is interesting that Mencius takes it as an undisputed desideratum that the government should not standardize prices regardless of quality—if only Mao et al. had brushed up on their Mencius before imposing crude forms of "communist" equality!

[6] See Miles Menander Dawson, *The Ethics of Confucius* (New York: G. P. Putnam's Sons, 1915), 206.

this system forced the people to use inferior products and enriched a tiny class of corrupt officials and powerful racketeers. The Legalists replied that government control of vital industries was necessary to protect the people from exploitation by unscrupulous private traders.[7] The Confucians eventually won the debate,[8] and most government monopolies were abolished.[9]

There is no doubt that Confucians would also oppose Soviet-style planned economies.[10] Does it follow, however, that "Confucians require a private-property economy"?[11] Not quite. There are possibilities between the extremes of total state control and a libertarian-style property rights regime. As we will see, Confucian prescriptions for the economy lie somewhere in this intermediate zone. Confucians do oppose state control of the economy, but they also defend values that justify constraints on private property rights.

One obvious point of difference between the Confucian and the libertarian regards the morally permissible means of acquiring wealth. The modern-day libertarian would justify the acquisition of wealth so long as the starting points were fair and wealth has been acquired by free

[7] The debate also turned on security matters. The Legalists argued that state control of vital industries was necessary to secure government revenues and thus to maintain defensive warfare against the surrounding tribes who threatened the empire, whereas the Confucians argued that China should make peace with its neighbors and be content to remain safely within its traditional boundaries.

[8] Some self-described Confucian thinkers subsequently adopted Legalist-inspired economic policies (just as self-described Confucian thinkers adopted Legalist-inspired political means of control from the Han dynasty onward). In the Song dynasty, the leading "Confucian" thinker, Wang Anshi (1021–1086), argued for "a variety of reform measures that clearly followed Legalist rather than Confucian principles [including the] State Monopoly of Commerce." Hahm Chaibong and Paik Wooyeal, "Legalistic Confucianism and Economic Development in East Asia," *Journal of East Asian Studies*, vol. 3, no. 3 (September–December 2003), 477.

[9] See the extract in Wm. Theodore de Bary et al., *Sources of Chinese Tradition* (New York: Columbia University Press, 1960), 218–23.

[10] Neither would the Legalists, it should be added. While Legalists may have favored state control of vital industries, the Legalist-inspired sociopolitical system (what John E. Schrecker calls the *junxian* system) would allow for the free sale of nonvital land, labor, and goods. See Schrecker, *The Chinese Revolution in Historical Perspective* (New York: Greenwood Press, 1991), 21. In contrast, Confucians favor less state control of vital industries but more regulation of economic activity at the local level, such as the well-field system (see below).

[11] Ruiping Fan, "Confucian and Rawlsian Views of Justice: A Comparison," *Journal of Chinese Philosophy*, vol. 24 (1997), 443. The Confucian requirement of a private-property regime is meant to contrast with John Rawls, who "wants his theory of justice to be consistent with either privately-owned or publicly-owned economy" (ibid., 442). Fan, however, tends to read Mencius through the lenses of contemporary libertarianism—overlooking, for example, Mencius's discussion of the well-field system. In my view, Mencius is neither a right-wing liberal (or libertarian) nor a left-wing liberal (or Rawlsian). Rather, Confucian values justify nonliberal constraints on property rights.

exchanges between consenting individuals, whereas the Confucian would place greater ethical constraints upon the means employed to acquire wealth:[12] as Confucius put it, "Wealth and rank acquired through unrighteous means are like floating clouds to me" (7.16).[13] Mencius provided an example of "unrighteous" acquisition of wealth: a husband who begs for food and drink from people offering sacrifices at graveyards and misleads his wife about how he had acquired his wealth. This man would not have done anything wrong from a libertarian point of view, but he causes his wife (and concubine) to "weep with shame" (4B.33). The libertarian could reply that the husband's behavior may be morally reprehensible, but it would not justify legal constraints on such means of acquiring wealth, and the Confucian aversion to legal punishments (see, e.g., *The Analects*, 2.3) may well lead to a convergence of views in this respect. To sharpen areas of difference, this chapter will therefore discuss Confucian values that justify *legal* constraints on property rights.

On the Selection of Feasible and Desirable Confucian Values for Modern Societies

But which Confucian values should one appeal to? How does one select values from the complex and changing centuries-long Confucian tradition, interpreted differently in different times and places and complemented in sometimes conflicting ways with Legalism, Daoism, Buddhism, and, more recently, Western liberalism? In this chapter, I limit myself to values that bear on the question of legal constraints on property rights. Beyond that, I employ the following criteria:[14]

First, I limit myself to the values espoused and defended by the two "founding fathers" of Confucianism: Confucius and Mencius.[15] *The*

[12] See the discussion in Jiang Qing, *Zhengzhi Rujia: Dangdai Rujia de zhuanxiang, tezhi yu fazhan* [Political Confucianism: Contemporary Confucianism's Change, Special Quality, and Development] (Beijing: San lian shu dian, 2003), 314–20.

[13] The translator of *The Analects of Confucius* is indicated following the quoted package. I indicate my own modifications with the word "modified." If no translator is noted, it is my own translation.

[14] I do not mean to imply that present-day Confucians should necessarily follow these criteria for selecting Confucian values. My only claim is that these criteria can generate results that shed some light on the potential clash between Confucian values and property rights in contemporary societies. Some of these criteria may be of more general applicability, but one must also leave room for other ways of selecting Confucian values for modern societies.

[15] In this chapter, I do not need to take sides in disputes regarding the authenticity of arguments and values allegedly put forward by Confucius and Mencius. What matters (for my purposes) is that the two classic Confucian texts—*The Analects of Confucius* and *The Works of Mencius*—have been transmitted in more or less intact form for well over two thousand years and continue to command a great deal of moral and political authority in contemporary East Asian societies.

Analects of Confucius is, of course, the central, founding text in the Confucian tradition. Mencius, who elaborated and systematized Confucius's ideas, is the second most influential figure in the Confucian tradition.[16] Thus, basing one's interpretation of Confucianism on Confucius and Mencius is, arguably, the least controversial starting point.

Second, I exclude Confucian values that have been explicitly repudiated by contemporary Confucian intellectuals.[17] East Asian political leaders such as Lee Kuan Yew have also invoked Confucian values, but these leaders often seem to be motivated primarily by the need to justify their authoritarian rule in the face of increasing demands for democracy at home and abroad rather than by a sincere commitment to the Confucian tradition. Whatever the truth of such views, we can avoid controversy by limiting our focus to values that have not been criticized by Confucian philosophers and social critics. These contemporary Confucians typically reject such (apparent) classical Confucian values as the inherent superiority of men over women, the complete exclusion of commoners from the political decision-making process, the three-year mourning period for deceased parents, or the idea that "Heaven" somehow dictates the behavior of political rulers. Passages in *The Analects of Confucius* and *The Works of Mencius* that seem to lend themselves to these views have been either reinterpreted or relegated to the status of uninformed prejudices of the period, with no implications for contemporary societies.

Third, I limit myself to Confucian values that contrast in some way with Western-style democracy. Contemporary Confucian intellectuals often endorse values that are consistent with liberal-democratic norms—more precisely, some liberal-democratic ideas and practices have been invoked to complement and enrich Confucian values.[18] But skeptics may reply that liberal Confucians—in their zeal to oppose authoritarianism—are sanitizing their own tradition, that is, choosing among Confucian values according to whatever fits with the best of contemporary liberal

---

[16] Xunzi (c. 310–219 B.C.E) is sometimes held to be the third "founding father" of the philosophy known as Confucianism. Xunzi, however, is a controversial character because he is also "blamed" for being a major influence on Legalism (Confucianism's main ideological competitor in Chinese history), with the consequence that he "was excluded from the Confucian orthodoxy." Shu-hsien Liu, *Understanding Confucian Philosophy* (Westport, CT.: Greenwood Press, 1998), 55. For this reason, I do not discuss the works of Xunzi in this chapter.

[17] For a discussion of contemporary Confucian intellectuals, see ibid., epilogue. Needless to say, I do not mean to imply that I have surveyed the thoughts of all contemporary Confucian intellectuals, and my claims here may need to be further qualified.

[18] For example, Confucius and Mencius both argue that the ruler must gain the trust of the population, but neither drew the implication that democratic elections are the best means to achieve this end. Thus, contemporary Confucians need to draw on the Western liberal-democratic tradition for the purpose of implementing a crucial Confucian value.

democratic norms. Thus, it is important to respond to the potential objection that contemporary Confucians defend the values of Confucius and Mencius on purely strategic grounds because they are seen as means to promote Western-style democracy in East Asia. For this purpose, I tried to identify, where relevant, areas of actual and potential conflict with liberal-democratic norms. The only real way to "prove" that Confucian norms have independent value, after all, is to show that Western liberal-democratic norms do not automatically have priority in cases of conflict (from the perspective of contemporary Confucian intellectuals). No doubt there are also substantial areas of overlap with Western-style democracy, but this is not my concern here.

Fourth, I focus on Confucian values that still inform—at least in part—the practices and institutions of countries in the East Asian region.[19] If one can plausibly point to some contemporary manifestations, this might help to respond to the potential objection that classical Confucian values are no longer influential in contemporary societies.

Fifth, I discuss values that are still defensible today, in the sense that they help to address contemporary social, economic, and/or political needs. This criterion helps to differentiate my approach from that of "Orientalist" scholars who recognize the contemporary impact of Confucian values while also regarding Confucianism as something "bad," a tradition that serves to obstruct or delay "modernization" and "progress."[20] But I also want to avoid the other extreme of equating "actually existing" Confucian values with the most practicable ideal. It is important to leave room for the possibility that Confucian values can provide a critical perspective on political practices in East Asia, and I do not want to argue that Confucian values are necessarily manifested in their *most desirable form* in contemporary East Asia. If need be, I will suggest different interpretations of Confucian values, or different combinations of Confucian and other values, that are more defensible than the status quo.

Let us now turn to the actual content of Confucian values. I will discuss two values that meet the criteria noted above: (1) the overriding

[19] See *Confucianism for the Modern World*, ed. Bell and Hahm.

[20] There is a long and (un)distinguished tradition of Western "Orientalists" who discuss Confucianism merely in order to put it down, from Hegel, Marx, and Mill in the nineteenth century to Weber in the twentieth. A recent book adopts this approach with regard to intellectual property in China. William Alford argues for the contemporary relevance of traditional values on Chinese notions of intellectual property rights, but he seems to regard (without explicitly arguing so) the effects of tradition as entirely negative, as something to be overcome by "modern" (i.e., Western) notions of property rights. Alford, *To Steal a Book Is an Elegant Offense: Intellectual Property Law in Chinese Civilization* (Stanford: Stanford University Press, 1995), esp. chap. 6.

value of basic material welfare, and (2) the value of care for needy family members.[21] These Confucian values continue to exert moral and political influence in East Asia, and any property rights regime in the region is likely to be shaped by them.[22]

THE OVERRIDING VALUE OF MATERIAL WELFARE

According to *The Analects*, the government has an obligation to secure the conditions for people's basic means of subsistence and intellectual/moral development. In cases of conflict, however, the former has priority:

> Ranyou drove the Master's carriage on a trip to Wey. The Master said: "What a huge population!" Ranyou said: "When the people are so numerous, what more can be done for them?" The Master said, "Make them prosperous." Ranyou asked, "When the people are prosperous, what more can be done for them?" The Master replied, "Educate them." (13.9; Ames and Rosemont, modified)

This does not mean the blind pursuit of a higher GNP. The main obligation is to help the worst-off:[23] "Exemplary persons help out the needy;

---

[21] There may be other Confucian values that meet some of the criteria mentioned above. For example, A. T. Nuyen argues that the value of harmony "entails that the state should make laws to ensure the balance of economic forces, laws that prevent anti-competitive behavior, laws that strengthen the mutual dependencies of all units on each other." Nuyen, "Chinese Philosophy and Western Capitalism," *Asian Philosophy*, vol. 8, no. 1 (March 1999), 6 (Internet version). The contrast with left-liberal values and the practices of Western-style social democratic states may not be obvious, however.

[22] Of course, one may ask, why worry about the topic of property rights in the region? My assumption is that some form of capitalism is here to stay for the foreseeable future, and any realistic defense of economic arrangements in East Asia needs to take this fact into account.

[23] The reader will pardon the use of anachronistic terminology. My point is to suggest that Confucius (if he were around today) may well have endorsed something like Rawls's difference principle. Confucians, however, might dispute Rawls's assumption that basic liberties should have priority over the fair distribution of material goods in cases of conflict— and here lies one basic contrast with liberalism. In the West, as Will Kymlicka notes, "the assumption that civil and political rights should have priority is widely shared. . . . As a result, the disputes between Rawls and his critics have tended to be on other issues. The idea that people should have their basic liberties protected is the least contentious part of his theory. . . . Some people reject the idea of a theory of fair shares of economic resources, and those who accept it have very different views about what form such a theory should take." Kymlicka, *Contemporary Political Philosophy: An Introduction*, 2nd ed. (Oxford: Clarendon Press, 2002), 56. *A Theory of Justice* has been translated in Chinese three times, and many of the disputes center around the protection of basic liberties; the idea that people should have a fair share of economic resources is the least contentious part of his theory. Perhaps this area of concern can be partly explained by the ongoing relevance of the Confucian tradition that prioritizes the fair distribution of material goods.

they do not make the rich richer" (6.4, Ames and Rosemont; see also 16.1). One important reason for helping the needy is that poverty is conducive to negative emotions, whereas wealth makes it easier to act in ethical ways: "To be poor without feeling resentful is difficult; to be rich without feeling arrogant is easy" (14.11).

Mencius echoes these concerns. People must be educated so that they can develop their moral natures. First, however, the government must provide for their basic means of subsistence so that they won't go morally astray:

> The people will not have dependable feelings if they are without dependable means of support. Lacking dependable means of support, they will go astray and fall into excesses, stopping at nothing. To punish them after they have fallen foul of the law is to set a trap for the people. How can a humane person in authority allow himself to set a trap for the people? Hence when determining what means of support the people should have, a clear-sighted ruler ensures that these are sufficient for the care of parents and for the support of wives and children, so that the people will always have sufficient food in good years and escape starvation in bad; only then does he drive them towards goodness. In this way, the people find it easy to follow him. (1A.7; Lau, modified; see also 3A.3 and *The Analects*, 14.10)

There is no point promoting moral behavior if people are worried about their next meal.[24] Thus, the government's first priority is to secure the basic means of subsistence of the people.[25]

[24] The importance of food as a precondition for moral behavior is vividly expressed by means of the character *he* (和), or "harmony." The character is composed of two parts: (禾), meaning "grain," and (口), meaning "mouth." In other words, a decent supply of food (grain in the mouth) underpins social harmony, and conversely the absence of food leads to conflict. See Tan Huay Peng, *Fun with Chinese Characters: The Straits Times Collection* (Singapore: Federal Publications, 1980), 147.

[25] This view was forcefully opposed by the Legalist Han Fei Zi on grounds that will be familiar to contemporary libertarians: "When the educated officers [i.e., Confucian scholars] of the day talk about governing, they often say, 'One should give land to the poor and destitute in order to provide for their lack of resources.' " . . . Now if there are some people who, having the same opportunities as everyone else, are able to keep themselves fully supplied even without the benefits of a good harvest or some additional source of income, it is either because they are industrious or because they are frugal. If there are some people who, having the same opportunities as everyone else, still fall into poverty and destitution even without the misfortunes of famine, sickness, and natural disasters, it is either because they are wasteful or because they are lazy. Those who are wasteful and lazy become poor, while those who are industrious and frugal become wealthy. Now if a superior imposes taxes on the rich in order to redistribute their wealth among the families of the poor, this is stealing from the industrious and frugal and giving to the wasteful and lazy. If a ruler does this and expects his people to be industrious in their work and frugal in their expenditures, he is going to be disappointed." "Han Feizi," in *Readings in Classical Chinese Philosophy*, ed. Ivanhoe and Van Norden, 337–38.

This does not necessarily translate into opposition to the free market. Absolute private property rights might still be justified on the instrumental grounds that they have the consequence of securing the basic means of subsistence of the people. Mencius, however, does not take this line.[26] While he opposes high taxes and restrictions on commerce that lead to economic inefficiency, he explicitly argues that the state can and should control the distribution and use of land to secure people's means of subsistence. And how does the government realize this aim? Mencius proposes the "well-field system":[27]

> Humane government must begin by defining the boundaries of the land. If the boundaries are not correctly defined, the division of the land into squares will not be equitable, and the produce available for official salaries will not be fairly distributed. Therefore oppressive rulers and corrupt officials are sure to neglect the defining of the boundaries. If the boundaries are correctly defined, the division of land and the regulation of salaries can be settled without difficulty. Although Teng's territory is limited, there will be exemplary persons and there will be common people. Without exemplary persons, there would be none to rule the common people, and without common people, there would be none to support the exemplary persons. I suggest that in the country the tax should be one in nine, but in the capital it should be one in ten, to be levied in kind. From the chief ministers on down,[28] [each family] should have fifty *mu* as sacrificial land, and an additional twenty-five *mu* for each additional household. When there are deaths or changing of abodes there will be no quitting of the district. In the fields of the district, those who belong to the same nine squares will render friendly service to one another at home and outside, help each other in keeping watch, and sustain each other in sickness. In this way, the people will live in affection and harmony. Each "well-field" unit is one *li* square and consists of nine-hundred *mu*. The center square is public field. The eight households each privately own a hundred *mu* and together they cultivate the public field. Only when the public work is done may they attend to their work. (3A.3; Chan, modified)

[26] I do not mean to imply that Mencius was motivated by the desire to distinguish his view from the libertarian defense of the free market (an argument that may not have been made in Mencius's day). More likely, Mencius felt the need to respond to Mozi's critique that Confucians preferred to lavish funds on expensive weddings and funerals and leave the rest to "fate" rather than think about how agricultural policy can address the material needs of the poor. On Mozi's critique, see Mozi, section 39, "Against Confucians."

[27] The well-field system, with its mixture of private and public property, predates Mencius. See Zhang Chuanxi, *Zhongguo gudai shi gang* [An Outline of the History of Ancient China] (Beijing: Beijing daxue chubanshe, 1991), 77, 101. This should not be surprising, given that Confucians aimed to restore an ideal said to exist in the past.

[28] According to Yang Bojun, the well-field system is meant to be restricted to ministers with sacrificial land, not to ordinary farmers. Yang Bojun, *Mengzi* [Mencius] (Beijing: Zhonghua shuju, 1960), 118–19.

This might seem like a rather rigid set of guidelines for establishing boundaries of land within states, but Mencius adds that "this is a rough outline. As for embellishments, it is up to you and your ruler" (3A.3). The important point is for the state to maintain a relatively equitable distribution of land at the local community level, to allow individual households to make productive use of land for their families, and to qualify farmers' rights to the produce of the land in order to ensure that enough food is supplied to the nonfarming classes. These principles, Mencius suggests, will secure basic material welfare for all members of the state.

Chinese rulers did subsequently adapt the principles of the well-field system to their own circumstances. In the early Tang dynasty, land was owned by the state and distributed to farming families,[29] roughly in accordance with the well-field system.[30] The system eventually broke down, however. By the Song dynasty (960–1279) there were many landowner-ship patterns,[31] including some forms of private ownership. The state did, however, maintain some control on the sale and purchase of land in order to secure people's basic means of subsistence. In the Ming and Qing dynasties, the state protected peasants against subsistence uncer-tainties by means of local community granaries. As R. Bin Wong notes, "the explicit logic of community granaries put responsibility for the cre-ation and maintenance of these institutions in the hands of local people. The state's willingness to depend on the gentry and others to promote local grain reserves assumed a basic commitment to subsistence security as a key element in social stability."[32] Moreover, the Qing penal code secured the right to food by punishing local officials who failed to pro-vide aid to the needy.[33]

Of course, the Chinese Communist Party put on end to "Confucian" principles of land distribution by abolishing all forms of local commu-nity autonomy and household responsibility for farming and forcing

[29] I will avoid use of the demeaning term "peasants." I was only made aware of the con-notations when a Chinese friend asked me about "peasants" in Canada.

[30] In the Tang, women also received land in the equal-field system. As John Schrecker notes, "It is probably no coincidence that the only female emperor of China, Wu Zhao, reigned at this time." Schrecker, *The Chinese Revolution in Historical Perspective*, 36.

[31] See Joseph P. McDermott, "Charting Blank Spaces and Disputed Regions: The Prob-lems of Sung Land Tenure," *Journal of Asian Studies*, vol. 44, no. 1 (November 1984), 13, 33–34.

[32] R. Bin Wong, "Confucian Agendas for Material and Ideological Control in Modern China," in *Culture & State in Chinese History*, ed. Theodore Huters, R. Bin Wong, and Pauline Yu (Stanford: Stanford University Press, 1997), 307.

[33] The "right to food" is not anachronistic here because it is a right in the modern sense of a legally enforceable norm.

farmers to work for state-owned communes.[34] Far from enriching the people, however, this system led to massive inefficiencies.[35] In 1978 Deng Xiaoping's launched a rural land reform program that can be seen as an "updated version of Mencius's economic ideals."[36] The program was not directly justified with reference to Mencius, but the Communist Party was aware of, and perhaps inspired by, the well-field system at the time that it was thinking about its reforms.[37] The household responsibility system that replaced state-owned communes bears striking resemblance to the broad outlines of Mencius's system: "individual households in a village are now granted the right to use the farmland, whereas the village cooperative, as the village-based governing body, retains other rights associated with ownership."[38] Farmers have an obligation to supply a quota of produce (which typically occupies one-sixth of the household's land) at a fixed low price to the state, but beyond that they are allowed to keep and sell the produce on the open market.[39] This system has been widely credited with underpinning China's rapid economic development (and the consequent improvement of the material welfare of the people) since that time.[40]

[34] The means may have been "communist," but the ultimate end—securing the material well-being of the people—may still have been inspired by the traditional Confucian concern for the material well-being of the common people. The Confucian scholar Liang Shuming shared many of his concerns regarding the need to focus first and foremost on the economic well-being of rural farmers with the Marxist Mao. Alitto, *The Last Confucian*, chaps. 6, 9–11. Mao turned on Liang in 1953 because Liang had attacked Mao's government for its decision to adopt the Soviet model of economic development that laid the heaviest burden on the backs of peasants while benefiting the urban workers (ibid., 1–3). Given subsequent developments (e.g., the famine that followed the Great Leap Forward), it seems unfortunate that Mao did not take heed of Liang's "Confucian" critique.

[35] Most obviously, it has been estimated that over twenty million Chinese died in the famine in the late 1950s and early 1960s. Arguably, however, this famine was due to the faulty policies of the Great Leap Forward, not to the commune system. It can be further argued that at least the commune system succeeded in feeding most, if not all, Chinese people (other than the period of famine noted above), which is an improvement upon what preceded the rule of the Communist Party (I thank Ci Jiwei for these points). On the other hand, one can argue that the Chinese Communist state could have done even better at feeding its people if it had implemented the Deng/Mencius agricultural reforms earlier.

[36] Schrecker, *The Chinese Revolution in Historical Perspective*, 186.

[37] Mencius's well-field system was explicitly praised in secondary schools in mainland China at the time of Deng's reforms (I thank Song Bing for this information).

[38] Xiao-Yuan Dong, "Two-Tier Land Tenure System and Sustained Economic Growth in Post-1978 Rural China," *World Development*, vol. 24, no. 5 (1996), 915.

[39] R. H. Folson, J. H. Minan, and L. A. Otto, *Law and Politics in the People's Republic of China* (St. Paul: West Publishing Co., 1992), 254.

[40] Some free-market economists have blamed this two-tier land tenure system for the problems in land allocation and in land-specific investment observed in postreform China.

It also worth noting that the four "Confucian tigers" (Korea, Taiwan, Hong Kong, and Singapore) have all significantly curtailed property rights, notwithstanding a commitment to free-market principles. Taiwan and Korea both engaged in massive land distribution programs after World War II (in part due to American pressure), which has underpinned the relatively egalitarian economic development since then. The Singapore government expropriated land shortly after independence and used it for industrial development and public housing[41] (today, 85 percent of Singaporeans live in quasi-public housing). The Hong Kong government technically owns all land in the territory, and much of it has been set aside for public housing projects (today, approximately half of Hong Kong residents live in public housing, and the Hong Kong government is the world's largest landlord).

This is not to suggest that there is a direct causal link between the sayings of Mencius and contemporary patterns of land distribution in East Asian states—no doubt other factors such as national defense, the requirements of holding on to power, pragmatic economic considerations, and ad hoc improvisation had more immediate impact on policy outcomes. But Confucian values that justify constraints on landownership were influential in East Asian history, and contemporary decision makers concerned with securing the basic material welfare of the people can and do draw on background Confucian values to justify constraints on private property in ways that would not be nearly as compelling in cultures largely untouched by Confucianism. It is difficult to otherwise explain the lack of opposition to constraints on property rights in East Asia, even in societies (such as Hong Kong and Korea) that allow for open dissent and contestation of the government's policies.

To sum up, the value of the priority of material welfare seems to meet the five criteria discussed above:

- Confucius and Mencius argue that the government has an overriding obligation to secure the conditions for basic means of subsistence.
- Contemporary Confucian intellectuals have not repudiated this value. Some have explicitly endorsed it.
- This value has not been so prominent in Western political tradition(s). It conflicts, for example, with Rawls's "lexical priority" for the first principle

---

Xiao-Yuan Dong, however, argues that their proposed solution—full land privatization—is unlikely to provide a solution to these agricultural problems. Dong, "Two-Tier Land Tenure System and Sustained Economic Growth in Post-1978 Rural China." Still, if the empirical evidence does support the view that absolute private property rights in land is the best mechanism to secure the "right to food," then presumably Confucians would endorse this solution.

[41] See Tan, "Economic Development, Legal Reform, and Rights in Singapore and Taiwan," 268.

of justice that secures civil and political rights. For Confucians, economic rights come first.

- This value is still relevant in East Asia. Many governments argue that their first obligation is to secure the basic material welfare of the people. East Asian governments often curtail property rights for the sake of this value.
- This value may still be desirable. The success of East Asian governments (relative to other parts of the world) in rapidly reducing severe material deprivation in the post–World War II period has been at least partly the result of policies designed to secure material welfare. In China, adaptations of Mencius's well-field system have served to promote the material welfare of the rural population. In the four "Confucian tigers," land has been expropriated and redistributed, thus contributing to the egalitarian form of subsequent economic development.

Let us now turn to the second Confucian value that justifies constraints on property rights. Libertarian or "capitalist-style" style property rights usually refer to maximal alienation of property as well as identification of property with the individual.[42] I have tried to show that the right to own and transfer (landed) property was limited by the government's responsibility to secure the people's basic material welfare. Next, I argue that Confucian ownership rights are vested in the family, not the individual.

THE VALUE OF CARE FOR NEEDY FAMILY MEMBERS

A basic assumption of Confucian ethics is that the moral life is possible only in the context of particularistic personal ties.[43] For the general population, the most important relationship by far is the family. As Ruiping Fan notes, "Familial relationships are so important that they assume three out of five basic human relations [emphasized by] Confucianism. It is a Confucian moral requirement that one should take one's family as an autonomous unit from the rest of society, flourishing or suffering as a whole."[44]

---

[42] See H. F. Schurmann, "Traditional Property Concepts in China," *Far Eastern Quarterly*, vol. 4 (1956), 507.

[43] Mencius targeted Mozi, who "speaks of love with discrimination, which amounts to denial of [the special relationship with] one's father" (3B.9). Mencius does not mean to argue, however, that love should stop at the family. Quite the opposite—the family is the springboard for the natural emotion of sympathy that is eventually extended to all human beings. See Qingping Liu, "Is Mencius' Doctrine of Extending Affection' Tenable?," *Asian Philosophy*, vol. 14, no. 1 (March 2004), 79–90.

[44] Ruiping Fan, "Self-Determination vs. Family-Determination: Two Incommensurable Principles of Autonomy," *Bioethics*, vol. 11, nos. 3–4 (1997), 317. Fan draws on

Within the family context, individuals owe each other certain obligations. Most important, economically productive adults must care for needy family members. This obligation is literally "beyond choice." From the political standpoint, as Mencius points out, it means that the government should try to ensure that economically productive members of families have sufficient means of support "for the care of parents, and for the support of wife and children" (1A.7).[45] The value of caring for children is widely shared in other cultures, but Confucianism places special emphasis on filial piety, the care for elderly parents. Quite simply, we are not free to neglect elderly parents. As Confucius said:

> Meng Yizi asked about filial piety. The Master said: "Do not oppose it." Fan Chi was driving the Master's chariot, the Master told him: "Meng Yizi asked about filial piety and I replied: 'Do not oppose it.'" Fan Chi said: "What does that mean?" The Master said: "When they [your parents] are alive, serve them according to ritual. When they die, bury them according to ritual and make sacrifices to them according to ritual." (2.5; Ames and Rosemont, modified; see also 1.2, 2.6, 2.8, 4.19, 19.17)

Filial piety is not simply a matter of providing material comfort to aged parents:

> Zixia asked about filial piety. The Master said: "It is the attitude that matters. If young people merely offer their services when there is work to do, or let their elders drink and eat when there is wine and food, how could this be [sufficient for] filial piety?" (2.8, Leys, modified; see also Mencius, 6B.3)

The only real test of filial piety, Confucius seems to imply, is the willingness to serve elderly parents even when this requires sacrificing one's

---

the Confucian idea of "family self-determination" to explain the fact that in East Asia both the patient and family members must reach an agreement before a clinical decision can be made (as opposed to the West, where a competent patient generally has the final word regarding medical decisions). See also Pang Mei Che, "From Virtue to Value: Nursing Ethics in Modern China," Ph.D. thesis, Dept. of Philosophy, University of Hong Hong, 1999, esp. chaps. 1, 3, and 7. For other examples of the different implications of "autonomy" and "family self-determination" (e.g., the latter allows for veto power by parents over marriage mates), see Andrew Brennan and Ruiping Fan, "Autonomy and Interdependence: A Dialogue between Liberalism and Confucianism," ms. on file with author.

[45] Confucians have also addressed the question of how to provide care for needy elderly people without family members. According to Mencius, the government has an overriding obligation to care for "elderly people without wives, husbands, and children, and children without fathers" (IB.5; *guan gua gu du*, 鰥寡孤獨, for short, an expression that is still used in contemporary Chinese). In the Han dynasty (the first dynasty to officially adopt Confucianism as its ruling ideology), this obligation was met by such indirect means as giving tax breaks for merchants that provided material support for elderly people without family members.

own interests. Confucius does allow for exceptions in extreme circumstances,[46] but in most cases people must subordinate their own desires for the sake of serving their elderly parents.[47]

Filial piety is also meant to take precedence over competing moral obligations. Mencius condemns those who are "selfishly attached to wives" (4B.30)—instead, people should be particularly mindful of the "greatest" duty of all, the duty to one's own parents (4A.20). And both Confucius and Mencius suggest that care for elderly parents should take priority over public duties in cases of conflict.[48]

In short, Confucians argue that productive adults have an obligation to care for needy family members, with special emphasis upon the need to care for elderly parents. Barring exceptional circumstances, these duties have priority over both narrowly defined individual self-interest and competing moral obligations. These duties have been implemented in

[46] Most notably, Confucius says that adult children should not *blindly* obey their parents. Confucius said: "In serving your father and mother, remonstrate with them gently" (4.18; Ames and Rosemont). See the discussion in Joseph Chan, "A Confucian Perspective on Human Rights," 223–24. But see Mencius, 4B.30, who seems to advocate blind obedience to parents' wishes.

It is also assumed that people are somehow reciprocating for the love and care given earlier by their own parents. In response to a disciple who suggests a one-year mourning period (instead of the traditional three-year period), Confucius says:

"The reason exemplary persons prolong the mourning period is because fine food seems tasteless to him, music offers no enjoyment, and the comfort of home does not provide peace. Thus, he prefers to do without all these pleasures. But now, if you can enjoy them, go ahead!"

Zaiwo left. The Master said: "Zaiwo is devoid of humanity. After a child is born, for the first three years of his life, he does not leave his parents' bosom. The custom of a three-year mourning period is practiced in the whole world. Surely Zaiwo received three years of loving care from his parents!" (17.21; Ames and Rosemont, modified)

This passage allows for the possibility that the obligation to care for elderly parents may not apply in cases where parents neglected their caring duties earlier (but for an argument that filial piety is an unconditional obligation that allows for no exceptions, see John Schrecker, "Filial Piety as a Basis for Human Rights in Confucius and Mencius," *Journal of Chinese Philosophy*, vol. 24 [1997], 402–4). It is interesting to note that Singapore, which explicitly (legally) enforces the right to be cared for by adult children, allows for exceptions where parents neglected parental duties earlier (e.g., if the parents did not provide material security for their children or resorted to extreme physical punishment).

[47] A Straussian political theorist may be tempted by the argument that Confucians went out of their way to stress filial piety precisely because it is the least natural of the family-centered caring relationships (i.e., the one that requires the most ongoing, conscious, and effortful commitment).

[48] See, e.g., Qingping Liu, "Filiality versus Sociality and Individuality: On Confucianism as 'Consanguinitism,'" *Philosophy East & West*, vol. 53, no. 2 (April 2003), 234–50; and Lijun Bi and Fred D'Agostino, "The Doctrine of Filial Piety: A Philosophical Analysis of the Concealment Case," *Journal of Chinese Philosophy*, vol. 31, no. 4 (December 2004), 451–67.

various ways by East Asian states, but I will discuss one means—the practice of joint family ownership—that contrasts with the liberal emphasis on individual ownership of property.

In traditional Chinese society, property was considered owned by the family, not the individual.[49] The family clan lived together and pooled family property, and it was assumed that economically productive members of the family would fulfill their duties of care for needy family members within this context.[50] The practice of joint family property, which "existed in China for at least two millennia,"[51] also carried certain legal implications. According to law, junior members of the family could not be accused of stealing, but only of appropriating (for their own use) family property.[52] As late as the Qing dynasty (1644–1911), family property could not be divided when parents and grandparents were still alive: "If sons or grandsons should divide up family property during the lifetimes of their parents or grandparents, they will be punished by 100 blows with the heavy bamboo stick."[53] The idea of joint family property also meant that family members could be made to serve jail time for the property crimes of elderly family members, as noted by an apparently surprised late-nineteenth-century Western observer: "It is quite usual for sons to go to prison, and into banishment, for offences committed by their parents. In 1862, I found in the district city of Tsung-fa, a youth suffering incarceration instead of his grandfather, who had been committed to prison for bankruptcy."[54]

Contemporary societies in East Asia do not, of course, resort to physical punishment to enforce the ideal of family property. But the duty to share one's property with one's parents is still legally enshrined in some East Asian states. In Singapore, for example, parents above sixty years old who cannot support themselves can appeal to the Tribunal for the

[49] The only exception to the joint ownership of property, according to Madeleine Zelin, "was a woman's dowry, which became her individual property and by extension the property of the nuclear family created by her and her husband." Zelin, "Economic Freedom in Late Imperial China," in *Realms of Freedom in China*, ed. William C. Kirby (Stanford: Stanford University Press, 2004), 73.

[50] There may be significant overlap between the two Confucian values identified in this chapter, and they may not always be easy to distinguish in practice. For example, the duty to aid needy members of the family is one of the ways of securing the "right to food" identified in the previous section. Also, the ruler's economic policies should not allow people to impoverish themselves as they carry out their expensive obligations to care for needy family members (e.g., Mencius argues that rulers should not force economically productive people to incur debt in carrying out their filial duties; 3A.3).

[51] Schurmann, "Traditional Property Concepts in China," 510.

[52] Ibid., 511–12.

[53] Qing code, no. 87. Quoted in Philip C. C. Huang, *Civil Justice in China: Representation and Practice in the Qing* (Stanford: Stanford University Press, 1976), 25.

[54] Quoted in Hugh D. R. Baker, *Chinese Family and Kinship* (New York: Columbia University Press, 1979), 102–3.

Maintenance of Parents to claim maintenance from their children.[55] The constraints on property rights are even more striking when we look at an individual's right (or lack thereof) to dispose of property after his or her death. In traditional China, testate transfers by will rarely existed, as there was little room left for individual discretion.[56] In 1931 the Nationalist Party of China promulgated the Civil Code of China, which was an explicit attempt to modernize Chinese law and do away with the injunction against household division. It was divided into five parts, and the last part dealt with succession. On the face of it, the new Civil Code encouraged the "Western" idea of "disposal by the testator of his property by will."[57] Most notably, women were given equal rights of succession for the first time.[58] Like Western-style common law, the free disposal of property was constrained by the need to maintain young children. However, the Civil Code of China also maintained traditional Confucian limitations on the disposal of property. It specified a detailed ranking of family members who were entitled to a share of the inheritance, including parents and grandparents.[59] Moreover, needy family members who were dependent on the support of the deceased during his or her lifetime also had rights of succession, with the precise details to be sorted out by "the family council."[60] In short, the intergenerational transfer of property through bequest and inheritance was constrained by the Confucian value of care for needy family members, including elderly parents (and grandparents). An individual was not free to neglect these obligations, even after his or her death.

Surprisingly, perhaps, inheritance practices in "Communist" China also embody traditional Confucian ideas about inheritance. On April 10, 1985,

[55] According to social workers in Singapore, however, such legal sanctions can be counterproductive. Most needy elderly parents would rather make do on their own or live on charity than ask the tribunal for help because it hurts their pride to have their children ordered to support them and to have family matters discussed in front of strangers ("They prefer charity to forcing children to pay," *Straits Times* [weekly edition], 10 April 1999, 5). There have also been reports that some adult children who once gave freely to their parents (the law that makes it mandatory to provide financial support for elderly parents was passed in 1995) now ask for receipts, just in case the government comes to check on them. One can imagine the impact this has on the amount of trust informing family relationships.

[56] See Folsom, Minan, and Otto, *Law and Politics in the People's Republic of China*, 281; and Louis B. Schwarz, "The Inheritance Law of the People's Republic of China," in *Law in the People's Republic of China*, ed. R. H. Folsom and J. H. Minan (Dordrecht: Kluwer Academic Publishers, 1989), 470.

[57] William S. H. Hung, *Outlines of Modern Chinese Law* (Shanghai: Kelly and Walsh, 1934), 197.

[58] Previously, property was divided equally among all sons following the death of parents, and daughters had a secondary right of succession.

[59] Ibid., 198. Note that it was not a matter of individual will—this ranking of family members overrides preferences of the deceased.

[60] Ibid., 203.

the National People's Congress promulgated the first inheritance law in the history of the People's Republic of China. Like the 1931 Civil Code of China, the Inheritance Law was meant to challenge patriarchal practices and emphasize individual autonomy. Women were given equal rights of inheritance and the law allows for inheritance by will. Under inheritance by will, however, the decedent choice is constrained by the requirement that he or she must provide for heirs who are elderly, infirm, or under age. Moreover, heirs who abandon or maltreat the decedent with serious consequences forfeit their right of inheritance. The Inheritance Law also provides for intestate succession (i.e., the deceased dies without a will), to be accomplished through statutory inheritance. In this case, traditional ideas regarding the disposal of property also operate. Article 10 specifies that an estate is inherited first by spouse, children, and parents, then by siblings, paternal grandparents, and maternal grandparents. Statutory heirs are also subject to important exceptions, based on the relative financial needs of the heirs and the extent to which the heirs have fulfilled their obligation to provide for the decedent (article 13). As Louis Schwartz notes, these exceptions are self-consciously drawn from traditional Confucian ideas about the family as the basic welfare unit of society: "Chinese legal scholars emphasize that the failure of family members to support one another is both immoral and illegal. Article 13 continues 'with the force of law' the traditional Chinese practice of providing for one another within the family. In this sense, mutuality of obligations and benefits may be analogized to the traditional practice of enforcing Confucian ethical principles (*li*) with law (*fa*)."[61]

The Hong Kong legal system, largely modeled on the English common law system, also allows for Confucian values to occasionally override the imperatives of individual autonomy. For example, it is mandatory for part of an inheritance to be used to support disabled members of the family, even if they have been explicitly left out of the deceased person's will.[62]

---

[61] Schwartz, "The Inheritance Law of the People's Republic of China," 477. Schwartz notes that this Inheritance Law, which reinforced the role of the family as the basic welfare unit in Chinese society, "parallels the reemergence of the family as the basic production unit in China (at least in the countryside)" (478). Technically speaking, land cannot be inherited, but "article 4 of the Inheritance Law permits the inheritance of the right of possession and use of land pursuant to a land contract. Inheritance of land contract rights flows from the constitutional right of citizens to enter into contracts to engage in private economic activity. The right to inherit land contract rights under article 4 creates a strong incentive for peasants to make investments in the land they work" (472).

[62] For a more detailed discussion of laws of succession in Hong Kong, see Lusina Ho, "Traditional Confucian Values and Western Legal Frameworks: The Law of Succession," in *Confucianism for the Modern World*, ed. Daniel A. Bell and Hahm Chaibong (New York: Cambridge University Press, 2003).

From a contemporary Confucian perspective, in short, the intergenerational transfer of property through bequest and inheritance should be constrained by the need to provide aid for less well-off members of the family, including children and aged parents. One cannot justly (and legally, it turns out) disinherit needy members of the family, and potential heirs forfeit their inheritance rights if they failed to fulfill their obligations to the deceased during his or her lifetime.[63]

It might be argued that there is nothing particularly distinctive about the Confucian system of family-based property rights. Social-welfare states in the West, for example, often treat property as a "family-based" resource in divorce cases, with children and former spouses (but not elderly parents) having rights to property. Some civil law codes (as in Quebec) also secure the "Confucian" right to be cared for by adult children (though the extent of enforcement is questionable).[64] Still, it is difficult to think of modern societies outside East Asia that similarly emphasize, in both law and public morality, the duty to regard property as an asset of the whole family, including elderly parents. East Asian societies have incorporated "individualistic" conceptions of property rights to a certain extent, but they still draw the line closer to family-based property rights in comparison with their liberal Western counterparts.

Is the value of care for needy family members still desirable? The moral justification for the tendency of East Asian governments (relative to most Western governments) to use different combinations of legal sanctions and financial incentives that facilitate the realization of the "right" of needy family members to a share of the family property is presumably the worry that more individual-centered property rights would have corrosive effects on family life.[65] The legal mode of implementation, however, may not be as ideal as it can be. Lusina Ho argues that "the limited and haphazard Confucian influences in the succession laws of the Chinese communities considered may be due in great part to the

---

[63] This assumes that the property was justly acquired in the first place—or at least that it was not appropriated in ways that current generations consider to be unjust. For example, conquered territory cannot justifiably be passed down to descendants. As Confucius said, "Zang Wuzhong, having occupied Feng, requested that it be acknowledged by Lu as his hereditary fief. Whatever may be said, I cannot believe that he did not exert pressure upon his lord" (14.14, Leys). It is not made explicit, but Confucius leaves open the possibility that the original inhabitants have rights to the conquered land, or at least more rights than the occupier's descendants.

[64] I thank Gary Bell for this information.

[65] I do not mean to deny that other factors may also have influenced the decision-making process. For example, East Asian government officials may also be attracted to the idea that adult children should care for elderly parents because it reduces the financial burden on the state.

fact that some of these communities have adopted Western laws as a foundation and then simply tinkered with them to suit local values."[66] This approach has unintentionally contributed to anti-Confucian consequences, such as benefits for the less filial. To remedy such flaws, Ho develops a proposal for a two-tiered law of succession where the Confucian order of the hierarchy of social relationships corresponds more systematically to the order of the rights of inheritance. Perhaps Ho's proposal can inspire proposals for reform of succession laws in East Asian societies.

Here too, in short, the value of care for needy family members seems to meet the five criteria above:

- This value, along with the implication that economically productive adults must care for needy family members (including elderly parents), has been widely discussed by Confucius, Mencius, and other Confucian scholars.

- The value of care for needy family members has not been repudiated by contemporary Confucian intellectuals. Quite the opposite, Confucian familism is still central to contemporary Confucian discourse.

- The political implication of this value—the state should promote obligations to care for needy family members, including (especially) elderly parents—conflicts with certain versions of liberal democratic theory that prioritize individual autonomy such as liberal neutrality (a policy can't be justified by appealing to the superiority of one comprehensive comprehension of the good) and republicanism (citizens should seek the good in political life outside the family).

- The value of care for needy family members still informs the practices of East Asian societies with a Confucian heritage; for example, policies to promote filial piety, profamily ads on TV, profamily moral education in schools, and inheritance laws that secure the interests of elderly parents, regardless of the will of the adult child. At the social level, even same-sex couples invoke these themes—in Taiwan, for example, much of the gay literature deals with relationships with parents.

- This value still serves important purposes. It provides psychological stability for family members and buttresses the family against the individualizing tendencies of global markets. The relatively low rates of divorce in East Asia benefit the children, and the relatively high rates of at-home care and support for elderly parents benefit the latter. The fact that needy family members have access to the means of subsistence may help to explain the relatively equal distribution of wealth in some East Asian societies (since needy family members, who might be left to fend for themselves in more libertarian economic systems, are not as poor as they

[66] Ho, "Traditional Confucian Values," 309.

might otherwise be). Still, actually existing Confucian familism can be criticized for its haphazard legal implementation, and it can and should be improved.

EXPORTING CONFUCIANISM?

To what extent are Confucian values realizable in societies that have not been shaped by the Confucian tradition? More grandly, perhaps, could Confucian values ever command international legitimacy? Let us review the two values surveyed in this chapter and assess the potential for exporting them to societies that have not been shaped by Confucianism.

From a Confucian standpoint, the government's first priority is to secure the basic means of subsistence of the people, and this obligation has priority over civil and political rights in cases of conflict. Property rights in particular must be constrained by the need to secure the basic material welfare of the people. To this end, Mencius suggested the well-field system, which involves state intervention to claim a share of produce to secure the basic means of subsistence of nonfarming members of the state and intervention to secure an equitable distribution of land at the local community level. Beyond that, individual households have the right to make productive use of land and sell their produce on the free market. Alternative distributions of property rights are (in principle) acceptable if they more effectively secure the end of improving the basic material welfare of the people. However, the well-field system has been influential in Chinese history, and it continues to be relevant in the contemporary era—Deng Xiaoping's rural land reform program represents (in effect, if not in theory) a "return" to Mencius's well-field system, and it has led to a dramatic improvement of material welfare in China. Any challenge to principles informing the well-field system would therefore need to (sur)pass a high bar of historical and present-day success.

Needless to say, the overriding value of basic material welfare and Mencius's idea for implementation would be more applicable in primarily agricultural societies. The lessons for North Korea and Vietnam—both "Communist" countries with Confucian characteristics—are obvious.[67] But there is no reason why non–East Asian societies cannot also experiment with Mencius's well-field system. The "founding fathers" of Confucianism defended ideals and practices that were held to be universalizable;[68] they did not view Confucianism as being necessarily confined

[67] Vietnam is self-consciously looking to the Chinese experience with agricultural reform as a model for its own reforms.

[68] I do not know of any evidence that early Confucians discussed the possibility that cultural differences might justify different normative and political standards.

to a particular group such as the Chinese. In terms of its actual history, Confucianism helped to inspire political reform in countries outside its area of origin (most notably, Korea, Japan, and Vietnam). Perhaps the well-field system can help to correct imbalances arising from too much or too little state intervention in the rural sector. China has shown that it is possible to move from Communist-style collectivism to this Mencian mixture of private and public property,[69] which could provide guidance for reform in Cuba. In the Philippines, the concentration of land in the hands of a few wealthy landlords is often cited as one of the reasons for widespread poverty and lack of economic development,[70] and the well-field system may help to remedy these problems.

The Confucian prioritization of material welfare will also manifest itself at the level of foreign policy. In societies shaped by a Confucian heritage, it seems obvious that the first priority of global justice should be the alleviation of severe poverty. This helps to explain why members of East Asian societies, including independent intellectuals, are often baffled by the Western insistence on promoting democracy in poor Third World countries and suspect that deeper or more sinister motives may be doing the real work. If nondemocratic forms of government can do better at alleviating poverty, then what's the hurry with democracy? Given that most East Asian societies underwent rapid development under less-than-democratic political arrangements, the potential trade-off between democracy and poverty alleviation seems very real. Such views are not likely to challenge dominant Western outlooks, however. Whatever the empirical facts regarding the relationship between democracy and poverty, the centrality of civil and political liberties in the moral framework of Western political traditions means that Western countries will continue to devote "excessive" resources to the promotion of democracy abroad, just as East Asian governments will continue to draw upon background Confucian concerns to press for economic justice first. The tendency to dismiss either position as motivated entirely by crude realpolitik can only inflame international tensions. In such cases, it may be necessary to tolerate, if not respect, cultural difference.

I also discussed the Confucian value of care for needy family members, including children and elderly parents. This value entails granting

---

[69] "Mencian" principles may have inspired agricultural reform in China, but other forms of property rights exist in other sectors of the economy. For an account of the different processes that have informed China's economic reforms, see Andrew G. Walder and Jean C. Oi, "Property Rights in the Chinese Economy: Contours of the Process of Change," in *Property Rights and Economic Reform in China*, ed. Oi and Walder (Stanford: Stanford University Press, 1999), 22.

[70] See, e.g., Donald Kirk, *Looted: The Philippines after the Bases* (New York: St. Martin's Press, 1998).

property rights to families rather than individuals, since it is assumed—and legally enforced, if need be—that economically productive persons find it easier to aid less well-off members of their families under a system of joint family property. In principle, Confucians would endorse alternative distributions of property rights that more effectively secure the value of care for needy family members. In East Asia, however, contemporary decision-makers have opted to maintain some Confucian-style property rights. In comparison with their Western counterparts, Asian governments go out of their way to use different combinations of legal sanctions and financial incentives that facilitate the realization of the "right" of elderly parents to a share of the family property—and there is little, if any, opposition to these policies in society at large. Moreover, it is noteworthy that the Nationalist Party of China (the KMT), the Chinese Communist Party, and the Hong Kong government—notwithstanding radically different political ideologies—have all passed laws that curtail the freedom of individuals to disinherit needy members of their families. The worry, presumably, is that more individual-centered property rights would undermine, rather than promote, the Confucian value of care for needy family members.

Those who would want to universalize Confucian familism face an additional hurdle relative to universalist defenders of Confucian concern for material welfare. The Confucian-inspired government has an obligation to promote material welfare because material welfare is necessary for the good life.[71] This view is, in principle, compatible with diverse conceptions of the good life. Confucian familism, however, is the good life. More precisely, the Confucian view is that the good life consists first and foremost of relationships of care and affection between family members, including elderly parents, with the political implication that the state has an obligation to promote profamily policies even if they place constraints upon individual autonomy (and property rights). The Confucian view may resonate in non-Western societies that similarly prioritize relationships between family members. But Western societies shaped by the liberal emphasis on individual autonomy will likely reject this Confucian value along with its political manifestations. This is not to deny that Western communitarians have articulated worries about the corrosive effects of liberal individualism on family life.[72] Such concerns, however, are rarely put in terms of the need to promote close relationships between adult children and their elderly parents. At best, then, Western-style

---

[71] For common people, that is. According to Mencius, exemplary persons can lead good lives even without dependable means of support (1A.7).

[72] See my entry on "Communitarianism" in the online *Stanford Encyclopedia of Philosophy* (http://plato.stanford.edu/entries/communitarianism).

Confucianism is likely to be "Confucianism lite," without the emphasis on filial piety and the attendant restrictions on the property rights of adult children.

The next two chapters deal more directly with contemporary capitalist phenomena in East Asia. Both chapters discuss East Asian–style responses to economic globalization. Chapter 10 is an overview of contemporary East Asian capitalism, and I try to sort out what is worth defending from what is not. Chapter 11 focuses on the issue of migrant domestic workers in East Asia, and here too I try to sort out what is worth defending from what is not. As we will see, the increased movement of domestic workers from impoverished countries and regions to the homes of relatively well-off East Asian families has led to several ethical and policy dilemmas that would likely be solved differently by Western liberals and Confucian-minded East Asians.

10

East Asian Capitalism in an Age of Globalization

IN EARLY 1998 the Asian economic crisis seemed to have dealt a fatal blow to the Asian economic model. U.S. Federal Reserve Board Chairman Alan Greenspan noted that the Asian crisis accelerated a worldwide move toward "the Western form of free market capitalism" and away from the competing Asian approach that only a few years ago looked like an attractive model for nations around the world. "What we have here is a very dramatic event towards a consensus of the type of market system which we have in this country."[1] In English-language newspapers, business schools, investment banks and Anglo-American government circles, one heard the same refrain: East Asian countries must shed old interventionist habits and adopt American-style shareholder capitalism in order to remain competitive. The shareholder model—based on flexible labor markets with high interfirm mobility, characterized by the rapid creation and failure of enterprises, with managers who are agents of shareholders and responsive to their demands, and with high-performing individuals rewarded handsomely for their contributions[2]— is best suited to promote creativity and innovation and withstand the disciplinary forces of global capital in an age of globalization. Thus, Asian countries should change to a mode of corporate governance that makes managers concentrate single-mindedly on creating shareholder value and sack workers who fail to perform, favors deregulation and un-linking of the government-business nexus, and promotes tax adjustments to let wealth-creators keep more of the wealth they create. Anything less was held to be a recipe for economic and social decline.

Shortly thereafter, however, it became clear that the Asian crisis was not caused solely by the "Asian approach" to capitalism. The "single most important cause of the crisis," according to Joseph Stiglitz, was excessively rapid financial and capital market liberalization, the kinds of policies that had been advocated by the U.S. Treasury and the International Monetary

---

[1] Alan Greenspan quoted in D. Sanger, "Greenspan Sees Asian Crisis Moving World to Western Capitalism," *New York Times*, 13 February 1998, D1.

[2] See D. Eleanor Westney, "Japanese Enterprise Faces the Twenty-First Century," in *The Twenty-First Century Firm: Changing Economic Organization in International Perspective*, ed. Paul DiMaggio (Princeton: Princeton University Press, 2001), 139.

Fund (IMF).[3] Moreover, the shortcomings of Anglo-American capitalism soon began to reassert themselves in the public eye. Corporate scandals at Enron and Worldcom showed that "crony capitalism" was not confined to Asia. Alan Greenspan himself orchestrated an "Asian-style" bailout for Long-Term Capital Management, the flagship hedge-fund that threatened to bring down the whole financial system with its reckless billion-dollar gambles. The collapse of the high-tech bubble in Silicon Valley sent stock prices tumbling worldwide. The launching of the Iraq War was widely perceived to have been encouraged by oil giants and well-connected corporations such as Halliburton and Bechtel that stood to gain huge economic benefits.[4] To many observers, such events stem from the structural inadequacies of American-style capitalism: the pursuit of short-term profit regardless of the impact on workers and local communities and the long-term health of companies; the militarization of the economy; and economically unproductive protectionist benefits for wealthy contributors to elected politicians. In the span of few years, the U.S. economic model has become a hard sell abroad,[5] and Asian countries are reasserting their own economic ways,[6] almost to the point of neglecting necessary economic reform.

In this chapter, I will try to steer between the extremes of universalizing claims for the "Western form of free market capitalism" and glorification of the traditional "competing Asian approach." On the one hand,

[3] Joseph E. Stiglitz, *Globalization and Its Discontents* (New York: Norton, 2003), 89. See also Robert Wade, "The Asian Crisis: The High Debt Model versus the Wall Street–Treasury–IMF Complex," *New Left Review*, no. 228 (March/April 1998), 5. Rodney Bruce Hall argues that it is not just the IMF's policies, but also its normative language, that exacerbated the Asian economic crisis. Hall, "The Discursive Demolition of the Asian Development Model," *International Studies Quarterly*, vol. 47 (2003), 87–88. In my view, Hall overstates his case somewhat by arguing that the IMF's normative language has contributed to the "demolition" of the Asian development model: even in Korea during the darkest days of the crisis (the context for Hall's article), there was a giant gap between official lip service to the IMF's language and continuing adherence to "East Asian–style" practices. For an argument that Korea continues to adhere to a distinctive (neither Anglo-American nor European corporatist) political economic model that is socially inclusive but not politically so, see Tat Yan Kong, "Neo-liberalization and Incorporation in Advanced Newly Industrialized Countries: A View from South Korea," *Political Studies*, vol. 52, no. 1 (March 2004).

[4] See Chalmers Johnson, "The War Business: Squeezing a Profit from the Wreckage in Iraq," *Harpers*, November 2003, 53–58.

[5] Evelyn Iritani, "After Scandals, U.S. Economic Model Is Hard Sell Abroad," *International Herald Tribune*, 8 July 2002, 1.

[6] In the case of Japan, it never stopped asserting its own ways (on the World Bank and developing countries), even (especially) in the midst of its decade-long recession in the 1990s: see Robert Wade, "Japan, the World Bank, and the Art of Paradigm Maintenance: *The East Asian Miracle* in Political Perspective," *New Left Review*, no. 217 (May/June 1996), 34.

I will assume that much remains desirable about the East Asian economic model: the combination of rapid economic growth with decreasing poverty and income inequality; companies that emphasize the interests of workers, local communities, and the national good and take a more long-term view regarding the need to make profit; and rapid modernization that preserves social stability and civil harmony. East Asian states should do their best to hold on to these features. On the other hand, I will assume that the intensified competitive pressures of globalization and the need for creativity and innovation in modernized economies require substantial economic restructuring in East Asia.

My strategy will be to sketch the features of an East Asian model of capitalism that may still be feasible and desirable in the contemporary globalizing world. They are feasible, in the sense that they do not contradict, and may in fact be beneficial for, the need to improve economic efficiency in an increasingly competitive global marketplace. They are desirable, in the sense that they preserve some of the social advantages of Asian capitalism. Thus, the features of this model that seem transparently undesirable or incompatible with the requirements of economic efficiency (e.g., rigidly patriarchal work practices, corrupt bailouts of unproductive enterprises, preferential loans to favored businesses with close ties to the governing elite)[7] will be deliberately left out. I will only discuss features that seem, prima facie, feasible and desirable, though it is recognized that any full-fledged defense of these features would need to be an empirically detailed argument showing that the advantages associated with these features outweigh the disadvantages.

The area of focus includes South Korea, Japan, Taiwan, Singapore, Hong Kong,[8] and one less-developed but rapidly growing economic power—mainland China. These generally secular countries partake of a Confucian heritage that values commitment to the family, education, saving, and hard work.[9] Confucianism informs the "habits of the heart" of ordinary East Asians, habits that have been transmuted into economic

---

[7] Seiichi Masuyama and Donna Vanderbrink, "Industrial Restructuring in East Asian Economies for the Twenty-First Century," in *Industrial Restructuring in East Asia: Towards the 21st Century*, ed. Seiichi Masuyama, Donna Vanderbrink, and Chia Siow Yue (Tokyo: Nomura Research Institute; Singapore: Institute for Southeast Asian Studies, 2001), 42–43.

[8] Hong Kong's economy may not seem to fit the "East Asian model," if only because it was structured by a British-led regime (before 1997) and is better known as a kind of libertarian paradise. However, the Hong Kong government, even under British rule, was notoriously interventionist in areas such as land policy. See my article, "Hong Kong's Transition to Capitalism," *Dissent* (Winter 1998), 15–23. Hence, I will assume that Hong Kong fits the category of the "East Asian model," but my view can be falsified by evidence of a non–East Asian country that partakes of more of the features listed here than does Hong Kong.

[9] See Robert Wade, *Governing the Market*, 2nd ed. (Princeton: Princeton University Press, 2003), 221.

behavior such as high rates of personal and corporate saving, a commitment to the firm as a collectivity, and a willingness to forgo leisure in favor of long hours at work.[10] The political leaders of East Asia have also
been inspired by Legalist ideas that justify "the institution of powerful,
centralized, and activist government that arrogates for itself the role of
fostering economic development and political reforms."[11] This combination of the two main East Asian political traditions—what Paik Wooyeal
terms "Legalistic Confucianism"[12]—underpins the East Asian economic
model.

Of course, I do not mean to imply that there is a direct causal relation
between cultural traditions and policy outcomes. Other factors also help
to explain the special characteristics of East Asian capitalism in the
post–World War II era.[13] The United States secured the international environment for an Asian economic take-off: to help build up solid capitalist

---

[10] Jeffrey Henderson and Richard P. Appelbaum, "Situating the State in the East Asian
Development Process," in *States and Development in the Asian Pacific Rim*, ed. Appelbaum
and Henderson (Newbury Park: Sage Publications, 1992), 16. See also Wei-bin Zhang,
*Confucianism and Modernization: Industrialization and Democratization of the Confucian
Regions* (Houndsmills: Macmillan Press, 1999), chap. 10; Tu Wei-ming, ed., *Confucian Tra-
ditions in East Asian Modernity: Moral Education and Economic Culture in Japan and the
Four Mini-Dragons* (Cambridge: Harvard University Press, 1996); Ezra Vogel, *The Four
Little Dragons: The Spread of Industrialization in East Asia* (Cambridge: Harvard Univer-
sity Press, 1991); Michio Morishima, *Why Has Japan Succeeded?: Western Technology and
the Japanese Ethos* (Cambridge: Cambridge University Press, 1982); Lucian W. Pye, *Asian
Power and Politics: The Cultural Dimensions of Authority* (Cambridge: Belknap Press,
1985); David Aikman, *Pacific Rim: Area of Change, Area of Opportunity* (Boston: Little,
Brown, 1986); Francis Fukuyama, *Trust: The Social Virtues and the Creation of Prosperity*
(New York: The Free Press, 1995); Hahm Chaibong, *Postmodernism and Confucianism*
(Seoul: Jontong gua Hyundai, 1998); Ju Song Hwan, "East Asian Economic Development
and Confucian Culture," *North East Asian Economic Review*, vol. 11, no. 1 (1999), 1–32;
Ju Song Hwan, "The Economic Development Theory of East Asia and Confucian Market
Economy Model," *Comparative Economics*, vol. 8 (2000), 303–37; Hahm Chaibong, *Con-
fucianism, Capitalism and Democracy* (Seoul: Jontong gua Hyundai, 2002).

[11] Hahm and Paik, "Legalistic Confucianism," 485. Legalist-inspired rulers such as Park
Chung Kee of Korea and Lee Kuan Yew of Singapore would typically try to justify their
rule in Confucian terms (ibid., 486), similar to "Legalist Confucians" in Chinese history,
but occasionally Legalist principles stood out starkly: for example, article 11 in the Japanese Seventeen Article Constitution stated that the government should "give clear appreciation to merit and demerit, and deal out to each its sure reward and punishment" (quoted
in Lin Ka, "Confucian Welfare Cluster: A Cultural Interpretation of Social Welfare," academic dissertation, University of Tampere, 1999, 31), a passage that could have been taken
straight out of Han Fei Zi.

[12] See Paik Wooyeal, "Confucianism with Legalistic Features: Its Contribution to Political-
Economic Development in East Asia," M.Phil. thesis, Department of Public and Social
Administration, City University of Hong Kong, September 2003.

[13] See Ian Holliday, "Productivist Welfare Capitalism: Social Policy in East Asia," *Political Studies*, vol. 48, no. 4 (September 2000), 716–19.

economies in the East Asian region as part of its Cold War struggle with the Soviet Union, the United States gave unimpeded access to its markets while allowing East Asian governments to protect their own industries. The legacies of British and Japanese colonial rule shaped subsequent economic development and social policy. East Asian policymakers were often trained in American universities and transplanted Western-style economic ideas to Asia. More immediate political and economic constraints, not to mention ad hoc decision making, help to explain key differences between the various East Asian countries.

In any case, my main aim is not to *explain* the features of East Asian capitalism; it is to *describe* those features that may still be feasible and desirable in the contemporary globalizing world. The features to be sketched below are not necessarily distinctive to East Asian societies, nor does every East Asian country partake of every single one of these features. However, my hypothesis is that developed East Asian countries informed by the Legalistic Confucian heritage partake of more of these features compared to developed societies in North America and Western Europe. To prove this model wrong, in other words, the critic must identify a society outside East Asia that partakes of more of these features.

The first part of the chapter surveys the main features of East Asian capitalism that serve to promote economic productivity, and the second part surveys the features of East Asian capitalism that serve to secure the welfare of those vulnerable to the negative effects of capitalism development. Capitalism is defined here as an economic system dominated by owners of capital who hire wage laborers and produce for profit. Globalization is defined as technology-driven growth and increased global trade and (especially) money flows that pressure companies to change and innovate at historically unprecedented levels.[14]

East Asian Capitalism and Economic Productivity

The main virtue of capitalism, as Karl Marx himself recognized, is that it promotes economic and technological development by means of competition between capitalists forced to innovate to stay competitive.[15] East Asian capitalism is no exception. It is organized for the purpose of promoting economic productivity, but it is characterized by several features that, taken together, may be distinctive.

---

[14] In chapter 11, globalization will refer primarily to increased labor migration between and within countries.

[15] This section draws on my article, "East Asian Capitalism: Towards a Normative Framework," *Global Economic Review*, vol. 30, no. 3 (2001), 75–80.

An Autonomous and Interventionist State

First, East Asian capitalism is characterized by a relatively strong, autonomous state that takes an active role in regulating the economy and promoting economic productivity.[16] The state is composed of "able and well-paid administrators who [are] insulated to a significant degree from political pressures and empowered to take development initiatives aimed at maximizing the growth of output and employment."[17] The bureaucrats are selected from the "best and brightest" in the elite university sector.[18] By global standards, East Asian bureaucrats are capable and highly motivated to contribute to economic development.[19] Conversely, government downsizing in Thailand and Malaysia led to bureaucratic brain drain to the private sector.[20] The loss of expertise and cohesion among the policy-making elite may lie behind the failure to upgrade technologically.[21] Another feature of the elite bureaucracy is that it is composed of generalists more than professional economists, allowing for broader perspectives on policy issues. Japan, Korea, and Taiwan have explicitly curbed the number and influence of economists in the industrial policy-making process, partly because neoclassical economics has little to say about how to exploit opportunities opened by new information technologies.[22] Finally, East Asian bureaucrats have

[16] Henderson and Appelbaum argue that the East Asian state (with the exception of Hong Kong) has been uniquely interventionist relative to corporatist state-business partnerships in other societies, "Situating the State in the Development Process," 20–23.

[17] Shahid Yusuf, "The East Asian Miracle at the Millenium," in *Rethinking the East Asia Miracle*, ed. Joseph E. Stiglitz and Shahid Yusuf (New York: Oxford University Press, 2001), 6.

[18] In contrast, the personnel policies of the U.S. federal government are designed to attract "competent people, not the best and most talented people," who should be encouraged to migrate to the private sector. Quoted in Wade, *Governing the Market*, 381.

[19] Ibid., 339, 341.

[20] K. S. Jomo notes that criticisms of the role of government since the 1980s, mainly from the Anglophone world, have "demoralized much of state personnel in Southeast Asia." Jomo, "Rethinking the Role of Government Policy in Southeast Asia," in *Rethinking the Asian Miracle*, 488. Singapore may be a counterexample because the "best and brightest" university students still aspired to be bureaucrats (judging from my experience teaching at the National University of Singapore in the 1990s). The high salaries in the public sector, of course, played a role, but the lasting influence of a Confucian tradition that values public service above other forms of the good life may also have provided some motivational resources. It could be that countries with a Confucian heritage are better able to psychologically withstand attacks on "Big Government" from the Anglophone world.

[21] Linda Weiss, "Is the State Being 'Transformed' by Globalization?," in *States in the Global Economy: Bringing Domestic Institutions Back in* (New York: Cambridge University Press, 2003), 300.

[22] Wade, *Governing the Market*, 372. To the extent that neoclassical economists have articulated thoughts on the subject of the high-tech economy, as in Alan Greenspan's overly optimistic pronouncements about the "new economy" prior to the collapse of the high-tech bubble, the results have not always been positive.

shown an unusual "willingness to play the pupil with respect to other countries—always on the assumption that the diligent pupil can eventually do better than the master."[23]

Industrial policy is the most famous—and controversial[24]—mechanism deployed by East Asian bureaucrats to promote the overall economic good.[25] The state decides on strategic industries to be protected and promoted and then proceeds to aid those industries in various ways. Most obviously, industrial policy takes the form of direct intervention in the affairs of the business sector. Some governments take direct equity stakes in desirable investment projects in the private sector. For example, the Singapore government invested in a semiconductor wafer fabricator, SemiTech, together with Texas Instruments and Hewlett Packard of the United States and Canon of Japan.[26] Large firms can be forced to cooperate with the government. In Japan, for example, powerful firms are compelled to participate in government-led research.[27] Joint government-business research can have the benefit of pooling the resources required for large-scale research and development of cutting-edge technologies.

More often than not, however, "government leadership" does not aim to replace private enterprise or to force companies to follow its dictates. Robert Wade argues that East Asian economic success owes more to

> a synergistic connection between a public system and a mostly private market system, the outputs of each becoming inputs for the other, with the government setting rules and influencing decision-making in the private sector in line with its view of an appropriate industrial and trade profile for the economy. Through this mechanism the advantages of markets (decentralization, rivalry, diversity, and multiple experiments) have been combined with the advantages of partially insulating producers from the instabilities

---

[23] Ibid., 334.

[24] Scott Callon, for example, draws on the case of the failures of Japan's Ministry of Trade and Industry to argue that defenders of industrial policy have overemphasized the positive effects of state intervention and the advantages of market failure. Callon, *Divided Sun: MITI and the Breakdown of Japanese High-Tech Industrial Policy, 1975–1993* (Stanford: Stanford University Press, 1995), 200–2. Callon, however, does not advocate the end of industrial policy per se; rather, he argues that MITI's industrial policies should swing away from large companies and toward smaller ones (207).

[25] Industrial policy is not distinctive to the East Asian region. As Joseph Stiglitz notes, "industrialization occurred within the United States behind the protection afforded by industrial tariffs." Stiglitz, "From Miracle to Crisis to Recovery: Lessons from Four Decades of East Asian Experience," in *Rethinking the East Asian Miracle*, 518.

[26] Masuyama and Vanderbrink, "Industrial Restructuring in East Asian Economies for the Twenty-First Century," 43.

[27] Charles Polidano, "Don't Discard State Autonomy: Revisiting the East Asian Experience of Development," *Political Studies*, vol. 49 (2001), 525.

of free markets and of stimulating investment in certain industries selected by government as important for the economy's future growth. This combination has improved upon the results of free markets.[28]

One recent example of using indirect means to encourage the buildup of indigenous innovation capacity is the Taiwanese government's "success in developing IT enterprises through technology transfer from the Industrial Research Institute (ITRI) and in providing high-technology infrastructure through the Hsin Chu Science Park."[29]

The East Asian state also induces economic actors to cooperate more effectively with each other. When firms coordinate more effectively, their performance will be better, and the result will be better overall economic performance.[30] Once again, this need not take the form of governments simply telling economic actors what to do: direct intervention is usually counterproductive because the outcomes are too complex to be dictated by regulation, and states lack the information needed to specify appropriate strategies. By tapping into and organizing already existing social organizations such as strong business associations, trade unions, and other parapublic organizations, the East Asian state can find it easier to effectively enhance nonmarket coordination.[31]

None of this is to deny that further deregulation, liberalization, and privatization is (and should be) taking place in East Asia. Even then, however, it may not mean that the state is "really" withdrawing from its central role in economic life. Linda Weiss argues that the pressures of globalization generate incentives for governments to take initiatives that will strengthen national systems of innovation and government-business cooperation.[32] After the Asian economic crisis, the role of the Korean

---

[28] Wade, *Governing the Market*, 5. Wade draws most of his support from the Taiwan case, but Yongping Wu argues that strongman tactics were responsible for the success of industrial policy in Taiwan. Wu, "Rethinking the Taiwanese Developmental State," *The China Quarterly*, vol. 177 (March 2004), 91–114.

[29] Masuyama and Vanderbrink, "Industrial Restructuring in East Asian Economies for the Twenty-First Century," 43–44.

[30] See Peter A. Hall and David Soskice, "An Introduction to Varieties of Capitalism," in *Varieties of Capitalism: The Institutional Foundations of Comparative Advantage*, ed. Hall and Soskice (Oxford: Oxford University Press, 2001), 45–46.

[31] In contrast, the U.S. government has largely failed to develop cooperation between business organizations and other interest groups, due (partly) to a deeply rooted adversarial culture that presents near-insurmountable obstacles for introducing cooperation. This has led to the dysfunctional consequence that the U.S. government regulates more than any other industrialized country yet with comparatively poor results in such fields as environmental regulation and the protection of work-related injuries. See Derek Bok, *The Trouble with Government* (Cambridge: Harvard University Press, 2001), chap. 6.

[32] Linda Weiss, "Introduction: Bringing Domestic Institutions Back in," in *States in the Global Economy*, 15–19.

state in relation to the market has become larger:[33] for example, it has pumped millions of dollars to finance a public-private venture industry designed to support high-technology startups.[34] In Japan, the state used strong incentives to promote competition in the telecommunications sector starting in 2000, with the result that the country has emerged as a leader in deploying high-speed broadband and the latest mobile-phone technology.[35] Even straightforward privatization need not mean relinquishing de facto state control. In mainland China, state-run enterprises sell shares to the public (including foreign markets) while maintaining control over management, usually by retaining the largest proportion of shares that allows them to choose the board of directors. This allows companies to raise funds and inject an element of professionalism and transparency while minimizing the damage to the workers and the communities in which they operate. In short, the relevant question is not whether the East Asian state will withdraw from economic life in response to the pressures of globalization. Rather, the question is how globalization will change the nature of the intervention. Indirect intervention that involves cooperation with the business sector and aid to cutting-edge sectors rather than to particular companies is more likely to be functional in the future.

The East Asian state is also characterized—and here the contrast is with European-style corporatism—by the fact that labor has been largely left out from the government-business decision-making nexus.[36] The freedom of association and the freedoms to organize and bargain have been greatly restricted in most East Asian states.[37] Frederic Deyo has referred to the political subordination and exclusion of workers as the

---

[33] Kap-Young Jeong and Yeon-ho Lee, "Convergence or Divergence? The South Korean State after the Asian Financial Crisis," *Global Economic Review*, vol. 30, no. 3 (2001), 66–67.

[34] Linda Weiss, "Guiding Globalization in East Asia," 256–57.

[35] In contrast, the United States dropped from fourth to thirteenth place in global rankings of broadband Internet usage in the first three years of the Bush administration, a lag that "is arguably the result of the Bush administration's failure to make a priority of developing these networks. In fact, the United States is the only industrialized state without an explicit national policy for promoting broadband." Thomas Bleha, "Down to the Wire," *Foreign Affairs* (May/June 2005), 1, http://www.foreignaffairs.org/20050501faessay84311/thomas-bleha/down-to-the-wire.html.

[36] Wade, *Governing the Market*, 327–28.

[37] Western Europe is the comparison here. Asian states are more protective of labor rights than the Middle East, North Africa, and Latin America (see the references in Peerenboom, "Show Me the Money," 76n.4). In some areas, East Asian states do better on labor rights than the United States. For example, the Chinese government has been insisting that Wal-Mart do what it refuses to do in the United States: allow all its workers to join unions. Howard W. French, "Investors Trump Unions in China," *New York Times*, 17 December 2004, A1.

"dark underside of the East Asian 'miracle.' "[38] Still, the marginalization of workers has had some benefits. It has prevented strikes and curbed collective bargaining that could interfere with the imperatives of economic productivity. Less obviously, the subordination of labor rights can contribute to overall economic equality: "strong unions, particularly in their earliest periods, are typically successful in creating substantial wage differentials between unionized and non-unionized workers. Ironically, therefore, the very absence of unions in the rapidly developing NICs serves as a partial explanation for income equality, at least among the large mass of relatively low-income manufacturing workers."[39] As states have moved up the industrial ladder, labor's representation in the governing process has increased by such means as joint consultation forums.[40] Moreover, there have been compensations for restrictions on "Western-style" labor rights. In Japan, they "take the form of the Labor Standards Law and a legally developed right to 'lifetime employment.' In Hong Kong and Singapore, they take the form of very good individual contracts of employment that incorporate many elements derived from the protective International Labor Organization (ILO) Conventions and, especially in the case of Singapore, very substantial citizenship rights with respect to housing and education."[41] These informal pacts between the state and relatively weak unions—material benefits and a sense of belonging without substantial participation in the decision-making process—can be functional in good economic times. When things go sour, however, the state has an interest in giving more rights of political representation to labor. For the first time in Korean history, Meredith Woo-Cumings notes, "the [Kim Dae-Jung government] has given labor a strong voice at the bargaining table with business and government— certainly a major achievement of reform and one that has generally kept labor from (truly) major strikes and disruptions in the fact of unemployment that tripled in one year."[42]

[38] Frederic C. Deyo, *Beneath the Miracle: Labor Subordination in the New Asian Industrialism* (Berkeley: University of California Press, 1989), 1.

[39] T. J. Pempel, "Of Dragons and Development," *Journal of Public Policy*, vol. 12, no. 1 (1992), 89–90.

[40] Anthony Woodiwiss, *Globalization, Human Rights and Labor Law in Pacific Asia* (Cambridge: Cambridge University Press, 1998), 67.

[41] Anthony Woodiwiss, " 'Community in the East': Towards a New Human Rights Paradigm," in *Communitarian Politics in Asia*, ed. Chua Beng-Huat (London: Routledge/Curzon, 2004), 176.

[42] Woo-Cumings, "Miracle as Prologue," in *Rethinking the East Asia Miracle*, ed. Joseph E. Stiglitz and Shohid Yusuf (New York: Oxford University Press, 2001), 369. The practice by many *chaebols* (large industrial conglomerates) of continuing to pay striking workers their wages for as long as several months, reflective of "Asian-style" company concern for employees (Elmar Rieger and Stephan Leibfried, *Limits to Globalization: Welfare*

In addition, the state radically reengineers the local force to suit its economic plans, especially by changing the forms of labor supply to the market. As short-term measures, East Asian states have been modifying their immigration procedures to allow for the import of foreign talent beneficial for the country's economy. Singapore currently has the highest proportion of skilled foreign workers of any developed country (except for Persian Gulf states), even hiring foreign CEOs for state-owned firms such as Singapore Air. In Hong Kong, the state has modified its immigration procedures to allow for the import of thousands of mainland Chinese with scientific and technological skills. As long-term measures, states are implementing rapid changes to their educational systems to promote creativity, technology, and more global outlooks. In Singapore, the state has been at the forefront of promoting global ties between its publicly funded universities and the outside world.[43] In Japan, the state has cut 30 percent of the curriculum in its primary schools to deemphasize rote memorization and promote creative thinking. This ability to swiftly respond to new trends, and to override vested interests (e.g., local workers and teachers set in their ways) and protectionist impulses, may be useful in rapidly changing modern economies.

Another feature of the East Asian state is that it accumulates large financial reserves. In line with Legalist thinking that the state should be rich,[44] most East Asian states have massive foreign exchange reserves. In 1997 Japan's foreign exchange reserves of U.S. $217 billion were far larger than those of the United States, Germany, and France combined.[45] The financial reserves of Hong Kong and Singapore are the world's largest in per capita terms.

One justification for huge national savings is that they would come in handy in the event of a "rainy day," such as the Asian economic crisis. In

---

States and the World Economy [Cambridge: Polity Press, 2003], 325), further reduces the likelihood of major worker uprisings. I do not mean to imply that the state and business groups strategically plan and successfully control the outcomes regarding labor's role in the state-business nexus (in South Korea, labor has been particularly militant relative to other East Asian states, and this militancy may have contributed to material and political gains for labor).

[43] The gap between the ideal and the reality in Singapore, however, is rather glaring. The government frequently launches drives to promote creativity among its population, but it has been unwilling to do the one thing that would really free people to explore new directions, viz., remove the fear factor stemming from a repressive political system.

[44] See, e.g., Han Fei Zi, in *Readings in Classical Chinese Philosophy*, eds. P. J. Ivanhoe and Bryan W. Van Norden (Indianapolis: Hackett Publishing Company, 2003), 332. Machiavelli, in *The Discourses*, similarly argued that the state should be rich so as to wield more power than any other societal agent, but this sort of argument has not been mainstream in Western political theory and practice.

[45] *International Herald Tribune*, 7 May 1997.

early 1998 Hong Kong's stock market underwent a precipitous decline, triggered largely by speculators who faced an apparently "win-win" scenario. The speculators bet against the currency knowing that the government would prop up interest rates in order to protect the pegged exchange rate. At the same time, they bet more against the stock market with the knowledge that the property-sensitive stocks would get pummeled. To fight back currency speculators, the Hong Kong government spent U.S. $10 billion in one day, and the market subsequently turned around. Even George Soros belatedly praised the Hong Kong government for its one-off "deviation" from free-market principles.

The Singapore government also draws on its huge reserves to mitigate the effects of severe economic downturns. In mid-2001 Singapore experienced its worst quarterly contraction of economic output in more than thirty years. In response to the slowdown, the government announced a U.S. $6.2 billion package of economic-stimulus measures equivalent to 7 percent of annual GDP, including the free provision of government "shares" to all citizens (with an emphasis on the worst-off). In short, large public savings can help shield people from the effects of sudden economic downturns, an eventuality that becomes more likely in an age of globalization due to the rapid increase in the speed and scale of international money flows.

The state can also draw on these reserves for more long-term measures, to ensure that all sectors of society, including the worst-off, can compete effectively in the "new economy." This includes job-training programs and material support, as well as more innovative schemes. In Singapore, for example, the state supplies subsidized computers to all families, thus ensuring that no one is left behind in the race for globalization. As a consequence, Singapore is one of the world's most "wired" nations in per capita terms.

Social Networks

Second, East Asian capitalism is characterized by relatively heavy reliance on social networks to "grease the wheels" of economic transactions.[46] These networks—rooted in school ties, marriage, work, hometown, and region—are used to pursue profit, but they are modeled on the extended family and thus are less characterized by naked instrumentality. As Lew Seok-Choon points out, the social trust embedded in these networks lowers the costs of supervision and provides for economic efficiency: "When a person is recruited by a company through recommendation or connection, he/she tends to work harder [so as] not to disappoint those

---

[46] See, e.g., Yunxiang Yan, "Managed Globalization," 23–24.

who recommend him/her and to secure his/her position within the network of personal relations tied by connections."[47] Such affective networks can also promote stability within firms, thus alleviating firms' worries about losing valued employees and allowing them to engage in long-term planning. The networks can also reduce transaction costs, as the strong trust reduces the need for detailed contracts and modes of enforcement.[48] Affective networks can break down hierarchy in economically functional ways, as when the former chairman of Daewoo, Kim U-jung, gathered a group of small people for brainstorming in ways that resemble Silicon Valley upstarts.[49] This is not to imply that legally enforceable contracts between strangers should be entirely displaced, but if contracts are complemented and/or cemented by social networks, then economic actors need not worry as much about defection, supervision, and enforcement, and the economy as a whole can benefit.

Needless to say, social networks can be corrupt, time-consuming, and economically dysfunctional.[50] For example, it was difficult for the managers of Chinese rural enterprises to make fellow villagers work hard until the enterprises were sold to outsiders not part of the network.[51] Still, the short-term economic costs (e.g., buying goods from a member of a social network instead of a cheaper competitor) can sometimes be outweighed by the long-term benefits (e.g., members of social networks will help those in trouble).[52] The deeper problem lies with single, all-powerful networks permeating legal, government, and business circles; such networks rooted in ties to college fraternities have been blamed for economic and social problems in the Philippines.[53] Korean-style affective networks, however, are more functional because they are not exclusive or closed to outsiders. An individual can belong to several affective networks simultaneously, and boundaries between groups are flexible and

[47] Lee Seok-Choon, Chang Mi-Hye, and Kim Tae-Eun, "Affective Networks and Modernity: The Case of Korea," in *Confucianism for the Modern World*, ed. Daniel A. Bell and Hahm Chaibong (New York: Cambridge University Press, 2003), 211.

[48] I'm told that the contracts for teaching staff at Yonsei University (in Seoul) rarely run for more than half a page. At Tsinghua University (in Beijing), I taught for one year without having seen any contract. In Singapore and Hong Kong, perhaps due to the British heritage, university contracts are "Western-style" legalistic documents.

[49] Lee Seok-Choon, "Social Capital in Korea: The Affective Linkage Group," *Korea Journal*, vol. 41, no. 3 (Autumn 2001), 219.

[50] See, e.g., Dwight H. Perkins, "Law, Family Ties, and the East Asian Way of Doing Business," in *Culture Matters: How Values Shape Human Progress*, ed. Lawrence E. Harrison and Samuel P. Huntington (New York: Basic Books, 2000), esp. 240–43.

[51] Jean Oi made this point at a Center for East Asian Studies seminar, Stanford University, October 2003.

[52] I thank Jongryn Mo for this insight.

[53] Mark Mitchell, "Frat Brats," *Far Eastern Economic Review*, 15 February 2001, 62–63.

changing depending on circumstances. In this globalizing world of fast-paced, relatively unpredictable change, such open networks can facilitate rapid adjustment and economic restructuring as required by the disciplinary forces of globalization. Korean-style networks are also characterized by the fact that they are bound within patriotic attachment to the nation (the rush to donate gold to the government following the 1997–98 crisis is a particularly vivid example), and broader attachments of this sort can help to counter the most perverse manifestations of "selfish" networks.

Family-run Firms

Third, East Asian capitalism is characterized by a greater tendency (relative to capitalisms in other developed societies) to rely on family members in management and ownership positions of firms. Put another way, East Asian capitalism rests on a form of social organization that is legitimated through kinship principles. This form of organization is more typical of small and medium-sized firms in China, Taiwan, Hong Kong, and Southeast Asia,[54] and less so in South Korea and Japan where the economy is dominated by large conglomerates (though many such conglomerates are also controlled by family members).

The most obvious problem with family-run firms is that they have a tendency to shut off talent, favoring family ties over professionalism and nepotism over merit.[55] In modern economies, firms run by highly educated and capable managers are more likely to succeed. But family-run firms are adapting. In some cases, the patriarchs of Chinese family firms hire the brightest sons educated in U.S. business schools[56] (on occasion, the less able sons are actually paid off to stay away from the family business[57]), and to a growing extent capable female descendants are given an important role as well.

Moreover, the very features that help to explain the success of family-run firms in the nineteenth and twentieth centuries may still be functional

[54] On Southeast Asia, see Gordon C. K. Cheung, "Chinese Diaspora as a Virtual Nation: Interactive Roles between Economic and Social Capital," *Political Studies*, vol. 52 (2004), 664–84. On China, see Christopher A. McNally, "The Contours of China's Emerging Capitalism," ms. on file with author, esp. 72–81; and Gilles Guiheux, "The Revival of Family Capitalism: A Zhejiang Entrepreneur," *China Perspectives*, no. 58 (March–April 2005), 22–31.

[55] Family-run firms can also have eccentric traits that may not be consistent with rational economic behavior. For example, an owner of a large family-run watch-making firm operating out of Hong Kong told me that his family does not allow family members involved in the business to become (or marry) lawyers because lawyers are not supposed to be sufficiently "trustworthy" (this comment was made in the presence of my wife, a Chinese lawyer, thus generating a few laughs).

[56] "Corporate, Maybe: But Governance?" *The Economist*, 21 July 2003, 11.

[57] I thank Chua Beng-Huat for this point.

in the contemporary context. Gary Hamilton explains how these firms first succeeded:

> This household-based economy produces a type of petty capitalism. It is a nonpolitically based form of capitalism that is very flexible and readily adaptable to external economic opportunities, such as those offered with the expansion of Western capitalism in Asia. The Chinese integrated themselves into the expanding world economy; they followed the current of Western capitalism and, using their flexible networks, quickly monopolized selected economic niches in many countries throughout the world.[58]

Far from being out-of-date, such responsiveness to new market demands is particularly functional now that globalization can overhaul the character of markets almost overnight. The small family firm may be particularly adept "at some high-tech industries in which efficiency and flexibility are important and can be achieved on a small scale."[59]

Still, family ownership might seem to place a constraint on the economic benefits that large-scale firms can provide (economies of scale, etc). But "family" does not necessarily refer to the fixed nuclear family. In the Chinese context, it is a flexible network that can be extended to include a great number of people, including non–blood relations.[60] Thus, ownership and control of firms need not refer to small firms run by tightly knit blood families. Although most family-run firms in a Chinese business network are small or medium in size, the family-owned network of firms can also include some very large individual firms. In Hong Kong, the typical family run-business expands by offering minority stakes in a public company within the network of family firms.[61] Moreover, family-run firms can also tap into *guanxi* (relationship) networks that can serve as the basis for creating production, distribution, and investment

---

[58] Gary Hamilton, "Overseas Chinese Capitalism," in *Confucian Traditions in East Asian Modernity: Moral Education and Economic Culture in Japan and the Four Mini-Dragons*, ed. Tu Wei-ming (Cambridge: Harvard University Press, 1996), 335.

[59] Edwin A. Winckler, "Statism and Familism in Taiwan," in *Ideology and National Competitiveness: An Analysis of Nine Countries*, ed. George C. Lodge and Ezra F. Vogel (Boston: Harvard Business School Press, 1987), 185.

[60] Family-like appellations (e.g., "sister" or "brother") and practices can also be extended to nonfamily members in the enterprise, thus generating, at least temporarily, family-like relations at work. Another personal anecdote: I am part owner of a Thai restaurant/café in Beijing, and one of the shareholders makes clothes and offers personal gifts to the waitresses and waiters as well as taking them out for karaoke sessions. It is my perception (though I may be wrong) that such "family-like" treatment helps to explain why the waitresses and waiters generally seem to be loyal and hardworking and committed to the good of the restaurant (of course, we also rely on economic incentives, such as bonuses for waitresses and waiters if business does particularly well).

[61] Woo-Cumings, "Miracle as Prologue," 352.

networks,[62] thus helping to solve some coordination problems of small
and medium-sized firms. Family-run firms have also relied on clan organizations and ancestral trusts to establish networks and business associations in Europe and North America.[63] Such networks can serve as
alternative sources of capital abroad, thus protecting family-run firms
against the tight monetary policies, credit rationing, and high interest
rates characteristic of macroeconomic stabilization policies.[64]

Business Networks

Fourth, East Asian capitalism is characterized by group-based business
cooperation, especially in Japan and South Korea. In Western European
countries such as Germany, coordination depends on business associations and trade unions that are organized primarily along sectoral lines. By
contrast, the dominant business networks in Japan are built on *keiretsu*,
families of companies with dense interconnections cutting across sectors,
the most important of which is the vertical *keiretsu* with one major company at its center.[65]

The *keiretsu* system, as it has been traditionally practiced, may not meet
the requirements of innovation in the "new economy." The group-based
organization of Japanese political economy allows firms to take advantage
of the capacities for cross-technology transfer and rapid organizational
redeployment, which translates into comparative institutional advantages
in the large-scale production of consumer goods, machinery, and electron-
ics that exploit existing technologies and capacities for organizational
change.[66] But globalization involves a shift from industrial technology to
information technology, and the latter emphasizes radical innovation
(one-off discrete inventions) instead of cumulative knowledge. Japanese
firms are said to lack the capacities for radical innovation in the high-tech
world that American firms have by virtue of fluid market settings.[67]

It is possible, however, to overstate the need for *radical* innovation in
modern economies. Radical innovation may be particularly important in
the computer industry, but even at the height of the high-tech boom
(bubble) in 1999, the American computer industry represented only 1.2

---

[62] Ibid., 340.

[63] Teema Ruskola, "Conceptualizing Corporations and Kinship: Comparative Law and
Development Theory in Comparative Perspective," *Stanford Law Review* (July 2000),
1726.

[64] Woo-Cumings, "Miracle as Prologue," 351.

[65] Hall and Soskice, "An Introduction to Varieties of Capitalism," 34.

[66] See Alice H. Amsden, *Asia's Next Giant: South Korea and Late Industrialization*
(New York: Oxford University Press, 1992), 320.

[67] Hall and Soskice, "An Introduction to Varieties of Capitalism," 35.

percent of American GNP.[68] Sophisticated manufacturing constitutes a larger share of most modern economies, and Japanese-style workplaces are beneficial for building and accumulating the tacit knowledge so crucial in the manufacturing process.[69] Still, Japanese firms are trying to reposition themselves for high-tech innovation without abandoning the merits of the *keiretsu* system. This involves delegating decision making to lower levels in the organization,[70] internal diversification, the setting up of new "child companies" in the *keiretsu*,[71] and the tapping of foreign sources of talent by setting up corporate R&D establishments in Europe, the United States, and, increasingly, China.[72] In short, Japanese-style "nonliberal capitalism"[73] has shown considerable institutional resilience, and path-dependent incremental change is the most likely scenario in the foreseeable future.

EAST ASIAN CAPITALISM AND SOCIAL WELFARE

The sole purpose of the state is not just to promote economic development. It must also provide for the people's material welfare. If the market fails to do so, then the state must ensure that nobody falls too far behind. This requires paying attention not just to securing the welfare of those left behind, but also to reduce the number of people left behind. To secure the latter aim, the East Asian state has sought to promote a relatively egalitarian form of development that reduces the number of poor and ensures that more people have an opportunity to earn a decent living.

The East Asian state has relied on two main strategies for securing egalitarian development: an expansive educational system and restrictions on property rights. Public expenditure on education, particularly at the primary and secondary levels, has been high relative to capitalisms elsewhere. As Elmar Rieger and Stephan Leibfried explain, "Public expenditure on education remains very high today, and the pressure to achieve on pupils and students is enormous. The educational system is thus structured far

[68] Ronald Dore, *Stock Market Capitalism: Welfare Capitalism, Japan and Germany versus the Anglo-Saxons* (Oxford: Oxford University Press, 2000), 238.

[69] Robert Boyer, "Distinctive Features and Innovations," in *The End of Diversity? Prospects for German and Japanese Capitalism*, ed. Kozo Yamamura and Wolfgang Streeck (Ithaca: Cornell University Press, 2003), 182.

[70] Masuyama and Vandenbrink, "Industrial Restructuring in East Asian Economies for the Twenty-First Century," 33.

[71] Westney, "Japanese Enterprise Faces the Twenty-First Century," 141.

[72] Dore, *Stock Market Capitalism*, 238.

[73] See Streeck and Yamamura, "Introduction: Convergence or Diversity?" in *The End of Diversity? Prospects for German and Japanese Capitalism*, ed. Kozo Yamamura and Wolfgang Streeck (Ithaca: Cornell University Press, 2003), 3, 5, 11.

more universally than the system of social policy. Education—and not just compensation for status loss—serves as an engine for social policy."[74] The East Asian state has also curtailed property rights to provide housing and secure the means of subsistence for the poor in ways that go beyond countries with similar levels of economic development (I discussed East Asian–style constraints on property rights in chapter 9).

Informal Care

If the East Asian state has relied on relatively interventionist methods to reduce the number of poor and the needy, it has relied on relatively informal, less-than-interventionist methods to secure the conditions for those who do need care. East Asian–style social policy has been characterized by an approach that relies on informal, relational bonds to secure care for the needy.[75] In comparison with Western welfare states, East Asian governments are relatively low spenders on social welfare. In 1992, for example, Sweden and the United Kingdom spent over 40 percent of public expenditure on welfare provision; the figures for Japan, South Korea, Taiwan, Singapore, and Hong Kong range from 14 to 31 percent.[76] With the exception of Hong Kong where the welfare system (first put in place by the British colonial regime) is financed by the state, the East Asian state does not play an important role in providing direct finance for welfare programs. Instead of state agencies, quasi-governmental

[74] Rieger and Leibfried, *Limits to Globalization*, 267. See also 255, 268, 271.

[75] For an argument that Confucian values inform the East Asian particularist and relational approach to social welfare—in marked contrast to the Judaeo-Christian values that inform the European-style universalist, egalitarian, rights-based approach to welfare— see Elmar Rieger and Stephan Leibfried, *Limits to Globalization*, chap. 5. Rieger and Leibfried's argument is fascinating, though the precise mechanism that connects the values and the policy outcomes remains somewhat obscure in their account. In contrast, M. Ramesh argues that "a complete understanding of social policy [in East and Southeast Asia] requires consideration of both broad political economy and immediate political conditions." Ramesh, *Social Policy in East and Southeast Asia: Education, Health, Housing and Income Maintenance* (London and New York: Routledge/Curzon, 2004), 8. Ramesh provides a rich and detailed discussion of policy outcomes and differences in four Asian societies, but he says hardly anything about the normative underpinnings that would motivate politicians to promote certain policies and people to live by them. In my view, a "complete understanding" of social policy in East and Southeast Asia would marry both approaches.

[76] Huck-ju Kwon, "Democracy and the Politics of Social Welfare: A Comparative Analysis of Welfare Systems in East Asia," in *The East Asian Welfare Model: Welfare Orientalism and the State*, ed. Roger Goodman, Gordon White, and Huck-ju Kwon (London: Routledge, 1998), 28. See also Rieger and Leibfried, *Limits to Globalization*, 254–55. Ramesh, however, argues that the characterization of Hong Kong, Singapore, Korea, and Taiwan as low-spending countries masks significant differences among them with respect to details (Ramesh, *Social Policy in East and Southeast Asia*, 25–28).

bodies often manage the various funds to which social welfare contributions are made.[77] Beyond that, much welfare provision is left to institutions and groups outside the state. As Gordon White and Roger
Goodman argue, "The notion of state-provided or guaranteed welfare
as a social right of citizens is weakly developed [in East Asia]. Rather,
non-state agencies—community, firm and family—have been expected to
play a major welfare role in both financing and providing welfare services in an ideological context where self-mutual help is encouraged and
dependence on the state is discouraged, indeed stigmatized."[78] Consider
the following examples.[79]

THE MINSEEIN SYSTEM OF SOCIAL WELFARE PROVISION IN JAPAN

In this system, care is provided by "social workers" who are appointed on
renewable three-year contracts. They are supposed to have lived in their
designated area "for a long time," to have a clear understanding of its social situation, and to display enthusiasm for carrying out the promotion
of social welfare. In contrast to professional social workers from other industrialized countries who live outside the communities in which they
work, *minseiin* are usually respected seniors who volunteer their time to
help needy members of their own community. This system of "help by in-
timates" has flaws (for example, rebellious young people may not want to
discuss their problems with elderly neighbors), but it has the advantage of
relying on inexpensive means to ensure that needy members of the community receive help tailored to their distinctive circumstances.[80]

THE LIFE-LONG EMPLOYMENT PRACTICES OF LARGE JAPANESE
FIRMS WITHIN THE KEIRETSU NETWORK

The cross-share holdings of the *keiretsu* mean that individual companies
need not worry (much) about hostile takeovers, which contributes to

---

[77] Kwon, "Democracy and the Politics of Social Welfare," 66.

[78] Gordon White and Roger Goodman, "Welfare Orientalism and the Search for an East
Asian Welfare Model," in *The East Asian Welfare Model*.

[79] Another distinctive feature (relative to Western societies) of East Asian-style informal
welfare, discussed in chapter 11, is the aversion to institutionalized (state-funded or private) day care for children. Instead, there seems to be a preference for at-home care of children. Traditionally, of course, mothers provided at-home care for children, but with growing number of women who work outside the home, mother's care has been complemented
(or, more rarely, replaced) by at-home care of children by foreign domestic workers (especially in Hong Kong and Singapore), grandparents (especially in mainland China and Korea), and fathers (especially in urban Chinese cities).

[80] For a positive assessment of *minseiin*, see Eyal Ben-Ari, *Changing Suburbia: A Study
of Two Present-Day Localities* (London and New York: Kegan Paul International, 1991).
For a relatively critical account, see Roger Goodman, "The 'Japanese-style Welfare State'
and the Delivery of Personal Services," in *The East Asian Welfare Model*.

security for employees. Workers within *keiretsu* are encouraged to acquire firm or group-specific skills, and in order to persuade workers to invest in skills of this specificity the large firms have customarily offered
many of them life-time employment and promotion tied to seniority
rather than merit. Although employees have no formal representation
on the board of directors (in contrast to labor representation in several
European countries) and lack representation among the leading shareholders, they have been recognized as privileged stakeholders in the
company. For their part, employees have been willing to sacrifice for
the company's good in ways that go far beyond the employees of most
capitalist firms elsewhere. The security of lifelong employment, for example, makes employees far more willing to propose productivity-enhancing
innovations to management compared to employees in Western companies who fear that rationalization processes will cost them their jobs.[81]

FAMILY CARE FOR THE SICK

In the 1990s several East Asian countries made steps toward de facto
universal health coverage.[82] One important reason for this development
is that high-quality services can be maintained without high expenditure.
Taiwan and Korea rely more on private provision and competition
among providers, whereas Hong Kong and Singapore rely more on the
provision of in-patient health care by the public sector. The result is
that Hong Kong and Singapore have better health-care outcomes, yet
they spend *less* on health care. As M. Ramesh explains, "competition in
the health-care sector may actually increase costs by promoting over-
supply."[83]

But the tendency to universalize health care coverage does not come at
the cost of support from nonstate groups. The family in particular plays
an important role in caring for the sick in East Asia, including societies
that provide direct subsidies for universal health care: "Even in hospi-
tals, family members often assume the lion's share of the burden in the
treatment and care of the sick."[84] The economic benefit of family care, of
course, is that it reduces the state's burden in the treatment and care of
the sick, thus helping to explain why East Asian states are low spenders

[81] See Rieger and Leibfried, *Limits to Globalization*, 315.

[82] M. Ramesh and Ian Holliday, "The Health Care Miracle in East and Southeast Asia:
Activist State Provision in Hong Kong, Malaysia and Singapore," *Journal of Social Policy*,
vol. 30, no. 4 (2001), 637–51.

[83] Ramesh, *Social Policy in East and Southeast Asia*, 189. Another economic disadvantage of private provision of health care is that it substantially increases administrative costs
(for example, the U.S. health-care system has substantially higher administrative costs than
the publicly funded Canadian system).

[84] Rieger and Leibfried, *Limits to Globalization*, 261.

on health care relative to capitalisms elsewhere.[85] There may be cultural roots underpinning family care for the sick, but the state's policies, as in Singapore's medical insurance scheme that holds individuals financially responsible for the care of close family members, also encourage the practice.

FAMILY-CENTERED SUPPORT FOR THE ELDERLY

In East Asia, public expenditure on pensions is low or nonexistent. Forced savings for retirement, as in Singapore's Central Provident Fund, reduces the government's role in providing welfare benefits for retired workers.[86] The striking aspect of care for elderly in East Asia, however, is the high rate of at-home care by adult children[87] and the lack of institutionalized care, public or private. South Korea, for example, has the maxim "Family care first, social security second," which is reflected in the high rate of elderly Koreans living with their families.[88] In contemporary Japan, two-thirds of Japan's elderly are cared for by their children.[89] In Beijing and Shanghai, 55 percent of the aged live with their children, and in wealthy Singapore and Hong Kong nearly four-fifths of the elderly reside with their offspring.[90] In Western societies, by contrast, the proportion of coresidence between the elderly and adult children has dropped to below 20 percent.[91]

The Economic Advantages of Informal Care

The East Asian practice of delegating welfare responsibilities from the state to other levels has an obvious economic advantage. In the context of a globalized "race to the bottom" that pressures states to cut back on

[85] The psychological benefits of family care for the sick are perhaps less evident, but they may be at least as important as the economic benefits (most people would be pleased to have a home-cooked meal brought to the hospital rather than hospital food, given the choice).

[86] Jomo, "Rethinking the Role of Government Policy in Southeast Asia," 487. With the erosion of the *danwei* (workplace)-based welfare system for urban residents in China, the government has been shifting responsibilities for welfare provision from state-owned enterprises to a combination of government, enterprises, communities, and individuals, including the imposition of Singapore-style arrangements for compulsory savings. Edward X. Gu, "Beyond the Property Rights Approach: Welfare Policy and Reform of State-Owned Enterprises in China," *Development and Change*, vol. 32 (2001), 142.

[87] Ramesh, *Social Policy in East and Southeast Asia*, 194.

[88] Reiger and Leibfried, *Limits to Globalization*, 265–66.

[89] Gosta Esping-Andersen, "Hybrid or Unique? The Japanese Welfare State between Europe and America," *Journal of European Social Policy*, vol. 7, no. 3 (August 1997), 181.

[90] Ka, *Confucian Welfare Cluster*, 139.

[91] "Japanese, American Approaches Differ on Aging, Long-Term Care," *JEI Report*, no. 14A (10 April 1992), 13.

state-funded welfare, informal safety nets allow states to lower taxes and hence provide for a more "business-friendly" environment that will be attractive to foreign investors. Moreover, the state's resources can be diverted from welfare provision to directly productive purposes, job-creating infrastructural projects, and job-training schemes, thus helping to reposition East Asian economies for future growth.[92] Yet another advantage of informal welfare is that it can underpin egalitarian forms of development. Multigenerational families, for example, help to promote income equality because income is privately transferred from productive members of families to individuals without income (youth, women, and the elderly).[93]

But will the informal welfare system last? In this harsh economic climate, greater numbers are falling outside the informal welfare net, and there may be a growing need for some universal, state-enforced welfare rights (e.g., to help the unemployed).[94] Globalization generates economic uncertainty, and societies with competitive political systems, such as Korea, are facing greater pressure from welfare constituencies to establish comprehensive social security programs.[95] Still, aspects of East Asian–style informal welfare may be long lasting. I will discuss the practice of Japanese-style lifelong employment and at-home care for the elderly because both practices seem to be "threatened," as Gosta Esping-Andersen argues, by economic and social pressures.[96] I will argue, in contrast, that the two practices can be reformed without losing their distinctive features.

The practice of Japanese-style lifelong employment appears to be resilient in the face of economic challenges. Security for employees has of course been difficult to sustain since the burst of the Japanese bubble, and similar pressures have been felt in other Asian countries with Japanese-style organization. But there may be ways of adapting the system without "throwing the baby out with the bathwater." Faced with an economic downturn, large firms in Japan have typically resorted to other measures to cut costs before sacking employees, such as setting up spin-off

[92] See also Reiger and Leibfried, *Limits to Globalization*, 266–67.

[93] Ramesh, *Social Policy in East and Southeast Asia*, 22.

[94] Unemployment insurance does not exist in the region except in Japan, South Korea (Rieger and Leibfried, *Limits of Globalization*, 263), and, to a lesser extent, Taiwan (Ramesh, *Social Policy in East and Southeast Asia*, 188). In Hong Kong, it is quite striking that the rise in the rates of unemployment since the 1997 economic crisis from 2 percent to 7 or 8 percent did not lead to widespread demand for unemployment insurance, a phenomenon that may be (at least partly) explained by relatively high (compared to Western societies) rates of family support for the unemployed.

[95] See M. Ramesh, "Globalization and Social Security Expansion in East Asia," in *States in the Global Economy*.

[96] Esping-Anderson, "Hybrid or Unique?", 188.

enterprises to provide employment, shifting workers to other companies within the *keiretsu*, eliminating management bonuses, slashing recruitment of new employees, reducing overtime, freezing wages, and even reducing top management salaries. To increase the productivity of their employees, companies have shifted from a seniority-based system to a merit-based system of promotion, or at least have placed greater emphasis on merit without completely eliminating the relevance of seniority.[97] Even with all these changes, however, Japanese employees of large firms "continue to enjoy secure employment and an income enviable to many U.S. workers."[98]

There may also be resources for maintaining the practice of at-home care for the elderly. The practice reflects the centrality of the value of filial piety in Confucian culture, and continued commitment to this value will nourish and maintain the practice.[99] Public policies can also help. In Singapore, mainland China, and Taiwan, it is mandatory for children to provide financial support for elderly parents. East Asian states also make use of indirect methods such as the Respect the Aged Day in Japan, designed to increase awareness of people's obligations to the elderly,[100] as well as tax breaks and housing benefits, as in Korea, Hong Kong, and Singapore, that simply make caring for the elderly easier.[101]

In the case of Japan, Esping-Anderson suggests that at-home care for the elderly may not be sustainable, given an aging population and the fact that women, who do most of the caring, may no longer be willing to sacrifice their careers for this cause.[102] But it does not follow that Japan will move to Western-style state pensions and institutionalized care for the elderly. Men could take on more caring responsibilities, as in Chinese cities

---

[97] See D. Eleanor Westney, "Japanese Enterprise Faces the Twenty-First Century," 133–34, 139–40. The system of promotion according to seniority has roots going back to the employment practices of the Edo period (1603–1867), and it is not the first time that adjustments were made to correct an overemphasis on seniority: adjustments were made in 1944 and 1960. Tamotsu Aoki, "Aspects of Globalization in Contempary Japan," in *Many Globalizations*, ed. Peter L. Berger and Samuel P. Huntington (Oxford: Oxford University Press, 2003), 82–83.

[98] Wolfgang Streeck and Kozo Yamamura, "Introduction: Convergence or Diversity? Stability and Change in German and Japanese Capitalism," in *The End of Diversity? Prospects for German and Japanese Capitalism*, ed. Yamamura and Streeck (Ithaca: Cornell University Press, 2003), 11.

[99] Opinion surveys in China and Japan indicate that most adult children want to support their elderly parents, and that the elderly depend on their children for emotional attachment, not simply for material support (Ka, *Confucian Welfare Cluster*, 143).

[100] Ibid., 144.

[101] M. Ramesh and Mukul G. Asher, *Welfare Capitalism in Southeast Asia: Social Security, Health and Education Policies* (Houndmills: Macmillan Press, 2000), 59, 67–68. See also chapter 3.

[102] Ibid., 186–88.

like Shanghai. Japan could import domestic workers to help with at-home care, as in Hong Kong, Singapore, and Taiwan.[103] Even robots can help with the task of caring for the aged.[104] Such practices and policies would allow Japanese women to lead productive lives outside the home without undermining the system of at-home care for elderly parents.

Implications for Public Policy

This chapter has been an effort to identify the features of East Asian capitalism that seem, prima facie, to serve desirable social and political purposes while also being compatible with, if not beneficial for, the requirements of economic productivity in an age of intense international competition that is enforcing innovation on many fronts. For East Asian countries, the lesson is clear: to be skeptical of calls for shedding all the old ways of doing things in favor American-style shareholder capital-ism.[105] Of course there is room for reform, but East Asian countries should also build on areas of comparative advantage and seek to develop new ones. As Peter A. Hall and David Soskice put it, "nations often prosper, not by becoming more similar, but by building on their institutional differences."[106]

Prosperity, however, is not the end goal. It provides the material basis for people to lead good lives. In the East Asian context, the good life is defined partly, if not mainly, in terms of the affective ties that inform familial, work, and communal relationships.[107] Therefore, the defense of East Asian–style family enterprises, social networks, and informal welfare does not simply rest on their economic utility: more important, ultimately, is that they help to maintain and promote affective ties between members of particular communities. But not all good things go together,

---

[103] See chapter 11.

[104] James Brooke, "Japan Seeks Robotic Help in Caring for the Aged," *The New York Times*, 5 March 2004, A1.

[105] As things stand, the American economic model could not be replicated even if other countries wanted to do so. As Tony Judt notes, "Americans are the world's consumers of last resort. But their national deficits on budget and current account are reaching unprecedented levels. The collapsing dollar is sustained only by foreigners willingness to hold it: Americans are currently spending other people's money on other people's products. Were the US any other country it would by now be in the unforgiving hands of the IMF." Judt, "Europe vs. America," *The New York Review of Books*, 10 February 2005, 38n.8.

[106] Hall and Soskice, "An Introduction to Varieties of Capitalism," 60. See also Streeck and Yamamura, "Introduction: Convergence or Diversity?" 38–50.

[107] See *The Politics of Affective Relations: East Asia and Beyond*, ed. Hahm Chaihark and Daniel A. Bell (Lanham, MD: Lexington Books, 2004); and Lee, Chang, and Kim, "Affective Networks and Modernity," 213–16.

and affective ties can also have economically harmful effects: for example, the emphasis on harmonious relations in the corporate enterprise may negatively affect the quality of products.[108] In such cases, affective ties may still be worth promoting (assuming that the economic costs do not result in high rates of bankruptcy and unemployment). Just as Europeans can sacrifice some economic productivity to safeguard the "right to leisure,"[109] so East Asians may choose to absorb some economic costs for the sake of nourishing affective ties in the workplace.

From a normative point of view, perhaps the more serious problem with affective ties in the workplace is that they can undermine ties in other spheres of life. Japanese-style lifelong employment, for example, entails the obligation to identify with and sacrifice oneself for the good of the enterprise in ways that leave little time for anything else. As Tatsuo Inoue points out, strong communal identity based on the workplace sometimes leads to *karoshi* ("death from overwork") and frequently deprives workers of "the right to sit down at the dinner table with their families."[110] To be sure, it's not all work, because affective ties developed within the workplace also entails the "right" to play, and no doubt there are some pleasures derived from late-night karaoke sessions with fellow workers.[111] But such benefits only exacerbate the tendency of Japanese firms to turn into all-consuming "constitutive communities that engage the self-identity of all their employees."[112]

---

[108] Lee, "Social Capital in Korea," 222.

[109] Europe's productivity is falling relative to that of the United States, but this "mainly reflects a series of policy choices that have tended to put a premium on leisure and equality at the expense of greater wealth." Katrin Bennhold, "Continent Guards Its Right to Leisure," *International Herald Tribune*, 19 July 2004, 1. The implication that Americans have chosen to work harder for more wealth, however, is only true of the well-off: "So more American adults are at work and they work much more than Europeans. What do they get for their efforts? Not much, unless they are well off." Tony Judt, "Europe vs. America," *The New York Review of Books*, 37.

[110] Tatsuo Inoue, "The Poverty of Rights-Blind Communality: Looking through the Window of Japan," *Brigham Young University Law Review* (January 1993), 534.

[111] It is an open secret that late-night karaoke sessions often include pleasures of the flesh. Doing business in Japan, South Korea, mainland China, and Hong Kong typically involves visits to karaoke bars that culminate in sessions with sex workers. There are regional differences—for example, Korean business partners often strip naked with sex workers in a communal room, with heavy drinking further contributing to the social trust that underpins business transactions—but the similarities in East Asia may outweigh the differences. Such benefits may also help to explain why the East Asian region is attractive to foreign investors: one Canadian friend who operates factories in mainland China told me that his buyers prefer to come to China (as opposed, say, to predominantly Islamic, relatively puritanical countries such as Bangladesh) partly because they can enjoy late-night karaoke sessions.

[112] Tatsuo Inoue, "Predicament of Communality: Lessons from Japan," in *Communitarian Politics in Asia*, ed. Chua Beng-Huat (London: Routledge/Curzon, 2004).

Single-minded devotion to the good of the workplace is not necessarily problematic if it satisfies the deeper emotional longings of workers. But workers—largely men—will be deprived of the possibility of nourishing affective ties within the family context. And since family responsibilities will be devolved almost entirely to women, they will be deprived of the possibility of nourishing ties in the workplace. The system may be breaking down precisely because those with experience of relatively balanced affective commitments seem to prefer that way of life:[113] today it is more common to see Japanese men in public parks with baby carriages, and Japanese firms are making more room for female employees.

In short, it may not be impossible to reconcile the profit motive in a globalizing world with the idea that East Asian societies can promote affective ties within the workplace. But the larger challenge will be to develop public policies that allow for individuals to develop commitments to both the family and the workplace, without one commitment radically undermining the other.

The next chapter discusses one specific feature of East Asian capitalism in more detail, trying to sort out what is defensible from what is not. Focusing on the case of migrant domestic workers, I argue that patterns of labor migration may justify unequal rights between citizens and noncitizens and also between citizens of the same state. I also suggest ways of improving the status quo so that the practice better conforms to Confucian norms regarding the treatment of nonfamily members.

---

[113] John Stuart Mill argued that "Of two pleasures, if there be one to which all or almost all who have experience of both give a decided preference, irrespective of any feeling of moral obligation to prefer it, that is the more desirable pleasure." Mill, "Utilitarianism," in John Stuart Mill and Jeremy Bentham, *Utilitarianism and Other Essays*, ed. Alan Ryan (London: Penguin Books, 1987), 279. I am assuming that people with experience of affective ties to both family members and fellow workers and experience of affective ties to only one of the two prefer the former way of life, but my suggestion would need to be empirically validated.

11

Justice for Migrant Workers? The Case of Migrant Domestic Workers in East Asia

GLOBALIZATION IS characterized by trade, capital, financial flows, as well as exchanges of people between increasingly porous national borders. An estimated 175 million people, or roughly 3 percent of the world's population, currently reside outside their country of origin.[1] Cross-border migration is not a new phenomenon, but the rate of migration has been accelerating rapidly, more than doubling since 1965.[2] The patterns of international migration have also undergone considerable changes of late, the most important of which is the increased feminization of these flows. The large bulk of these female migrants originate from the poorer regions of the world, seeking better economic opportunities in industrialized countries to support their families.

The Asian region is no exception to these global trends. In Hong Kong and Singapore, the rapid increase of the rate of labor force participation by women has led to demand for foreign domestic workers (FDWs).[3] In relatively poor sending countries, new opportunities for emigration arose through the relaxation of emigration policies and the establishment of recruitment agencies. By 2002 there were at least 1.3 million migrant women working legally in the major labor-importing countries of the region (Singapore, Malaysia, Thailand, Taiwan, Hong Kong, Korea, and Japan).[4] Most of these women migrate from Southeast Asia, notably the Philippines and Indonesia, but increasing numbers of women have also migrated from South Asia, particularly Sri Lanka and Bangladesh, to destinations in the Middle East as well as East and Southeast Asia.[5] The

---

[1] Kristin Gilmore, "Convention Established Rights of All Migrant Workers and Their Families," United Nations Chronicle online edition (http://www.un.org/Pubs/chronicle/2003/webArticles/070203_migrantworkers.html, visited 8 January 2006).

[2] Daiva K. Stasiulis and Abigail B. Bakan, *Negotiating Citizenship: Migrant Women in Canada and the Global System* (Houndsmills: Palgrave Macmillan, 2003), 1.

[3] For more details on the Hong Kong case, see Vicky C. W. Tam, "Foreign Domestic Helpers in Hong Kong and Their Role in Childcare Provision," in *Gender, Migration and Domestic Service*, ed. Janet Henshall Momsen (London: Routledge, 1999), 265.

[4] Keiko Yamanaka and Nicola Piper, "An Introductory Overview," *Asian and Pacific Migration Journal*, vol. 12, nos. 1–2 (2003), 5–6.

[5] R. Gamburd, *The Kitchen Spoon's Handle: Transnationalism and Sri Lanka's Migrant Housemaids* (Ithaca: Cornell University Press, 2000); T. Siddiqui, *Transcending Boundaries—Labour Migration of Women from Bangladesh* (Dhaka: The University Press Limited, 2001).

majority of female migrants in East and Southeast Asia still work in a narrow range of unskilled, reproductive, and productive labor. Domestic work, helping with housework and caring for children and the elderly, has been the most common occupation among migrant women throughout the region.[6] These workers often experience abuse and exploitation hidden in the "privacy" of the home, and they may well be the most vulnerable of all migrant workers. But what is the best way of securing their basic interests and needs?

Liberal democratic theorists typically argue that equal citizenship is the solution.[7] There may be a case for differential rights in the short term, but foreign resident workers, including FDWs, should not be treated as permanent second-class citizens. They belong, and belonging matters morally. As the political theorist Joseph Carens puts it, "long term membership in civil society creates a moral entitlement to the legal rights of membership, including citizenship itself."[8] After a certain time, say five or ten years, the state should give equal rights to workers in its territory, regardless of their background.[9]

---

[6] For exact statistics, see Yamanaka and Piper, "An Introductory Overview," 1–20. For in-depth ethnographic data, see N. Constable, *Maid to Order in Hong Kong: Stories of Filipina Workers* (Ithaca: Cornell University Press, 1997); Christine Chin, *In Service and Servitude: Foreign Female Domestic Workers and the Malaysian "Modernity" Project* (New York: Columbia University Press, 1998); B. Yeoh, S. Huang, and J. Gonzalez, "Migrant Female Domestic Workers in the Economic, Social and Political Impacts in Singapore," *International Migration Review*, vol. 33, no. 1 (1999), 114–36.

[7] Will Kymlicka, the leading theorist of minority rights, argues that justice requires equality between ethnocultural groups in the same state, and he has suggested that this principle also applies to the case of long-term migrants in Asia. See Kymlicka, "Models of Multicultural Citizenship: Comparing Asia and the West," in *Challenging Citizenship: Group Membership and Cultural Identity in a Global Age*, ed. Sor-hoon Tan (Hampshire, England: Ashgate, 2005), 129. He notes that the expectations that they would return "home" were misguided, as in the West, and that in most cases citizenship rules have subsequently been liberalized to enable some members of the migrant group to gain or regain citizenship. Where perceptions of security or unjust privilege exist, however, the trend toward citizenship is unlikely to take place without international pressure. As we will see, the case of FDWs in Asia does not fit Kymlicka's categories. The expectation that they would return "home" has not proven to be misguided, citizenship rules have not been liberalized to enable them to gain citizenship, and neither perceptions of security nor perceptions of unjust privilege have played significant roles.

[8] Joseph H. Carens, "Citizenship and Civil Society: What Rights for Residents?", ms., 3, 5. For a similar view, see Alexander Aleinikoff and Douglas Klusmeyer, *Citizenship Policies in an Age of Migration* (Washington, DC: Carnegie Endowment for International Peace, 2002), 43, 60. Aleinikoff and Klusmeyer suggest that the required period of residence (before citizenship is granted) "should not exceed five years" (21).

[9] This moral argument for citizenship seems less plausible in the case of wealthy, skilled immigrants—for example, it would be difficult to argue that, say, a state such as Switzerland would be committing a fundamental injustice by denying full citizenship rights to a well-paid corporate lawyer who has spent the last ten years working out of that country's branch office (I am grateful to John Holbo for raising this point). The case for equal

This argument, as Carens recognizes, mirrors the emerging pattern in most Western liberal democracies. There is a trend toward extending to long-term residents most if not all the legal rights of citizens and improving access to citizenship for the descendants of immigrants and immigrants themselves.[10] This situation is different in East Asian societies, however, and this gives rise to potentially troubling questions. This chapter will focus on the case of FDWs, who do much of the paid housework and childrearing, with particular focus on Hong Kong and Singapore.[11] These workers are denied the rights of citizenship and have no realistic hope that they will ever be equal members of the political community. In Hong Kong, for example, the contracts of FDWs can be renewed indefinitely (it is not uncommon to find women who have been working in the territory for fifteen years or more[12]), but the individuals cannot apply for permanent residence (the functional equivalent of citizenship).[13] This situation gives rise to many injustices. It does not follow, however, that the prescriptions of Western liberal democracies will help to secure the interests of these women.[14]

The Political Concerns of Foreign Domestic Workers in Hong Kong and Singapore

Singapore and Hong Kong have the largest number of legally contracted FDWs in Asia, in both absolute and relative terms. In 2002, 140,000

---

citizenship seems more compelling for relatively poor, unskilled foreign resident workers who would likely derive substantial benefits from citizenship rights. Even in such cases, however, I will argue that the case for citizenship rights is not as straightforward as it might seem.

[10] See Patrick Weil, "Access to Citizenship: A Comparison of Twenty-Five Nationality Laws," in *Citizenship Today: Global Perspectives and Practices*, ed. T. Alexander Aleinikoff and Douglas Klusmeyer (Washington, DC: Carnegie Endowment for International Peace, 2001), 32–33.

[11] I have selected Hong Kong and Singapore because they have the highest proportion of foreign domestic workers in East Asia. I have also lived and worked in both societies.

[12] "Reflections on Racism," *Migrant Focus Magazine*, vol. 1, no. 3 (January–March 2001), 11.

[13] The Hong Kong government's policy in this regard is relatively generous compared to other Asian countries. In Japan, the large bulk of migrants must return home after two or three years. Nicola Piper and R. Irendale, *Identification of the Obstacles to the Signing and Ratification of the UN Convention on the Protection of the Rights of All Migrant Workers 1990—The Asia Pacific Perspective* (UNESCO: Paris, 2003), 28. In Taiwan, the maximum is six years.

[14] I am grateful to Joseph H. Carens, who has commented at length on earlier versions of this chapter. However, I have failed to persuade Carens of the main argument against Western-style equal rights for long-term migrant workers in East Asia. It is worth noting that I wholeheartedly endorse (and have learned much from) Carens's contextual approach

women, mostly from the Philippines, Indonesia, and Sri Lanka, registered as FDWs in Singapore, accounting for more than 40 percent of the
country's unskilled foreign labor force.[15] That same year, over 240,000
FDWs were working in Hong Kong, comprising the most significant minority group in the territory. The majority of them were from the Philippines (151,990), followed by those from Indonesia (78,110), Thailand
(6,920), and other countries (4,000).[16]

In terms of their legal status, there are some commonalities in Singapore and Hong Kong.[17] There is no limit to work hours, and FDWs are
not allowed to bring in dependants or other members of their families.
Overall, however, FDWs are far better off in Hong Kong than in Singapore.[18] The minimum wage in Hong Kong is set at HK$3,270 (U.S.$419)
per month, including room and board. There is no minimum wage in Singapore, but average pay is about half of Hong Kong's minimum wage.
Employers in Singapore must also pay a "maid levy"—in effect, a luxury
tax—of U.S.$225 per month to the government (the tax is not sub-
sequently used for the benefit of FDWs). In Singapore, FDWs can stay
a maximum of eight years (four two-year contracts), but there is no legal limit in Hong Kong. FDWs have more statutory holidays in Hong
Kong—every Sunday and eleven public holidays, and two other floating
holidays, compared to one day per month off in Singapore (after three
months of probation). Employers in Singapore are supposed to provide
FDWs with medical insurance, but this does not always happen; in Hong

---

to political theory. See his book, *Culture, Citizenship, and Community*, esp. chap. 1. The
likelihood of persuading the large majority of Anglo-American liberal theorists who do not
share the contextual approach to political theory is, I confess, even more remote.

[15] Brenda S. A. Yeoh and Shirlena Huang, "The Difference Gender Makes: State Policy
and Contract Migrant Workers in Singapore," *Asian and Pacific Migration Journal*, vol.
12, nos. 1–2 (2003), 75–98.

[16] Chow Chiu-tak and Antonio Tsui Chung-man, *A Survey of the Living and Working
Conditions of Catholic Migrant Domestic Helpers in Hong Kong* (Hong Kong: Catholic
Diocese of Hong Kong, 2003), 1.

[17] Data compiled from S. Samydorai, "Who Is the Domestic Worker and How Is She/He
Protected?", paper presented at the annual consultation with the UN Special Rapporteur
for the Human Rights of Migrants, Kuala Lumpur, 30 September to 2 October 2003, and
Hong Kong government (Nicola Piper interview, February 2003).

[18] On 7 December 2005, Human Rights Watch released a report detailing the range of
abuses endured by domestic workers in Singapore, including the point that domestic workers are far worse off in Singapore than in Hong Kong. "Singapore: Domestic Workers
Suffer Grave Abuses" (http://hrw.org/English/docs/2005/12/07/Singap12125.htm, visited
27 December 2005). According to this report, Malaysia's laws and regulations offer even
less protection to domestic workers than those in Singapore. See also Nisah Varia et al.,
"Help Wanted: Abuses against Female Migrant Domestic Workers in Indonesia and
Malaysia," *Human Rights Watch*, vol. 14, no. 9 (July 2004) (http://hrw.org/reports/2004/
indonesia0704/index.htm, visited 24 April 2005).

Kong, FDWs enjoy the same (nearly free) medical benefits as other residents. FDWs have the right to bring complaints to a labor tribunal in Hong Kong, but not in Singapore. FDWs in Singapore are obliged to sign a Statement of Undertaking that prohibits them from marrying or cohabiting with any Singapore citizen or permanent resident; there are no such restrictions in Hong Kong. The Hong Kong government blocks off main roads in the financial district every Sunday to allow FDWs to congregate; there are no comparable public spaces for workers in Singapore. In Hong Kong, it is unlawful to terminate an FDW because of pregnancy after five weeks, and they have ten weeks of maternity leave; in Singapore, they have to undergo pregnancy tests every six months and are immediately deported if they are pregnant. In Hong Kong, FDWs have two weeks to find a new employer; in Singapore, they are repatriated if they change employers. In Singapore, FDWs are subject to the death penalty;[19] capital punishment is illegal in Hong Kong. Perhaps the most telling sign of better conditions is that most FDWs prefer to work in Hong Kong, given the choice.

What explains the better protections and benefits for FDWs in Hong Kong? One important factor is that they (like other residents) are free to organize self-help groups and public protests to secure their interests.[20]

---

[19] In 1995 the Philippine FDW Flor Contemplacion was hanged in Singapore for killing another FDW and the five-year-old Singaporean she was caring for. The controversial circumstances of the trial and the extreme punishment triggered huge demonstrations in the Philippines and put the two countries on a collision course (both nations recalled ambassadors) that lasted for about a year. See Tim Healy, "Exorcizing Flor's Ghost: Singapore and the Philippines Make Up," *Asia Week*, 26 July 1996.

[20] More controversially, the relative lack of political rights in Hong Kong may be another factor that favors the interests of FDWs. See my article, "Equal Rights for Domestic Workers?", *Dissent* (Fall 2001), 26–28. In Singapore, there are substantial constraints on the democratic process, but elections are still competitive, and political parties must be seen to campaign for the interests of their constituents. Since employers are constituents, their interests are more likely to be manifested in the political process than those of disenfranchised FDWs (one Singaporean civil servant told me that the government feels constrained by a large constituency that opposes recommendations by a Human Right Watch report issued in December 2005, such as more days off for FDWs). In Hong Kong, there is no pretense that the people choose their leaders, and it is quite likely that many political leaders (including Tung Chee-hwa, the first chief executive in the posthandover period) would not have been chosen by the people in free and fair competitive elections. Hong Kong decision makers, in other words, are less constrained by the interests of Hong Kong citizens (more precisely, permanent residents), and they can rely to a greater extent on their own sense of justice and decency to implement policies that favor FDWs (not surprisingly, prodemocracy parties in Hong Kong have been very cautious about articulating proposals that favor FDWs). In the case of Taiwan, the development of a more democratic, responsive government has been bad for FDWs—under increasing pressure from specific domestic groups that (mistakenly?) blamed foreigners for growing unemployment of indigenes and blue-collar workers, in September 2000 President Chen Shui-bian promised to cut the number of foreign workers by fifteen thousand annually, the goal being to reduce the number by sixty thousand by

Thus, groups of FDWs can and do publicly express their grievances, such as campaigning against government proposals to cut the minimum wage. In Hong Kong, more than twenty nongovernmental organizations cater to the interests of FDWs,[21] compared to three severely constrained NGOs in Singapore. These NGOs have been at the forefront of political activism, and they offer a good window into the actual political concerns of FDWs.[22]

Surprisingly, perhaps, NGOs do not seem to be actively struggling for citizenship rights for their constituents in either Hong Kong or Singapore.[23] The fact that Asian governments sanction two classes of residents with unequal rights and privileges—in effect, relegating FDWs to permanent second-class citizenship—is not, at least on the surface, an issue of great concern for pro-FDW NGOs. As we will see, there are normative and political reasons explaining silence in this matter. What, then, are the concerns of these NGOs and their constituents? My findings are based on interviews with pro-FDW NGOs as well as interviews with individual FDWs.[24]

2004. Anne Loveband, "Positioning the Product: Indonesian Migrant Women Workers in Contemporary Taiwan," *Working Papers Series*, no. 43, City University of Hong Kong, April 2003, 3. I do not mean to imply, needless to say, that the Asian public is uniquely "reactionary": Christian Joppke notes the findings of Virginia Guiraudon that episodes of rights expansion for immigrants in Germany, the Netherlands, and France "were conditional upon keeping the public out and containing the issue behind the "closed doors of bureaucracy and judiciary." Joppke, "The Evolution of Alien Rights in the United States, Germany, and the European Union," in *Citizenship Today*, ed. T. Alexander Aleinikoff and Douglas Klusmeyer (Washington, DC: Carnegie Endowment for International Peace, 2001), 56.

[21] Most pro-FDW NGOs in Hong Kong are organized and managed by Filipino nationals, but it is worth noting that Christian NGOs composed primarily of members of the Hong Kong Chinese community have also taken stands defending the interests of FDWs, such as opposing government plans to reduce their minimum wage. See, e.g., Chow Chiutak, "Waiyong xiaoxin, bu hehu gongyi" [Reducing the Salary of FDWs: Not Consistent with Justice], *Ming Pao*, 24 November 2001.

[22] This is not to imply that some NGOs may not have mixed motives. According to a political science lecturer at the University of Indonesia in Jakarta, some Indonesian NGOs have used the issue of migrant workers to get money from donor agencies for other purposes (Nicola Piper interview, 19 March 2003).

[23] But NGOs run by and for Filipinas engage in active citizenship rights' struggle directed at their country of origin. See Robyn M. Rodriguez, "Migrant Heroes: Nationalism, Citizenship and the Politics of Filipino Migrant Labor," *Citizenship Studies*, vol. 6, no. 3 (2002), 341–56. The Philippines has implemented the "Absentee Voting Bill," which allows overseas migrants to vote in general elections, starting with the 2004 election.

[24] I owe much to Nicola Piper, who coauthored an earlier version of this chapter that appeared in *Multiculturalism in Asia: Theoretical Perspectives*, ed. Will Kymlicka and He Baogang (Oxford: Oxford University Press, 2005). Piper interviewed many NGOs, government officials, academic researchers, and other individuals as part of a report written (coauthored with Robyn Iremdale), for UNESCO (www.unesco.org/most/apmrn_unconv.htm, visited 27

Interaction between employers and FDWs occurs mainly in the privacy of the home, consequently, the informal rules of engagement within the home have great impact on the welfare of FDWs. The laws, as they stand, typically leave large amounts of discretion to the employer—for example, contracts between employers and FDWs do not specify maximum number of work hours, and in some countries (e.g., Singapore) the wage levels are set by the employer. So from the point of view of FDWs, one of the most important considerations is to find a "nice" employer and to avoid "exploitative" ones.[25]

There is growing recognition of the need to counter the "education" provided by agencies that benefit from the trade in FDWs. In Hong Kong, "agencies routinely warn domestic workers against crying, displaying 'long faces,' touching employers with any part of a broom, sweeping the house the first day of the Chinese lunar New Year, or wearing all white or all black (colors associated with death), because some Hong Kong employers believe these behaviors will bring them bad fortune."[26] One officially sanctioned private agency in Singapore distributes a pamphlet that offers the following advice to FDWs regarding prayers:

1. You are discouraged to bring your White Prayer Uniform along. This is because the Employer does not want this Uniform to scare their children. Most of the employers dislike their domestic helpers to pray while

---

December 2005). I conducted interviews in Hong Kong in December 2002 with Cynthia CA Abdon-Thellez, director of the Mission for Filipino Migrant Workers; and Holly Allen, director of Helpers for Domestic Helpers; one volunteer helper at that organization; and four Filipina domestic workers with experience in both Singapore and Hong Kong interviewed at the YMCA in Tsimshatsui, Hong Kong. I have also done volunteer work for Helpers for Domestic Helpers, and I thank the helpers I have met during the course of this work. It may also be relevant to note that I have been an employer of FDWs in both Singapore and Hong Kong, and my experience has provided some of the motivation for writing this chapter. I have tried not to let my "class position" determine my arguments, and the reader can judge whether I have been successful.

[25] In Singapore, however, this is relatively difficult because FDWs have no power over their placement, and they are legally tied to one employer and not allowed to swap. Employers also have to pay a $5,000 bond to the government to make sure their domestic workers do not "run away." As a result, FDWs usually have their passports confiscated by employers and are often locked up in apartments during the day. A hotline set up at the Indonesian Embassy in Singapore receives on average three distress calls per day, typically by FDWs locked into an apartment, and the Labor Desk receives three to four runaway cases each day. The restriction on pregnancy reinforces this problem—an employer would lose his or her bond if the FDW becomes pregnant, which leads to such restrictions as bans on receiving phone calls from males in the employer's home.

[26] Nicole Constable, "Filipina Workers in Hong Kong Homes: Household Rules and Regulations," in *Global Woman: Nannies, Maids, and Sex Workers in the New Economy*, ed. Barbara Ehrenreich and Arlie Russell Hochschild (New York: Henry Holt, 2002), 119.

working in their house. This condition has been stated earlier and we as your agent have agreed on your behalf in order to be able to secure you a job.

2. Another thing due to various reasons such as a conflict between two Gods, employer does not want to have different kinds of prayers in their house, does not understand the domestic helper's religion, etc.

3. But if you are lucky, you may be allowed to pray in the morning before your employer and the family members [have woken up].

4. Subject to Employer's Approval. If this should happen, please pray in your heart and you may make it up when you return to your country.

5. Thus, you should have an attitude by thinking that you are lucky to be able to work here whereas your friends are still in the village waiting for their employment.[27]

The main concern, apparently, is to minimize conflict between employer and FDW so that the agency will not be blamed if things go wrong, but the strategy is entirely focused on ensuring that docile FDWs defer to the wishes of employers. The Singapore government has published pamphlets that aim for a more balanced approach. Once again, the aim is to promote a harmonious working relationship between employer and employee, but this is meant to be achieved by means of mutual cultural understanding, open communication, and mutual respect.[28] These desiderata are stated in vague language, however, and their effect on the behavior of employers is questionable.

An ad hoc working group made up of individuals and organizations that seek to promote respect for FDWs has recently published a guide for employers of FDWs that spells out their moral obligations in substantial detail. The bulk of this guide seems designed to appeal to the conscience of the employers, rather than invoking threats of legal punishment. To counter the myth that "My maid can't manage money well, so I should keep her passbook," for example, the guide notes that "In the Philippines, one in every two households depends on the remittances of overseas workers." On the issue of religious requirements, the guide notes the requirements of different religions and urges employers to respect those requirements.[29] A devout Muslim, for example,

---

[27] Advance Link Pte Ltd, *Maids Handbook: An Essential Guide to Hiring and Keeping a Foreign Domestic Helper* (Singapore: Raffles, 2000), 35. This pamphlet might be particularly relevant in the case of Muslim FDWs from Indonesia, though it is not made explicit.

[28] Jean Tan, "Report Maid Abuse to MoM or Police," *The Straits Times*, 30 January 2002.

[29] It could be argued that the employer does not have any moral obligation to respect the religious requirements of the FDW, since the employer is the "boss" of the home and employees need to abide by the employer's religious requirements during work (so long as the employer sticks to the contractual requirements). My view is that work at "home" blurs the

is required to pray five times a day and fast in the month of Ramadan. These constitute two of the five pillars of Islam that must be observed. Allowing your FDW breaks to perform her prayers does not take up much of her time. Each prayer takes ten minutes at the most and are spread out at convenient intervals from dawn until bedtime. For most Muslims, as the conduct of Singaporean Muslims shows, life goes on as normal during the fasting month of Ramadan: they work while fasting from dawn till dusk. A Muslim FDW expects to perform her usual duties during this month, but you should show understanding of her need to eat before dawn, so that she does not work all day on an empty stomach.

Such informal "calls to the conscience" might seem naïve, but they are crucial, given the nature of interaction between employers and FDWs. If the concern is to improve the welfare of FDWs, the informal rules of engagement within the home are often just as fundamental, if not more so, than the set of rights guaranteed by law. It is important to emphasize this point only because liberal-democratic theorists (and Western NGOs) are inclined to think, first and foremost, of legalistic solutions for securing the welfare of the weak and vulnerable.

Of course, this is not to deny that laws also affect the welfare of FDWs. In Hong Kong, the minimum wage of FDWs is guaranteed by law, and pro-FDW NGOs (along with the Philippines government) have campaigned on three separate occasions since the 1997 economic crisis against proposals by political parties and employers' interest groups to cut the minimum wage for FDWs (once, in 2002, with successful opposition to the cut). Another prominent issue for NGOs has been opposition to the New Conditions of Stay implemented in April 1987 under the Immigration Ordinance, more popularly known as the "two-week rule," which allows two weeks for FDWs to find new domestic employment when their contracts are completed or if their employer unexpectedly terminates them. If they are unsuccessful, they must immediately return to their home country or face heavy fines and imprisonment.[30] This rule effectively means that FDWs must put up with exploitative conditions since it is difficult for them to find an alternative employer on such short

---

boundaries between the personal and the commercial (particularly in the case of live-in help), and hence employers have greater obligations to respect the religious beliefs of their employees than might be the case in a purely commercial setting. An employer who does not want to make any allowance for different religious practices should hire an FDW who follows the same religion. But if, say, a Christian employer prefers to hire a Muslim Indonesian FDW because it costs less than hiring a Filipina FDW, then the employer should make special allowances for the religious practices of the FDW.

[30] Neetu Sakhrani, "A Relationship Denied: Foreign Domestic Helpers and Human Rights in Hong Kong," *Civic Exchange*, Hong Kong, 2002, 5, 12–14.

notice. According to my interviewees, there is no other legal regulation
that is as damaging to the interests of FDWs. NGOs in Hong Kong have
suggested going back to the pre-1987 system, when FDWs were given
six-month renewable visas and had more time to find alternative employers if things went sour.

Another major concern for NGOs, at least in Singapore, is the issue
of domestic workers not being covered by the national Employment
Law, which covers all other (male) migrant workers. The recently formed
ad hoc working group campaigns for the inclusion of FDWs under this
law. Last but not least, there is the "one day off" campaign in Singapore. Unlike Hong Kong, many FDWs (mainly non-Filipinas) do not get
a day off per week for their own recreation.[31]

Should Foreign Domestic Workers Be Given Equal Rights?

From the perspective of FDWs and their representative NGOs, in short,
the main concerns relate to informal interaction within the home, improved working conditions, and labor rights. The fight for equal citizenship is not the most pressing issue, and equal citizenship is not typically
seen to be the key to alleviating the high level of abuse that FDWs often
experience. Still, it may seem that the fight for equal citizenship matters,
at least as a long-term goal. After all, citizenship rights confer a wide
range of benefits (and duties, however, such as paying taxes and a two-
and-a-half-year period of national service for Singaporean males). Even
in nondemocratic Hong Kong, citizenship matters—it provides access to
valued passports, public housing, education, as well as a certain degree of
political representation—all benefits currently denied to FDWs.

One possibility might be to invoke the United Nations International
Convention on the Protection of the Rights of All Migrant Workers and
Members of Their Families, which officially entered into force as an in-
strument of international law on July 1, 2003.[32] In comparison to the
two previous ILO conventions dealing with migrant workers (no. 97
from 1949 and no. 143 from 1975), this convention sets new ground by:

[31] Interestingly, no NGO in Singapore campaigns to abolish the rule that prevents locals
from marrying FDWs.

[32] This convention was passed by the General Assembly on 18 December 1990, but a
minimum number of ratification by twenty countries was required to let it come into force.
During the ten years of deliberation regarding the content of this convention, no Asian
country was present, apart from Japan, which joined in the last year. The main countries
involved in the drafting process were the European MESCA group (seven Mediterranean
and Scandinavian states) and the Group 77, which is mainly composed of sending countries (with specific engagement by Algeria, Mexico, and Morocco). It is not surprising that
the content of this convention reflects the situation of migrant workers in Europe and
North America at the time.

1. emphasizing that both host and origin countries often lack protective/ rights legislation on migrants, and encouraging states to establish legislation in harmony with recognized standards
2. providing a comprehensive international definition of migrant worker, categories of migrant workers and members of their families
3. establishing that migrant workers are social entities with families as well as laborers or economic entities
4. specifying the specific fundamental human rights of all migrant workers, including unauthorized migrants, and elaborating on other rights of regular migrant workers in a number of legal, civil, economic, social and cultural rights
5. seeking international cooperation in eliminating exploitation of migrants, and in ending clandestine movements and irregular or undocumented situations.

The convention, however, has been less than successful,[33] particularly if the test of commitment to an international accord is that it would affect (change) the policies of member states.[34] Only two sending countries in Asia (Sri Lanka and the Philippines) have ratified it, and not one single receiving country has done so. The concern among receiving countries is not that the convention specifies equal citizenship rights for migrant workers—states are still largely free to design their own visa and immigration policies—but that it would lead to settlement by admitting family members of labor migrants. As Ryszard Cholewinski explains,

> States are still under a duty in Part IV of the Convention to facilitate family reunification (Article 44(2)), which must mean that any outright or deliberate moves to restrict or prohibit the entry of family members without good

---

[33] Yasemin Nuhoglu Soysal has argued that migrants have been protected by international human rights norms and conventions that provide universal standards applicable to international migrants. Soysal, *Limits and Citizenship: Migrants and Postnational Membership in Europe* (Chicago: University of Chicago Press, 1994). Soysal is explicit that "my discussion draws on cases from western Europe" but then goes on to assert (without any evidence) that "the arguments I develop are not exclusive to Europe. As the transnational norms and discourse of human rights permeate the boundaries of nation-states, the postnational model is activated and approximated world-wide" (155–56). I do not want to make the (now familiar) critique about Eurocentric approaches. Let me simply note that Soysal's findings may not even apply in the European context: Christian Joppke has argued that domestic constitutions have been responsible for increasing immigrant rights in Europe (and the United States) and that international human rights codes and conventions "are plainly irrelevant." Joppke, "The Evolution of Alien Rights," 58.

[34] Twenty-two states have ratified the treaty, protecting 2.5 percent of the migrant worker population worldwide. UN Secretary General Kofi Annan said that this number is "small," and he stated that "only when it [the Convention] is ratified by a large number of countries, including those receiving significant numbers of immigrants, will we be able to say that the promise of the Convention is being translated into reality. Gilmore, "Convention Establishes Rights of All Migrant Workers and Their Families," 1.

reason would be a violation. And the longer the worker stays few good reasons can be given. So the concerns of some government officials are probably justified, particularly in the Asian context where migrant workers are essentially single persons with little or no prospect of settlement.[35]

In short, most labor-receiving countries do not want permanent settlement programs, and they feel that extending rights to the families of migrants will encourage settlement.[36] These views are not likely to change in the foreseeable future. The authors of a recent report identifying the obstacles to the signing and ratification of the convention conclude that the focus in receiving countries should therefore be on changing domestic policies and laws before mounting a ratification campaign. In fact, this is exactly what NGOs in receiving countries are already doing: they refrain from lobbying their government to ratify the convention because they fear that focusing on the promotion of the convention would result in a backlash with smaller-scale improvements slipping away.[37]

Whatever the legal issues, the normative question remains—should FDWs be put on the road to citizenship, as liberal democratic theorists advocate? In East Asia, as we will see, the arguments for denying equal rights to FDWs are not simply the crude justifications of narrowly self-interested elites or quasi-racist peoples.[38]

---

[35] Ryszard Cholewinski, e-mail sent to Nicola Piper, 27 January 2004.

[36] Piper and Irendale, *Identification of the Obstacles*.

[37] Ibid., 55. This is not to deny that the Convention can be useful for other purposes. In Singapore, for example, a working group of pro-FDW individuals (the word "NGO" can be sensitive in Singapore!) notes that "practices such as withholding of salaries, not providing adequate and proper food, use of threats, degrading methods of punishment such as compelling FDWs to stand facing a wall for hours or to perform repeated 'squats' as means of disciplining them are in direct violation of Articles 10 and 11 of the Convention, which stipulate that migrant workers (who include FDWs) should not be treated in a cruel, inhumane and slave-like manner. Depriving FDWs of freedom to follow practices required by their religious faiths such as praying, going to mass or a place of worship and fasting contravene Article 12, on freedom of religious practice. This convention came into force in July 2003." Of course, the Singaporean government did not ratify this convention, so it is not legally binding in that country. However, the hope is that invoking this convention can have rhetorical and political effects anyway. It would seem rather pedantic on the part of exploitative employers to argue that they can treat their FDWs in a slavelike manner because the government had not yet ratified the convention.

[38] Stephen Castles and Alastair Davidson argue that "it is very difficult for aliens to obtain nationality in any East and South-Asian or Pacific country . . . because of the strongly ethnic basis of nationality laws in most countries. . . . In many Asian countries, discrimination borders on racism." Castles and Davidson, *Citizenship and Migration: Globalization and the Politics of Belonging* (Houndsmills: Macmillan, 2000), 194. But racism cannot be the main explanation in the societies considered in this chapter: Singapore and Hong Kong both grant citizenship to several diverse ethnic groups, and the *hukou* system in China is not motivated by racism (the main people affected are Han Chinese).

The most obvious justification for unequal rights is that FDWs could be seen as consenting to the arrangement that brings them to the receiving countries. Restrictions on the rights of domestic workers are publicly announced, and FDWs know about them before they come.[39] Why do they come? The large majority are driven by economic concerns.[40] Many FDWs are university-educated mothers,[41] and they seek relatively high-paying jobs as domestic workers abroad to support their children's education. As the Philippine labor secretary put it, they "make a choice for more money but less prestige."[42] Poverty at home may not be the only motivating factor. For many workers, as Janet Henshall Momsen notes, "the search for personal freedom and the accompanying rejection of traditional gender roles is as important as economic reasons."[43] Another factor is that divorce is illegal in the Philippines, and "it is often the case for women unhappy in marriage to decide to migrate in order to escape an unsatisfying, unpleasant life."[44] In short, unequal rights for foreign domestic workers may be justified given that they accept these terms before they go abroad.

The problem with this argument, as Joseph Carens points out, is that

> every plausible moral view sets limits to consent. For example, no liberal democratic state permits people to sell their organs or to sell themselves into slavery. It is no doubt true, given the conditions in the world today, that many immigrants would readily agree to severe restrictions on their rights, even including terms of indentured servitude. But consent alone cannot legitimate that sort of arrangement. There are standards of fairness and justice beyond actual consent for assessing the ways in which states treat their own citizens and others.[45]

[39] There is an important difference, however, with regard to the different nationality groups and their respective governments' actions: Filipinas are generally well informed due to better predeparture training; Indonesians are not typically as well informed and often only find out about rights issues after arrival in Singapore and Hong Kong.

[40] Brenda S. A. Yeoh and Shirlena Huang, "Singapore Women and Foreign Domestic Workers," in *Gender, Migration and Domestic Service*, ed. Janet Henshall Momsen (London: Routledge, 1999), 291.

[41] One recent survey of Filipina FDWs in Hong Kong found that 57 percent had university or tertiary education (Chow and Tsui, *A Survey of the Living and Working Conditions*, 25).

[42] Quoted in "Maid Wage Cut a Political Football," *South China Morning Post*, 23 December 2001.

[43] Janet Henshall Momsen, "Maid on the Move," in *Gender, Migration, and Domestic Service*, 10–11.

[44] Liane Mozere, "Conceptualising Social Networks and Migration: Empirical Contributions and Theoretical Challenges," ms., May 2003, 10.

[45] Joseph H. Carens, "Citizenship and Civil Society: What Rights for Residents?", ms., 24.

Still, it is difficult to compare the terms of FDWs to "terms of indentured servitude."[46] In some cases, it is true that FDWs must take out
high-interest loans from private agencies, and much of their salary goes
to pay their loans. One interviewee said that she did not get to keep any
of her salary the first six months she worked in Singapore, and she never
had a day off. But these are abuses of the system, more typical in Singapore than elsewhere, and the Singapore government is finally getting serious about cracking down on unscrupulous agencies.[47] If the system
works as it is supposed to, the choice is between low-paying jobs (or unemployment) at home and (relatively) high-paying jobs as FDWs. Moreover, in Hong Kong (but not in Singapore), FDWs can change employers
if they so choose (though they have only two weeks to find another employer). In both Singapore and Hong Kong they can return home on moment's notice, so the comparison with indentured service is misleading.
In the large majority of cases, it cannot be denied that FDWs consented
to an unequal rights regime because they calculated that the benefits of
this arrangement outweigh the costs. Still, consent is only a prima facie
argument for justifying particular arrangements (one can not consent to
slavery). Let us consider some possibilities that may override the argument from consent and see if they hold water for FDWs in the East Asian
context.

One argument might be that one-off consent, while sufficient to legit-
imize market transactions, cannot justify the subjugation of foreign resident workers. For one thing, foreign workers do not simply sign contracts with their employers. They have another "boss"—the state in
which they live and work. As Michael Walzer puts it,

> These guests [foreign resident workers] experience the state as a pervasive
> and frightening power that shapes their lives and regulates their every
> move—and never asks for their·opinion. Departure is only a formal option;
> deportation, a continuous threat. As a group, they constitute a disenfran-
> chised class. They are typically an exploited or oppressed class as well, and

[46] The illegal employment of FDWs in American homes more closely resembles terms of
indentured servitude. As Pierrette Hondagneu-Sotelo notes, "In the United States today,
these jobs remain effectively unregulated by formal rules and contracts. Consequently, even
today they often resemble relations of servitude that prevailed in earlier, precapitalist feudal societies. These contemporary work arrangements contradict American democratic
ideals and modern contractual notions of employment." Quoted in Caitlin Flanagan,
"How Serfdom Saved the Women's Movement: Dispatches from the Nanny Wars," *The
Atlantic* (March 2004), 9.

[47] All agencies in Singapore must now be registered (starting in 2004). The Hong Kong
government, for its part, recently established a commission, including participation of pro-
FDW NGOs, to investigate such abuses and prosecute rogue agencies (*South China Morning Post*, 4 January 2003).

they are exploited or oppressed at least in part because they are disenfranchised, incapable of organizing effectively for self-defense. Their material condition is unlikely to be improved except by altering their political status.[48]

These are not just theoretical musings. In the East Asian context, states have unilaterally altered the terms of contracts—for example, the Hong Kong government has twice cut the minimum wages of FDWs since the economic crisis of 1997.

Having said that, FDWs would not necessarily prefer contracts where all parties are indefinitely bound by original consent. They may discover new possibilities, learn about unexpected problems, compare their situation with FDWs in other countries, and realize that they were given a raw deal that needs to be challenged. This helps to explain why, as mentioned earlier, many pro-FDW NGOs in Hong Kong are campaigning for an end to the "two-week rule" and more severe punishment for employers who mistreat domestic workers. It is also possible that they may campaign for increases in salaries in inflationary and/or economic boom times. In short, we have good reasons to doubt the argument that FDWs consented to the exact terms that brought them to the receiving countries—many discover upon arrival that the state can and should do more to improve their condition.

Compared to guest workers in Europe and immigrant groups in North America, however, one is still struck by the absence of the demand for equal rights in East Asia. Yes, FDWs are the victims of many injustices and many are actively campaigning for better conditions, but this rarely translates into the request that they be put on the road to citizenship. They may not be satisfied with the status quo, but they do not aspire to equal citizenship. At some basic level, it seems that FDWs in East Asia really do consent to unequal rights. Is there a sufficiently powerful reason to trump this argument from consent?

One possibility is that FDWs are subject to coercion, and this is what prevents them from articulating the demand for equal citizenship. Thus, they are not genuinely consenting to unequal rights, it is just that they are forced into acceding to this arrangement and fearful about articulating or even contemplating an alternative. In a just world without this element of coercion, they would be pushing for equal rights, and the state would be morally required to accede to this demand. But is it really coercion that explains this apparent lack of interest in the demand for equal rights?

If guest workers in Europe or long-term immigrants in North America were to refrain from articulating the demand for equal citizenship, one

---

[48] Michael Walzer, *Spheres of Justice* (Oxford: Basil Blackwell, 1983), 59.

would be tempted to explain this frame of mind with reference to either fear or false consciousness. In Singapore, there is much merit to the argument from coercion—FDWs cannot freely organize and/or publicly articulate their demands and are likely to be deported if they try to do so. In Hong Kong, however, the situation is more complicated. Hong Kong is a small, crowded territory where the cost of living is very high— not an ideal location for establishing long-term homes. Even the locals frequently move abroad when they have the means to do so. Whereas most immigrant workers to, say, the United States or Canada aim to establish roots in their new country, the large majority of FDWs plan to return "home" once they have earned enough money.[49] As one of my interviewees put it, "I'm not interested to stay in another place. I love my country."

Another key difference is that guest workers in Europe were given longer visas for certain jobs and were allowed to bring their families. Their children often learn the language and culture of their resident country and develop the desire to stay there. Even if their parents consented to return "home," the consent of parents cannot be construed as the consent of the children. No doubt many parents want to stay in their new country for the sake of their children. In contrast, FDWs come to Hong Kong without their families and rarely make an effort to learn the local culture and way of life, though a few do pick up some Cantonese.[50]

Still, it may be difficult to dispel the suspicion that coercion plays an important role when FDWs "consent" to unequal rights. More rights are better than fewer, and it seems irrational not to want equal rights. Given the choice, some FDWs may well choose to settle down in their new country. Even those who plan to return "home" because of emotional ties to family and native land may change their mind and hence would prefer

---

[49] One important factor, as noted below, is that FDWs in East Asia leave their families behind in sending countries. Another factor is that they spend most of their waking lives working in the homes of their employers, with limited opportunities to partake of civic and cultural life outside the home, which further reduces the likelihood that they would develop psychological attachments to the receiving country and the desire to stay there. On their days off, they typically spend time with relatives and friends from their home country: according to one recent survey, 75.3 percent of Filipina FDWs had relatives in Hong Kong, and nearly 50 percent had "many friends," which may help to explain why "57.6 percent of the interviewees said they were 'Very happy' or 'Happy' with their current jobs and only 6.3 percent said that they were 'Unhappy' or 'Very unhappy'" (Chow and Tsui, A Survey of the Living and Working Conditions, 25, 20, 27). More anecdotally, the seemingly joyous scenes of Filipina FDWs in central Hong Kong on Sundays and public holidays suggests that they may not be as unhappy as their "objective" class status would predict.

[50] It could be argued that more FDWs would make more of an effort to learn Cantonese if they had the prospect of permanent residence.

to be given the choice of membership on the basis of equal rights. So why not ask for equal rights?

In the real political world, struggling for what seems like the ideal solution may lead to worse outcomes than settling for the second best. The simple fact of the matter is that locals would never agree to this demand, and it may be counterproductive even to raise it. Let us take the case of Hong Kong. Urban areas in the territory are already among the most crowded on earth (only the Gaza strip is more densely populated). Land is expensive, and decent housing is beyond the reach of most people. As a result, the government provides massively subsidized housing for more than half the population. There is a waiting list of five to seven years that would expand even further if FDWs were given equal rights and allowed to join the queue. This would be an obvious source of discontent among locals.

Besides practical obstacles, there are also questions of fairness at stake. Many FDWs recognize this. As one interviewee put it, "there are so many mainland Chinese waiting in the queue." To control population growth and prevent the territory from being "flooded" with relatively impoverished mainland Chinese "compatriots," there are strict border controls between Hong Kong and mainland China (the functional equivalent of an international border). While the majority of the population in Hong Kong arguably benefits from this arrangement, some families in Hong Kong cannot sponsor their own family members as immigrants. In recent "right of abode" controversies, the Hong Kong government has been fighting hard to prevent mainland Chinese not born in Hong Kong, even if they have close relatives in the territory, from getting residence rights. From the perspective of Hong Kong residents with relatives on the mainland, it would seem unfair if the Hong Kong government were to grant permanent residence to FDWs without relatives in the territory, even if only a minority took up the offer.

For FDWs, the fact that the door is closed to equal rights does have one practical benefit—it means that there are more doors open to temporary contract workers. The only reason that so many FDWs are allowed to work in Hong Kong—and Singapore—is that all sides assume they will eventually return home. In Canada, by way of comparison, FDWs can become permanent residents after two years, but the government can afford to be relatively "generous" because it lets in only a few thousand such workers every year—in 1996, for example, only 1,710 domestic workers were admitted under the Live-in Caregiver Program.[51] The

---

[51] On the experience of FDWs in Canada, see Geraldine Pratt (in collaboration with the Philippine Women Center), "Is This Canada? Domestic Workers' Experiences in Vancouver, BC," in *Gender, Migration and Domestic Service*.

choice, in reality, is between few legal openings for migrant workers with the promise of equal citizenship and many openings for migrant workers without the promise of citizenship. So FDWs in Hong Kong who benefited from the latter system generally refrain from raising the demand for equal rights because they know it is a nonstarter.[52] Were they to raise this issue, populist politicians would propose replacing them with contract domestic workers from other countries. That is already happening in the struggles against pay cuts—Filipinas are gradually being replaced by the more compliant and less well-organized Indonesians,[53] and employers' groups point out that they can also be replaced with contract domestic workers from mainland China if they complain too much. The Hong Kong government has also hinted at such possibilities. For FDWs in Hong Kong, it seems, the feasible alternatives to unequal rights are considerably worse.

Notwithstanding the consent of FDWs, liberal democratic theorists may reply that the situation is still unjust. The institutionalization of second-class citizenship—permanent unequal legal rights for a group of residents—is a violation of fundamental liberal-democratic principles and should never be allowed, no matter what the circumstances. As Will Kymlicka puts it, "it violates the very idea of a liberal democracy to have groups of long-term residents who have no right to become citizens."[54] No decent government will ever compromise on these principles. The

[52] There is, however, one legal challenge seeking to overthrow the law that bars FDWs from obtaining permanent residence in Hong Kong. Cannix Yau, "Maid in Abode Bid," *The Standard*, 29 September 2003. As of early 2006, the case has not been resolved. If the legal challenge is successful, it could have the implication that 15,000 FDWs who have been in Hong Kong for more than seven years will be entitled to permanent residence. (But not necessarily so, as it depends on the job situation: one unemployed expatriate was recently refused permanent residence even though he had stayed in Hong Kong for more than seven years.) But this legal challenge, if successful, would also likely have the implication that the government radically cuts back on the number of FDWs in Hong Kong, which may help to explain why pro-FDW NGOs have not been actively supporting this case.

[53] Compared to Filipinas, Indonesian FDWs tend to be less well-educated and less well-organized, and their government does not offer the same level of support, with the consequence that many are underpaid and abused. Asian Migrant Center, "Racial Discrimination in Hong Kong," 8 November 2001, p. 2, http://www.december18.net/paper33 Hongkong.htm. In Taiwan, the proportion of Filipinas has also been decreasing, as they are gradually being replaced by less expensive Indonesian and Vietnamese women (there is no minimum wage in Taiwan). Anne Lovebond notes that "according to the common truth [in Taiwan,] Indonesian women are best suited as carers of the chronically ill, the paralysed and elderly patients because they are more 'caring' and 'loyal' and they can cope with the repetition of washing, cleaning of people, clothes and households more easily than the cleverer Filipinas who tended to argue about their rights and precise job specifications. Indonesians are also supposedly more accepting because, as one employer suggested to me, they are Muslims" ("Positioning the Product," 6).

[54] Will Kymlicka, *Contemporary Political Philosophy: An Introduction*, 2nd ed. (Oxford: Oxford University Press, 2002), 359.

argument for granting full rights to long-term residents may be politically infeasible in current circumstances in Asian societies,[55] but none of
the counterarguments shows that it is not correct in principle. It is just a
matter of how best to persuade Asian governments to recognize the
moral imperative of equal citizenship.

Let us assume, for the sake of argument, that policy makers in East
Asia are persuaded by this view. The laws are changed, and all FDWs
are automatically entitled to equal citizenship following a period of, say,
seven years. All FDWs are permitted to settle down in receiving countries and are given the same rights as locals. What would be the likely effect of this policy switch?

It is almost certain that the door to further immigration from major
sending countries such as the Philippines would be officially closed. I say
"officially," because the door to illegal migration would likely open wide,
as happens in Europe, in North America, and in other Asian destinations.
Filipina domestic workers may still come (illegally) to Hong Kong and
Singapore and "choose" to work in even more exploitative conditions
without any legal protection whatsoever. As it stands, there are few illegal
worker migrants from the Philippines in Hong Kong.[56] But that may
change if the legal doors to immigration are closed. Judging from the experience in the United States and Canada—where illegal employment of domestic workers from the Third World is quite widespread—one can expect
that people from impoverished countries will migrate to rich countries,
with or without the legal rights to do so. Canada, for example, effectively
cut back on the number of FDWs legally entitled to work in the country,
and this led to an increase in the number who came to work illegally.[57] The

---

[55] In Korea and Taiwan, the situation is more complicated, and counterarguments are
often cast in normative (as opposed to purely pragmatic) language. In the post–World War
II era, there was, arguably, an implicit contract between workers who agreed to be "exploited" (sixty-hour weeks, minimal worker safety regulations, curbs on union activity,
etc.) in exchange for accumulation of wealth that was meant to benefit the next generation.
Hence, there is strong resistance to granting citizenship rights to foreigners who should not
be seen to benefit from their sacrifices. As one Korean interviewee put it, "We Koreans
have worked hard, if foreigners come, they will get the benefits of our work without any of
the sacrifice" (Nicola Piper, interview May 2003).

[56] The situation is more complex in Singapore, where the large majority of Filipina FDWs
came as "tourist workers" without work permits from the Philippines, an arrangement that
is legal in Singapore but not considered so by the Philippines government. The purpose of
this arrangement appears to be that of circumventing the regulations in the Philippines designed to protect the interests of their migrant workers and therefore allowing for relatively
exploitative conditions (e.g., very low wages; the Philippines government requires a minimum wage, but not the Singapore government) for Filipina FDWs in Singapore.

[57] Abigail B. Bakan and Daiva Stasiulis, "Introduction," in *Not One of the Family: Foreign Domestic Workers in Canada*, ed. Bakan and Stasiulis (Toronto: University of Toronto
Press, 1997), 19–20.

same is true in Asian countries. Following the 1997–98 economic crisis in South Korea, the government announced a moratorium on admitting low-skilled migrant workers (such workers would normally have been eligible for all the rights Korean workers possess, following a two-year period), but this led to a large influx of illegal workers.[58] From a normative standpoint, it is not obvious that formal equal rights for all workers combined with high rates of illegal employment of foreigners is preferable to reliance on large numbers of contract workers with legal protection but without the hope of equal rights. In the West, the political culture places higher priority on the justice of legal forms, and there may be greater willingness to accept substantial harms in the social world for the sake of preserving laws that conform to liberal-democratic principles.[59] That may not be the case in East Asia. Their governments prefer to enact nonliberal laws that allow for huge numbers of FDWs to temporarily engage in legally protected work in their territories.[60] And from the perspective of sending countries, the East Asian approach may be preferable.

For the sake of argument, once again, let us assume that illegal immigration can be controlled, and that this would not turn out to be a prob-

---

[58] Deborah J. Milly, "The Rights of Foreign Migrant Workers in Asia: Contrasting Bases for Expanded Protections," in *Human Rights and Asian Values: Contesting National Identities and Cultural Representations in Asia*, ed. Michael Jacobsen and Ole Bruun (Richmond, Surrey: Curzon Press, 2000), 310.

[59] In January 2004 the Bush administration proposed legislation that would in effect replace illegal immigration and work by millions of Mexicans with a guest-worker program that would allow previously illegal immigrants and future migrants to work on three-year contracts, with a maximum of six years (in early 2006, the legislation had yet to be enacted, mainly because some Republicans reject it as too close to an amnesty for illegal immigrants). This proposed legislation does not provide for opportunities for contract renewal and/or access to citizenship rights via the guest-worker program (because it would effectively sanction illegal immigration and would seem unfair to those waiting to migrate to the United States via the legal route, and perhaps also because it would be more difficult to enact this kind of legislation in the U.S. Congress). So the obvious question is what to do with workers that seek to stay for more than six years. If the choice is between renewable contracts without the opportunity for citizenship that would effectively sanction permanent second-class citizenship for a group of foreign-born workers and short-term contracts with many illegal overstayers, it is predicted that the United States will opt for the latter option. This Western liberal democratic approach—which emphasizes the need to preserve the legal form of equal citizenship while sanctioning illegal immigrant workers—can be viewed as a cultural preference. However, this approach would not be favored by illegal migrants who are subject to unmonitored exploitation by employers.

[60] Note, however, that FDWs are excluded from National Employment Acts in Asian countries like Singapore and hence are not officially defined as "workers" (male migrant workers, by contrast, are covered by labor and employment laws). This means that whatever protection FDWs get comes from their contracts, and Filipinas typically have better contracts than Indonesians as the Filipino government is more actively involved in ensuring decent contracts. Still, even the worse-off group—Indonesian FDWs—typically has more rights and legally defined obligations than illegal workers.

lem in territories such as Hong Kong and Singapore. It is then worth considering the effects of granting equal rights to FDWs in Hong Kong and Singapore on people in sending countries such as the Philippines. The most likely effect of this policy switch would be to close off further emigration. This would mean that many young Filipinas would lose the opportunity to work abroad to support themselves and family members. The country's economy as a whole would eventually suffer as well—Hong Kong's Filipinos make the fourth biggest contribution of remittances to the Philippines, a total of U.S.$116 million in the year to October 2000.[61] That is the main reason they are so appreciated by the Philippine government,[62] even though the state is not supposed to officially promote overseas employment as a means to sustain economic growth and achieve national development.[63] In 1998 President Cory Aquino, speaking to a group of domestic workers in Hong Kong, coined the term "national heroes" for overseas workers,[64] a term that has been frequently invoked in national rhetoric since then.[65] The government recognizes that FDWs experience hardship and loneliness abroad for the sake of earning money for their families, and their remittances help to sustain

[61] South China Morning Post, 7 May 2001.

[62] Another economic reason is that Filipino workers overseas are obliged to file income tax returns and pay tax to the Philippine government (Rodriguez, "Migrant Heroes," 348). The Philippines' Department of Labor and Employment invoked a political reason: "[t]here is evidence the deployment of OCWs [overseas contract workers] may have blunted the Communist insurgency as well, by draining the sea of rural discontent in which the guerillas thrive" (quoted in ibid., 347).

[63] Joaquin L. Gonzalez III, Philippine Labour Migration: Critical Dimensions of Public Policy (Singapore: Institute of Southeast Asian Studies, 1998), 78. Fortunately, the Philippines does not let official hypocrisy get in the way of its efforts to help migrant workers. Its efforts (once again, in sharp contrast to the more passive Indonesian state) include "predeparture orientation seminars, the appointment of labor attachés and welfare staff in many embassies . . . a Welfare Fund to assist workers and their families in times of illness or death; and the prosecution of labor recruiters who charge illegal fees or engage in deception. The state also negotiates bilateral labor and social security agreements that include protective clauses commonly absent in labor importing countries." Michael Pinches, "Migrant Workers and the Reconstruction of Class Relations in East Asia," in East Asian Capitalism: Conflicts, Growth and Crisis, ed. Luigi Tomba (Milano: Fondazione Giangiacomo Feltrinelli, 2002), 497–98.

[64] Interestingly, there have been parallel developments in Mexico: President "Fox has called Mexicans working in the United States heroes, mostly for the money they send home—an estimated $13.3 billion last year. Those remittances are the second largest source of foreign revenue, after oil." Tim Weiner, "Fox Seeks to Allow Mexicans Living Abroad to Vote in 2006," The New York Times, 16 June 2004. As in the Philippines, President Fox has put forward a proposal that would allow citizens working abroad to vote in presidential elections.

[65] Lisa Law, "Sites of Transnational Activism: Filipino Non-government Organizations in Hong Kong," in Gender Politics in the Asian-Pacific Region, ed., Brenda S. A. Yeoh, Peggy Teo, and Shirlena Huang (London: Routlege, 2002), 208.

some 34 to 54 percent of the Filipino population[66] (about 9 percent of the Philippines population live and work overseas, two-thirds of whom are women, and their remittances account for 10 percent of the country's GNP). *The Economist* has noted the more general advantages of remittances: "Recent research ties rising remittances directly to increasing GDP and reducing poverty. Another study finds a positive link between remittances and the probability that children stay in school. At this year's G8 summit, rich-world politicians noted the importance of remittances in financing small businesses, education and housing in recipient countries."[67] The workings of realpolitik also point to the economic importance remittances: the United States punished the Philippines for withdrawing its troops from Iraq by pressuring the Japanese government to curb the flow of Filipina hostesses and entertainers to Japan.[68]

Of course, the situation may not be so dire for workers in poor countries if wealthy receiving countries decide to increase foreign aid to sending countries so as to help develop their economies. But there is no reason to expect that this will happen. According to the World Bank, the worldwide remittances of migrant workers are second only to the earnings of crude-oil trading and bigger than all the developmental aid combined.[69] Certainly the experience of Western countries does not provide grounds for optimism. Canada has recently increased standards of edu-

---

[66] Cynthia Fuchs Epstein, "Working Moms under Attack," *Dissent* (Fall 2004), http://www.dissentmagazine.org/menutest/articles/fa04/epstein/htm.

[67] "Economics Focus: Monetary Lifeline," *The Economist*, 31 July 2004. Some economists argue that remittances actually harm the Philippines economy in the long term: "There is a reluctance to go for bold reforms that would essentially try to absorb more labor because there are huge foreign exchange inflows that cushion the government's balance of payments." Florian Alburo, quoted in Peter Kammerer, "Philippines Is Too Reliant on Its Workers Overseas, Experts Say," *South China Morning Post*, 17 February 2004, A8. Even if it is true that the harm done to the Philippines economy by curbing the flow of remittances would be outweighed by the long-term economic good of "bold reforms," there would likely be substantial suffering in the short to medium term, and it may not be feasible to enact such "bold reforms" in the democratic political context of the Philippines. Another possibility is that remittances are not deployed in the most economically efficient ways. Noeleen Heyzer and Vivienne Wee have proposed that the governments of sending countries ensure that remittances be used in productive ways as opposed to items of conspicuous consumption that may not aid the local economy. Heyzer and Wee, "Domestic Workers in Transient Overseas Employment: Who Benefits, Who Profits," in *The Trade in Domestic Workers*, ed. Noeleen Heyzer, Geertie Lycklamaa Nijehort, and Nedra Weerakoon (Kuala Lumpur: Asian and Pacific Development Center, 1994). However, it would be politically difficult (and difficult to morally justify) for the government to extend this level of control to uses of remittances among family members.

[68] Comment at conference on Multiculturalism and Nationalism in Asia, Ritsumeikan University, 22 March 2005.

[69] "The Lucrative Business That Is Labor Export," *Migrant Focus Magazine*, vol. 1, no 2 (October–December 2000), 5.

cation and experience for immigrant domestic workers, with the consequence that the poorest and least-skilled domestic workers have fewer opportunities to come in, but this has not been accompanied by increased aid to affected countries. Even if receiving countries were to increase foreign aid, this would not necessarily (or even probably) translate into an improvement of the sending countries' economy to the point that its people would not need to consider working abroad. It is far from certain that channeling foreign aid to (often corrupt) government officials would do more to benefit the people of sending countries than direct remittances from family members working abroad.[70]

The liberal democrat may reply that there are other feasible ways to secure the benefits of the trade in migrant workers without comprising on the ideal of equal citizenship. It can be conceded that we will not be able to do away with the fact that workers from poor countries will seek to make their fortunes in the industrialized world and also that rich countries are not about to offer full citizenship rights to huge numbers of migrants from poor countries. One proposal, consistent with liberal democratic principles, might be to limit the work visas of FDWs to, say, six years, as in Taiwan (or eight as in Singapore, for the more "flexible" liberal democrats).[71] That way, they will not have stayed long enough to be morally entitled to equal citizenship rights.

The problem with this proposal, however, is all too evident—it harms the interests of FDWs, who would rather have the opportunity to work longer in rich countries. If the choice is between Hong Kong–style work visas that can be renewed indefinitely without the hope of equal citizenship rights and six-year, nonrenewable work visas that may be more

---

[70] See Thomas Pogge's argument that governmental development "aid is generally ineffective in protecting the global poor and is rarely even intended to do so" ("Migration and Poverty," ms., 7–8). Pogge also argues that citizens and governments from developed countries can more effectively aid needy foreigners by donating to efficient antipoverty organizations such as UNICEF and Oxfam, and by creating global institutional mechanisms for raising a stable flow of international financing for global poverty eradication than by admitting needy foreigners into rich countries and supporting citizenship for those already there. In his paper, Pogge does not consider the possibility that the Asian-style practice of admitting large numbers of needy foreigners on contract terms without the possibility of citizenship is an important mechanism for helping needy foreigners. The sorts of global institutional mechanisms that Pogge defends (such as the Tobin tax) may be ideal long-term solutions, but the most efficient short- to medium-term mechanisms for eradicating global poverty may be a combination of donations to efficient antipoverty organizations and millions of slots for needy contract workers in rich countries.

[71] It is worth noting that the constitutional court in Germany turned temporary guest workers into permanent settlers "only because the state had failed to be explicit about limits and deadlines." Joppke, "The Evolution of Alien Rights," 47. If the German state had imposed contracts with clear indications of nonrenewability on guest workers, the constitutional court would not have argued for the constitutional incorporation of aliens.

consistent with liberal democratic principles, no rational FDW would choose the latter.[72]

Why is it that liberal democratic theorists typically fail to identify the conflict between their ideals and the actual needs and interests of migrant workers? One reason is that liberal democratic theorists often write as though justice applies only within the nation-state.[73] Justice is realized once meaningful rights are given to free and equal citizens—and usually this means citizens in Western-style liberal democracies. Thus, much theorizing about justice is carried out with the liberal democratic context in mind, and the interests of Third World peoples fade into the background.

There is increased recognition, however, of the need to consider our obligations to relatively deprived people in foreign lands. If it turns out that equal rights for all long-term resident workers in rich countries have negative implications for people in impoverished countries, this should be a source of concern. By drawing on the case of FDWs in East Asia, I have tried to show that equal citizenship rights can harm the same group they are meant to protect. The condition of FDWs can be criticized on many grounds, but putting them on the road to citizenship may well worsen their overall situation—if not for FDWs currently working abroad, then for people in sending countries potentially denied the opportunity to improve their living standards.

Let me then put forward the following hypothesis: Unequal rights between citizens and migrant workers may be justified if (1) this arrangement works to the benefit of migrant workers (as decided by the migrant workers themselves), (2) it creates opportunities for people in relatively impoverished societies to improve their lives, and (3) there are no feasible alternatives to serve the ends identified in (1) and (2). Of course, the "East Asian" system of long-term residency without hope of equal citizenship is far from perfect; it is something to be tolerated, not celebrated. The trade in migrant workers is founded on global injustice—the global economy is thoroughly unjust, it is unfairly skewed toward the interests of rich countries, and it perpetuates poverty in the Third World.[74] The

---

[72] That is, no rational FDW among the current batch. Future potential FDWs may have an interest in shortening the contracts of the current batch of FDWs so as to increase opportunities for others (I thank Thomas Pogge for this point). See the section on culture in this chapter for more on the conflict between the interests of the current batch of FDWs and future potential FDWs.

[73] Thomas Pogge is a welcome exception to this trend. See, e.g. Thomas Pogge, ed. *Global Justice* (Oxford: Blackwell, 2001).

[74] See, e.g., Thomas Pogge, "Moral Priorities for International Human Rights NGOs," in *Ethics in Action: The Ethical Challenges of International Human Rights Nongovernmental Organizations*, ed. Daniel A. Bell and Jean-Marc Coicaud (New York: Cambridge University Press, 2006); and Stiglitz, *Globalization and Its Discontents*.

long-term aim should be to eliminate global inequalities, or at least to reduce them so that people are not forced to leave loved ones to seek decent
work opportunities abroad.[75] Unfortunately, that day does not seem to be
forthcoming, and the short- to medium-term task (next one hundred
years?) is to think about other ways of dealing with Third World poverty.

The exportation of migrant workers is one way. From the perspective
of poor migrant workers, arguably, it may in fact be better than liberal
democratic prioritization of equal citizenship for all resident workers.
Equal citizenship, to repeat, can have negative implications for people in
poor countries. In the case of FDWs in East Asia, putting them on the
road to citizenship is most likely to result in one-way tickets back home
and to deny opportunities to improve the living standards of people in
sending countries.

THE ROLE OF CULTURE

Given the relative advantages of "East Asian–style" differential citizenship rights,[76] does it mean wealthy people in Western countries should

[75] Reevaluating contemporary perspectives on the lack of importance of care would be
one way of reducing the international trade in FDWs. As William A. Christian Jr. and
Josefa Martinez Berriel put it, "It is paradoxical that societies we think of as 'developed'
have an acute shortage of the kind of caring that makes life worth living. As a result, their
families are attempting to buy the milk of human kindness that, proverbially, 'money can't
buy.' What would be the ranking of countries by gross national product of kindness?
Countries can be net exporters or net importers of loving care. Should the world community not cherish and cultivate the societies that produce the best caregivers, and learn from
them? It does not yet, because by and large domestic care is not yet valued." Christian and
Berriel, "Edgar and Eunice: International Traffic in Care," in *Miniature etnografiche*, ed.
Henk Driessen and Huub de Jonge (Nijmegen: SUN, 2000), 121. Valuing care in a non-
monetary sense would mean that more people would be willing to be care-givers (because
it would offer more status, even if the economic benefits are not significant), and this
would reduce the international trade in FDWs. Valuing care in a monetary sense would
mean that domestic workers get paid more, which would also reduce the international
trade in FDWs (because more locals in rich countries would do it if it pays more, and those
in sending countries would receive higher salaries at home, and not have to go abroad).
Unfortunately, it seems unlikely that care work will be socially prestigious and economically profitable in the foreseeable future. Even some feminist defenders of the interests of
FDWs continue to refer to care work as "shit work" (Flanagan, "How Serfdom Saved the
Women's Movement," 4). Doing dishes may be "shit work," but is that the right way to
think about caring for children, elderly, and people with disabilities?

[76] Another advantage of this system is that domestic workers can provide around-the-
clock day care, which could help to remedy the growing problem of inadequate "night
care" in Western countries (that results from the increasing tendency toward shift work
with nonstandard hours). See Harriet B. Presser, *Working in a 24/7 Economy: Challenges
for American Families* (New York: Russell Sage, 2003).

open their homes to contract domestic workers from the Third World?[77] Whatever the moral imperatives at stake, there are cultural particularities underpinning the system in East Asia that may not be shared elsewhere, which poses difficulties for those favoring exportability of this system.

One interviewee—a volunteer at the Hong Kong NGO Helpers for Domestic Helpers—noted that Asian people have a more recent history of living in homes with extended family members, and there may be greater acceptance of domestic workers in one's home and caring for needy members of the family. Given the choice between at-home care for children and elderly parents (and the chronically ill) and day care for children and nursing homes for elderly parents, most East Asians seem to prefer the former. In East Asia, the day-care and nursing-home systems are relatively undeveloped, even in the wealthiest countries. One important factor seems to be the reluctance to commit one's children and elderly parents to anonymous carers in publicly funded institutions. Most people in East Asia would rather hire domestic workers to provide family-like care for needy family members. Conversely, the disadvantages of living with a nonfamily member in the "privacy" of one's home would seem relatively high in Western countries.[78]

Of course, it is difficult to prove that a cultural preference for at-home family care is the main explanation for the predominance of this practice in East Asia—other factors, such as policy making and economic forces, may be equally, if not more, important.[79] The role of culture may be more evident in the way people actually deal with each other within the home. Consider the treatment of FDWs. FDWs with diverse experiences

[77] This is already happening in southern European countries such as Italy, Spain, and Greece, but the numbers are much lower than in Hong Kong and Singapore. See B. Anderson, *Doing the Dirty Work? The Global Politics of Domestic Labour* (London: Zed Books, 2000); and Rogelia Pe-Pua, "Wife, Mother, and Maid: The Triple Role of Filipino Domestic Workers in Spain and Italy," in *Wife or Worker? Asian Women and Migration*, ed. Nicola Piper and Mina Roces (Lanham, MD: Rowman & Littlefield, 2003).

[78] One way of dealing with the lack of privacy is to employ FDWs who do not speak the local language (and thus cannot partake of intimate secrets), which may help to explain why some Hong Kong employers prefer to hire English-speaking FDWs over Cantonese ones, even given the choice (I thank Ming Chan for this point).

[79] The fact that Western expatriates in East Asia often hire domestic workers casts some doubt on cultural explanations—one could argue that people are forced to rely on at-home care because of the relatively undeveloped day-care system, and there would not be "cultural" differences if people had the same opportunities to make use of day care. In fact, however, the average waiting period for nursery care in Hong Kong is only 1.6 months (Tam, "Foreign Domestic Helpers," 266), i.e., it is not obvious that people are "forced" to rely on at-home care. More importantly, the lack of public demand for widespread day care, even in East Asian societies with open political systems and vibrant civil societies, is rather striking, and cultural biases against formal care seems to be part of the explanation (ibid., 269–70).

say that typically, different sorts of employers act in very different ways, depending on their background and set of cultural expectations. Western employers, for example, generally treat FDWs differently than Chinese employers. Two social scientists at the Chinese University of Hong Kong who administered a questionnaire to Filipina FDWs in Hong Kong found that the domestic workers were generally more satisfied with their Western employers, who allow them more personal space and are more likely to treat them on equal terms. The authors of this study suggest that Chinese and Western employers may have different conceptions of the Filipina domestic worker as a human being.[80] Respect appears to be more important to the Western employer.

Respect per se, however, may not be sufficient. That is, the very best employers—only a small minority—treat FDWs with more than respect; they also treat them as valued members of the family. Most of these employers tend to be Chinese. The aforementioned study provides a good example of family-like treatment by a Chinese employer. A Filipina domestic worker valued her employer's parents because she was treated as the daughter that they never had. The ties between the employee and the employer's family were based on mutual concern and caring, not simply fairness and respect, and this manifested itself in gestures such as watching television together, mutual teasing, and the employer's sincere concern for the FDW's biological family in the Philippines.[81] My own interviews with FDW revealed similar reactions. One FDW praised her former employer in Singapore for her use of affectionate family-like appellations and for including her in weekend family outings. Another FDW was made a godmother of the employer's child, and they would go to church together. Her biological family in the Philippines made regular visits to her employer's home in Hong Kong, and she hoped that her employer's family would visit her in the Philippines when she returned.

Of course, Western employers can also treat FDWs as family members, but this is relatively rare.[82] The Hong Kong study found that Western employers were more homogenous as a group compared to Chinese employers. One of our interviewees said that Western employers often treat FDWs with respect and tend to be fair-minded,[83] but it typically

[80] Tak Kin Cheung and Bong Ho Mok, "How Filipina Maids Are Treated in Hong Kong—A Comparison between Chinese and Western Employers," *Social Justice Research*, vol. 2, no. 2 (1998), 191.

[81] Ibid., 184.

[82] One reason may be that expatriates do not expect to stay too long and thus do not seek to develop family-like bonds with FDWs.

[83] In Hong Kong, several of Nicola Piper's interviewees noted that foreign employers often allow FDWs to be politically active and give them time off to attend NGO meetings, participate in demonstrations, and organize themselves. The Western employers seem more used to the idea (and to appreciate the importance) of civil society/political activism.

does not go beyond that. Good treatment means paying beyond the minimum wage and giving more free time to employees, but the affective component may not be as prominent. Such "distance" has its advantages. The idea that the FDW belongs to the family can be used as an excuse to impose extra burdens on the worker, such as asking her to work during public holidays.[84] This may help to explain why some FDWs will refuse to address their employers by their given names, even if they are asked to do so, preferring such formal labels as "Sir" and "Ma'am."[85]

Still, the feeling of being treated as a valued member of the family—of feeling loved and trusted—usually outweighs the cost.[86] Once again, it is difficult to directly trace the influence of culture, but it is not unreasonable to suggest that Confucian ethics makes this kind of family-like treatment more likely, or at least more deeply entrenched when it happens.[87] In Confucianism, there is a firm distinction between family insiders and nonfamily outsiders, but the concept of family is relatively flexible, and ethical relationships grow when family-type labels and norms are applied to nonfamily members.[88] This is reflected in the Chinese language. Good friends and alumni will refer to each other as younger or older siblings, and—in the best cases—so will FDWs and employers.

The critic may reply that the argument moves too quickly from fact to value. Whatever the facts, some Confucian cultural norms are morally problematic and should not be encouraged. Cultural values change, and

[84] Bakan and Stasiulis, "Introduction," in *Not One of the Family*, 11.

[85] Another "distancing" tactic, with the aim of minimizing work, is to feign linguistic incomprehension: "Filipinas [in Taiwan] often say they don't wish to learn or speak Chinese because then they would have to work harder. One woman told me how she could avoid many tasks by pretending not to understand what she was being asked 'then they just give up (she laughs) . . . if it is really important they can telephone the grand-daughter who speaks English and she can tell me (laughs again)' " (Loveband, "Positioning the Product," 5).

[86] Some FDWs would rather put up with overwork than risk endangering family-like relations. As one Indonesian FDW put it, "I find my current working conditions quite stressful. I do not have any spare time at all to myself. My friends have suggested other employers but I don't think I want to change employers just yet. My current employers treat me like one of the family and I do not want to be ungrateful to them." Quoted from "Dignity Overdue: A Guide to Employers of Foreign Domestic Workers."

[87] There may be substantial overlap between Confucian "familism" and Filipino culture, which may increase the likelihood of family-like sentiments developing between Chinese employers and Filipina FDWs. On the importance of "familism" in Filipino culture, see Liane Mozere, "Conceptualizing Social Networks and Migration," 5–8. What is clear is that Filipina FDWs often develop warm, maternal-like feelings for employers' children. This kind of sentiment is well depicted in fictitious form in S. J. Rozan's *Reflecting the Sky* (New York: St. Martin's Minotaur, 2001).

[88] For an account of how "Confucian" extension works in twentieth-century Chinese society, see Liang Shuming, *Zhongguo wenhua yaoyi* [Essentials of Chinese Culture] (Hong Kong: San lian shu dian, 1987), chap. 12.

the undesirable ones should be challenged rather than promoted. For example, Confucianism is (in)famous for its patriarchal values,[89] and this can (and often does) pose obvious dangers for FDWs working in Chinese homes. On the other hand, it is worth noting that the whole FDW system would not be feasible in thoroughly patriarchal cultures. Rigidly patriarchal countries like Pakistan do not send their women to work abroad, no matter what the potential economic benefits. The Philippines, the main sending country, is relatively egalitarian compared to many other Asian countries, which is one of the factors explaining the trade—women must be regarded as free and autonomous agents to an important extent if they are "allowed" to work abroad. While most FDWs go abroad to earn money, as mentioned earlier, many are also seeking adventure, freedom, and independence. Moreover, well-off but rigidly patriarchal countries, like Japan and Korea, do not import many FDWs, no matter what the potential benefits. Opportunities for decent employment for local women are few and far between, and most are "confined" to the household, thus reducing the need for FDWs.

More controversially, the FDW system may itself help to transform patriarchal cultures, on both ends. In receiving countries, it frees women from many household and caring duties and allows them to develop their talents in the "public" sphere, paving the way for future generations of women freed from patriarchal (mis)understandings regarding the "proper" role of women. (Of course, the fact that FDWs are women also serves to remind them that household and caring duties tend to be "women's work," and this aspect still needs to be challenged.) In sending countries, it helps to transform the way child-rearing has been conceived. The fact that many Filipina mothers work abroad, for example, means that Filipino fathers have become the primary child-minders, notwithstanding the ideology that mothers should be responsible for the emotional care of children.[90] Of course, the fact that mothers are forced to leave their biological children behind is not something to celebrate.

The FDW system, in short, may help to challenge patriarchal aspects of Confucianism, thus allowing the more desirable aspects of the Confucian tradition—the application of family-like norms and practices to

[89] But for an argument that Confucian principles should not be held responsible for patriarchal practices and that Confucianism can be reconciled with feminist principles without altering its major values, see Chan, "The Confucian Conception of Gender in the Twenty-First Century."

[90] Rhacel Salazar Parrenas, "Mothering from a Distance: Emotions, Gender, and Intergenerational Relations in Filipino Transnational Families," *Feminist Studies*, vol. 27, no. 2 (Summer 2001). Not all Filipino fathers turn into what wives jokingly call "househusbands," as some will leave the family and/or openly find girlfriends. Liane Mozere, "Filipina Women as Domestic Workers in Paris: A National or a Transnational Labor-Market?," ms., 15.

nonrelatives such as FDWs within homes[91]—to do their work without being tainted by past abuses. The critic may then reply that Confucian valuation of family-like ties is beside the point because there is no conflict between this value and the "Western" emphasis on respect and fairness. Both should be promoted, there is no trade-off between them. Unfortunately, things are not so simple. At the level of public policy, the Western emphasis on fairness takes the form of legal regulations designed to protect the rights of FDWs. Some regulations are of course necessary, but taken to an extreme they can undermine affective ties between employer and employee. In the family context, emphasizing rights can be inappropriate if it leads members to view themselves as subjects possessing rights upon which they make claims against their partners. Rights can motivate us to see each other's interests more as limitations on ours than as interests we wish to promote, and this can undermine family relationships that should be informed by love and caring.[92]

Of course, the relationship between FDW and employer is also a market relationship, and there needs to be a balance between concern for rights and the quality of affective ties. The point here, however, is that these concerns often conflict in practice, and considerations of justice should not always have priority. For example, one interviewee praised her former Singapore employer for providing shampoo and other toiletries. Such seemingly trivial gestures were deeply appreciated because they went beyond formal legal obligations, and they strengthened bonds of trust between employer and employee. If the employer had provided toiletries because that obligation had been spelled out in contract form, it would not have had the same beneficial effect on their relationship.

Consider also the debate over whether to legislate the maximum number of work hours. In Hong Kong, contracts between employers and FDWs do not set a maximum number of work hours. There is nothing illegal about making FDWs work sixteen-hour days, which is not uncommon. At first glance, this seems morally suspect.[93] However, one reason

[91] The point here is not to suggest that such an ideal is typically realized in homes with Chinese employers (as suggested above, only a minority of homes may come close to realizing this ideal). Rather, the point is that Confucian familism resonates in countries with a Confucian heritage and hence may be relatively easy to implement (compared to Western countries), and that East Asian governments should promote public policies designed to implement Confucian familism because it is desirable from the perspective of both employers and FDWs.

[92] See Joseph Chan, "A Confucian Perspective on Human Rights for Contemporary China," 220.

[93] Interestingly, it is employers who are calling for specified work hours (though many employers still prefer FDWs available around the clock). An urban councilor in Hong Kong named Jennifer Chow, herself an employer of three FDWs, told the press: "The working hours for live-in maids in Hong Kong are not specified and should be in the contract. We

for not specifying a maximum number of work hours is that it would be difficult to enforce within the "privacy" of the home and to adjudicate cases of conflict. Another reason is of greater concern for our purposes. The best employers can offer to limit work hours to "reasonable" amounts, and this may have the effect of strengthening affective ties between the employer and the FDW. Conversely, the FDW may offer to work beyond agreed-upon hours, and this will also have the effect of strengthening trust and caring relationships within the household. Eventually, the lines between economic activity and family duties may become blurred, and the process of negotiating work between employer and FDW will more closely resemble the distribution of tasks within biological family members;[94] put differently, it allows for the "Confucian" extension of family-like norms and practices to FDWs. Such an outcome is less likely to develop if legal contracts specify in great detail the rights and duties of FDWs within the family context.

The liberal may reply that the proposal for not specifying maximum work hours still benefits the employer, who ultimately controls the levers of power. Why should the employer have the right to decide whether or not to exploit the FDW? From the perspective of the FDW, it might seem preferable to have the right to limited work hours, which can be invoked if need be. If the FDW wants to strengthen affective ties with her employer, then she can waive this right, and the employer would be grateful. In practice, unfortunately, this is not likely to happen—consider the case of Canada, where FDWs rarely work beyond the specified work hours. Once the right is formalized, there is a strong tendency to invoke

---

should look at the system in Singapore where they set the work at 16 hours a day, which seems reasonable. I have had complaints from several employers saying their domestic helpers started work around 8 a.m. and are going into their rooms at 9 p.m. and will not do any more work—if we set working hours these situations would not happen." Quoted in Ceri Williams, "Workers Starting at 8 am are Stopping at 9 pm, Grumbles Councilor; 16-Hour Day for Maids Urged," *South China Morning Post*, 9 November 1998. Cynthia CA Abdon Thellez, director of the Mission for Filipino Migrant Workers Society in Hong Kong, explained NGO public silence on the matter of compulsory works hours, notwithstanding heated internal debates (interview with Bell). On the one hand, the NGO felt a need to push for an eight-hour maximum, so that FDWs would be treated on par with Hong Kong workers. On the other hand, it recognized that many FDWs would oppose this policy because many work fourteen to sixteen hour a days, and FDWs fear they would price themselves out of the market if they cut that by half. The NGO eventually decided not to take a stand on the issue of maximum work hours.

[94] I have been using the term "domestic worker" because the more commonly used term, "domestic helper," masks the market relationship that (arguably) lies at the root of the arrangement between employer and employee. But when relations between employer and employee do take the form of family-like relations, then the term "domestic helper" may be more appropriate.

it, even against "good" employers where it might not be necessary to do so.[95] Moreover, the fact that this right is so difficult to enforce may lead to endless conflicts that could poison the atmosphere in the household.

The suggestion here is not that legal protections for FDWs be entirely abolished. As noted above, FDWs should be given more legal rights, such as longer periods to find employers between jobs. The state should also strengthen its control on employment agencies and investigate dubious ones.[96] Hong Kong would benefit from greater use of Singapore-style punishments, such as public humiliation and stiff penalties to deal with employers who resort to sexual or physical abuse of FDWs. There should be legal ways of punishing employers that force FDWs to work beyond humanly tolerable amounts. Still, the imperatives of justice should not always have priority over Confucian ethics. In some cases, justice should trump other concerns, but concern for the quality of affective ties matters most in other situations. There is no universally right or wrong way of deciding particular cases; it depends on such factors as the severity of the injustice and the likelihood that curbing rights will promote Confucian family values.[97] In hard cases, however, one's normative position may lead to different conclusions. The liberal individualist may prefer to err on the side of justice, but the Confucian may opt for norms and practices more likely to secure harmony and trust within the family.

Let me draw one final implication from Confucian familism. Confucian ethics, as noted above, starts with special, particularistic feelings for members of the family, which are then extended to nonfamily members. In the case of domestic workers, it means that (in the best cases) they are eventually treated as valued members of the family, that market relationships are gradually displaced by family-like relations. But this process takes time: love and trust cannot be cultivated overnight. That is why the best relations tend to be between employers and domestic workers who have been together for several years.

This need for prolonged interaction between employer and FDW is an important justification for public policy that favors the interests of current FDWs over those of potential FDWs in cases of conflict. The latter group, for example, may have an interest for shortening the contracts of the current batch of FDWs to, say, three years, so as to increase the opportunities for future FDWs. They may also have an interest in reducing the minimum wage, on the assumption that labor demand will go up

---

[95] The tendency to invoke rights may be more characteristic of employees working in "legalistic" liberal societies, but similar tendencies (if not to the same extent) may also be present in East Asian societies. I do not know of any empirical work on the subject.

[96] Chow and Tsui, *A Survey of the Living and Working Conditions*, 34.

[97] Another variable may be the age of the FDW. Younger FDWs may prefer more autonomy, whereas older ones may care more about family-like relations within the home.

when costs come down, hence increasing opportunities for future FDWs.[98] However, if the effect of these policies would be to limit the opportunities for the development of family-like relations between employer and FDW (because such relations require an extended period to develop[99]), then Confucians would prefer to opt for the interests of the current batch of FDWs.[100] Given the continuing normative relevance of Confucianism in an East Asian context, the need to promote affective relations would be an important justification for long-term contracts with minimum wages that motivate the current batch of FDWs.[101] Let us now turn to the case of migrant domestic workers in Chinese cities: as we will see, similar questions and prescriptions arise at the national level.

Migrant Domestic Workers in Mainland China

China has been propelled into the capitalist age at a speed and scale far exceeding anything experienced in Western countries.[102] Chinese-style

[98] It could be, however, that the market for FDWs is saturated in Hong Kong, so that reducing costs would not increase demand. Moreover, the strength of opposition to reducing the minimum wage by pro-FDW NGOs in Hong Kong suggests that they do not see any potential benefit whatsoever from this proposal. Whatever the outcome of reducing costs, the point of this argument is to suggest that there would still be an important normative reason to favor the interests of the current batch of FDWs (e.g., not cutting the minimum wage) over those of future potential FDWs in cases of conflict.

[99] If not an unlimited period—it could be that employers and domestic workers would be less motivated to develop family-like relations if they knew that the workers must return "home" after a fixed number of years.

[100] Shortening contracts and cutting wages would also impact negatively on affective relations between employer and FDW, because the FDW may become demoralized and seek to return home or find employment elsewhere. (Of course, the employer is free to pay more than the minimum wage, but in most cases that doesn't seem to happen, and public policy should be based on the realistic assumption that it won't usually happen.) Two of my interviewees said they left Singapore for Hong Kong largely because the salaries are higher in Hong Kong, though one noted that she preferred her employers in Singapore and said that she would have stayed in Singapore if the salary had been higher.

[101] I do not mean to imply that the Hong Kong government was motivated by the need to promote affective relations when it implemented the minimum wage. But awareness of the link between decent salaries and the development of affective relations between employer and FDW could be invoked as a reason to maintain or increase the minimum wage in future policymaking. And if the government of Singapore really cared about affective relations in the home, it would force employers to pay decent wages to FDWs instead of maid levies to the government.

[102] As Michael Mann notes, the industrial "takeoff" in England led to an average growth rate of only 1 percent between 1660 and 1760, rising to nearly 3 percent (and never higher) in the midnineteenth century (see chap. 6, n. 62). Since 1979, China has averaged 9.4 annual economic growth rates. See http://www.iadb.org/idbamerica/index.cfm?thisid=2561, visited 27 December 2005.

development has been characterized by massive internal migration, composed largely of impoverished farmers migrating to urban areas in search of better work opportunities and higher earnings. China's "floating population" consists of about 120 million migrants, and by 2020 it is estimated that another 300–350 million migrant workers will have relocated to urban areas.[103]

Perhaps the most distinctive feature of internal migration is that it has been *regulated* by means of a household registration system (*hukou*, 戸口) that allows the state to control the extent of migration to urban areas and makes it more difficult for those born in rural areas to establish permanent homes in cities. The hukou is a politically sanctioned, hereditary distinction between those born in rural and urban areas, and migrants from rural areas must make known their presence in cities and apply for labor permits to work there. Urban household registrants are granted an extra share of rights and entitlements, and migrants are precluded from partaking of these benefits as a result of their rural backgrounds, regardless of how long they have actually lived in urban areas. As Dorothy Solinger has argued, the plight of China's migrant workers can be compared to foreign migrant workers in countries such as Japan and Germany (one might add Hong Kong and Singapore), who are similarly prevented from enjoying full citizenship rights as a result of their background.[104] In Japan and Germany, foreign domestic workers actually receive better treatment (in the sense of entitlement to some civil and political rights) than Chinese migrants. Even some developing countries grant migrant workers basic political rights (such as the right to vote) and basic civil rights (such as the right to move freely) that Chinese migrants are denied.[105] From a liberal democratic perspective, in other words, the hukou system is just as problematic as denying equal rights to FDWs in Hong Kong and Singapore:[106] it is the functional equivalent of

[103] *Together with Migrants* (Beijing: UNESCO Office Beijing, 2004), 26.

[104] See Dorothy J. Solinger, "Human Rights Issues in China's Internal Migration: Insights from Comparisons with Germany and Japan," in *The East Asian Challenge for Human Rights*, ed. Joanne R. Bauer and Daniel A. Bell (New York: Cambridge University Press, 1999), 285–312.

[105] Indonesia under Suharto, however, went beyond restricting the rights of migrants in urban areas: the government implemented a transmigration program that involved the forced migration of millions of people from heavily populated areas to remote islands. See http://dte.gn.apc.org/ctrans.htm, visited 27 December 2005. The Chinese government also forcefully transported farmers to other areas in the name of economic development, such as the farmers moved during the construction of the Three Gorges Dam, but such forced migration has not been a central plank of development policy in the era of economic reform.

[106] In some ways, more problematic: for example, FDWs in Hong Kong usually get the same kind of medical benefits that locals are entitled to, which is not typically the case for rural migrants in Chinese cities.

a caste system that marks a group of people as second-class citizens just because they were unlucky enough to be born in the countryside. Solinger herself scathingly indicts the hukou system for precisely this reason, arguing that the more economically developed areas in China have "drawn upon the country's own domestic peasants to serve as drudges, in the process denying them the rights that international norms of justice decree should belong to all human beings."[107]

Such concerns are not merely theoretical: the hukou system is hugely unpopular within China itself.[108] The legal discrimination against rural migrants also has social consequences: they are routinely subject to the scorn of urbanites and suspected of criminal activity. Moreover, their search for work opportunity and higher earnings does not always go as planned: "In surveys conducted in Beijing, in 2002 as much as 45.4% of *mingong* [rural migrants] had unemployment problems. Roughly one in four got no payment or was being paid in arrears. For various reasons, 36.3% of them were penniless. Approximately 60% had to work over ten hours a day, one third over 12 and 16% over 14. In 2002, 46% suffered from disease and 93% received nothing from their employer for medical treatment."[109] Even relatively privileged and educated students from rural areas experience practical difficulties and narrowed opportunities as a result of the hukou system: in Beijing, for example, university students from rural areas compete hard for jobs with the civil service so that they can get a Beijing hukou after they graduate. (Many quit their jobs in the civil service after a few years, once they obtain a hukou, to find higher-paying employment in the private sector.)[110]

It is worth asking what could possibly motivate what seems like a transparently unjust system. One way of answering this question is to anticipate the likely consequences of economic development without the hukou system. Consider what happened when Tibet—for Han Chinese, the most remote, inhospitable, and hostile part of the country—was exempted from the hukou system: "To encourage economic development in Tibet, Beijing had exempted Tibet from the general rule that one must be a permanent

---

[107] Ibid., 286.

[108] I asked one of my Tsinghua University graduate students (from outside Beijing) to help find articles on the pros and cons of the hukou system, and he responded (by e-mail), "I hate the system." Fortunately, he located several articles that expressed a range of views and did not let his own views get in the way of the research.

[109] Tan Shen, "Rural Workforce Migration: A Summary of Some Studies," *Social Sciences in China* (Winter 2003), 91. The majority of migrant workers do seem to earn money, and they send remittances back home (ibid., 96), similar to Filipino migrant workers.

[110] Another anecdote: a graduate student in journalism from Beijing University has obtained employment with one of China's most prestigious newspapers, but she will be posted in the United States rather than Beijing because it is easier for her to obtain a foreign working visa than to obtain a Beijing hukou.

resident of a given area to start a business there. The result was that Tibetan cities, Lhasa in particular, were inundated with a so-called 'floating population' of Han Chinese from other provinces."[111] Wu Ming spells out the likely consequences of abolishing the hukou system in more desirable (from a Han Chinese perspective) locations such as Beijing and Shanghai:

> If the urban hukou is abolished, not only will this cause difficulties of technical and human management in cities, there will also be a flood of laborers from the countryside. This will lead to many "urban illnesses" [*chengshi bing*, 城市病], particularly in developed cities on the East Coast. Perhaps we can say that there are already huge numbers of rural migrants in cities? But there aren't many "urban illnesses." That's because the urban hukou system has not been abolished. The rural migrants don't have a fixed residence, and their life is like that of migratory birds [*hou niao*, 侯鳥]. Without the hukou system, they would travel in groups, if they could establish their residence [in cities], they would bring their whole families to live in the outskirts of cities and there would be a huge amount of poverty stricken people. Urbanization in Latin America is the best example of this kind of situation.[112]

In other words, the hukou system has prevented the emergence of shanty towns and slums that characterize the big cities of other developing countries such as Brazil, Mexico, India, and Indonesia.[113] The benefits for economic development of urban areas are obvious: there is more social peace and less crime, as well as a more welcoming (stable) environment for foreign investors.

Wu Ming argues that the hukou system also benefits the less-developed parts of the country. The medium-sized and small cities of the less-

---

[111] Baogang He, "Minority Rights with Chinese Characteristics," in *Multiculturalism in Asia*, 64. Note that He draws on this example to make a different point, viz., the economic development alone cannot deal with the question for fair treatment for minorities (as it turns out, the Han Chinese took business away from Tibetans, and this only exacerbated tensions between the two groups).

[112] Wu Ming, "*Zhongguo huji zhidu: Zanshi bu neng quxiao*" [The Chinese Household Registration System: Cannot be Abolished in the Near Term], *Xin xi bu*, 26 November 2001.

[113] Lee Kuan Yew, strangely enough, notes the differences in patterns of labor migration between China and Brazil without mentioning the hukou system: "To drive development, look at these migrant workers in the cities, their aim is not just to become residents of Beijing or Shanghai. Their drive is to make money, send it back to their families, and one day to go back and build similar factories and apartments in their home towns. Why? Because their family is rooted there. You do not find that in Brazil. Having migrated to Rio, they stay in Rio." Transcript of Senior Minister Lee Kuan Yew's interview with Joshua Cooper Ramo from Foreign Policy Centre, UK, 6 April 2004, appendix to Joshua Cooper Ramo, *The Beijing Consensus: Notes on the New Physics of Chinese Power* (London: The Foreign Policy Centre, 2004), 67 (http://fpc.org.uk/fsblob/244.pdf). Lee's off-the-cuff comment points to the danger of monocausal cultural explanations.

developed western part of the China find it easier to retain the talent that helps to develop their economies[114] (without the hukou system, talent would migrate to cities like Beijing and Shanghai). One might add that the benefits of economic investment in relatively wealthy east coast cities can eventually be redistributed for purposes of developing impoverished regions (the Chinese government has recently announced funding for expensive infrastructure projects in the west). In short, the disadvantages of the hukou system may be outweighed by the positive contribution of the system to the long-term economic development of the country. Once the country attains the requisite level of economic development, the system can be abolished.[115]

There is a lively debate in China regarding the merit of such claims for the hukou system,[116] but the argument turns largely on the consequences of the system relative to other possibilities (as opposed to the "fundamentalist" liberal position that the system is inherently unjust because of its castelike characteristics, and should be abolished regardless of the consequences). Free marketers argue that free mobility will produce such beneficial consequences as less crime and more employment opportunities for city residents.[117] The sociologist Li Qiang argues that social order can be secured by administrative means such as property rights, diplomas, and know-how certificates that lend "social status to a person based upon his or her postnatal endeavors rather than congenital conditions."[118]

Whatever the validity of such arguments for and against the hukou system (and they turn on empirical considerations as well as the willingness to risk untested possibilities), the system is no longer deployed as the "one size fits all" solution to the problem of maintaining social order in China. The levels of economic development vary greatly across China, and different resident requirements apply in different contexts. In more than twenty thousand small towns, "the requirements to get a *hukou* are

---

[114] Ibid.

[115] Of course, the hukou system has not put an end to illegal migration, but it has minimized it. The illegal migrants that do come and get caught are subject to detention and repatriation (in June 2003, the State Council removed the compulsory detention component): a form of administrative detention that has been severely criticized, particularly by Western human rights groups. For an argument that eliminating administrative detention at this time would have significant negative consequences for most of the intended beneficiaries, see Randall Peerenboom, "Out of the Pan and into the Fire: Well-Intentioned but Misguided Recommendations to Eliminate All Forms of Administrative Detention in China," *Northwestern University Law Review*, vol. 98, no. 3 (2004).

[116] See Ibid., 1006–8.

[117] See Xia Xianliang and Wang Yingxi, "Zhongguo hukou zhidu gaige de lilun fenxi" [A Theoretical Analysis of China's Institutional Reform for Residence Registration], *Chenshi fazhan yanjiu* [Urban Studies], vol. 9, no. 4 (2002), 23.

[118] Tan, "Rural Workforce Migration," 97.

reduced to no more than 'stable living sources and legal housing in towns.' Any qualified non-local person or family may apply for *hukou* there."[119] In middle-sized and some big cities, the requirements to get a hukou have been greatly reduced. In Beijing and Shanghai, however, the requirements have actually been tightened in some respects.[120] In early 2005, one deputy of the Chinese People's Political Consultative Committee argued for even further restrictions in Beijing: "Beijing's population must be limited. . . . The population already exceeds 17 million people. . . . The resident population already exceeds the resources available, restricting Beijing's economic development. . . . It's like two hundred people trying to fit into a bus with one hundred seats. . . . There are shortages of water and electricity, so restricting the population is a necessity. . . . More than 50 percent of crime in Beijing is caused by outsiders."[121] The crime statistic may be contestable, but there is a widespread perception in Beijing that the city is bursting at the seams. Given this reality, it is not likely that the hukou system will be abolished in Beijing (and Shanghai) in the foreseeable future.[122]

Let us now draw implications for the question of how best to secure the interests of mainland Chinese domestic workers.[123] Like everything else in China, the numbers involved are staggering: according to one estimate, there are ten million domestic workers in the mainland, generating approximately 4 percent of China's GDP.[124] In Beijing alone, 223,000 households hire full-time domestic workers, and another 225,000 employ part-time workers.[125] The large bulk of domestic workers—over

[119] Cai Fang, "How the Market Economy Promotes Reform of the Household Registration System," *Social Sciences in China*, no. 4 (2003), 122.

[120] In one respect, however, the Beijing hukou has been loosened: a child born before 7 August 2003 could only obtain a Beijing hukou if his or her mother had one, but since then a child can get a Beijing hukou if either parent has one.

[121] "Interview with Zhang Wei Yin," "*Zhengxie weiyuan jianyi dui jin jing renkou shixing zhun ru zhidu*" [CPPCC Deputy Suggests Implementing System for Standardizing the System of Entering Beijing]," *Xin jing bao*, 25 January 2005.

[122] It may be tempting to condemn a city like Beijing for "selfishly" holding onto its resources, but is there a moral difference between seventeen million Beijingers establishing de facto boundaries to prevent a flood of impoverished migrants from the countryside and, say, nineteen million Australians establishing boundaries to prevent a flood of impoverished migrants from Indonesia? And Beijingers need to make do with a city the size of Sydney—as well as promise eventually to use some of their resources to develop the impoverished hinterlands.

[123] The official Chinese term is *jiazheng fuwuzhe*, 家政服務者, translated literally as "House Management Service People."

[124] "Another 5 Million Domestic Helpers Needed, Says Group," *South China Morning Post*, 17 February 2004, A4.

[125] "Beijingers Just Cannot Get the Staff These Days," *China Daily*, 7 February 2005, http://www.china.org.cn/english/Life/120051.htm.

90 percent—are migrant workers from the countryside who are subject to the restrictions of the hukou system.[126]

Just as the impossibility of equal rights in Hong Kong and Singapore does not seem to be the major concern of FDWs, so the hukou system per se—meaning the lack of access to permanent residency rights—does not seem to be the major concern of migrant domestic workers in Beijing. Instead, my interviewees mentioned some practical disadvantages associated with not having the Beijing hukou,[127] such as lack of access to subsidized housing, free schooling for their children, and health insurance.[128] Another key issue is the lack of work accident insurance: in one recent case, a migrant domestic worker was run over by a car, and only the active involvement of an NGO helped the worker to secure any compensation.[129]

The most commonly cited grievance in Beijing is the low salary for domestic workers.[130] Monthly salaries for migrant domestic workers range from 545 to 800 yuan (approx. 60–80 U.S. dollars), low even by the standards of other mainland Chinese cities such as Shanghai and Shenzhen. Translated into policy, this means that the hukou system may not be the right target for those concerned with promoting the interests of

[126] See http:www.beijing.org.cn/3825/2004/01/18/182@1832825.htm (visited 18 January 2004).

[127] Interviews carried out with three migrant domestic workers at the Jiezu Jiazheng Fuwu Gongsi [The "Fast Responding" Domestic Service Company] in Beijing, 17 April 2005. As in the case of Hong Kong and Singapore, my views may be colored by the fact that I am personally an employer of a domestic worker, though I have tried not to let my "class position" influence my judgments.

[128] The interviewees also mentioned that there are ways around these obstacles. For example, one interviewee from nearby Henan province noted that she could return to her hometown for treatment of serious illnesses. Another interviewee (from impoverished Guizhou province) actually had three children in Beijing, including one elder son who attended Tsinghua University and two younger ones attending secondary school. This particular worker needs to pay extra for kids to attend school in Beijing (an extra 500 yuan per year for secondary school), but he said he could afford the expense because his wife also worked in Beijing as a domestic worker. This case points to another particular (distinctive?) feature of domestic workers in China: approximately 15 percent are male ("Zhongguo jiazheng fuwu hangye fenxi yanjiu baogao" [Chinese Domestic Workers' Industry Analysis Research Report], http://www.icinet.com.cn/ReadNews.asp?NewsID=312), and they tend to care for elderly people. Perhaps there is more need for physical strength with respect to caring for elderly people; e.g., the person being cared for may need to be lifted into a bathtub.

[129] Interview with Geneviève Domenach of UNESCO's Beijing office, 29 April 2005. UNESCO is actively involved in funding pro–migrant worker NGOs and funding projects (such as art exhibits) that aim to raise consciousness about the plight of domestic workers. See *Together with Migrants* (Beijing: UNESCO office Beijing, 2004).

[130] See the following (Chinese-language) websites: http://www.sina.com.cn/c/2004-11-16/17144935474.shtml, http://www.people.com.cn/GB/shehui/8217/34282/34284/2697861.html, and http://finance.memail.net/041221/129,5,450305.00.shtml (visited 1 July 2004). All three of my interviewees also noted the low salary as the main problem.

migrant domestic workers in Beijing. If the *hukou* were abolished in Beijing (to repeat, a highly unlikely proposition), the likely result would be further migration from the countryside and more competition for jobs as domestic workers: in other words, the salaries for domestic workers would decrease! So from the perspective of migrant domestic workers, challenging the hukou system would be just as counterproductive as challenging the system of unequal rights for FDWs in Hong Kong and Singapore.[131] Once again, the good intentions of liberals would harm the very constituency they are supposed to be helping.

If the concern is to improve the well-being of migrant domestic workers, then policymakers should consider measures that have the effect of increasing wages, such as training programs that upgrade the skill level of domestic workers.[132] The government can also consider setting minimum wages, as in Hong Kong. This measure would involve formalizing contractual relationships between employer and employee—at the moment, almost all migrant domestic workers work without a contract. Standardized contracts, as in Hong Kong, should also ensure that employees are guaranteed health insurance and work accident insurance. These policies would require reform of the Beijing hukou, but such reforms can be implemented without across-the-board abolishment that would likely lead to a huge influx of rural migrants.

The concern to promote affective relations also bears on the question of formalizing contractual arrangements. Similar to Hong Kong and Singapore, the interviewees in Beijing specifically noted "being treated as a member of the family" as an important desideratum.[133] From this point

---

[131] To be more precise, once again, it would be counterproductive from the perspective of the current batch of migrant workers (the potential batch might benefit from more opportunities, even if the salaries are lower). But the need to increase the likelihood of family-like relations within the home speaks in favor of erring in favor of the interests of the current batch of workers, as in Hong Kong and Singapore.

[132] At present, only one-third of migrant domestic workers receive prior training before they work in Beijing, and the common complaint among employers is that the migrant workers tend to be of "low quality" (http://www.people.com.cn/GB/shehui/8217/34282/34284/2697861.html), meaning that they are not trained to perform basic tasks like cooking and ironing, and some may be barely literate. If domestic workers are more skilled, they could presumably command higher salaries (though it is worth noting that some employers cannot afford to pay more than the current market rate—for example, one Beijing University professor told me that half of her elderly mother's pension of 1,600 yuan per month goes to pay for her live-in domestic worker).

[133] Family-like relations (as in Hong Kong and Singapore) within the home means that the employer expresses genuine concern for the domestic worker's family (and vice versa) and shares information not directly related to the work. Another anecdote: in Beijing, I live with my mother-in-law, and she often forms an ideological alliance with our domestic worker to engage in almost daily critiques of my supposedly "wasteful" habits. Such an alliance is tolerated because it is regarded as an expression of family-like relations between employer and worker.

of view, specifying longer terms of engagement (say, two or three years) in the contract would be desirable, because domestic workers would be more likely to stick with their employers, thus increasing the likelihood that family-like ties develop between employer and employee.[134] On the other hand, an important advantage for domestic workers under the current, informal system of engagement is that they can easily change jobs and therefore do not have to put up with abusive employers.[135] So the contract would need to allow for some form of exit, but not to the point that employer and employee do not have any motivation to deal with minor conflicts in family-like ways.[136] Such contracts would therefore need to be combined with further measures that protect the domestic worker from abuse, such as Singapore-style punishments for employers who physically abuse or otherwise mistreat domestic workers. The government can also use informal means such as TV programming designed to increase consciousness about the need to treat domestic workers well.[137]

To sum up. The global inequalities of late capitalism force some hard choices upon policy-makers concerned with morally defensible outcomes. From the perspective of foreign domestic workers, perhaps the most vulnerable group of long-term residents, East Asian–style contract terms for hundreds of thousands of FDWs may be more just (less unjust) than liberal democratic–style citizenship rights for relatively few legal FDWs and hundreds of thousands of illegal ones. In the Chinese domestic context, the hukou system is the functional equivalent of an unequal rights regime, but challenges to the system in cities such as Beijing are likely to

[134] Other features of contracts designed to promote (or not undermine) family-like relations would also apply in Beijing, such as limits on detailed lists of rights and duties that decrease the likelihood of nonlegalistic acts of generosity and solidarity.

[135] Yet another anecdote: an eighty-year-old woman in my building (a self-described "capitalist") hit her sixteen-year-old domestic worker from the countryside and refused to pay her wages. The domestic worker quit the next day. In Singapore and Hong Kong, by contrast, the difficulty of changing employers means that FDWs often need to tolerate abusive employers.

[136] There may be some parallels with debates over divorce law. The liberal view is that spouses should be able to decide for themselves when to divorce (so long as the interests of children are secured). Translated into policy, it means granting spouses the right to instant divorce. The Confucian (or communitarian) concern for affective relations would justify some constraints on the right to exit, such as a waiting period of one year so that spouses are not likely to make hasty decisions to divorce that they may subsequently regret.

[137] Consider, for example, the fact that the television program on the eve of the Spring Festival draws an audience of roughly 500 million people (the Super Bowl, the most watched television event in the United States, draws an audience of roughly 150 million people). This program consists of songs and skits that convey moral messages in humorous

be just as counterproductive as challenges to the unequal rights regime in Hong Kong and Singapore. Defenders of justice should instead focus their energies addressing problems that migrant workers themselves care about. But justice is not all that matters. In cultures that prioritize the quality of affective relations over individual autonomy, policymakers should also be sensitive to arrangements, formal and informal, that increase the likelihood of affective ties within the home, even if they conflict with the rights and duties that an exclusive focus on the imperatives of justice might mandate.

---

ways (for example, one skit in the 2005 show portrayed a migrant worker who complained that his wages were not being paid on time, and the audience clapped loudly in sympathy). In future programming, perhaps one skit can depict the importance of promoting family-like relations between employers and migrant domestic workers and refraining from abuse of the latter.

12

Responses to Critics: The Real and the Ideal

THIS BOOK is divided into three parts—human rights, democracy, and capitalism—that correspond to the three main pillars of liberal democracy. I have tried to show the problems associated with transferring Western-style liberal ideas about human rights, democracy, and capitalism, and I argued for alternative justifications and practices appropriate for an East Asian context. My approach should not be too controversial: upon reflection, who can deny that political thinkers concerned with putting forward effective and respectful suggestions for political reform in East Asia need to consider empirical realities and the values of local traditions and allow for the possibility of justifiable difference? Only the most dogmatic imperialists would insist that political thinkers cannot look beyond Western-style liberal democratic norms and practices for inspiration. To the extent that there is any controversy (or originality) in this book, it will lie in the particular way I have applied this methodology, not in the methodology itself.

Nonetheless, I have often run into controversy when I have tried to spell out my methodology in seminars and lectures. The main problem, I freely confess, lies in my own responses following critical questions, and I have often regretted my initial, off-the-cuff responses, particularly when I have presented this material in the United States. My responses were not necessarily wrong, but they were often inappropriate. Instead of clarifying my methodology and my intentions, they had the opposite effect. Only later, after some introspection and a few of glasses of wine did I realize what I should have said. So let me set the record straight here. What follows is a list of critical questions that I typically encountered when I presented ideas from this book. I begin with the general methodological questions, and I end with the personal attacks that tended to follow after my responses needlessly poisoned the atmosphere. Each question (Q) is followed by two responses: what I actually said (real response: RR) and what I should have said (ideal response: IR).

> Q1: A theorist thinks about ideals, and a practitioner thinks about implementation, but you seem to be doing two tasks at once. You're trained as a political theorist, so why don't you just stick to ideals and let others worry about implementation?

RR: You can't do one without the other. When people try, it's a disaster. Mao Zedong had great ideals—the equality of men and women, respect for farmers and workers, taking power from bureaucrats and giving it to the people—but he let others worry about implementation. And what's the result? The Cultural Revolution: a good idea badly implemented. At the other extreme, we have Adolf Hitler. He had terrible ideals—anti-Semitism, the biological superiority of the German race, a love of warfare—but he had brilliant technocrats with the ability to implement them. And what's the result? The Nazi Holocaust: a bad idea ably implemented.

IR: I'm not sure if there's a rigid division between theorists and practitioners. Political theorists also have a view about the world as it actually works and how their ideals might operate in it. At some level, all theorists agree that principles should be assessed partly by the extent to which they can be usefully implemented in practice. Otherwise they'd be doing science fiction. Practitioners, for their part, also have ideals, not always fully articulated, that partly motivate what they're doing. At some level, they seek to morally justify what they do; they're not just blindly implementing ideals handed down to them by others. I guess I'm proposing that we should be more self-conscious about the interaction between the ideal and the feasible, about how the empirical world sets constraints on workable moral principles and also about how sensitivity to different ideals should shape one's practical work.

Q2: You seem to be impatient with theory of a more abstract kind or anything that bears little relevance to the contemporary world. But surely theorists have to be given room to focus on fundamental moral issues such as the nature and justification of rights and the basis of social justice. In these questions, there are moral issues of a more philosophical character that need to be tackled.

RR: Let me tell you something about theorists who work at a high level of abstraction. It's striking just how many happened to be gifted mathematicians as children. Naturally, they're enamored by beautiful theories and formulae, and less so by the messy world of real politics and people's less-than-beautiful moral aspirations. The same quest for beauty and perfection in math occasionally leads them to apply their talent to the realm of moral and political philosophy. They do come up with beautiful and rigorously formulated theories, but their principles can rarely be translated into practical guidance for action. I sometimes wonder if they stumbled upon the wrong profession.

IR: Fair enough. There are different approaches to political thinking; each has its advantages and disadvantages. The utility of the abstract approach may not always be immediately evident, but one virtue of framing arguments at a high level of abstraction is that they can be useful in as-yet-unforeseen contexts: consider the way that great philosophers of the past have inspired people of future ages. Of course, my own approach is more down-to-earth, so to speak. I work at the intersection of theory and practice, I have a particular context in mind when I'm arguing for something, and I try not to lose sight of the question of effectiveness. But both approaches are valuable, as well as other approaches to political thinking such as the history of political thought. I think such methodological pluralism is healthy. In fact, I'd worry about academic departments that emphasize only one approach: there's more to learn from a diversity of approaches.

Q3: You claim to be doing political thinking "for an East Asian context," but you're still using Western methods of scholarship. For example, a Chinese scholar of classical Chinese would rarely dive right into the original source and draw implications for present-day societies (it seems like you're just searching for whatever fits your preexisting views). He or she would review the history of interpretations and of interpretations of interpretations before drawing any conclusions. Why don't you adopt local methods of scholarship?

    RR: You've got to be joking! At my pace reading Chinese-language material, can you imagine how long it would take me to review the history of interpretations?

    IR: Once again, I think different approaches have different advantages and disadvantages. One advantage of the "Chinese" approach is that the scholar isn't likely to reinvent the wheel, because he or she knows what has already been said. One disadvantage is that the scholar's own viewpoint often gets buried in the analysis of interpretations, and there's rarely a systematic effort to draw implications for modern-day societies. The advantages and disadvantages are reversed for my approach. The choice of approach deployed also depends on the question being asked: I happen to be concerned with drawing implications for present-day East Asian societies— that's what I find interesting. If the reader has the same concern, he or she should be willing to engage with what I'm saying. If not, he or she should be reading a different book. It doesn't really matter where the methodology comes from if we agree that it helps to shed light on what are considered to be important questions. And by the way, it's not always true that I look at the sources for whatever fits my preexisting views. There may be a bit of that, but I've also changed my views in response to the sources. I didn't know about

Mencius's defense of punitive expeditions, for example, and what I learned from the text shaped the conclusions I try to draw for contemporary societies. And the reading I've done about filial piety and political elitism in Confucianism and state-building in Legalism has definitely changed my perspective.

Q4: You claim to be looking for local knowledge, but you're still importing Western categories—human rights, democracy, and capitalism, not to mention points you make about "the right to food," "property rights," "evil deeds," and so on. These are all categories that derive from the experience of Western societies.

  Rr: I know, I know. I've been living in East Asia since 1991, and I can't get the Western stuff out of my system, no matter how hard I try. It's really frustrating.

  Ir: In present-day East Asian societies, these "Western" categories have also become part of everyday political discourse; they're no longer "owned" by the societies in which they originated. The scholar of contemporary East Asian political thinking can't help being a comparativist. I've also looked at the classical sources, and I do recognize that I've used modern categories to make sense of the argument. But one shouldn't worry too much about labels: the point is to improve understanding for the contemporary reader, and as long as I haven't distorted the substance of what the classical thinkers were saying, it should be OK. If I've distorted the substance, please tell me!

Q5: Culture isn't fixed or permanent, it's always changing. So why are you making essentialist claims about particular cultural values, as though people must have certain values just because they're born in a certain culture?

  Rr: Of course cultures change, nobody denies that. I can't believe postmodernists can get so much mileage out of such a trivial claim!

  Ir: Fair enough. But some values and practices, for whatever concatenation of historical reasons, are deeply entrenched for now and the foreseeable future. If the aim is to understand social phenomena— say, the role of affective relations in Korea—then knowledge of traditional cultural outlooks is helpful, if not essential. The normative question of whether or not traditional values are worth maintaining isn't entirely separate from the question of understanding the function of traditional values in contemporary societies. If it turns out that people really are attached to certain traditional values, there's a strong presumption in favor of respecting those values. But only a presumption; it's not the end of the investigation. The case for maintenance and promotion of traditional values is much stronger if those values contribute positively to contemporary needs and requirements. If they don't, then traditional values can be challenged, no matter how much people still care about them.

Q6: You're exaggerating the importance of culture. People will respond in similar ways to incentives, no matter where they're from. Take an American, put him in China with the same constraints and incentives that Chinese experience, and he will make the same rational choices as the Chinese.

> RR: Cultural identity is very deep—it's shaped by forces and values imbibed in one's childhood. It's hard to have a clear sense of how it influences one's life, much less establish conscious control over it. Put an American in China and he will still act like an American, I can assure you, and if it's not obvious to the American it will be to the Chinese.

> IR: Of course we need to be aware of politics and economics—about how power and money shapes outcomes—but neither should we deny the possibility that cultural values can contribute something important to people's motivation and behavior. Values may play a greater role in hard cases: if the "right" solution to an ethical or political dilemma isn't obvious—there are advantages and disadvantages on both sides—then choices can differ depending upon which value has greater priority in one's cultural background. Given similar sets of incentives, a Chinese is more likely to opt for at-home care for needy family members over institutionalized care, even if this entails certain costs to her lifestyle. In this book, I've focused on hard issues that may sharpen areas of cultural difference.

Q7: You're making empirical claims without any empirical evidence. Why not make more use of polling data and values surveys, instead of relying on unscientific anecdotes and "feelings" about culture?

> RR: Polls! How deep can you get with polls! People will give you their unreflective, off-the-top-of-their-head responses, and who knows if those responses have any impact on behavior. In cross-cultural surveys, it's not always easy to translate questions about values, and the set of options may reflect the biases of the pollster rather than the values the respondent really cares about. In East Asia, there are additional problems: people are generally quite reticent with strangers, and they may not immediately reveal their true views. And let's not mention the political constraints in countries like China: people are more likely to be frank with those they trust. I think we should treat such "data" with some skepticism. If I have

to choose, I'll rely on other ways of generating cultural understanding: in-depth interviews, historical research, movies, novels, not to mention the simple fact of living in a particular place for prolonged periods. It's not a coincidence that I write more about the places I've lived in.

IR: I do try to support my claims with empirical evidence, including values surveys and polling data. For example, there's plenty of evidence that East Asians are more favorably inclined to at-home caring for elderly people, and I invoke such evidence in the book. The section on capitalism makes extensive use of empirical data. Of course, I'd welcome more relevant evidence that casts doubt on some of my empirical claims. Please show me where I've gone wrong!

Q8: Don't you think universal values like human rights should have priority over Asian values? It looks like you're arguing for the opposite.

RR: What's universal? I'm contesting this whole idea of universality. As far as I'm concerned, it's a clash between different forms of local values, not between universal and local values. If proponents of human rights and democracy derive their ideas entirely from Western liberal societies, are they really universal? It's a very parochial form of "universalism," if you ask me.

IR: In my view, it's an encounter between different universalisms, not between universal and local values. It's not just human rights values that are meant to be universal. Several Asian philosophies and religions also share the aspiration to universalize their values. The founding fathers of Confucianism, for example, believed that their theories were universalizable; they were not intended only for one culture. Of course, one needs to ask if Confucian values and practices should be applied in contexts unforeseen by their founding theoreticians. But one needs to ask the same question of other theories designed for all human beings, such as human rights. In the case of Confucianism, it did spread to non-Chinese cultures in East Asia, such as Korea, and it was modified in the process. The same may happen to human rights. I'm interested in the question of how human rights, democracy, and capitalism are being received and modified during the course of encounters with East Asian cultures.

Q9: You're a relativist, aren't you? What works for Asians is fine, what works for Westerners is fine, and there's no higher principle that would allow us to distinguish between good and bad values.

RR: That's ridiculous, you haven't been listening to my argument. Just because I question the idea that liberal values should be universalized doesn't mean that I'm a relativist. It's liberals who often sound like relativists, as when Isaiah Berlin endorses the view that we should realize the relativity of our ideas but still stand for them unflinchingly. I'm not sure why he would bother standing for anything if he really thought all ideas were equally valid. In the same vein, an American liberal theorist once told me that when people say, "Oh, they do it differently in country X," she responds, "So what." The right response is to show curiosity and to ask how what's being done in country X can help us to improve our own ways.

IR: To be more precise, I'm a pluralist. I want to allow for the possibility that there are different legitimate ways of prioritizing values and organizing societies. It's not to say that anything goes, but there can be justifiable moral diversity; we needn't rank all values according to a common scale. In this sense, I'm no different from liberals like Isaiah Berlin.

Q10: You seem to be idealizing East Asian societies. It's as though you're comparing the "best of the East" with the "worst of the West."

RR: If I do that, I'm compensating for the other extreme that's more typical in the West: idealizing the practices of Western societies and denigrating those elsewhere. It's a bit tiring to read one China-bashing article after another in the *New York Times* and the *New York Review of Books*. When things are working in East Asia, I do think we need to defend the status quo, even if it happens to deviate from liberal ideals and Western-style practices.

IR: That's not my intention. In nearly every single chapter, I've tried to identify flaws with political practices in East Asia and suggested proposals for reform.

Q11: Is East Asia really a unified region? There are huge differences between the various countries, and you support your arguments with examples from some East Asian countries, but the experience of other East Asian countries may cast doubt on your arguments.

RR: Yes, I admit there's something pretty ad hoc about what I'm doing. I've lived and worked in Singapore, Hong Kong, and mainland China, and much of what I say stems from that experience. I feel most comfortable talking about countries I'm more familiar with personally. I've also been to conferences in Korea, Japan, and Taiwan a few times, and I have close friends in those countries, so I feel I can also draw on examples from there. Of course, I've also done lots of reading, but somehow information seems more reliable if it comes from my own experience or the voices of trusted friends and family members.

IR: Yes, I agree there are huge differences between, as well as within, the countries of East Asia. However, several societies in East Asia are also bound by common political traditions. China, Korea, Japan, Hong Kong, Singapore, Taiwan, and Vietnam have all been shaped by their Confucian and Legalist legacies. Several East Asian countries have also been shaped by the experience of rapid economic development in the post–World War II era, which provides another element of commonality. And the region of East Asia seems to have an institutional reality. Investment banks and multinational companies often have East Asian divisions. The region's stock markets and currencies are intimately linked, as we found out during the Asian financial crisis. Regional economic and political organizations such as the Asia Pacific Economic Cooperation Organization (APEC) add another element of reality.

Q12: Your choice of traditions seems arbitrary. Why do you choose Confucianism and Legalism? Why not Buddhism, Islam, or Daoism?

RR: It so happens I'm more familiar with Confucianism and Legalism, and that's what I feel most comfortable writing about. Also, because I know those traditions best, I can think more about contemporary implications. What I know about Daoism seems pretty eccentric, but I may be wrong. If I study more Daoism, I might discover there are political implications for the modern world, and then I'd have more to say about it.

IR: There are other political traditions, of course, but Confucianism and Legalism are the two dominant ones that continue to influence people's "habits of the hearts" as well as shape economic and political outcomes. Confucianism is perhaps less controversial because it was the official ideology of several East Asian countries for such a long time. So let me say something about Legalism because the attempt to trace its influence is a bit more speculative. The first Chinese dynasty, led by the tyrant Qin Shihuang, was inspired by Legalist principles, but it was so brutal that Legalism was given a bad name after it collapsed. The theories of Legalist thinkers such as Han Fei Zi were debated in the succeeding Han dynasty, but after that few thinkers adopted the Legalist label, and Legalism was not perpetuated as a philosophic tradition. However, the vastness of empire and the increasing complexity of government required compromise with Legalist calls for strong states and bureaucratic coordination. Consequently, Confucianism assimilated, and remained in tension with, Legalist elements. The need for state-building in East Asia since the late nineteenth century has reinvigorated the Legalist tradition, explicitly so in the case of Mao. So it's important to understand Legalism if the aim is to understand political developments in East Asia. From a normative point of view, however, any defensible version of Legalism will have to rest on a Confucian foundation. Legalists believed that the purpose of politics is to strengthen the state, and thinkers such as Han Fei Zi explicitly argued that this aim conflicts with the interests of the ordinary people (as well as that of ministers, and even the interests of the ruler, who is supposed to conceal his true needs lest he weaken the power of the state). That's a strange idea: what's the point of a strong state if nobody benefits from it? The Confucian view, which I endorse, is that the state should serve the people. So there may be a case to draw on Legalist ideas for strengthening the state, but the case must be justified with reference to the interests of the people.

Q13: Why do you discuss some Confucian and Legalist values, but leave out others? The ones you leave out, like Confucian patriarchy, are often just as influential as the ones you discuss.

RR: Yes, that's driven by my normative agenda. My main constructive purpose is to propose desirable alternatives to Western-style liberal democracy. So I won't spend much time on values that I find objectionable, even if they're still influential in modern-day societies. I don't like patriarchal values, and if Confucians want to defend patriarchy, well, that's their business, not mine.

IR: Yes, I didn't mean to imply that I've covered all the relevant territory of Confucian and Legalist values. I'd like to hear more about others, and I hope to think more and write about them in the future. But let me say something about "Confucian patriarchy." It may be somewhat unfair to link the two. Contemporary scholars have argued that the core values of Confucianism don't support patriarchy, and that it's both possible and desirable to reinterpret Confucianism so that it's compatible with feminist goals. In Korea, there's a group of feminists who refer to themselves as "Confucian feminists."

Q14: You raise some doubts about the desirability of Western-style "liberal democracy" in East Asia, but look at what's been happening: Korea, Japan, and Taiwan are democratic, their leaders are elected by the people, and nobody's saying we need to go back to the old authoritarian ways.

RR: You're working, if I may say so, with a pretty crude dichotomy. The world is divided into "good" Western liberal democracies and "bad" authoritarian others. Why is it that Westerners—politicians, journalists, political scientists, Joe Six-Pack—so often succumb to this less-than-nuanced way of thinking?

IR: Yes, that's right, to a certain extent. From a normative point of view, however, it's not obvious that electoral democracies do better on all dimensions compared to nondemocratic regimes. I tried to argue that democratization, in the sense of political leaders elected by the majority, won't necessarily work well for minority groups. And if you compare democracy with as-yet-unrealized alternatives, like governments composed of meritocratically selected deputies, I think you'd get even more advantages for nondemocratic alternatives. We shouldn't foreclose any possibilities. Governments led by elected politicians have some advantages over those that don't, but they also have some disadvantages. We need to investigate claims about the virtues of democracy closely, by looking at how it actually works in particular contexts and doing one's best to leave aside biases that may be the products of other settings.

Q15: This debate about the pros and cons of democracy versus authoritarianism is academic. Eventually, all societies are bound to abandon their authoritarian ways as they modernize.

RR: That's what I used to think. In May 1989 I met a Chinese woman. It was a joyous time, divided equally between romance and support of the democratic revolution in China. We ended up getting married, but our democratic aspirations were, how shall I say, set back somewhat by what the government calls the Tiananmen Square "incident." By the way, I used to say that it was a failed revolution and a successful marriage, but a Chinese friend once replied that it's too early to tell: in both respects . . . [nobody laughs]. In 1991 I moved to ultramodern Singapore to teach at the National University. A new prime minister had replaced Lee Kuan Yew, and opposition forces seemed energized. A colleague and friend, Dr. Chee Soon Juan, joined an opposition party. Shortly thereafter, he was sacked from the university on trumped-up charges, publicly humiliated, and bankrupted. That was the end of a period that local wits term the "Prague Spring of Singapore." In 1996 I moved to Hong Kong. Chris Patten enacted some democratic reforms, although this time I was less sympathetic, why did the British take so long to do it, and why go out of your way to antagonize the Chinese government? Not surprisingly, the reforms were rolled back after the handover to China. The Chinese government has put off substantial political reform in Hong Kong till 2012, at the earliest. Now I'm living in Beijing, and you'll understand if I'm going to hedge my bets this time.

IR: Perhaps. But I'm not sure if "modernization" is the key to democratization, the middle classes in East Asia often seem to be politically conservative when the economy is booming. It could be the

opposite, that economic setbacks spur democratization. Look at
what happened after the 1997 economic crisis. Newly impoverished
members of the bourgeoisie had an incentive to question the old
ways, and this contributed to democratization in Indonesia, Korea,
and Thailand. But for the sake of argument, let's assume that all
modernized East Asian countries end up being governed by elected
leaders. If the aim is to understand economic and political phenomena, we'd need to look at other factors. Elected governments in East
Asia may be serving very different purposes than democratically
elected governments in the West. The political discourse may not be
liberal, and policies may be serving nonliberal aims. What they do
may have more in common with their predemocratic days than with
the workings of democratic governments in the liberal West. In any
case, for purposes of my book, liberal democracy isn't just competitive elections for political leaders. There are other ways of ap-
proaching this topic, of course, but I define liberal democracy as being composed of three main pillars—human rights, democracy, and
capitalism—that have originated and been developed in Western
countries. I've tried to show that those three features of liberal
democracy are substantially modified when they're exported to East
Asian societies that have not been shaped by liberalism to nearly the
same extent. In the constructive part of my book, I propose alternative models of human rights, democracy, and capitalism that may
be more appropriate—more feasible and desirable—for East Asian
societies.

Q16: Aren't you exaggerating the differences between liberal Western societies and supposedly nonliberal East Asian ones? After all, you agree that
all societies need human rights, democracy, and capitalism, and you're
just suggesting that different societies can adopt different variations. The
differences between "East" and "West" seem pretty minor; they're differences of degree rather than kind.

   RR: I'm reminded of a philosopher's joke: Is the difference between a
   difference of degree and a difference of kind a difference of degree
   or a difference of kind? . . . [nobody laughs]. Let me answer your
   question. What liberals may view as minor wouldn't necessarily be
   viewed as minor by East Asians. Most disputes turn on the centrality of values in particular traditions, which matters when the state
   must decide how to distribute scarce resources.

   IR: Yes, some differences are minor, but others are less so. I've been
   questioning the priority of civil and political rights that has been so
   fundamental to the liberal tradition. I've been arguing against equal
   citizenship for all long-term residents—doesn't that challenge liberal

theory at its very core? I've also been arguing for empowering political leaders chosen by competitive examinations, and I believe liberal societies wouldn't sanction this kind of political system. And
I've suggested that the East Asian state will play an active role in
promoting the value of filial piety, whereas the Western state is
more likely to take a hands-off approach to what's perceived to be a
matter of individual choice.

Q17: Confucian values, like filial piety, aren't unique to Confucianism.
Other cultures also value care for elderly parents—for one thing, it's a
Biblical commandment—so why are you making such a big deal about
Confucian values?

RR: I'm not saying that Americans have less love for their parents than
East Asians. But there are key differences. Look at how much time
adult children spend with their parents and how East Asian governments and social institutions promote at-home care for parents. In
the United States, the prevailing approach for dealing with elderly
parents was summed up by a bumper sticker I once saw: "Be Nice
to Your Kids: They'll Choose Your Nursing Home."

IR: You're perfectly right: other cultures, such as the predominantly
Catholic societies of southern Europe, also place special value upon
care for elderly parents. And if you agree that filial piety is a desirable value, then we should celebrate commonality: all the better if defensible values are shared by many cultures! If the point of contrast is between Confucian and liberal values, however, I do think there are key
differences. There are different justifications for the practice of filial
piety: in Confucianism, it's viewed as the means of linking generations and generations of family members—one isn't just caring for an
elderly parent, it's also a way of maintaining ties with dead ancestors.
The different justifications also translate into different rituals: ancestor worship, for example, is practiced by most Korean families. And
filial piety has greater importance in Confucianism: comparable, perhaps, to the importance of the value of fidelity among married couples in the West. The central importance of filial piety in Confucianism matters for explanatory purposes, say, if the aim is to explain
differences regarding the treatment of the elderly in Japan and the
United States. It also matters for normative purposes. The value of individual autonomy has far greater importance in predominantly liberal societies, and consequently it often overrides the requirements of
filial piety in particular areas of controversy, whereas societies influenced by Confucian values typically side with filial piety. Politics is
usually about choosing between competing goods, and East Asian societies that emphasize filial piety typically choose to spend more time

and money on filial piety compared to predominantly liberal societies, and they're not necessarily wrong in doing so.

Q18: What about the supposed Confucian defense of political elitism? The same sorts of arguments were made by nineteenth-century liberals such as John Stuart Mill, who argued for extra votes for educated people. There's nothing distinctive about Confucianism, except that it's a bit old-fashioned by now.

> RR: You're working with an old-fashioned theory of progress, if I may say so. I don't believe that Western history is the story of linear progress that sets the model for everybody else. What you view as "old-fashioned" isn't typically regarded as such in East Asia, I can assure you.

> IR: But I'm comparing the centrality of values in different *contemporary* societies. If you compare the centrality of the value of political elitism in contemporary East Asian societies with, say, the centrality (or lack thereof) of the same value in, say, the United States, I think you'd find huge differences that matter for both explanatory and normative purposes.

Q19: The supposed Asian emphasis on family and affective relations isn't distinctive, it's similar to the discourse of communitarian theorists in the West.

> RR: Yes, I know, that's why I'm attracted to it. My first book was a defense of Western communitarianism.

> IR: Again, I don't mean to argue for the distinctiveness of particular values, my point is that there may be differences regarding the centrality of particular values in particular contexts that matter for both explanatory and normative purposes. In East Asian societies, the "communitarian" discourse is central, whereas it's marginal compared the more individualistic liberal discourse in Western societies. Also, there are key differences of emphasis between the different communitarians. The Western communitarians tend to be republicans, meaning that they favor active, public-spirited participation by the many. The Asian communitarians tend to be more family oriented and more accepting of the idea that active political participation should be reserved for the educated few.

Q20: How can you, as a Westerner, defend proposals meant for East Asians? You condemn Western liberals for their cultural imperialism, but aren't you doing the same thing?

> RR: I'm not a "pure" Westerner any more. I've been living and working in East Asia since 1991. I have Chinese family members and lots

of friends in the region. I've spent years learning the Chinese language. It's different from Western liberals lecturing East Asians about
the virtues of Western-style liberal democracy. Why should anybody
listen to people with rudimentary knowledge and no particular affection for the societies where their ideas are meant to apply?

IR: At the end of the day, I hope that people pay more attention to the
substance of my arguments, rather than the source. I guess the
same would be true anywhere. If an East Asian intellectual proposes ways of understanding and ideas for dealing with problems
in contemporary American society, I would hope that the American audience listens with an open mind, leaving open the possibility of being persuaded, rather than dismissing the ideas out of hand
simply on account of the East Asian's racial and cultural background.

Q21: If your book is meant for East Asians, then why are you publishing it
in English, with Princeton University Press?

RR: I can't write well in any East Asian language, but fortunately most
East Asian academics read English. My last book, *East Meets West*,
was published by Princeton, and it was subsequently translated in
Chinese and Japanese, thus increasing the likelihood of wider read-
ership in East Asia. Also, my son was born in Princeton and I have a
soft spot for the place, notwithstanding the lack of good restaurants.

IR: My book is meant for an "East Asian" context; the main point
is to provide ideas for people thinking about how to improve
East Asian societies. Of course I hope East Asians will read it. But
Westerners—representatives of the U.S. government, human rights
NGOs, international organizations such as the IMF and the World
Bank, even academics—also have the power to shape events in East
Asia, and I hope they'll also read the book. Some Westerners may
simply be curious about China's increasing power in the world, and
they may also benefit from the book. And perhaps Western political
theorists will learn something from East Asian theories discussed in
this book.

Q22: Don't you think it's dangerous to question the value of democracy
and consider Asian alternatives? This sort of argument can easily play
into the hands of Asian autocrats.

RR: It's not just Asian politicians who misuse arguments. Aren't you
worried about the way American rulers misuse arguments for freedom and democracy? Vietnam, Central America, Iraq . . . need I
go on?

IR: Yes, I agree. So I should try to anticipate possible misuses and clearly explain what I really mean. If it turns out that my ideas are picked up by politicians for dubious purposes—though I'd be very surprised, I doubt that my name would add much credibility!—I'd have the responsibility to publicly expose their misuses.

Q23: What happened to you? You used to favor more power to the people, not less.

RR: It's true, I've changed. As an undergraduate at McGill, I remember being shocked when I read about how East Asian governments suppress people's voices. Surely authoritarian rulers had to be motivated by nothing more than the thirst for power, and I'd question the integrity of anybody who suggested otherwise. I've learned more, and I now think my earlier reactions were simplistic. I guess there's something more emotional about the idea of participating in the political process, and I've lost that too. I'm not sure why. It could be related to my own experience in politics. I ran for president of student government at St. Antony's College, Oxford, in 1989, and I was soundly defeated. At least the smarter ones voted for me—that consoled me somewhat . . . [nobody laughs]. That was a joke. In any case, I've been living abroad since then. It hit me the other day, I haven't voted in any national election for about two decades. I felt bad, once I thought about it: I've benefited from the democratic system growing up in Canada, and I haven't done anything to repay my political ancestors or to maintain the system. All the others are doing the work, even if "work" just means putting an "X" on a piece of paper every four or five years. So I honestly hope that not too many Canadians follow my example. From a scholarly point of view, however, I'm not sure my lack of commitment has hurt, and it may have helped. Perhaps I can evaluate the pros and cons of democracy—especially the cons—in a less biased way. I may also have more "emotional space," so to speak, to consider the actual and potential merits of nondemocratic forms of rule. There seems to be something less-than-rational that prevents most Westerners from being able to do so.

IR: It's not a question of being for "more" or "less" people's power. There are always constraints on people's rule, and these constraints can vary from context to context. In the United States, the decisions of elected politicians are circumscribed by a constitutional bill of rights enforced by unelected judges holding final powers of review. The idea is that values central to the liberal tradition, like the freedom of speech, should be protected and not be subject to the political trade-offs of the ordinary democratic process. In East Asia, people's participation in the political process may be constrained by values grounded in nonliberal traditions. The question of whether or not the constraints are legitimate is separate. It depends on whether the constraints are necessary to promote traditional values, the centrality of those values in the moral system, people's ongoing attachment to those values, and whether those values serve the requirements of contemporary societies. All I'm saying is that we should leave open the possibility of legitimate constraints on people's power that may be different from those characteristic of liberal societies.

Q24: You're very complacent about political dissidents who fall out of favor in authoritarian systems. There aren't any dissidents in democratic societies.

> RR: You don't have to lecture me. I'm also against the way political dissidents are treated in certain East Asian countries. In fact, I've helped colleagues and friends that got into political trouble.

> IR: If the aim is to protect people from arbitrary state power, it's the rule of law that's important, not democracy per se. In theory, it's possible to imagine a nondemocratic society that's committed to the rule of law. In practice, Hong Kong is a good example: it's a nondemocratic society, and it generally secures the rule of law. Nobody goes to jail for expressing political viewpoints in Hong Kong.

Q25: You work in China. Interesting. You must experience constraints on what you can say and write. Can we really assume that you're speaking the truth, if the truth will get you in political trouble?

> RR: It's all relative to one's experience, and to me, it's not so bad in China. My first academic job was at the National University of Singapore, and I had to submit my reading lists to the head of department. There were government spies in my classroom, and students would clam up when I mentioned local politics. China is a paradise of academic freedom compared to Singapore: even if they want to control you in China, they can't—it's so big and there are so many diverse viewpoints. Besides, there's something to be said for political constraints: if the political authorities think my work matters, then I don't have to worry about its practical relevance!

> IR: In China, there are different sorts of constraints in different spheres. Among friends, anything goes. In the classroom, it's surprisingly free, so long as one doesn't launch frontal attacks on government leaders. Newspapers are tightly controlled, but academic publications are much more critical. In my case, I'm publishing an English-language book with an American publisher, and there aren't any political constraints: the Chinese authorities rarely care about what's published in English.

Q26: Aren't you a hypocrite? You call yourself a communitarian, and you're telling East Asians to stick to their own traditions, but you've long ago abandoned your own community and ventured outside.

RR: I haven't abandoned my own community. I still go back to Canada once or twice a year, and I'm teaching hockey to my kid.

IR: In the past, "communitarianism" may have meant living one's life in a totalizing, all-consuming community. Today, however, our identities are composed of many communal attachments that pull in different directions. I don't know of any contemporary communitarian who argues that we should restrict ourselves to the good of one community. My own view is that we should be open, not closed, to the ways of life of other communities.

Q27: You're a liberal, deep in your heart, aren't you? You urge tolerance and understanding of other ways, surely that's no different from what liberals are saying.

RR: Please, let's refrain from personal insults. Liberals such as John Stuart Mill had nothing but contempt for the non-Western civilizations of "barbarians" that supposedly needed to learn liberal ways with the "help" of Western imperialists. Contemporary liberals show more tolerance in theory, but we should look at liberal practice as well. It turns out that there's a great deal of hypocrisy among defenders of liberal values. Far from showing tolerance, the way liberals seek to promote their supposedly universal values abroad has more in common with religious fundamentalism than anything else. That's why I call them liberal fundamentalists, the secular missionaries of our age. Today, of course, it's more of an American phenomenon; I wouldn't condemn the West as a whole.

IR: In that sense, perhaps. Fortunately, liberals don't have a monopoly on tolerance. Several Asian religions and philosophies also emphasize tolerance, in theory as well as historical practice. Take the case of Confucianism. Confucius famously expressed epistemological uncertainty about the world of "ghosts and spirits," which has allowed for tolerance of, if not active respect for, different metaphysical systems. Confucian tolerance may help to explain why highly diverse modes of thought and religions have coexisted in Chinese history, and also why it's not uncommon for contemporary East Asians to identify with both Confucianism and Christianity.

Q28: No reflective liberal today defends nineteenth-century missionary imperialism. Most liberals today, including Americans, recognize the value of tolerance for other communities and forms of life. If you spent more time listening rather than condemning, you'd recognize that you're just defending a form of liberal multiculturalism.

RR: Unfortunately, it's not the "reflective liberals" who are calling the shots. In any case, there's still a deep problem with liberal multiculturalism. When reflective liberals think about engaging with other cultures, they realize there may be something to learn, and they're ready to employ the resources of particular cultures to construct their own individual personal and social lives. But they don't show any preference for any particular culture, except their own (and they don't usually make it explicit). As for myself, I recognize that my attachments are limited, and that I won't treat all cultures equally. I'm attached to the Canadian community, and I've also grown attached to the Chinese community. I'm prepared to do more for the sake of my particular communities, and in cases of conflict I'll usually side with the interests of my communities. That's what multiculturalism means for me.

IR: No doubt we have a lot in common. But I think liberal multiculturalists might object to some of my arguments, such as the view that constraints on the democratic process can be beneficial for minority groups. In any case, we shouldn't worry too much about labels: let's discuss the ideas, and try to improve our starting positions through rational persuasion.

Q29: Your multicultural sympathies end abruptly at the American border, don't they?

RR: And why shouldn't they? You invaded us twice, in 1775 and 1812: fortunately we repelled the attacks both times . . . [audience gasps]. That was a joke: no hard feelings anymore, seriously. The truth of the matter, I guess, is that I cheer for the underdog. The world is a competitive place, and it's not always obvious to me why the United States should win. For example, an American newspaper recently noted that the United States is losing its dominance in science, that a greater proportion of patents are being created in Europe and East Asia. That was presented as bad news, but I read it as good news: why shouldn't scientific innovations be more widely distributed around the world? American politicians complain about manufacturing jobs going to Asian countries, but if there really are limited numbers of jobs, then I think they should go to people in poorer countries. Even liberals such as Paul Krugman can't resist flaunting their patriotic credentials: he called for blocking the sale of an oil company to a Chinese firm because he worried the United States would lose its privileged access to oil resources. And I confess, those "We're number one!" chants for American sports teams don't warm my heart. You see, I'm not sure if we're always on the same side . . . [pause]. Of course, that doesn't mean I dislike Americans personally. Some of my best friends are American. My own son, if you must know, has an American passport. He's proud of being American, no matter what I tell him.

IR: I didn't mean to give that impression. Nobody doubts the global influence of American-style values and practices—that's why it's important to understand and evaluate their effects in East Asia. Some effects may be positive overall, some negative, some mixed, it depends on the particular issue. One should keep an open mind.

Q30: When people ask you critical questions, you tend to respond with personal stories and jokes. That's not very academic.

RR: Let's be frank: academic seminars can be boring at times. I prefer discussion that's fortified with good food and fine wine. The constraints on reasonable speech are loosened somewhat, and we often learn more, as well as enjoying the process. People ask, what's an academic like you doing in the restaurant business? Well, I'm hoping to create an appropriate setting for more intimate and free-flowing discussion. So I opened a restaurant in Beijing with family and friends: it's called Purple Haze (紫苏庭), on the small lane facing Workers' Stadium, and I also store my books there (except the politically sensitive ones). I'm usually there on Friday nights, and I look forward to the debate!

IR: I think academic ideas often owe much to people's life experiences, so why not try to be reflective about it? But I do recognize that we should focus, first and foremost, on the substance of the argument. So if you'd like to pursue the discussion, kindly send me an e-mail (daniel.a.bell@gmail.com). I'll be happy to respond.

SELECTED BIBLIOGRAPHY

Ackerly, Brooke A. "Is Liberalism the Only Way toward Democracy?" *Political Theory*, vol. 33, no. 4 (August 2005).

Aikman, David. *Pacific Rim: Area of Change, Area of Opportunity.* Boston: Little, Brown, 1986.

Aleinikoff, Alexander, and Douglas Kusmeyer. *Citizenship Politics in an Age of Migration.* Washington, DC: Carnegie Endowment for International Peace, 2002.

————, eds. *Citizenship Today: Global Perspectives and Practices.* Washington, DC: Carnegie Endowment for International Peace, 2001.

Alford, William. *To Steal a Book Is an Elegant Offense: Intellectual Property Law in Chinese Civilization.* Stanford: Stanford University Press, 1995.

Alitto, Guy S. *The Last Confucian: Liang Shu-ming and the Chinese Dilemma of Modernity,* 2nd ed. Berkeley: University of California Press, 1986.

Ambrosius, Lloyd A. *Wilsonianism: Woodrow Wilson and His Legacy in American Foreign Relations.* New York: Palgrave Macmillan, 2002.

Ames, Roger T. *The Art of Rulership: A Study of Chinese Political Thought.* Albany: State University of New York Press, 1994.

Ames, Roger T., and Henry Rosemont, Jr. *The Analects of Confucius: A Philosophical Translation.* New York: Ballantine Books, 1998.

Amsden, Alice H. *Asia's Next Giant: South Korea and Late Industrialization.* New York: Oxford University Press, 1992.

Anderson, B. *Doing the Dirty Work? The Global Politics of Domestic Labour.* London: Zed Books, 2000.

Angle, Stephen C. *Human Rights and Chinese Thought: A Cross-Cultural Inquiry.* New York: Cambridge University Press, 2002.

Angle, Stephen, and Marina Svensson, eds. *The Chinese Human Rights Reader.* Armonk, NY: M. E. Sharpe, 2002.

An-Na'im, Abdullahi A. "The Cultural Mediation of Human Rights: The Al-Arqam Case in Malaysia." In *The East Asian Challenge for Human Rights.* Ed. Joanne R. Bauer and Daniel A. Bell. New York: Cambridge University Press, 1999.

————. "Toward a Cross-Cultural Approach to Defining International Standards of Human Rights: The Meaning of Cruel, Inhuman, or Degrading Treatment or Punishment." In *Human Rights in Cross-Cultural Perspectives: A Quest for Consensus.* Ed. Abdullahi A. An-Na'im. Philadelphia: University of Pennsylvania Press, 1992.

————, ed. *Human Rights in Cross-Cultural Perspectives: A Quest for Consensus.* Philadelphia: University of Pennsylvania Press, 1992.

Aoki Tamotsu. "Aspects of Globalization in Contemporary Japan." In *Many Globalizations: Cultural Diversity in the Contemporary World.* Ed. Peter L. Berger and Samuel P. Hungtington. Oxford: Oxford University Press, 2003.

Arendt, Hannah. *The Human Condition*. New York: Doubleday, 1959.

Aristotle. *The Politics*. Ed. and trans. Ernest Barker. London: Oxford University Press, 1946.

Bakan, Abigail B. and Daiva Stasiulis, eds. *Not One of the Family: Foreign Domestic Workers in Canada*. Toronto: University of Toronto Press, 1997.

Baker, Hugh D. R. *Chinese Family and Kinship*. New York: Columbia University Press, 1979.

Bartley, Robert, et al. *Democracy and Capitalism: Asian and American Perspectives*. Singapore: Institute of Southeast Asian Studies, 1993.

Bauer, Joanne R., and Daniel A. Bell, eds. *The East Asian Challenge for Human Rights*. New York: Cambridge University Press, 1999.

Bell, Daniel. "The Old War: After Ideology, Corruption," *The New Republic*, 23 and 30 August 1993.

Bell, Daniel A. "Communitarianism," *Stanford Encyclopedia of Philosophy*, 2004. http://plato.stanford.edu/entries/communitarianism/.

———. "Deliberative Democracy with Chinese Characteristics: A Comment on He Baogang's Research." In *The Search for Deliberative Democracy in China*. Ed. Ethan J. Leib and He Baogang. New York: Palgrave Macmillan, 2006.

———. "East Asian Capitalism: Towards a Normative Framework," *Global Economic Review*, vol. 30, no. 3 (2001).

———. "The East Asian Challenge to Human Rights," *Human Rights Quarterly*, vol. 18, no. 3 (August 1996).

———. *East Meets West: Human Rights and Democracy in East Asia*. Princeton: Princeton University Press, 2000.

———. "Equal Rights for Domestic Workers?" *Dissent* (Fall 2001).

———. "From Mao to Jiang: China's Transition to Communism," *Dissent* (Summer 1999).

———. "Hong Kong's Transition to Capitalism," *Dissent* (Winter 1998).

———. "Human Rights and Social Criticism in Contemporary Chinese Political Theory," *Political Theory*, vol. 32, no. 3 (June 2004).

———. "Is Republican Citizenship Appropriate for the Modern World?" In *Forms of Justice: Critical Perspectives on David Miller's Political Philosophy*. Ed. Daniel A. Bell and Avner de-Shalit. Lanham, MD: Rowman and Littlefield, 2003.

———. "The Making and Unmaking of Boundaries," in *States, Nations, and Borders: The Ethics of Making Boundaries*. Ed. Allen Buchanan and Margaret Moore. New York: Cambridge University Press, 2003.

———. "Minority Rights: On the Importance of Local Knowledge," *Dissent* (Summer 1996).

———. "Teaching in a Multicultural Context: Lessons from Singapore," *Dissent* (Spring 2000).

———. "Toward an International Human Rights (and Responsibilities) Regime: Some Obstacles." In *Autonomy and Order: A Communitarian Anthology*. Ed. Edward W. Lehman. Lanham, MD: Rowman & Littlefield, 2000.

Bell, Daniel A., et al. *Towards Illiberal Democracy in Pacific Asia*. London and New York: Macmillan/St. Antony's College and St. Martin's Press, 1995.

Bell, Daniel A., and Joseph H. Carens. "The Ethical Dilemmas of International Human Rights and Humanitarian NGOs: Reflections on a Dialogue between Practitioners and Theorists," *Human Rights Quarterly*, vol. 26, no. 2 (May 2004).

Bell, Daniel A., and Jean-Marc Coicaud, eds. *Ethics in Action: The Ethical Challenges of International Human Rights Nongovernmental Organizations*. New York: Cambridge University Press, 2006.

Bell, Daniel A., and Avner de-Shalit, eds. *Forms of Justice: Critical Perspectives on David Miller's Political Philosophy*. Lanham, MD: Rowman and Littlefield Publishers, 2003.

Bell, Daniel A., and Hahm Chaibong, eds. *Confucianism for the Modern World*. New York: Cambridge University Press, 2003.

Bell, David A. "Paris Dispatch: Class Conflict," *The New Republic Online*, 6 June 2005.

Bell, Lynda S., Andrew J. Nathan, and Ilan Peleg, eds. *Negotiating Culture and Human Rights*. New York: Columbia University Press, 2001.

Bellah, Robert, et al. *Habits of the Heart*. Berkeley: University of California Press, 1985.

Berger, Peter L., and Samuel P. Hungtington, eds. *Many Globalizations: Cultural Diversity in the Contemporary World*. Oxford: Oxford University Press, 2003.

Bertrand, Jacques. "Democratization and Religious and Nationalist Conflict in Post-Suharto Indonesia." In *Democratization and Identity: Regimes and Ethnicity in East and Southeast Asia*. Ed. Susan J. Henders. Lanham, MD: Lexington Books, 2004.

Bi Lijun, and Fred D'Agostino. "The Doctrine of Filial Piety: A Philosophical Analysis of the Concealment Case," *Journal of Chinese Philosophy*, vol. 31, no. 4 (December 2004).

Bleha, Thomas. "Down to the Wire," *Foreign Affairs* (May/June 2005).

Blinder, Alan. "Is Government Too Political?" *Foreign Affairs*, vol. 76, no. 4 (November/December 1997).

Bob, Clifford. "Merchants of Morality," *Foreign Policy* (March/April 2002).

Bodde, Derk. *Chinese Thought, Society, and Science: The Intellectual and Social Background of Science and Technology in Pre-modern China*. Honolulu: University of Hawaii Press, 1991.

Bok, Derek. *The Trouble with Government*. Cambridge: Harvard University Press, 2001.

Boyer, Robert. "The Embedded Innovation Systems of Germany and Japan: Distinctive Features and Innovations." In *The End of Diversity? Prospects for German and Japanese Capitalism*. Ed. Kozo Yamamura and Wolfgang Streeck. Ithaca: Cornell University Press, 2003.

Brooks, E. Bruce, and Taeko A. Brooks. *The Original Analects*. New York: Columbia University Press, 1998.

Brown, David, and David Martin Jones. "Democratization and the Myth of the Liberalizing Middle Classes." In *Towards Illiberal Democracy in Pacific Asia*. Ed. Daniel A. Bell et al. London and New York: Macmillan/St. Antony's College and St. Martin's Press, 1995.

Brown, Widney. "Human Rights Watch: An Overview." In *NGOs and Human Rights: Promise and Performance.* Ed. Claude E. Welch, Jr. Philadelphia: University of Pennsylvania Press, 2001.

Buchanan, Allen, and Margaret Moore, eds. *States, Nations, and Borders: The Ethics of Making Boundaries.* New York: Cambridge University Press, 2003.

Buruma, Ian. *Inventing Japan: From Empire to Economic Miracle 1853–1964.* London: Weidenfeld & Nicolson, 2003.

Button, Mark. "A Monkish Kind of Virtue? For and Against Humility," *Political Theory,* vol. 33, no. 6 (December 2005).

Cai Fang. "How the Market Economy Promotes Reform of the Household Registration System," *Social Sciences in China,* no. 4 (2003).

Callon, Scott. *Divided Sun: MITI and the Breakdown of Japanese High-Tech Industrial Policy, 1975–1993.* Stanford: Stanford University Press, 1995.

Carens, Joseph H. *Culture, Citizenship, and Community: A Contextual Exploration of Justice as Evenhandedness.* Oxford: Oxford University Press, 2000.

Carpenter, Daniel P. *The Forging of Bureaucratic Autonomy: Reputations, Networks, and Policy Innovation in Executive Agencies.* Princeton: Princeton University Press, 2001.

Carracedo, Jose Rubio. "Globalization and Differentiality in Human Rights." In *Beyond Nationalism: Sovereignty and Citizenship.* Ed. Fred Dallmayr and Jose M. Rosales. Lanham, MD: Lexington Books, 2001.

Cassidy, John. "Fleeing the Fed," *The New Yorker,* 19 February 1996.

Castles, Stephen, and Alastair Davidson. *Citizenship and Migration: Globalization and the Politics of Belonging.* Houndsmills: Macmillan, 2000.

Chan, Joseph. "A Confucian Perspective on Human Rights for Contemporary China." In *The East Asian Challenge for Human Rights.* Ed. Joanne R. Bauer and Daniel A. Bell. New York: Cambridge University Press, 1999.

———. "Giving Priority to the Worst-Off: A Confucian Perspective on Social Welfare." In *Confucianism for the Modern World.* Ed. Daniel A. Bell and Hahm Chaibong. New York: Cambridge University Press, 2003.

———. "Territorial Boundaries and Confucianism." In *Boundaries, Ownership, and Autonomy.* Ed. David Miller and Sohail H. Hashmi. Princeton: Princeton University Press, 2001.

———. "The Asian Challenge to Universal Human Rights: A Philosophical Appraisal." In *Human Rights and International Relations in the Asia Pacific.* Ed. James T. H. Tang. London: Pinter, 1995.

Chan, Joseph, and Lo Manto, eds. *Zhengzhi lilun zai Zhongguo* [Political Theory in China]. Hong Kong: Oxford University Press, 2001.

Chan Sin Yee. "The Confucian Conception of Gender in the Twenty-First Century." In *Confucianism for the Modern World.* Ed. Daniel A. Bell and Hahm Chaibong. New York: Cambridge University Press, 2003.

———. "Gender and Relationship Roles in the Analects and the Mencius." *Asian Philosophy,* vol. 10, no. 2 (Summer 2000).

Chang Bi-yu. "From Taiwanisation to De-sinification: Culture Construction in Taiwan since the 1990s," *China Perspectives,* no. 56 (November–December 2004).

Chang Maukei. "Taiwan de zhengzhi zhuanxin yu zhengzhi de 'zuqunhua' guocheng" [The Political Transformation of Taiwan and the Emergence of Politically Significant Ethnic Identity], *Jiaoshou luntan zhuankan*, no. 4 (1997).

———. "Toward an Understanding of the Sheng-chi Wen-ti in Taiwan." In *Ethnicity in Taiwan*. Ed. Chen Chung-min, Chuang Ying-chang, and Huang Shu-min. Taipei: Institute of Ethnology, Academic Sinica, 1994.

Chen, Albert H. Y. "Mediation, Litigation, and Justice: Confucian Reflections in a Modern Liberal Society." In *Confucianism for the Modern World*. Ed. Daniel A. Bell and Hahm Chaibong. New York: Cambridge University Press, 2003.

Chen Chung-min, Chuang Ying-chang, and Huang Shu-min, eds. *Ethnicity in Taiwan*. Taipei: Institute of Ethnology, Academic Sinica, 1994.

Chen Huan-Chang. *The Economic Principles of Confucius and His School*, vol. 2. New York: Columbia University Press, 1911.

Cheung, Gordon C. K. "Chinese Diaspora as a Virtual Nation: Interactive Roles between Economic and Social Capital," *Political Studies*, vol. 52 (2004).

Cheung Tak Kin and Mok Bong Ho. "How Filipina Maids Are Treated in Hong Kong—A Comparison between Chinese and Western Employers," *Social Justice Research*, vol. 2, no. 2 (1998).

China Human Rights Strategy Study Group, "Promoting Human Rights in China," November 2001.

Chin, Christine. *In Service and Servitude: Foreign Female Domestic Workers and the Malaysian "Modernity" Project*. New York: Columbia University Press, 1998.

Ching, Julia. "Confucianism and Weapons of Mass Destruction." In *Ethics and Weapons of Mass Destruction: Religious and Secular Perspectives*. Ed. Sohail H. Hashmi and Steven P. Lee. New York: Cambridge University Press, 2004.

Chow Chiu-tak and Antonio Chung-man Tsui. *A Survey of the Living and Working Conditions of Catholic Migrant Domestic Helpers in Hong Kong*. Hong Kong: Catholic Diocese of Hong Kong, 2003.

Christian, William A., Jr., and Josefa Martinez Berriel. "Edgar and Eunice: International Traffic in Care." In *Miniature etnografiche*. Ed. Henk Driessen and Huub de Jonge. Nijmegen: SUN, 2000.

Christopher, Robert C. *The Japanese Mind*. Tokyo: Charles E. Tuttle, 1983.

Chua, Amy. *World on Fire: How Exporting Free Market Democracy Breeds Ethnic Hatred and Global Instability*. New York: Doubleday, 2003.

Chua Beng Huat. "The Cost of Membership in Ascribed Community." In *Multiculturalism in Asia: Theoretical Perspectives*. Ed. Will Kymlicka and He Baogang. Oxford: Oxford University Press, 2005.

———, ed. *Communitarian Politics in Asia*. London: Routledge/Curzon, 2004.

Ci Jiwei. "Taking the Reasons for Human Rights Seriously," *Political Theory*, vol. 33, no. 2 (April 2005).

Clarke, J. J. *Oriental Enlightenment: The Encounter between Asian and Western Thought*. London and New York: RoutledgeCurzon, 1997.

Constable, Nicole. "Filipina Workers in Hong Kong Homes: Household Rules and Regulations." In *Global Woman: Nannies, Maids, and Sex Workers in the*

New Economy. Ed. Barbara Ehrenreich and Arlie Russell Hochschild. New York: Henry Holt, 2002.

———. *Maid to Order in Hong Kong: Stories of Filipina Workers.* Ithaca: Cornell University Press, 1997.

Constant, Benjamin. *Ecrits Politiques.* Ed. Marcel Gauchet. Paris: Gallimard, 1997.

Cooper, Joshua. *The Beijing Consensus: Notes on the New Physics of Chinese Power.* London: The Foreign Policy Centre, 2004.

Creel, H. G. *The Origin of Statecraft in China.* Chicago: The University of Chicago Press, 1970.

Dallmayr, Fred. "Beyond Monologue: For a Comparative Political Theory," *Perspectives on Politics,* vol. 2, no. 2 (June 2004).

Dallmayr, Fred, and Jose M. Rosales, eds. *Beyond Nationalism: Sovereignty and Citizenship.* Lanham, MD: Lexington Books, 2001.

Dalrymple, William. "India: The War over History," *The New York Review of Books,* 7 April 2005.

Danopoulos, Constantine P., Dhirendra Vajpeyi, and Amir Bar-or, eds. *Civil-Military Relations, Nation-Building, and National Identity: Comparative Perspectives.* Westport, CT: Praeger, 2004.

Dawson, Miles Menander. *The Ethics of Confucius.* New York: G. P. Putnam's Sons, 1915.

de Bary, Wm. Theodore. *Asian Values and Human Rights: A Confucian Communitarian Perspective.* Cambridge: Harvard University Press, 1998.

———. *Nobility and Civility: Asian Ideals of Leadership and the Common Good.* Cambridge: Harvard University Press, 2004.

———. "The Trouble with Confucianism," *Institute of East Asian Philosophies (Singapore) Public Lecture Series,* no. 13 (1989).

———. *Waiting for the Dawn: A Plan for the Prince.* Huang Zongxi. New York: Columbia University Press, 1993.

de Bary, Wm. Theodore, Irene Bloom, and Joseph Adler. *Sources of Chinese Tradition.* New York: Columbia University Press, 1960.

de Bary, Wm. Theodore, and Tu Wei-ming, eds. *Confucianism and Human Rights.* New York: Columbia University Press, 1998.

de-Shalit, Avner. *Power to the People: Teaching Political Philosophy in Skeptical Times.* Lanham, MD: Lexington Books, 2006.

de Vos, George, and Hiroshi Wagatsuma, eds. *Japan's Invisible Race: Caste in Culture and Personality.* Berkeley: University of California Press, 1967.

de Waal, Alex. "The Moral Solipsism of Global Ethics Inc," *London Review of Books,* 23 August 2001.

Deyo, Frederic C. *Beneath the Miracle: Labor Subordination in the New Asian Industrialism.* Berkeley: University of California Press, 1989.

DiMaggio, Paul, ed. *The Twenty-First Century Firm: Changing Economic Organization in International Perspective.* Princeton: Princeton University Press, 2001.

Dittmer, Lowell. "Chinese Leadership Succession to the Fourth Generation." In *China after Jiang.* Ed. Gang Lin and Xiaobo Hu. Washington, DC: Woodrow Wilson Center Press, 2003.

Dobson, W.A.C.H. *The Works of Mencius.* London: Oxford University Press, 1963.

Dong Xiao-Yuan. "Two-Tier Land Tenure System and Sustained Economic Growth in Post-1978 Rural China," *World Development,* vol. 24, no. 5 (1996).

Donnelly, Jack. "Human Rights and Asian Values: A Defense of 'Western' Universalism." In *The East Asian Challenge for Human Rights.* Ed. Joanne R. Bauer and Daniel A. Bell. New York: Cambridge University Press, 1999.

Doré, Jean-François. *Y en aura pas d'facile: Dix clichés du sport et leurs raçines philosophiques* [There Won't Be Any Easy Ones: Ten Sports Clichés and Their Philosophical Roots]. Montréal: Leméac, 2003.

Dore, Ronald. *Stock Market Capitalism: Welfare Capitalism, Japan and Germany versus the Anglo-Saxons.* Oxford: Oxford University Press, 2000.

Doshi, Tilak, and Peter Coclanis. "The Economic Architect: Goh Keng Swee." In *Lee's Lieutenants: Singapore's Old Guard.* Ed. Lam Peng Er and Kevin Y. L. Tan. St. Leonards, Australia: Allen & Unwin, 1999.

Dowdle, Michael W. "How a Liberal Jurist Defends the Bangkok Declaration." In *Negotiating Culture and Human Rights.* Ed. Lynda S. Bell, Andrew J. Nathan, and Ilan Peleg. New York: Columbia University Press, 2001.

———. "Preserving Indigenous Paradigms in an Age of Globalization: Pragmatic Strategies for the Development of Clinical Legal Aid in China," *Fordham Journal of International Law,* vol. 24 (2000).

Dreyer, June Teufel. *China's Forty Millions: Minority Nationalities and National Integration in the People's Republic of China.* Cambridge: Harvard University Press, 1976.

Dryzek, John S. "Deliberative Democracy in Different Places." In *The Search for Deliberative Democracy in China.* Ed. Ethan J. Leib and He Baogang. New York: Palgrave Macmillan, 2006.

Dunn, John, ed. *Democracy: The Unfinished Journey 508BC to AD1993.* Oxford: Oxford University Press, 1993.

Dworkin, Ronald. *Freedom's Law.* Cambridge: Harvard University Press, 1996.

———. "Taking Rights Seriously in Beijing," *The New York Review of Books,* vol. 49, no. 14, 26 September 2002.

Edwards, Martha L. "The Cultural Context of Deformity in the Ancient Greek World: 'Let There Be a Law That No Deformed Child Shall Be Reared,'" *The Ancient History Bulletin,* vol. 10, nos. 3–4 (1996).

Edwards, Michael. *Future Positive: International Cooperation in the 21st Century.* London: Earthscan, 1999.

Ehrenreich, Barbara, and Arlie Russell Hochschild. *Global Woman: Nannies, Maids, and Sex Workers in the New Economy.* New York: Henry Holt, 2002.

Elvin, Mark. *The Pattern of Chinese Past.* Stanford: Stanford University Press, 1973.

Eno, Robert. *The Confucian Creation of Heaven.* Albany: State University of New York Press, 1990.

Epstein, Cynthia Fuchs. "Working Moms under Attack," *Dissent* (Fall 2004).

Esping-Andersen, Gosta. "Hybrid or Unique? The Japanese Welfare State between Europe and America," *Journal of European Social Policy,* vol. 7, no. 3 (August 1997).

Esposito, John L. "Political Islam: Beyond the Green Menace," *Current History*, vol. 93, no. 579 (January 1994).

Etzioni, Amitai. *The New Golden Rule*. New York: Basic Books, 1996.

———. *The Spirit of Community: Rights, Responsibilities, and the Communitarian Agenda*. New York: Crown Publishers, 1993.

Eyal, Ben-Ari. *Changing Suburbia: A Study of Two Present-Day Localities*. London and New York: Kegan Paul International, 1991.

Fadiman, Anne. *The Spirit Catches You and You Fall Down: A Hmong Child, Her American Doctors, and the Collision of Two Cultures*. New York: Farrar, Strauss, and Giroux, 1997.

Fairbank, John K., ed. *The Chinese World Order: Traditional China's Foreign Relations*. Cambridge: Harvard University Press, 1968.

———. "Introduction: Varieties of the Chinese Military Experience." In *Chinese Way in Warfare*. Ed. Frank A. Kierman, Jr., and John K. Fairbank. Cambridge: Harvard University Press, 1974.

Fairbank, John K., and Ssu-Yu Teng. "On the Ch'ing Tributary System." In *Ch'ing Administration: Three Studies*. Ed. John K. Fairbank and Ssu-Yu Teng. Cambridge: Harvard University Press, 1960.

———, eds. *Ch'ing Administration: Three Studies*. Cambridge: Harvard University Press, 1960.

Fan Ruiping. "Confucian and Rawlsian Views of Justice: A Comparison," *Journal of Chinese Philosophy*, vol. 24 (1997).

———. "Self-Determination vs. Family-Determination: Two Incommensurable Principles of Autonomy," *Bioethics*, vol. 11, nos. 3–4 (1997).

Feinberg, Walter. *Common Schools/Uncommon Identities: National Unity and Cultural Difference*. New Haven: Yale University Press, 1998.

Ferguson, R. James. "Inclusive Strategies for Restraining Aggression—Lessons from Classical Chinese Culture," *Asian Philosophy*, vol. 8, no. 1 (March 1998), http://search.epnet.com/direct.asp?an=2752805&db=aph.

Flanagan, Caitlin. "How Serfdom Saved the Women's Movement: Dispatches from the Nanny Wars," *The Atlantic* (March 2004).

Folsom, R. H., and J. H. Minan, eds. *Law in the People's Republic of China*. Dordrecht: Kluwer Academic Publishers, 1989.

Folsom, R. H., J. H. Minan, and L. A. Otto. *Law and Politics in the People's Republic of China in a Nutshell*. St. Paul: West Publishing Co., 1992.

Freedman, Amy. *Political Participation and Ethnic Minorities: Chinese Overseas in Malaysia, Indonesia, and the United States*. New York: Routledge, 2000.

Fu Zhengyuan. *Autocratic Tradition and Chinese Politics*. Cambridge: Cambridge University Press, 1993.

Fukuyama, Francis. *Trust: The Social Virtues and the Creation of Prosperity*. New York: The Free Press, 1995.

Fung, Edmund S. K. *In Search of Chinese Democracy*. Cambridge: Cambridge University Press, 2000.

Fung Yu-Lan and Derk Bodde. *A Short History of Chinese Philosophy*. New York: Macmillan, 1961.

Galston, William A. *Liberal Purposes: Goods, Virtues, and Diversity in the Liberal State*. Cambridge: Cambridge University Press, 1991.

Gamburd, R. *The Kitchen Spoon's Handle: Transnationalism and Sri Lanka's Migrant Housemaids.* Ithaca: Cornell University Press, 2000.

Gardels, Nathan. "Interview with Lee Kuan Yew," *New Perspectives Quarterly,* vol. 9, no. 1 (Winter 1992).

Ge Jianxiong. *Putianzhixia* [The World under Heaven]. Jilin: Jilin Jiaoyu Chubanshe, 1989.

Ge Yong Guang. *Wenhua duoyuanzhuyi yu guojia zhenghe* [Cultural Pluralism and National Integration]. Taipei: Zhengzhong shuju, 1991.

General Affairs Office of the CPPCC National Committee. *The Chinese People's Political Consultative Conference.* Beijing: Foreign Languages Press, 2004.

Gilley, Bruce. *China's Democratic Future: How It Will Happen and Where It Will Lead.* New York: Columbia University Press, 2004.

Ginsburg, Tom. "Confucian Constitutionalism? The Case of Constitutional Review in Korea and Taiwan," *Law & Social Inquiry,* vol. 27, no. 2 (Fall 2002).

Gladney, Dru C. "Ethnic Identity in China: The Rising Politics of Cultural Difference." In *Democratization and Identity: Regimes and Ethnicity in East and Southeast Asia.* Ed. Susan J. Henders. Lanham, MD: Lexington Books, 2004.

Gold, Thomas B. "Identity and Symbolic Power in Taiwan," *Asian Program Special Report,* Woodrow Wilson International Center for Scholars, no. 114 (August 2003).

Golden, Mark. *Sport and Society in Ancient Greece.* Cambridge: Cambridge University Press, 1998.

Gong Gang. "Shei shi quanqiu lunli de daidao shiwei?" [Who is the Armed Guard of Global Ethics?], *Nan feng chuang* (September 2003).

Gonzalez, Joaquin L., III. *Philippine Labour Migration: Critical Dimensions of Public Policy.* Singapore: Institute of Southeast Asian Studies, 1998.

Goodman, Roger. "The 'Japanese-style Welfare State' and the Delivery of Personal Services." In *The East Asian Welfare Model: Welfare Orientalism and the State.* Ed. Roger Goodman, Gordon White, and Huck-ju Kwon. London: Routledge, 1998.

Goodman, Roger, Gordon White, and Huck-ju Kwon, eds. *The East Asian Welfare Model: Welfare Orientalism and the State.* London: Routledge, 1998.

Gordon, Neve, ed. *From the Margins of Globalization: Critical Perspectives on Human Rights.* Lanham, MD: Lexington Books, 2004.

Graff, David A. *Medieval Chinese Warfare, 300–900.* London: Routledge, 2002.

Graham, A. C. *Disputers of the Tao: Philosophical Argument in Ancient China.* La Salle, IL: Open Court, 1989.

Gu, Edward X. "Beyond the Property Rights Approach: Welfare Policy and Reform of State-Owned Enterprise in China," *Development and Change,* vol. 32 (2001).

Guiheux, Gilles. "The Revival of Family Capitalism: A Zhejiang Entrepreneur," *China Perspectives,* no. 58 (March–April 2005).

Gurr, Ted. "Communal Conflicts and Global Security," *Current History,* vol. 94, no. 592 (May 1995).

Gutmann, Amy. *Democratic Education,* revised edition. Princeton: Princeton University Press, 1999.

Hagen, Kurtis. "A Chinese Critique on Western Ways of Warfare." *Asian Philosophy*, vol. 6, no. 3 (November 1996), http://search.epnet.com/direct.asp?an=9702072810&db=aph.

Hahm Chaibong. *Confucianism, Capitalism and Democracy*. Seoul: Jontong gua Hyundai, 2002.

———. "The Family vs. the Individual: The Politics of Marriage Laws in Korea." In *Confucianism for the Modern World*. Ed. Daniel A. Bell and Hahm Chaibong, New York: Cambridge University Press, 2003.

———. "The Ironies of Confucianism," *Journal of Democracy*, vol. 15, no. 3 (July 2004).

———. *Postmodernism and Confucianism*. Seoul: Jontong gua Hyundai, 1998.

Hahm Chaibong and Paik Wooyeal. "Legalistic Confucianism and Economic Development in East Asia," *Journal of East Asian Studies*, vol. 3, no. 3 (September–December 2003).

Hahm Chaihark and Daniel A. Bell, eds. *The Politics of Affective Relations: East Asia and Beyond*. Lanham, MD: Lexington Books, 2004.

Hall, David L., and Roger T. Ames. *Thinking through Confucius*. Albany: State University of New York Press, 1987.

Hall, Edith. "Drowning by Nomes: The Greeks, Swimming, and Timotheus' Persians." In *The Birth of European Identity: The Europe-Asia Contract in Greek Thought 490–322 B.C.* Ed. H. A. Khan, Nottingham Classical Literature Studies, vol. 2. Nottingham: University of Nottingham, 1994.

Hall, Peter A., and David Soskice. "An Introduction to Varieties of Capitalism." In *Varieties of Capitalism: The Institutional Foundations of Comparative Advantage*. Ed. Peter A. Hall and David Soskice. Oxford: Oxford University Press, 2001.

———, eds. *Varieties of Capitalism: The Institutional Foundations of Comparative Advantage*. Oxford: Oxford University Press, 2001.

Hall, Rodney Bruce. "The Discursive Demolition of the Asian Development Model," *International Studies Quarterly*, vol. 47 (2003).

Hamilton, Gary. "Overseas Chinese Capitalism." In *Confucian Traditions in East Asian Modernity: Moral Education and Economic Culture in Japan and the Four Mini-Dragons*. Ed. Tu Wei-ming. Cambridge: Harvard University Press, 1996.

Han Fook Kwang, Warren Fernandez, and Sumiko Tan. *Lee Kuan Yew: The Man and His Ideas*. Singapore: Times Editions, 1998.

Hashmi, Sohail H., and Steven P. Lee, eds. *Ethics and Weapons of Mass Destruction: Religious and Secular Perspectives*. New York: Cambridge University Press, 2004.

Harrison, Lawrence E., and Samuel P. Huntington, eds. *Culture Matters: How Values Shape Human Progress*. New York: Basic Books, 2000.

Hartcher, Peter. *The Ministry: How Japan's Most Powerful Institution Endangers World Markets*. Boston: Harvard Business School Press, 1998.

Hathaway, Robert M. "The Lingering Legacy of Tiananmen," *Foreign Affairs* (September/October 2003).

Hatzfeld, Jean. *History of Ancient Greece*. New York: W. W. Norton, 1966.

He Baogang. "Confucianism versus Liberalism over Minority Rights: A Critical Response to Will Kymlicka," *The Journal of Chinese Philosophy*, vol. 31, no. 1 (March 2004).

———. "Minority Rights with Chinese Characteristics." In *Multiculturalism in Asia: Theoretical Perspectives*. Ed. Will Kymlicka and He Baogang. Oxford: Oxford University Press, 2005.

———. "Participation and Deliberative Institutions in China." In *The Search for Deliberative Democracy in China*. Ed. Ethan J. Leib and He Baogang. New York: Palgrave Macmillan, 2006.

Helgesen, Geir. *Democracy and Authority in Korea: The Cultural Dimension in Korean Politics*. Richmond, England: Curzon, 1988.

Henders, Susan J. ed. *Democratization and Identity: Regimes and Ethnicity in East and Southeast Asia*. Lanham, MD: Lexington Books, 2004.

Henderson, Jeffrey, and Richard P. Appelbaum. "Situating the State in the East Asian Development Process." In *States and Development in the Asian Pacific Rim*. Ed. Appelbaum and Henderson. Newbury Park: Sage Publications, 1992.

———, eds. *States and Development in the Asian Pacific Rim*. Newbury Park: Sage Publications, 1992.

Heyzer, Noeleen, Geertie Lycklamaa Nijehort, Nedra Weerakoon, eds. *The Trade in Domestic Workers*. Kuala Lumpur: Asian and Pacific Development Center, 1994.

Heyzer, Noeleen, and Vivienne Wee. "Domestic Workers in Transient Overseas Employment: Who Benefits, Who Profits." In *The Trade in Domestic Workers*. Ed. Noeleen Heyzer, Geertie Lycklamaa Nijehort, and Nedra Weerakoon. Kuala Lumpur: Asian and Pacific Development Center, 1994.

Ho, Lusina. "Traditional Confucian Values and Western Legal Frameworks: The Law of Succession." In *Confucianism for the Modern World*. Ed. Daniel A. Bell and Hahm Chaibong. New York: Cambridge University Press, 2003.

Holliday, Ian. "Productivist Welfare Capitalism: Social Policy in East Asia," *Political Studies*, vol. 48, no. 4 (September 2000).

Honig, Emily. *Creating Chinese Ethnicity: Subei People in Shanghai, 1850–1980*. New Haven: Yale University Press, 1992.

Hornblower, Simon. "Creation and Development of Democratic Institutions in Ancient Greece." In *Democracy: The Unfinished Journey 508 BC to AD 1993*. Ed. John Dunn. Oxford: Oxford University Press, 1993.

Hsu Cho-yun. "Applying Confucian Ethics in International Relations," *Ethics and International Affairs*, vol. 5 (1991).

Hsu, Immanuel C. Y. *China's Entrance into the Family of Nations*. Cambridge: Harvard University Press, 1960.

Huang, Philip C. C. *Civil Justice in China: Representation and Practice in the Qing*. Stanford: Stanford University Press, 1976.

Hui, Victoria Tin-Bor. "The Emergence and Demise of Nascent Constitutional Rights: Comparing Ancient China and Early Modern Europe," *The Journal of Political Philosophy*, vol. 9, no. 4 (2001).

Hulme, David, and Michael Edwards. "Too Close to the Powerful, Too Far from the Powerless." In *NGOs, States and Donors: Too Close for Comfort?* Ed. David Hulme and Michael Edwards. Houndsmills: Macmillan, 1997.

———, eds. *NGOs, States and Donors: Too Close for Comfort?* Houndsmills: Macmillan, 1997.

Hung, William S. H. *Outlines of Modern Chinese Law*. Shanghai: Kelly and Walsh, 1934.

Huntington, Samuel P. "American Democracy in Relation to Asia," in *Democracy and Capitalism: Asian and American Perspectives*. Ed. Robert Bartley et al. Singapore: Institute of Southeast Asian Studies, 1993.

———. *The Clash of Civilizations and the Remaking of World Order*. New York: Simon & Schuster, 1996.

———. *Who Are We?: The Challenges to America's Identity*. New York: Simon & Schuster, 2004.

Huters, Theodore, R. Bin Wong, and Pauline Yu, eds. *Culture & State in Chinese History*. Stanford: Stanford University Press, 1997.

Hwang Kwang-Kuo. "The Deep Structure of Confucianism: A Social Psychological Approach," *Asian Philosophy*, vol. 11, no. 3 (2001).

Inoue Tatsuo. "Liberal Democracy and Asian Orientalism." In *The East Asian Challenge for Human Rights*. Ed. Joanne R. Bauer and Daniel A. Bell. New York: Cambridge University Press, 1999.

———. "Predicament of Communality: Lessons from Japan." In *Communitarian Politics in Asia*. Ed. Chua Beng-Huat. London: Routledge/Curzon, 2004.

Ivanhoe, Philip J. " 'Heaven's Mandate' and the Concept of War in Early Confucianism." In *Ethics and Weapons of Mass Destruction: Religious and Secular Perspectives*. Ed. Sohail H. Hashmi and Steven P. Lee. New York: Cambridge University Press, 2004.

Ivanhoe, Philip J., and Bryan W. Van Norden. *Readings in Classical Chinese Philosophy*. New York: Seven Bridges Press, 2001.

Jacobsen, Michael and Ole Bruun, eds. *Human Rights and Asian Values: Contesting National Identities and Cultural Representations in Asia*. Richmond, Surrey: Curzon Press, 2000.

Jarde, A. *The Formation of The Greek People*. London: Routledge, 1996.

Jeong Kap-Young, and Yeon-ho Lee. "Convergence or Divergence? The South Korean State after the Asian Financial Crisis," *Global Economic Review*, vol. 30, no. 3 (2001).

Jiang Qing. *Shengming xinyang yu wangdao zhengzhi: Rujia wenhua de xiandai jiazhi* [Life, Belief, and the Kingly Way of Politics: Cultural Confucianism's Contemporary Value]. Taibei: Yang zheng tang wenhua shiye gufen youxian gongsi, 2004.

———. *Zhengzhi Rujia: Dangdai Rujia de zhuanxiang, tezhi yu fazhan* [Political Confucianism: Contemporary Confucianism's Change, Special Quality, and Development]. Beijing: San lian shu dian, 2003.

Johnston, Alasdair Ian. *Cultural Realism: Strategic Culture and Grand Strategy in Chinese History*. Princeton: Princeton University Press, 1995.

Jomo, K. S. "Rethinking the Role of Government Policy in Southeast Asia." In *Rethinking the Asian Miracle*. Ed. Joseph E. Stiglitz and Shahid Yusuf. Oxford: Oxford University Press, 2001.

Jones, William C. "Chinese Law and Liberty." In *Realms of Freedom in Modern China*. Ed. William C. Kirby. Stanford: Stanford University Press, 2004.

Joppke, Christian. "The Evolution of Alien Rights in the United States, Germany, and the European Union." In *Citizenship Today: Global Perspectives and Practices*. Ed. T. Alexander Aleinikoff and Douglas Klusmeyer. Washington, DC: Carnegie Endowment for International Peace, 2001.

Ju Song Hwan. "East Asian Economic Development and Confucian Culture," *North East Asian Economic Review*, vol. 11, no. 1 (1999).

———. "The Economic Development Theory of East Asia and Confucian Market Economy Model," *Comparative Economics*, vol. 8 (2000).

Judt, Tony. "Europe vs. America," *The New York Review of Books*, 10 February 2005.

Kaplan, Robert D. *Warrior Politics: Why Leadership Demands a Pagan Ethos*. New York: Vintage Books, 2003.

Kausikan, Bilahari. "Asia's Different Standard," *Foreign Policy*, vol. 92 (1993).

Khan, H. A. ed. *The Birth of European Identity: The Europe-Asia Contract in Greek Thought 490–322 B.C.* Nottingham Classical Literature Studies, vol. 2. Nottingham: University of Nottingham, 1994.

Kierman, Frank A., Jr. "Phases and Modes of Combat in Early China." In *Chinese Way of Warfare*. Ed. Frank A. Kierman, Jr., and John K. Fairbank. Cambridge: Harvard University Press, 1974.

Kierman, Frank A., Jr., and John K. Fairbank, eds. *Chinese Way in Warfare*. Cambridge: Harvard University Press, 1974.

Kim Dae Jung. "Is Culture Destiny?" *Foreign Affairs* (November/December 1994).

Kim Dongkyu. *The World History of Physical Education*. Kyungsan: Young Nam University Press, 1999.

Kirby, William C. ed. *Realms of Freedom in Modern China*. Stanford: Stanford University Press, 2004.

Kirk, Donald. *Looted: The Philippines after the Bases*. New York: St. Martin's Press, 1998.

Kloter, Henning. "Language Policy in the KMT and DPP eras," *China Perspectives*, no. 56 (November–December 2004).

Knoblock, John, trans. *Xunzi: A Translation and Study of the Complete Works*. Stanford: Stanford University Press, 1990.

Korey, William. *NGOs and the Universal Declaration of Human Rights: "A Curious Grapevine."* New York: Palgrave, 1998.

Kristianasen, Wendy. "Débats entre femmes en terres d'islam," *Le Monde Diplomatique* (April 2004).

Kwon Huck-ju. "Democracy and the Politics of Social Welfare: A Comparative Analysis of Welfare Systems in East Asia." In *The East Asian Welfare Model: Welfare Orientalism and the State*. Ed. Roger Goodman, Gordon White, and Huck-ju Kwon. London: Routledge, 1998.

Kymlicka, Will. *Contemporary Political Philosophy: An Introduction*. 2nd ed. Oxford: Oxford University Press, 2002.

———. "The Future of the Nation-State," *Fifth Kobe Lecture* (December 1998).

———. "Models of Multicultural Citizenship: Comparing Asia and the West." In *Challenging Citizenship: Group Membership and Cultural Identity in a Global Age*. Ed. Sor-hoon Tan. Hampshire, England: Ashgate, 2005.

———. *Multicultural Citizenship*. Oxford: Clarendon Press, 1995.

———, ed. *The Rights of Minority Cultures*. Oxford: Oxford University Press, 1995.

Kymlicka, Will, and He Baogang, eds. *Multiculturalism in Asia: Theoretical Perspectives*. Oxford: Oxford University Press, 2005.

Lam Peng Er and Kevin Y. L. Tan, eds. *Lee's Lieutenants: Singapore's Old Guard*. St. Leonards, Australia: Allen & Unwin, 1999.

Langlois, Anthony J. *The Politics of Justice and Human Rights: Southeast Asia and Universalist Theory*. Cambridge: Cambridge University Press, 2001.

Lau, D. C., trans. *Mencius*. Hong Kong: The Chinese University Press, 1984.

Law, Lisa. "Sites of Transnational Activism: Filipino Non-government Organizations in Hong Kong." In *Gender Politics in the Asian-Region*. Ed. Brenda S. A. Yeoh, Peggy Teo, and Shirlena Huang. London: Routledge, 2002.

Lee, Desmond, trans. *The Republic*. Plato. 2nd ed. London: Penguin Books, 1987.

Lee Kuan Yew. *The Singapore Story*. Singapore: Prentice Hall, 1994.

Lee Seok-Choon. "Social Capital in Korea: The Affective Linkage Group," *Korea Journal*, vol. 41, no. 3 (Autumn 2001).

Lee Seok-Choon, Chang Mi-Hye, and Kim Tae-Eun. "Affective Networks and Modernity: The Case of Korea." In *Confucianism for the Modern World*. Ed. Daniel A. Bell and Hahm Chaibong. New York: Cambridge University Press, 2003.

Lee, Theresa Man Ling, "Intercultural Teaching in Higher Education," *Intercultural Education*, vol. 16, no. 3 (August 2005).

Lehman, Edward W., ed. *Autonomy and Order: A Communitarian Anthology*. Lanham, MD: Rowman & Littlefield, 2000.

Leib, Ethan J. "The Chinese Communist Party and Deliberative Democracy," *Journal of Public Deliberation*, vol. 1, no. 1 (2005), http://services.bepress.com/jpd/vol1/iss1/art1.

Lewis, Mark Edward. *Sanctioned Violence in Early China*. Albany: State University of New York, 1990.

———. "Warring States Political History." In *The Cambridge History of Ancient China: From the Origins of Civilization to 221 B.C.* Ed. Michael Loewe and Edward L. Shaughnessy. Cambridge: Cambridge University Press, 1999.

Leys, Simon, trans. *The Analects of Confucius*. New York: Norton, 1997.

Li Ming Han. "Cong Ruxue de guandian kan heping wenti" [Looking at the Issue of Peace from a Confucian Perspective]. In *Dangdai Ruxue fazhan zhi xin qiji* [Opportunities for the Development of Contemporary Confucianism]. Ed. Liu An Wu. Taipei: Wenjin chubanshe, 1997.

Liang Shuming, *Zhongguo wenhua yaoyi* [Essentials of Chinese Culture]. Hong Kong: San lian shu dian, 1987.

Liang Wei Xian. *Mengzi yanjiu* [Research on Mencius]. Taipei: Wenjin chuban-she, 1993.

Lie, John. "The Politics of Recognition in Contemporary Japan." In *Democratization and Identity: Regimes and Ethnicity in East and Southeast Asia*. Ed. Susan J. Henders. Lanham, MD: Lexington Books, 2004.

Lin Gang and Xiaobo Hu, eds. *China after Jiang*. Washington, DC: Woodrow Wilson Center Press, 2003.

Liu An Wu, ed. *Dangdai Ruxue fazhan zhi xinqiji* [Opportunities for the Development of Contemporary Confucianism]. Taipei: Wenjin chubanshe, 1997.

Liu Qingping. "Filiality versus Sociality and Individuality: On Confucianism as 'Consanguinitism,' " *Philosophy East and West*, vol. 53, no. 2 (April 2003).

———. "Is Mencius' Doctrine of 'Extending Affection' Tenable?", *Asian Philosophy*, vol. 14, no. 1 (March 2004).

Liu Shu-hsien. *Understanding Confucian Philosophy*. Westport, CT: Greenwood Press, 1988.

Lloyd, G.E.R. *Magic, Reason and Experience: Studies in the Origin and Development of Greek Science*. London: Gerald Duckworth, 1999.

Lodge, George C., and Ezra F. Vogel, eds. *Ideology and National Competitiveness: An Analysis of Nine Countries*. Boston: Harvard Business School Press, 1987.

Loewe, Michael, and Edward L. Shaughnessy, eds. *The Cambridge History of Ancient China: From the Origins of Civilization to 221 B.C.* Cambridge: Cambridge University Press, 1999.

Loveband, Anne. "Positioning the Product: Indonesian Migrant Women Workers in Contemporary Taiwan," *Working Papers Series*, no. 43. City University of Hong Kong, April 2003, http://www.cityu.edu.hk/searc/WP43_03_Loveband.pdf.

Macedo, Stephen. *Diversity and Distrust: Civic Education in a Multicultural Democracy*. Cambridge: Harvard University Press, 2000.

MacIntyre, Alasdair. "Questions for Confucians: Reflections on the Essays in Comparative Study of Self, Autonomy, and Community." In *Confucian Ethics: A Comparative Study of Self, Autonomy, and Community*. Ed. Kwong-loi Shun and David Wong. New York: Cambridge University Press, 2004.

———. *Whose Justice? Which Rationality?* London: Duckworth, 1988.

Mackerras, Colin. *China's Minorities: Integration and Modernization in the Twentieth-Century*. Hong Kong: Oxford University Press, 1994.

MacLennan, Hugh. *Two Solitudes*. New York: Duell, Sloan and Pearce, 1945.

Mandelbaum, Michael. *The Meaning of Sports: Why Americans Watch Baseball, Football, and Basketball and What They See When They Do*. New York: Public Affairs, 2004.

Martens, Kerstin. "An Appraisal of Amnesty's International's Work at the United Nations: Established Areas of Activities and Shifting Priorities since the 1990s," *Human Rights Quarterly*, vol. 26, no. 4 (November 2004).

Masuyama, Seiichi, and Donna Vanderbrink. "Industrial Restructuring in East Asian Economies for the Twenty-First Century." In *Industrial Restructuring in East Asia: Towards the 21st Century*. Ed. Seiichi Masuyama, Donna Vanderbrink, and Chia Siow Yue. Tokyo: Nomura Research Institute; Singapore: Institute for Southeast Asian Studies, 2001.

Masuyama, Seiichi, Donna Vanderbrink, and Chia Siow Yue, eds. *Industrial Restructuring in East Asia: Towards the 21st Century*. Tokyo: Nomura Research Institute; Singapore: Institute for Southeast Asian Studies, 2001.

McDermott, Joseph P. "Charting Blank Space and Disputed Regions: The Problems of Sung Land Tenure," *Journal of Asian Studies*, vol. 44, no. 1 (November 1984).

McLauchlan, Alastair. "Introduction." In Suchiro Kitaguchi, *An Introduction to the Buraku Issue: Questions and Answers*. Trans. Alastair McLauchlan. Richmond, Surrey: Japan Library, 1993.

Mechikoff, Robert A., and Steven G. A. Estes. *History and Philosophy of Sport and Physical Education*, 3rd ed. New York: McGraw-Hill, 2002.

Miller, David. *Citizenship and National Identity*. Cambridge: Polity Press, 2000.

Miller, Stephen G. *Ancient Greek Olympics*. New Haven: Yale University Press, 2004.

Millet, Paul. "The Economy." In *Classical Greece*. Ed. Robin Osborne. Oxford: Oxford University Press, 2000.

Milly, Deborah J. "The Rights of Foreign Migrant Workers in Asia: Contrasting Bases for Expanded Protections." In *Human Rights and Asian Values: Contesting National Identities and Cultural Representations in Asia*. Ed. Michael Jacobsen and Ole Bruun. Richmond, Surrey: Curzon Press, 2000.

Miners, Norman. *The Government and Politics of Hong Kong*, 5th ed. Hong Kong: Oxford University Press, 1995.

Ming Yongquan. "Youmeiyou zhengyi de zhanzheng? Yilun Rujia (wang ba zhi bian)" [Are There Just Wars? A Confucian Debate on True Kings and Hegemons], http://www.arts.cuhk.hk/~hkshp.

Mo Jongryn. "The Challenge of Accountability: Implications of the Censorate." In *Confucianism for the Modern World*. Ed. Daniel A. Bell and Hahm Chaibong. New York: Cambridge University Press, 2003.

Momsen, Janet Henshall. "Maid on the Move." In *Gender, Migration and Domestic Service*. Ed. Janet Henshall Momsen. London: Routledge, 1999.

———, ed. *Gender, Migration and Domestic Service*. London: Routledge, 1999.

Moody, Peter R. "The Legalism of Han Fei-tzu and Its Affinities with Modern Political Thought," *International Philosophical Quarterly*, vol. 19, no. 3 (September 1979).

Morishima, Michio. *Why Has Japan Succeeded? Western Technology and the Japanese Ethos*. Cambridge: Cambridge University Press, 1982.

Nathan, Andrew. "China's Constitutionalist Option," *Journal of Democracy*, vol. 7, no. 4 (October 1996).

———. *Chinese Democracy*. London: I. B. Tauris, 1986.

———. "Chinese Democracy: The Lesson of Failure," *Journal of Contemporary China*, no. 4 (1993).

Neher, Clark, and Ross Marlay. *Democracy and Development in Southeast Asia*. Boulder: Westview Press, 1995.

Nevinson, D., ed. *Confucianism in Action*. California: Stanford University Press, 1960.

Newberg, Paula, ed. *The Politics of Human Rights.*. New York: New York University Press, 1980.

Ni Lexiong. "Zhongguo gudai junshi wenhua guannian dui shijie heping de yiyi" [The Implications of Ancient China's Military Cultural Conceptions for World Peace], *Junshi lishi yanjiu* [Military History Research], vol. 2 (2001). http://www.meet-greatwall.org/gwjs/wen/jswhgn.htm.

Nisbett, Richard E. *The Geography of Thought: How Asians and Westerners Think Differently . . . and Why.* New York: The Free Press, 2003.

Nuyen, A. T. "Chinese Philosophy and Western Capitalism," *Asian Philosophy*, vol. 8, no. 1 (March 1999).

———. "Confucianism and the Idea of Equality," *Asian Philosophy*, vol. 11, no. 2 (2001).

O'Dwyer, Shaun. "Democracy and Confucian Values," *Philosophy East and West*, vol. 53, no. 1 (January 2003).

Oi, Jean C., and Andrew G. Walder, eds. *Property Rights and Economic Reform in China.* Stanford: Stanford University Press, 1999.

Onuma Yasuaki. "In Quest of Intercivilizational Human Rights: 'Universal vs. Relative' Human Rights Viewed from an Asian Perspective," Centre for Asian Pacific Affairs, The Asia Foundation, Occasional Paper no. 2 (1996).

———. "Toward an Intercivilizational Approach to Human Rights." In *The East Asian Challenge for Human Rights.* Ed. Joanne R. Bauer and Daniel A. Bell. New York: Cambridge University Press, 1999.

Osborne, Robin, ed. *Classical Greece.* Oxford: Oxford University Press, 2000.

Othman, Norani. "Grounding Human Rights Arguments in Non-Western Culture: *Shari'a* and the Citizenship Rights of Women in a Modern Islamic State." In *The East Asian Challenge for Human Rights.* Ed. Joanne R. Bauer and Daniel A. Bell. New York: Cambridge University Press, 1999.

Parrenas, Rhacel Salazar. "Mothering from a Distance: Emotions, Gender, and Inter-generational Relations in Filipino Transnational Families," *Feminist Studies*, vol. 27, no. 2 (Summer 2001).

Peerenboom, Randall. "Assessing Human Rights in China: Why the Double Standard?," *Cornell International Law Journal*, vol. 38, no. 1 (February 2004)

———. *China Modernizes: Threat to the West or Model to the Rest?* Oxford: Oxford University Press, forthcoming.

———. "Out of the Pan and into the Fire: Well-Intentioned but Misguided Recommendations to Eliminate All Forms of Administrative Detention in China," *Northwestern University Law Review*, vol. 98, no. 3 (2004).

———. "Show Me the Money—The Dominance of Wealth in Determining Rights Performance in Asia," *Duke International Law Journal*, vol. 15, no. 1 (2005).

Pempel, T. J. "Of Dragons and Development," *Journal of Public Policy*, vol. 12, no. 1 (1992).

Pe-Pua, Rogelia. "Wife, Mother, and Maid: The Triple Role of Filipino Domestic Workers in Spain and Italy." In *Wife or Worker? Asian Women and Migration.* Ed. Nicola Piper and Mina Roces. Lanham, MD: Rowman & Littlefield, 2003.

Perkins, Dwight H. "Law, Family Ties, and the East Asian Way of Doing Business." In *Culture Matters: How Values Shape Human Progress.* Ed. Lawrence E. Harrison and Samuel P. Huntington. New York: Basic Books, 2000.

Pettit, Philip. *Republicanism: A Theory of Freedom and Government*. Oxford: Clarendon Press, 1997.

Pinches, Michael. "Migrant Workers and the Reconstruction of Class Relations in East Asia." In *East Asian Capitalism: Conflicts, Growth and Crisis*. Ed. Luigi Tomba. Milano: Fondazione Giangiacomo Feltrinelli Milano, 2002.

Pines, Yuri. "The One That Pervades the All' in Ancient Chinese Political Thought: The Origins of the 'Great Unity' Paradigm," *T'oung Pao*, vol. 86 (2000).

Piper, Nicola, and R. Irendale. *Identification of the Obstacles to the Signing and Ratification of the UN Convention on the Protection of the Rights of All Migrant Workers 1990—The Asia Pacific Perspective*. UNESCO: Paris, 2003.

Piper, Nicola, and Mina Roces, eds. *Wife or Worker? Asian Women and Migration*. Lanham, MD: Rowman & Littlefield, 2003.

Pogge, Thomas, ed. *Global Justice*. Oxford: Blackwell, 2001.

Polidano, Charles. "Don't Discard State Autonomy: Revisiting the East Asian Experience of Development," *Political Studies*, vol. 49 (2001).

Pratt, Geraldine. "Is This Canada? Domestic Workers' Experiences in Vancouver, BC." In *Gender, Migration and Domestic Service*. Ed. Janet Henshall Momsen. London: Routledge, 1999.

Presser, Harriet B. *Working in a 24/7 Economy: Challenges for American Families*. New York: Russell Sage, 2003.

Pye, Lucian W. *Asian Power and Politics: The Cultural Dimensions of Authority*. Cambridge: Belknap Press, 1985.

Quah, Jon. "Government Policies and Nation Building." In *In Search of Singapore's National Values*. Ed. Jon Quah. Singapore: Institute of Policy Studies, 1990.

Quero, Yann. *Le Procès de l'Homme Blanc*. La Courneuve: Editions Arkuiris, 2005.

Ramesh, M. "Globalization and Social Security Expansion in East Asia." In *States in the Global Economy: Bringing Domestic Institutions Back in*. Ed. Linda Weiss. New York: Cambridge University Press, 2003.

———. *Social Policy in East and Southeast Asia: Education, Health, Housing and Income Maintenance*. London and New York: Routledge/Curzon, 2004.

Ramesh, M., and Mukul G. Asher. *Welfare Capitalism in Southeast Asia: Social Security, Health and Education Policies*. Houndsmills: Macmillan Press, 2000.

Ramesh, M., and Ian Holliday. "The Health Care Miracle in East and Southeast Asia: Activist State Provision in Hong Kong, Malaysia and Singapore," *Journal of Social Policy*, vol. 30, no. 4 (2001).

Rangarajan, L. N., ed. and trans. *Kautilya: Arthasastra*. New Delhi: Penguin Books, 1987.

Rappa Antonio L., and Sor-hoon Tan. "Political Implications of Confucian Familism," *Asian Philosophy*, vol. 13, nos. 2/3 (July 2003).

Rawls, John. *Lectures on the History of Moral Philosophy*. Cambridge: Harvard University Press, 2000.

———. *A Theory of Justice*. Cambridge, Mass.: Oxford University Press, 1971.

Reich, Rob. *Bridging Liberalism and Multiculturalism in Modern Education*. Chicago: Chicago University Press, 2002.

Rieger, Elmar, and Stephan Leibfried. *Limits to Globalization: Welfare State and the World Economy.* Cambridge: Polity Press, 2003.

Rodriguez, Robyn M. "Migrant Heroes: Nationalism, Citizenship and the Politics of Filipino Migrant Labor," *Citizenship Studies,* vol. 6, no. 3 (September 2002).

Rosenthal, Franz, trans. *The Muqaddimah: An Introduction to History, Vol. 1.* Ibn Khaldun. London: Routledge & Kegan Paul, 1958.

Roth, Kenneth. "Response to Leonard S. Rubenstein," *Human Rights Quarterly,* vol. 26, no. 4 (November 2004).

Rubenstein, Leonard S. "How International Human Rights Organizations Can Advance Economic, Social, and Cultural Rights: A Response to Kenneth Roth," *Human Rights Quarterly,* vol. 26, no. 4 (November 2004).

Ruskola, Teema. "Conceptualizing Corporations and Kinship: Comparative Law and Development Theory in Comparative Perspective," *Stanford Law Review* (July 2000).

Ryan, Alan, ed. *Utilitarianism and Other Essays. John Stuart Mill and Jeremy Bentham.* London: Penguin Books, 1987.

Ryden, Edmund. *Just War and Pacifism: Chinese and Christian Perspectives in Dialogue.* Taipei: Taipei Ricci Institute, 2001.

Sakhrani, Neetu. "A Relationship Denied: Foreign Domestic Helpers and Human Rights in Hong Kong," *Civic Exchange,* Hong Kong, 2002.

Sawyer, Ralph D., ed. and trans. *The Seven Military Classics of Ancient China.* Boulder: Westview Press, 1993.

Scanlon, Thomas F. *Eros & Greek Athletics.* Oxford: Oxford University Press, 2002.

Schrecker, John E. *The Chinese Revolution in Historical Perspective.* New York: Greenwood Press, 1991.

———. "Filial Piety as a Basis for Human Rights in Confucius and Mencius," *Journal of Chinese Philosophy,* vol. 24 (1997).

Schurmann, H. F. "Traditional Property Concepts in China," *Far Eastern Quarterly,* vol. 4 (1956).

Schwartz, Benjamin. "The Chinese Perception of Order, Past and Present." In *The Chinese World Order: Traditional China's Foreign Relations.* Ed. John Fairbank. Cambridge: Harvard University Press, 1968.

———. "Some Polarities in Confucian Thought." In *Confucianism in Action.* Ed. D. Nevinson. Stanford: Stanford University Press, 1960.

Schwarz, Louis B. "The Inheritance Law of the People's Republic of China." In *Law in the People's Republic of China.* Ed. R. H. Folsom and J. H. Minan. Dordrecht: Kluwer Academic Publishers, 1989.

Scott, Jeffrey T. "Evaluating Development-Oriented NGOs." In *NGOs and Human Rights: Promise and Performance.* Ed. Claude E. Welch, Jr. Philadelphia: University of Pennsylvania Press, 2001.

Se Teruhisa, and Rie Karatsu. "A Conception of Human Rights Based on Japanese Culture: Promoting Cross-Cultural Debates," *Journal of Human Rights,* vol. 3, no. 3 (September 2004).

Sen, Amartya. "Human Rights and Economic Achievement." In *The East Asian Challenge for Human Rights.* Ed. Joanne R. Bauer and Daniel A. Bell. New York: Cambridge University Press, 1999.

Shi Yuankang. "Tianming yu zhengdangxing" [The Mandate of Heaven and Political Legitimacy]. In *Zhengzhi lilun zai Zhongguo* [Political Theory in China]. Ed. Joseph Chan and Lo Manto. Hong Kong: Oxford University Press, 2001.

Shichor, Yitzhak. "Military-Civilian Integration in China: Legacy and Policy." In *Civil-Military Relations, Nation-Building, and National Identity: Comparative Perspectives*. Ed. Constantine P. Danopoulos, Dhirendra Vajpeyi, and Amir Bar-or. Westport, CT: Praeger, 2004.

Shils, Edward. "Reflections on Civil Society and Civility in the Chinese Intellectual Tradition." In *Confucian Traditions in East Asian Modernity*. Ed. Tu Weiming. Cambridge: Harvard University Press, 1996.

Shue, Vivienne. "China: Transition Postponed?" *Problems of Communism*, vol. 41, nos. 1–2. (January–April 1992).

Shun Kwong-loi and David Wong, eds. *Confucian Ethics: A Comparative Study of Self, Autonomy, and Community*. New York: Cambridge University Press, 2004.

Siddiqui, T. *Transcending Boundaries—Labour Migration of Women from Bangladesh*. Dhaka: The University Press Limited, 2001.

Snyder, Jack. *From Voting to Violence: Democratization and Nationalist Conflict*. New York: W. W. Norton, 2000.

Solinger, Dorothy J. "Human Rights Issues in China's Internal Migration: Insights from Comparisons with Germany and Japan." In *The East Asian Challenge for Human Rights*. Ed. Joanne R. Bauer and Daniel A. Bell. New York: Cambridge University Press, 1999.

Soysal, Yasemin Nuhoglu. *Limits and Citizenship: Migrants and Postnational Membership in Europe*. Chicago: University of Chicago Press, 1994.

Spence, Jonathan D. *The Search for Modern China*. London: Hutchinson, 1990.

Stasiulis, Daiva K., and Abigail B. Bakan. *Negotiating Citizenship: Migrant Women in Canada and the Global System*. Houndsmills: Palgrave Macmillan, 2003.

Stiglitz, Joseph E. "From Miracle to Crisis to Recovery: Lessons from Four Decades of East Asian Experience." In *Rethinking the East Asian Miracle*. Ed. Joseph E. Stiglitz and Shahid Yusuf. Oxford: Oxford University Press, 2001.

———. *Globalization and Its Discontents*. New York: Norton, 2003.

Stiglitz, Joseph E., and Shahid Yusuf, eds. *Rethinking the Asian Miracle*. Oxford: Oxford University Press, 2001.

Streeck, Wolfgang, and Kozo Yamamura. "Introduction: Convergence or Diversity? Stability and Change in German and Japanese Capitalism." In *The End of Diversity? Prospects for German and Japanese Capitalism*. Ed. Kozo Yamamura and Wolfgang Streeck. Ithaca: Cornell University Press, 2003.

Strong, Tracy B. *Friedrich Nietzsche and the Politics of Transfiguration*, expanded ed. Berkeley: University of California Press, 1988.

Sullivan, Michael. *The Meeting of Eastern and Western Art*. Berkeley: University of California Press, 1997.

Svensson, Marina. *Debating Human Rights in China: A Conceptual and Political History*. Lanham, MD: Rowman and Littlefield, 2002.

Tam, Vicky C. W. "Foreign Domestic Helpers in Hong Kong and Their Role in Childcare Provision." In *Gender, Migration and Domestic Service*. Ed. Janet Henshall Momsen. London: Routledge, 1999.

Tan, Eugene K. B. "Re-engaging Chineseness: Political, Economic and Cultural Imperatives of Nation-Building in Singapore," *The China Quarterly*, no. 175 (September 2003).

Tan, Kevin. "Economic Development, Legal Reform, and Rights in Singapore and Taiwan." In *The East Asian Challenge for Human Rights*. Ed. Joanne R. Bauer and Daniel A. Bell. New York: Cambridge University Press, 1999.

Tan Shen. "Rural Workforce Migration: A Summary of Some Studies," *Social Sciences in China* (Winter 2003).

Tan Sor-hoon. *Confucian Democracy: A Deweyean Construction*. Albany: State University of New York Press, 2003.

———, ed. *Challenging Citizenship: Group Membership and Cultural Identity in a Global Age*. Hampshire, England: Ashgate, 2005.

Tang, James T. H., ed. *Human Rights and International Relations in the Asia Pacific*. London: Pinter, 1995.

Tat Yan Kong. "Neo-liberalization and Incorporation in Advanced Newly Industrialized Countries: A View from South Korea," *Political Studies*, vol. 52, no. 1 (March 2004).

Taubman, William. *Khrushchev: The Man and His Era*. New York: W. W. Norton, 2003.

Taylor, Charles. "Conditions of an Unforced Consensus on Human Rights." In *The East Asian Challenge for Human Rights*. Ed. Joanne R. Bauer and Daniel A. Bell. New York: Cambridge University Press, 1999.

———. *Sources of the Self: The Making of the Modern Identity*. Cambridge: Harvard University Press, 1989.

Tomasevki, Katarina. "Unasked Questions about Economic, Social, and Cultural Rights from the Experience of the Special Rapporteur on the Right of Education(1998–2004): A Response to Kenneth Roth, Leonard S. Rubenstein, and Mary Robinson," *Human Rights Quarterly*, vol. 27, no. 2 (May 2005).

Tomba, Luigi, ed. *East Asian Capitalism: Conflicts, Growth and Crisis*. Milano: Fondazione Giangiacomo Feltrinelli, 2002.

Tremewan, Christopher. *The Political Economy of Social Control in Singapore*. Houndsmills: Macmillan/St. Antony's College, 1994.

Tu Wei-ming. *Confucianism in a Historical Perspective*. Institute of East Asian Philosophies, Occasional Paper and Monograph Series no. 13, 1989.

———, ed. *Confucian Traditions in East Asian Modernity: Moral Education and Economic Culture in Japan and the Four Mini-Dragons*. Cambridge: Harvard University Press, 1996.

Tucker, John. "Two Mencian Political Notions in Tokugawa Japan," *Philosophy East and West*, vol. 47, no. 2 (August 1997).

Tucker, Robert, ed. *Capital*, vol. 3, in *The Marx-Engels Reader*. Karl Marx. New York: W. W. Norton, 1978.

Turner, Karen. "War, Punishment, and the Law of Nature in Early Chinese Concepts of the State," *Harvard Journal of Asiatic Studies*, vol. 53, no. 2 (December 1993).

Twiss, Sumner B. "A Constructive Framework for Discussing Confucianism and Human Rights." In *Confucianism and Human Rights*. Ed. Wm. Theodore de Bary and Tu Wei-ming. New York: Columbia University Press, 1998.

Upham, Frank K. "Who Will Find the Defendant If He Stays with His Sheep? Justice in Rural China?" *The Yale Law Journal*, vol. 114, no. 7 (May 2005).

Van Dyke, Vernon. "The Individual, the State, and Ethnic Communication in Political Theory." In *The Rights of Minority Cultures*. Ed. Will Kymlicka. Oxford: Oxford University Press, 1995.

Van Ness, Peter, ed. *Debating Human Rights*. London: Routledge, 1999.

Vogel, Ezra. *The Four Little Dragons: The Spread of Industrialization in East Asia*. Cambridge: Harvard University Press, 1991.

———. "Japan: Adaptive Communitarianism." In *Ideology and National Competitiveness: An Analysis of Nine Countries*. Ed. George C. Lodge and Ezra F. Vogel. Boston: Harvard Business School Press, 1987.

Wade, Robert. "The Asian Crisis: The High Debt Model versus the Wall Street–Treasury–IMF Complex," *New Left Review*, no. 228 (March/April 1998).

———. *Governing the Market, 2nd* ed. Princeton: Princeton University Press, 2003.

Walder, Andrew G., and Jean C. Oi. "Property Rights in the Chinese Economy: Contours of the Process of Change." In *Property Rights and Economic Reform in China*. Ed. Jean C. Oi and Andrew G. Walder. Stanford: Stanford University Press, 1999.

Waley, Author, trans. *The Analects of Confucius*. London: Allen & Unwin, 1938.

Walzer, Michael. *Arguing about War*. New Haven: Yale University Press, 2004.

———. *Interpretation and Social Criticism*. Cambridge: Harvard University Press, 1987.

———. *Just and Unjust Wars: A Moral Argument with Historical Illustrations*. 3rd ed. New York: Basic Books, 2000.

———. *Spheres of Justice*. Oxford: Basil Blackwell, 1983.

———. *Thick and Thin*. Notre Dame: University of Notre Dame Press, 1994.

Wang Feng. "Can China Afford to Continue Its One-Child Policy?" *Asia Pacific Issues: Analysis from the East-West Center*, no. 77 (March 2005), 1–12.

Wang Juntao. "Confucian Democrats in Chinese History." In *Confucianism for the Modern World*. Ed. Daniel A. Bell and Hahm Chaibong. New York: Cambridge University Press, 2003.

Watson, Burton, trans. *Basic Writings of Mo Tzu, Hsun Tzu, and Han Fei Tzu*. New York: Columbia University Press, 1967.

Wei, J. L., R. H. Myers, and D. G. Gillin, eds. *Selected Writings of Sun Yat-sen*. Stanford: Hoover Institution Press, 1994.

Weil, Patrick. "Access to Citizenship: A Comparison of Twenty-Five Nationality Laws." In *Citizenship Today: Global Perspectives and Practices*. Ed. T. Alexander Aleinikoff and Douglas Klusmeyer. Washington, DC: Carnegie Endowment for International Peace, 2001.

Weiss, Linda. "Guiding Globalization in East Asia," in *State in the Global Economy: Bringing Domestic Institutions Back In*. Ed. Linda Weiss. New York: Cambridge University Press, 2003.

———. "Introduction: Bringing Domestic Institutions Back In." In *States in the Global Economy: Bringing Domestic Institutions Back In*. Ed. Linda Weiss. New York: Cambridge University Press, 2003.

———. "Is the State Being 'Transformed' by Globalization." In *States in the Global Economy: Bringing Domestic Institutions Back In*. Ed. Linda Weiss. New York: Cambridge University Press, 2003.

———, ed. *States in the Global Economy: Bringing Domestic Institutions Back In*. New York: Cambridge University Press, 2003.

Welch, Claude E., Jr. "Amnesty International and Human Rights Watch." In *NGOs and Human Rights: Promise and Performance*. Ed. Claude E. Welch, Jr. Philadelphia: University of Pennsylvania Press, 2001.

———. "Conclusion." In *NGOs and Human Rights: Promise and Performance*. Ed. Claude E. Welch, Jr. Philadelphia: University of Pennsylvania Press, 2001.

———, ed. *NGOs and Human Rights: Promise and Performance*. Philadelphia: University of Pennsylvania Press, 2001.

Westney, D. Eleanor. "Japanese Enterprise Faces the Twenty-First Century." In *The Twenty-First Century Firm: Changing Economic Organization in International Perspective*. Ed. Paul DiMaggio. Princeton: Princeton University Press, 2001.

White, Gordon, and Roger Goodman. "Welfare Orientalism and the Search for an East Asian Welfare Model." In *The East Asian Welfare Model: Welfare Orientalism and the State*. Ed. Roger Goodman, Gordon White, and Huck-ju Kwon. London: Routledge, 1998.

Winckler, Edwin A. "Statism and Familism in Taiwan." In *Ideology and National Competitiveness: An Analysis of Nine Countries*. Ed. George C. Lodge and Ezra F. Vogel. Boston: Harvard Business School Press, 1987.

Winston, Morton E. "Assessing the Effectiveness of International Human Rights NGOs: Amnesty International." In *NGOs and Human Rights: Promise and Performance*. Ed. Claude E. Welch, Jr. Philadelphia: University of Pennsylvania Press, 2001.

Wollheim, Richard, ed. "Considerations on Representative Government." In *Three Essays*. John Stuart Mill. Oxford: Oxford University Press, 1975.

Wong, David. "Comparative Philosophy: Chinese and Western," *Stanford Encyclopedia of Philosophy*, http://plato.stanford.edu/entries/comparphil-chiwes/.

———. "Relational and Autonomous Selves," *Journal of Chinese Philosophy*, vol. 31, no. 4 (December 2004).

Wong, R. Bin. "Confucian Agendas for Material and Ideological Control in Modern China." In *Culture & State in Chinese History*. Ed. Theodore Huters, R. Bing Wong, and Pauline Yu. Stanford: Stanford University Press, 1997.

Woo, Edward P. H. *In Search of an Ideal Political Order & an Understanding of Different Political Cultures*. Hong Kong: Novelty Publishers, 2002.

Woo-Cumings, Meredith. "Miracle as Prologue: The State and the Reform of the Corporate Sector in Korea." In *Rethinking the East Asia Miracle*. Ed. Joseph E. Stiglitz and Shahid Yusuf. New York: Oxford University Press, 2001.

Woodiwiss, Anthony. " 'Community in the East': Towards a New Human Rights Paradigm." In *Communitarian Politics in Asia*. Ed. Chua Beng-Huat. London: Routledge/Curzon, 2004.

———. *Globalization, Human Rights and Labor Law in Pacific Asia*. Cambridge: Cambridge University Press, 1998.

Wu Junsheng. "Tianxia yijia guannian yu shijie heping" [The Concept of One Family under Heaven and World Peace], *Dongfang zazhi*, vol. 10, no. 8 (September 1977).

Wu Ming. "Zhongguo huji zhidu: Zanshi bu neng quxiao" [The Chinese Household Registration System: Cannot Be Abolished in the Near Term], *Xin xi bu*, November 2001.

Wu Yongping. "Rethinking the Taiwanese Developmental State," *The China Quarterly*, no. 177 (March 2004).

Xu Jilin. "Reforming Peking University: A Window into Deliberative Democracy?" In *The Search for Deliberative Democracy in China*. Ed. Ethan J. Leib and He Baogang. New York: Palgrave Macmillan, 2006.

Xia Xianliang and Wang Yinxi. "Zhongguo hukou zhidu gaige de lilun fenxi" [A Theoretical Analysis of China's Institutional Reform for Residence Registration], *Chenshi fazhan yanjiu* [Urban Studies], vol. 9, no. 4 (2002).

Yamamura Kozo, and Wolfgang Streeck, eds. *The End of Diversity? Prospects for German and Japanese Capitalism*. Ithaca: Cornell University Press, 2003.

Yamanaka Keiko, and Nicola Piper. "An Introductory Overview," *Asian and Pacific Migration Journal*, vol. 12, nos. 1–2 (2003).

Yan Yunxiang. "Managed Globalization: State Power and Transition in China." In *Many Globalizations: Cultural Diversity in the Contemporary World*. Ed. Peter L. Berger and Samuel P. Huntington. New York: Oxford University Press, 2002.

Yang Bojun, ed. *Chun qiu zuo zhuan zhu* [Annotation on Spring and Autumn Zuo Zhuan], vol. 4. Beijing: Zhonghua shuju, 1981.

———. *Mengzi* [Mencius]. Beijing: Zhonghua shuju, 1960.

Yao Xinzhong, ed. *RoutledgeCurzon Encyclopedia of Confucianism*. London: RoutledgeCurzon, 2003.

Yeoh, Brenda S. A., and Shirlena Huang. "The Differences Gender Makes: State Policy and Contract Migrant Workers in Singapore," *Asian and Pacific Migration Journal*, vol. 12, nos. 1–2 (2003).

———. "Singapore Women and Foreign Domestic Workers." In *Gender, Migration and Domestic Service*. Ed. Janet Henshall Momsen. London: Routledge, 1999.

Yeoh, Brenda S. A., S. Huang, and J. Gonzalez. "Migrant Female Domestic Workers: Debating the Economic, Social and Political Impacts in Singapore," *International Migration Review*, vol. 33, no. 1 (1999).

Yeoh, Brenda S. A., Peggy Teo, and Shirlena Huang, eds. *Gender Politics in the Asian-Region*. London: Routledge, 2002.

Young, Stephen B. "Human Rights Questions in Southeast Asian Culture: Problems for American Response." In *The Politics of Human Rights*. Ed. Paula Newberg. New York: New York University Press, 1980.

Yusuf, Shahid. "The East Asian Miracle at the Millenium." In *Rethinking the East Asia Miracle*. Ed. Joseph E. Stiglitz and Shahid Yusuf. New York: Oxford University Press, 2001.

Zakaria, Fareed. *The Future of Freedom: Illiberal Democracy at Home and Abroad*. New York: W. W. Norton, 2003.

Zelin, Madeleine. "Economic Freedom in Late Imperial China." In *Realms of Freedom in China*. Ed. William C. Kirby. Stanford: Stanford University Press, 2004.

Zhang Chuanxi. *Zhongguo gudai shigang* [An Outline of the History of Ancient China]. Beijing: Beijing daxue chubanshe, 1991.

Zhang Junbo and Yao Yunzhu. "Differences between Traditional Chinese and Western Military Thinking and Their Philosophical Roots," *Journal of Contemporary China*, vol. 5, no. 1 (July 1996), http://search.epnet.com/direct.asp?an=9608225143&db=aph.

Zhang Wei-bin. *Confucianism and Modernization: Industrialization and Democratization of the Confucian Regions*. Houndsmills: Macmillan Press, 1999.

Zheng Hong Sheng. "Taiwan de dalu xiangxiang" [Taiwan's Imagination of the Mainland], *Du shu*, January 2005.

"Zhongguo jiazheng fuwu hangye fenxi baogao" [Chinese Domestic Workers' Industry Analysis Research Report], *Huanqiu zixun xinxiwang*, 2005, http://www.icinet.com.cn/ReadNews.asp?NewsID=1312.

Zhongguo Ruxue dabaike quanshu [Encyclopedia of Confucianism in China]. Beijing: Zhongguo dabaike quanshu chubanshe, 1997.

Zhou Qi. "Conflicts over Human Rights between China and the US," *Human Rights Quarterly*, vol. 27, no. 1 (February 2005).